Albert S. Bickmore

Travels in the East Indian archipelago

With maps and illustrations

Albert S. Bickmore

Travels in the East Indian archipelago
With maps and illustrations

ISBN/EAN: 9783743323773

Manufactured in Europe, USA, Canada, Australia, Japa

Cover: Foto ©Andreas Hilbeck / pixelio.de

Manufactured and distributed by brebook publishing software (www.brebook.com)

Albert S. Bickmore

Travels in the East Indian archipelago

WIVES OF ONE OF THE TWO HIGHEST PRINCES IN JAVA

TRAVELS

IN THE

EAST INDIAN ARCHIPELAGO.

By ALBERT S. BICKMORE, M.A.,

FELLOW OF THE ROYAL GEOGRAPHICAL SOCIETY OF LONDON,
CORRESPONDING MEMBER OF THE AMERICAN AND LONDON ETHNOLOGICAL SOCIETIES,
NEW YORK LYCEUM OF NATURAL HISTORY, MEMBER OF THE BOSTON SOCIETY
OF NATURAL HISTORY AND AMERICAN ORIENTAL SOCIETY, AND
PROFESSOR OF NATURAL HISTORY IN MADISON
UNIVERSITY, HAMILTON, N. Y.

WITH MAPS AND ILLUSTRATIONS.

LONDON:
JOHN MURRAY, ALBEMARLE STREET.
1868.

The right of Translation is reserved.

LONDON: PRINTED BY W CLOWES AND SONS, DUKE STREET, STAMFORD STREET,
AND CHARING CROSS.

TO

THE GENEROUS FRIENDS OF SCIENCE

IN

BOSTON AND CAMBRIDGE,

THROUGH WHOSE LIBERALITY THE TRAVELS

HEREIN DESCRIBED WERE MADE,

THIS VOLUME

Is Respectfully Dedicated.

GOVERNMENT BUILDINGS AT BATAVIA.

See page 30.

PREFACE.

The object of my voyage to Amboina was simply to re-collect the shells figured in Rumphius's "Rariteit Kamer," and the idea of writing a volume of travels was not seriously entertained until I arrived at Batavia, and, instead of being forbidden by the Dutch Government to proceed to the Spice Islands, as some of my warmest friends feared, I was honored by His Excellency, the Governor-General of "the Netherlands India," with the order given on page 40.

Having fully accomplished that object, I availed myself of the unexampled facilities to travel afforded me in every part of the archipelago, and all except the first six chapters describe the regions thus visited.

The narrative given has been taken almost entirely from my journal, which was kept day by day with scrupulous care. Accuracy, even at any sacrifice of elegance, has been aimed at throughout; and first impressions are presented as modified by subsequent observation.

My sincerest thanks are herein expressed to the liberal gentlemen to whom this volume is dedicated; to Baron Sloet van de Beele, formerly Governor-General of the Netherlands India; to Mr. N. A. T. Arriens, formerly Governor of the Moluccas; to Mr. J. F. R. S. van den Bosche, formerly Governor of the West Coast of Sumatra; to the many officers of the Netherlands Government, and to the Dutch and American merchants who entertained me with the most cordial hospitality, and aided me in every possible way throughout the East Indian Archipelago.

CAMBRIDGE, MASS., U. S. A.,
Sept. 1, 1868.

CONTENTS.

CHAPTER I.
THE STRAIT OF SUNDA AND BATAVIA.

Object of the Travels described in this volume—Nearing the coast of Java—Balmy breezes of the Eastern Isles—King Æolus's favorite seat—A veil of rain—First view of Malays—Entering the Java Sea—The Malay language—Early history of Java—Marco Polo—Hinduism in Java—History of Batavia—The roadstead of Batavia—The city of Batavia—Houses of Europeans—Mode of cooking—Characteristics of the Malays—Collecting butterflies—Visit Rahden Saleh—Attacked with a fever—receive a letter from the Governor-General 13–41

CHAPTER II.
SAMARANG AND SURABAYA.

Sail from Batavia for the Moluccas—My companions—Mount Slamat—The north coast of Java—Mount Prahu—Temples at Boro Bodo and Brambanan—Samarang—Mohammedan mosque—History of Mohammedanism—Mount Japara—The Guevo Upas, or Valley of Poison—Gresik—Novel mode of navigating mud-flats—Surabaya—Government dock-yard and machine-shops—Zoological gardens—History of Hinduism—The Klings—Excursion to a sugar plantation—Roads and telegraphic routes in Java—Malay mode of gathering rice—The kinds of sugar-cane . . 42–70

CHAPTER III.
THE FLORA AND FAUNA OF THE TROPICAL EAST.

Leave Surabaya for Macassar—Madura—The Sapi—Manufacture of salt—The Tenger Mountains—The Sandy Sea—Eruptions of Mount Papandayang and Mount Galunggong—Java and Cuba compared—The forests of Java—Fauna of Java—The cocoa-nut palm—The Pandanus—The banana—Tropical fruits—The mangostin—The rambutan—mango—duku—durian—bread-fruit—

Bali—Javanese traditions—Limit between the fauna of Asia and that of Australia—A plateau beneath the sea—Caste and suttee practices on Bali 71–96

CHAPTER IV.

CELEBES AND TIMOR.

History of Celebes—De Barros—Diogo de Cauto—Head-hunters of Celebes—The harbor of Macassar—Voyages of the Bugis—Skilful diving—Fort Rotterdam—The Societeit, or Club—A drive into the country—The tomb of a native merchant—Tombs of ancient princes—Sail for Kupang, in Timur—Flying-fish—The Gunong Api in Sapi Strait—Gillibanta—Sumbawa—Eruption of Mount Tomboro—The Eye of the Devil—Floris and Sandal-wood Island—Kupang—Fruits on Timur—Its barrenness and the cause of it—Different kinds of people seen at Kupang—Human sacrifice—Purchasing shells—Geology of the vicinity of Kupang—Sail for Dilli—Village of Dilli—Islands north of Timur—The Bandas—Monsoons in the Java and China Seas 97–129

CHAPTER V.

AMBOINA.

Description of the island and city of Amboina—Dutch mode of governing the natives—A pleasant home—A living nautilus is secured—Excursion to Hitu—Hassar steering—History of the cocoa-tree—Indian corn—Hunting in the tropics—Butterflies—Excursion along the shores of Hitu for shells—Mode of travelling in the Spice Islands—The pine-apple—Covered bridges—Hitulama—Purchasing specimens—History of the Spice Islands—Enormous hermit-crabs—An exodus—Assilulu—Babirusa shells from Buru—Great curiosities—Jewels in the brains of snakes and wild boars—Description of the clove-tree—History of the clove-trade—Watched by the rajah's wives—Lariki and Wakasihu—A storm in the height of the southeast monsoon—Variety of native dialects—Dangerous voyage by night—An earthquake—Excursion to Tulahu 130–176

CHAPTER VI.

THE ULIASSERS AND CERAM.

The arrival of the mail at Amboina—The Uliassers—Chewing the betel-nut and siri—Haruku—We strike on a reef—Saparua Island, village, and bay—Nusalaut—Strange reception—An Eastern banquet—Examining the native schools—Different classes of natives—Yield of cloves in the Uliassers—Nullahia, Amet, and Abobo—Breaking of the surf on the coral reefs—Tanjong O—Travel by night—Ceram—Elpaputi Bay and Amahai—Alfura, or head-hunters, come down from the mountains and dance before us—Land on the south coast of Ceram—Fiendish revels of the natives—Return to Saparua and Amboina 177–212

CHAPTER VII.

BANDA.

Governor Arriens invites me to accompany him to Banda—The Gunong Api—Road of the Bandas—Banda Neira and its forts—Geology of Lontar—The Bandas and the crater in the Tenger Mountains compared—The groves of nutmeg-trees—The canari-tree—Orang Datang—We ascend the volcano—In imminent peril—The crater—Perilous descent—Eruptions of Gunong Api—Earthquakes at Neira—Great extent of the Residency of Banda—The Ki and Arru Islands—Return to Amboina—Geology of the island of Amboina—Trade of Amboina—The grave of Rumphius—His history . 213–252

CHAPTER VIII.

BURU.

Adieu to Amboina—North coast of Ceram—Wahai—Buru—Kayéli—Excursions to various parts of the bay—A home in the forest—Malay cuisine—Tobacco and maize—Flocks of parrots—Beautiful birds—History of Buru—The religion and laws of the Alfura—Shaving the head of a young child—A wedding-feast—Marriage laws in Mohammedan countries—A Malay marriage—Opium, its effects and its history—Kayu-puti oil—Gardens beneath the sea—Roban—Skinning birds—Tropical pests—A deer-hunt—Dinding—A threatening fleet—A page of romance—A last glance at Buru 253–297

CHAPTER IX.

TERNATE, TIDORE, AND GILOLO.

Seasons in Ceram and Buru—Bachian and Makian—Eruptions of Ternate—Magellan—Former monopolies—The bloodhounds of Gilolo—Migrations—A birth-mark—The Molucca Passage—Malay pirates—They challenge the Dutch 298–322

CHAPTER X.

THE NORTHERN PENINSULA OF CELEBES.

Mount Klabat—Kema—A hunt for babirusa—A camp by the sea—Enormous snakes—From Kema to Menado—Eruption of Mount Kemaas—Population of the Minahassa—Thrown from a horse—The Bantiks—A living death—History of the coffee-tree—In the jaws of a crocodile—The bay of Menado—Lake Linu—A grove by moonlight 323–355

CHAPTER XI.

THE MINAHASSA.

The waterfall of Tinchep—A mud-well—A boiling pool—The ancient appearance of our earth—Lake Tondano—One of the finest views in the world—Palm-wine—Graves of the natives—Christianity and education—Tanjong Flasco—Gold-mines in Celebes—The island of Buton—Macassar—A raving maniac 356–383

CHAPTER XII.

SUMATRA.

Padang—Beautiful drives—Crossing the streams—The cleft—Crescent-shaped roofs—Distending the lobe of the ear—Cañons—The great crater of Manindyu—Immense amphitheatres—Ophir—Gold-mines . . 384–406

CHAPTER XIII.

TO THE LAND OF THE CANNIBALS.

Valley of Bondyol—Monkeys—The orang-utan—Lubu Siköping—Tigers and buffaloes—The Valley of Rau—A Batta grave—Riding along the edge of a precipice—Twilight and evening—Padang Sidempuan—Among the cannibals—Descent from the Barizan—The suspension bridge of rattan—Ornaments of gold—The camphor-tree 407–434

CHAPTER XIV.

RETURN TO PADANG.

Bay of Tapanuli—The Devil's Dwelling—Dangerous fording—Among the Battas—Missionaries and their brides—The feasts of the cannibals—The pepper trade—The English appear in the East—Struck by a heavy squall—Ayar Bangis and Natal—The king's birthday—Malay ideas of greatness 435–457

CHAPTER XV.

THE PADANG PLATEAU.

Thunder and lightning in the tropics—Paya Kombo and the Bua Valley—The Bua cave—Up the valley to Suka Rajah—Ancient capitals of Menangkabau—The reformers of Korinchi—Malay mode of making matchlocks—A simple meal—Geological history of the plateau—The Thirteen Confederate Towns—The flanks of the Mérapi—Natives of the Pagi Islands—Where the basin of the Indian Ocean begins 458–487

CHAPTER XVI.

CROSSING SUMATRA.

Bay of Bencoolen—Rat Island—Loss of Governor Raffles's collection—A trap for tigers—Blood-suckers—Pits for the rhinoceros—virgin children—Plateau of the Musi—From Kopaiyong to Kaban Agong—Natives destroyed by tigers—Sumatra's wealth—The Anak gadis—Troops of monkeys—From Tebing Tingi to Bunga Mas—We come upon an elephant—Among tigers—The Pasuma people—Horseback travel over—The land of game 486–520

CHAPTER XVII.

PALEMBANG, BANCA, AND SINGAPORE.

Mount Dempo—Rafts of cocoa-nuts—Floating down the Limatang—Cotton—From Purgatory to Paradise—Palembang—The Kubus—Banca—Presented with a python—The python escapes—A struggle for life—Sail for China. 521–542

APPENDIX A. Area of the principal islands, according to Baron van Carnbée 543
" B. Population of the Netherlands India, 1865 . . . 543
" C. A table of heights of the principal mountains in the archipelago 544
" D. Coffee sold by the government at Padang . . . 545
" E. Trade of Java and Madura during 1864 . . . 546
" F. A list of the birds collected by the author on the island of Buru 547
INDEX 549

"SAPIE" OXEN FROM MADURA.

See page 64.

LIST OF ILLUSTRATIONS.

Wives of one of the great Princes of Java (from a Photograph)		*Frontispiece*
Poultry Vendor, Batavia	,,	*Page* 27
Government Buildings in Batavia	,,	4
Sapis, or oxen from Madura	,,	11
Javanese and family	,,	33
Rahden Saleh	,,	37
Rahden Saleh's Palace	,,	37
Watering the streets, Java	,,	49
A Tandu	,,	49
A Kling		63
A Native of Beloochistan (from a Photograph)		63
Fruit-Market	,,	89
The Pinang, or Betel-nut Palm (from a Drawing by Rahden Saleh)		180
After the bath (from a Photograph)		182
Musical Instruments of the Malays (Batavia)		191
Dyak, or Head-hunter of Borneo (from a Photograph)		206
Landing through the Surf on the south coast of Ceram (from a Sketch)		209
The Lontar Palm		220
Ascent of the Volcano of Banda—saved by a fern (from a Sketch)		234
A Jungle		261
A Malay Opium-smoker (from a Photograph)		281
The Gomuti Palm (from a Sketch)		370
The Bamboo		374
Approach to the Cleft near Padang		390
Women of Menangkabau		395
Scene in the interior of Sumatra		404
Driving round a dangerous Bluff		419
Suspension Bridge of rattan		428
Native of Nias		445
Natives of the Pagi Islands		482
Singapore		521
River Scene in Sumatra, on the Limatang		525
Natives of Palembang } Palembang—high water }		530
Killing a Python		541
Map of Sumatra		*To face page* 384
Tomb of the Sultan—Palembang		546
Map of the Eastern Archipelago		*at the end*

TRAVELS

IN THE

EAST INDIAN ARCHIPELAGO.

CHAPTER I.

THE STRAIT OF SUNDA AND BATAVIA.

On the 19th of April, 1865, I was fifty miles east of Christmas Island, floating on the good ship "Memnon" toward the Strait of Sunda.

I was going to Batavia, to sail thence to the Spice Islands, which lie east of Celebes, for the purpose of collecting the beautiful shells of those seas.

I had chosen that in preference to any other part of the world, because the first collection of shells from the East that was ever described and figured with sufficient accuracy to be of any scientific value was made by Rumphius, a doctor who lived many years at Amboina, the capital of those islands. His great work, the "Rariteit Kamer," or Chamber of Curiosities, was published in 1705, more than sixty years before the twelfth edition of the "Systema Naturæ" was issued by Linnæus, "the Father of Natural History," who referred to the figures in that work to illustrate a part of his own writings. When Holland became a province of France, in 1811, and it was designed to make Paris the centre of science and literature in Europe, it is said that this collection was taken from Leyden to that city, and afterward returned, and that during these two transfers a large proportion of the specimens disappeared; and that, finally, what was left of this valuable collection was scattered through the great museum at Leyden. It was partly to restore Rumphius's specimens, and partly to bring into our own country such a standard collection, that I was going to search myself for the shells figured in the "Rariteit Kamer," on the very points and headlands, and in the very bays, where Rumphius's specimens were found.

As we neared the coast of Java, cocoa-nuts and fragments of sea-washed palms, drifting by, indicated our approach to a land very different at least from the temperate shores we had left behind; and we could in some degree experience Columbus's pleasure, when he first saw the new branch and its vermilion berries. Strange, indeed, must be this land to which we are coming, for here we see snakes swimming on the water, and occasionally fragments of rock drifting over the sea. New birds also appear, now sailing singly through the sky, and now hovering in flocks over certain places, hoping to satisfy their hungry maws on the small fishes that follow the floating driftwood. Here it must be that the old Dutch sailors fabled could be seen the tree—then unknown—that bore that strange fruit, the double cocoa-nut. They always represented it as rising up from a great depth and spreading out its uppermost leaves on the surface of the sea. It was guarded by a bird, that was not bird but half beast; and when a ship came near, she was always drawn irresistibly toward this spot, and not one of her ill-fated crew ever escaped the beak and formidable talons of this insatiable harpy.

But such wonders unfortunately fade away before the light of advancing knowledge; and the prince of Ceylon, who is said to have given a whole vessel laden with spice for a single specimen, could have satisfied his heart's fullest desire if he had only known it was not rare on the Seychelles, north of Mauritius.

The trades soon became light and baffling. Heavy rain-squalls, with thunder and lightning, were frequent; and three days after, as one of these cleared away, the high mountain near Java Head appeared full a quarter of a degree above the horizon, its black shoulders rising out of a beautiful mantle of the ermine-white, fleecy clouds, called *cumuli.*

Although we were thirty-five miles from the shore, yet large numbers of dragon-flies came round the ship, and I quickly improvised a net and captured a goodly number of them.

After sunset, there was a light air off-shore, which carried us to within a few miles of the land, and at midnight the captain called me on deck to enjoy " the balmy breezes of the Eastern isles;" and certainly to myself, as well as to the others, the air seemed to have the rich fragrance of new-mown clover, but far more spicy. At that hour it was quite clear, but at sunrise a thick haze rose up from the ocean, and this phenomenon was repeated each morning that we were trying to enter the Strait of Sunda. As we had arrived during the changing of the monsoons, calms were so continuous that for six days we tried in vain to gain fifty miles. When a breeze would take us up near the mouth of the channel, it would then die away and let a strong current sweep us away to the east, and one time we were carried most unpleasantly near the high, threatening crags at Palembang Point, near Java Head. Those who have passed Sunda at this time of the year, or Ombay Strait in the beginning of the opposite monsoon, will readily recall the many weary hours they have passed waiting for a favorable breeze to take them only a few miles farther on their long voyage.

During those six days, at noon the sun poured down his hottest rays, the thermometer ranging from 88° to 90° Fahr. in the shade, and not the slightest air moving to afford a momentary relief. Although constantly for a year I was almost under the equator, these six days were the most tedious and oppressive I ever experienced.

The mountain back of Java Head seemed to be King Eolus's favorite seat. Clouds would come from every quarter of the heavens and gather round its summit, while the sun was reaching the zenith; but soon after he began to pass down the western sky, lightnings would be seen darting their forked tongues around the mountain-crest: and then, as if the winds had broken from the grasp of their king, thick cloud-masses would suddenly roll down the mountain-sides, lightnings dart hither and thither, and again and again the thunders would crash and roar enough to shake the very firmament.

We are not alone. Six or eight vessels are also detained here—for this Strait of Sunda is the great gate through which pass out most of the valuable teas and costly silks of China and Japan, and these ships are carrying cotton goods to those lands to exchange in part for such luxuries. On the evening of the sixth day a more favorable breeze took us slowly up the channel past a group of large rocks, where the unceasing swell of the ocean was breaking, and making them sound in the quiet night like the howling and snarling of some fierce monster set to guard the way and unable to prevent his expected prey from escaping.

With the morning came a fine breeze, and, as we sailed up the strait, several small showers passed over the mountains, parallel to the shore, on the Java side; and once a long cloud rested its ends on two mountains, and unfolded from its dark mass a thin veil of sparkling rain, through which we could see quite distinctly all the outlines and the bright-green foliage of the valley behind it. The highly-cultivated lands near the water, and on the lower declivities of the mountains, whose tops were one dense mass of perennial green, made the whole view most enchanting to me; but our captain (who was a Cape Cod man) declared that the sand-hills on the outer side of Cape Cod were vastly more charming to him. On the shallows, near the shore, the clear sea-water took a beautiful tint of emerald green in the bright sunlight, and here we passed long lines of cuttle-fish bones and parts of mysterious fruits where the tides met, that were setting in different directions.

Nearly all the islands in the strait are steep, volcanic cones, with their bases beneath the sea; the bright-green foliage on their sides forming an agreeable contrast with the blue ocean at their feet when the waves roll away before a strong breeze; but when it is calm, and the water reflects the light, as from a polished mirror, they appear like gigantic emeralds set in a sea of silver.

As we approached Angir, where ships bound to and from China frequently stop for fresh provisions, we saw, to our great alarm, a steamship! Was it the pirate Shenandoah, and was our ship to be taken and burnt there, almost at the end of our long voyage? I must confess that was what we all feared till we came near enough to see the "Stars and Stripes" of the loyal flag of our native land.

Here many Malays paddled off in their canoes to sell us fruit. We watch the approach of the first boat with a peculiar, indescribable interest. It contains two young men, who row. They are dressed in trousers and jackets of calico, with cotton handkerchiefs tied round their heads. This is the usual dress throughout the archipelago, except that, instead of the trousers or over them, is worn the *sarong*, which is a piece of cotton cloth, two yards long by a yard wide, with the two shorter sides sewn together, so as to make a bag open at the top and bottom. The men draw this on over the body, and gather it on the right hip; the loose part is then twisted, and tucked under the part passing around the body, so as to form a rude knot. There is a man in the stern, sitting with his feet under him, steering the canoe, and at the same time helping it onward with his paddle. He is dressed in a close-fitting red shirt? No! He is not encumbered with any clothing except what Nature has provided for him, save a narrow cloth about his loins, the usual working-costume of the coolies, or poorer classes. He brings several kinds of bananas, green cocoa-nuts, and the "pompelmus," which is a gigantic orange, from six to eight inches in diameter. He seems perfectly happy, and talks with the most surprising rapidity. From an occasional word that may be half English, we suppose, like traders in the Western world, he is speaking in no moderate manner of the value of what he has to sell.

Mount Karang, back of Angir, now comes into view, raising its crest of green foliage to a height of five thousand feet; a light breeze takes us round Cape St. Nicholas, the northwest extremity of Java. It is a high land, with sharp ridges coming down to the water, thus forming a series of little rocky headlands, separated by small sandy bays. These, as we sail along, come up, and open to our view with a most charming panoramic effect. Near the shore a few Malays are seen on their *praus*, or large boats, while others appear in groups on the beaches, around their canoes, and only now and then do we catch glimpses of their rude houses under the feathery leaves of the cocoa-nut palm.

We are in the Java Sea. It seems very strange.

after being pitched and tossed about constantly for more than a hundred days, thus to feel our ship glide along so steadily; and after scanning the horizon by the hour, day after day, hoping to be able to discern one vessel, and so feel that we had at least one companion on "the wide waste of waters," now to see land on every side, and small boats scattered in all directions over the quiet sea. That night we anchored near Babi Island, on a bottom of very soft, sticky clay, largely composed of fragments of shells and coral. A boat came off from the shore, and, as the coxswain could speak a little English, I took my first lesson in Malay, the common language, or *lingua franca*, of the whole archipelago. As it was necessary, at least, that I should be able to talk with these natives if I would live among them, and purchase shells of them, it was my first and most imperative task, on reaching the East, to acquire this language. The Malay spoken at Batavia, and at all the Dutch ports and posts in the islands to the east, differs very much from the high or pure Malay spoken in the Menangkabau country, in the interior of Sumatra, north of Padang, whence the Malays originally came: after passing from island to island, they have spread over all Malaysia, that is, the great archipelago between Asia, Australia, and New Guinea. Perhaps of all languages in the world, the low or common Malay is the one most readily acquired. It contains no harsh gutturals or other consonants that are difficult to pronounce. It is soft and musical, and somewhat resembles the Italian in its liquid sounds; and one who has learned it can never fail

to be charmed by the nice blending of vowels and
consonants whenever a word is pronounced in his
presence. The only difficult thing in this language
is, that words of widely different meaning sometimes
are so similar that, at first, one may be mistaken for
another. Every European in all the Netherlands
India speaks Malay. It is the only language used in
addressing servants; and all the European children
born on these islands learn it from their Malay
nurses long before they are able to speak the language of their parents. Such children generally find
it difficult to make the harsh, guttural sounds of the
Dutch language, and the Malays themselves are
never able to speak it well; and, for the same
reason, Dutchmen seldom speak Malay as correctly as
Englishmen and Frenchmen.

We are now off the ancient city of Bantam, and
we naturally here review the voyages of the earliest
European navigators in these seas, and the principal
events in the ancient history of this rich island of
Java.

The word Java, or, more correctly, "Jawa," is
the name of the people who originally lived only in
the eastern part of the island, but, in more modern
times, they have spread over the whole island, and
given it their name. The Chinese claim to have
known it in ancient times, and call it Chi-po or
Cha-po, which is as near Jawa as their pronunciation of most foreign names at the present day.

It was first made known to the Western world by
that great traveller, Marco Polo, in his description
of the lands he saw or passed while on his voyage

from China to the Persian Gulf, in the latter part of the thirteenth century. He did not see it himself, but only gathered accounts in regard to it from others. He calls it Giaua, and says it produces cloves and nutmegs, though we know now that they were all brought to Java from the Spice Islands, farther to the east. In regard to gold, he says it yielded a quantity "exceeding all calculation and belief." This was also probably brought from other islands, chiefly from Sumatra, Borneo, and Celebes.

In 1493, one year after the discovery of America by Columbus, Bartholomew Dias, a Portuguese, discovered the southern extremity of Africa, which he called the Cape of Storms, but which his king said should be named the Cape of Good Hope, because it gave a *good hope* that, at last, they had discovered a way to India by sea. Accordingly, the next year, this king* sent Pedro da Covilham and Alfonso de Payva directly to the east to settle this important question. From Genoa they came to Alexandria in the guise of travelling merchants, thence to Cairo, and down the Red Sea to Aden. Here they separated—Payva to search for "Prester John," a Christian prince, said to be reigning in Abyssinia over a people of high cultivation; and Covilham to visit the Indies, it having been arranged that they should meet again at Cairo or Memphis. Payva died before reaching the principal city of Abyssinia, but Covilham had a prosperous journey to India, where he made drawings of the cities and harbors, especially of Goa and Calicut (Calcutta), and marked their

* Valentyn, "History of the Moluccas."

positions on a map given him by King John of Portugal. Thence he returned along the coast of Persia to Cape Guardafui, and continued south to Mozambique and "Zofala," where he ascertained that that land joined the Cape of Good Hope, and thus was the first man who *knew* that it was possible to sail from Europe to India. From Zofala he returned to Abyssinia, and sent his diary, charts, and drawings to Genoa by some Portuguese merchants who were trading at Memphis.

On receiving this news, King Emanuel, who had succeeded King John, sent out, during the following year, 1495, four ships under Vasco di Gama, who visited Natal and Mozambique; in 1498 he was at Calcutta, and in 1499 back at Lisbon.

In 1509 the Portuguese, under Sequiera, first came into the archipelago. During the next year Alfonso Albuquerque visited Sumatra, and in 1511 took the Malay city Malacca, and established a military post from which he sent out Antonio d'Abreu to search for the Spice Islands. On his way eastward, D'Abreu touched at Agasai (Gresik) on Java.

In 1511 the Portuguese visited Bantam, and two years later Alvrin was sent from Malacca with four vessels to bring away a cargo of spices from a ship wrecked on the Java coast while on her way back from the Spice Islands.

Ludovico Barthema was the first European who described Java from personal observation. He remained on it fourteen days, but his descriptions are questionable in part, for he represents parents as selling their children, to be eaten by their purchasers, and himself as quitting the island in haste for fear of being made a meal of.

In 1596 the Dutch, under Houtman, first arrived off Bantam, and, finding the native king at war with the Portuguese, readily furnished him with assistance against their rivals, on his offering to give them a place where they could establish themselves and commence purchasing pepper, which at that time was almost the only export.

The English, following the example of the Portuguese and the Dutch, sent out a fleet in 1602, during the reign of Queen Elizabeth. These ships touched at Achin, on the western end of Sumatra, and thence sailed to Bantam.

In 1610 the Dutch built a fort at a native village called Jacatra, "the work of victory," but which they named Batavia. This was destroyed in 1619, and the first Dutch governor-general, Bolt, decided to rebuild it and remove his settlement from Bantam to that place, which was done on the 4th of March of that year. This was the foundation of the present city of Batavia. The English, who had meantime maintained an establishment at Bantam, withdrew in 1683.

In 1811, when Holland became subject to France, the French flag was hoisted at Batavia, but that same year it was captured by the English. On the 19th of August, 1816, they restored it to the Dutch, who have held it uninterruptedly down to the present time.

In glancing at the internal history of Java, we find that, for many centuries previous to A. D. 1250,

Hinduism, that is, a mixture of Buddhism and Brahminism, had been the prevailing religion. At that time an attempt was made to convert the reigning prince to Mohammedanism. This proved unsuccessful; but so soon afterward did this new religion gain a foothold, and so rapidly did it spread, that in 1475, at the overthrow of the great empire of Majapahit, who ruled over the whole of Java and the eastern parts of Sumatra, a Mohammedan prince took the throne. Up to this time the people in the western part of Java, as far east as Cheribon (about Long. 109°), spoke a language called Sundanese, and only the people in the remaining eastern part of the island spoke Javanese; but in 1811 nine-tenths of the whole population of Java spoke Javanese, and the Sundanese was already confined to the mountainous parts of the south and west, and to a small colony near Bantam.

Soon after founding Batavia, the Dutch made an alliance offensive and defensive with the chief prince, who resided near Surakarta. Various chiefs rebelled from time to time against his authority, and the Dutch, in return for the assistance they rendered him, obtained the site of the present city of Samarang; and in this way they continued to increase their area until 1749, when the prince then reigning signed an official deed "to abdicate for himself and for his heirs the sovereignty of the country, conferring the same on the Dutch East India Company, and leaving them to dispose of it, in future, to any person they might think competent to govern it for the benefit of the company and of Java." Seven years before this time the empire had been nominally divided, the hereditary prince being styled Susunan, or "object of adoration," whose descendants now reside at Surakarta, near Solo; and a second prince, who was styled Sultan, and whose descendants reside at Jokyokarta. Each receives a large annuity from the Dutch Government, and keeps a great number of servants. Their wives are chosen from all the native beauties in the land, and the engraving we give from a photograph represents those of one of the highest dignitaries in full costume, but barefoot, just as they dress themselves on festive occasions to dance before their lord and his assembled guests.

The next day when the sea-breeze came, about one o'clock, we sailed up through the many islands of this part of the coast of Java. They are all very low and flat, and covered with a short, dense shrubbery, out of which rise the tall cocoa-nut palm and the waringin or Indian fig. This green foliage is only separated from the sea by a narrow beach of ivory-white coral sand, which reflects the bright light of the noonday sun until it becomes positively dazzling. Where the banks are muddy, mangrove-trees are seen below high-water level, holding on to the soft earth with hundreds of branching rootlets, as if trying to claim as land what really is the dominion of the sea.

This dense vegetation is one of the great characteristics of these tropical islands; and the constantly varied grouping of the palms, mangroves, and other trees, and the irregular contour and relief of the shores, afford an endless series of exquisite views.

POULTRY VENDER.

As we passed one of the outer islands, its trees were quite covered with kites, gulls, and other sea-birds.

The next evening we came to the Batavia road, a shallow bay where ships lie at anchor partially sheltered from the sea by the many islands scattered about its entrance. The shores of this bay form a low, muddy morass, but high mountains appear in the distance. Through this morass a canal has been cut. Its sides are well walled in, and extend out some distance toward the shipping, on account of the shallowness of the water along the shore. At the end of one of these moles, or walls, stands a small white light-house, indicating the way of approaching the city, which cannot be fully seen from the anchorage.

When a ship arrives from a foreign port, no one can leave her before she is boarded by an officer from the guardship, a list of her passengers and crew obtained, and it is ascertained that there is no sickness on board. Having observed this regulation, we rowed up the canal to the " boom " or tree, where an officer of the customs looks into every boat that passes. This word " boom " came into use, as an officer informed me, when it was the custom to let a *tree* fall across the canal at night, in order to prevent any boat from landing or going out to the shipping.

Here were crowds of Malay boatmen, engaged in gambling, by pitching coins. This seemed also the headquarters of poultry-venders, who were carrying round living fowls, ducks, and geese, whose feet had been tied together and fastened to a stick, so that they had to hang with their heads downward—the very ideal of cruelty.

Before we could land, we were asked several times in Dutch, French, and English, to take a carriage, for cabmen seem to have the same persistent habits in every corner of the earth. Meanwhile the Malay drivers kept shouting out, "Crétur tuan! crétur tuan!" So we took a "crétur," that is, a low, covered, four-wheeled carriage, drawn by two miniature ponies. The driver sits up on a seat in front, in a neat *baju* or jacket of red or scarlet calico, and an enormous hemispherical hat, so gilded or bronzed as to dazzle your eyes when the sun shines.

Though these ponies are small, they go at a quick canter, and we were rapidly whirled along between a row of shade-trees to the city gate, almost the only part of the old walls of the city that is now standing. The other parts were torn down by Marshal Daendals, to allow a freer circulation of air. Then we passed through another row of shade-trees, and over a bridge, to the office of the American consul, a graduate of Harvard; and, as Cambridge had been my home for four years, we at once considered ourselves as old friends.

Before I left America, Senator Sumner, as chairman of our Committee on Foreign Relations, kindly gave me a note of warm commendation to the representatives of foreign powers; and Mr. J. G. S. van Breda, the secretary of the Society of Sciences in Holland, with whom I had been in correspondence while at the Museum of Comparative Zoology in Cambridge, gave me a kind note to Baron Sloet van de Beele, the governor-general of the Netherlands India. I immediately addressed a note to His Excellency, enclosing these credentials, and explaining my plan to visit the Spice Islands for the purpose of collecting the shells figured in Rumphius's "Rariteit Kamer," and expressing the hope that he would do what he could to aid me in my humble attempts to develop more fully the natural history of that interesting region. These papers our consul kindly forwarded, adding a note endorsing them himself.

As the governor-general administers both the civil and military departments of all the Dutch possessions in the East, I could not expect an immediate reply. I therefore found a quiet place in a Dutch family, with two other boarders who spoke English and could assist me in learning their difficult language, and, bidding Captain Freeman and the other good officers of the Memnon farewell, took up my abode on shore.

Batavia at present is more properly the name of a district or "residency," than of a city. Formerly it was compact and enclosed by walls, but these were destroyed by Marshal Daendals, in 1811. The foreigners then moved out and built their residences at various places in the vicinity, and these localities still retain their old Malay names. In this part of the city there are several fine hotels, a large opera-house, and a club-house. There are two scientific societies, which publish many valuable papers on the natural history, antiquities, geography, and geology, of all parts of the Netherlands India. These societies have valuable collections in Batavia, and at Buitenzorg there is a large collection of minerals and geological specimens. The "King's Plain" is a very large open square, surrounded by rows of shade-trees and the residences of the wealthier merchants. Near this is the "Waterloo Plain." On one of its sides is the largest building in Batavia, containing the offices of the various government bureaus, and the "throne-room," where the governor-general receives, in the name of the king, congratulations from the higher officials in that vicinity.

The governor-general has a palace near by, but he resides most of the time at Buitenzorg, forty miles in the interior, where the land rises to about a thousand feet above the level of the sea, and the climate is much more temperate.

A river, that rises in the mountains to the south, flows through the city and canal, and empties into the bay. Many bridges are thrown over this river and its branches, and beautiful shade-trees are planted along its banks.

All the houses in these Eastern lands are low, rarely more than one story, for fear of earthquakes, which, however, occur in this part of the island at long intervals. The walls are of bricks, or fragments of coral rock covered with layers of plaster. The roof is of tiles, or *atap*, a kind of thatching of palm-leaves. A common plan is, a house part parallel to the street, and behind this and at right angles to it an L or porch, the whole building being nearly in the form of a cross.

In front is a broad veranda, where the inmates sit in the cool evening and receive the calls of their friends. This opens into a front parlor, which, with a few sleeping-rooms, occupies the whole house part.

EASTERN MODE OF COOKING.

The L, when there is one, usually has only a low wall around it, and a roof resting on pillars. It is therefore open on three sides to the air, unless shutters are placed between the pillars. This is usually the dining-room. Back of the house is a square, open area, enclosed on the remaining three sides by a row of low, shed-roofed houses. Here are extra bedrooms, servants' quarters, cook-rooms, bath-rooms, and stables. Within this area is usually a well, surrounded with shade-trees. The water from this well is poured into a thick urn-shaped vessel of coral rock, and slowly filters through into an earthen pot beneath; it is then cooled with ice from our own New-England ponds. Thus the cold of our temperate zone is made to allay the heat of the tropics. Several ship-loads of ice come from Boston to this port every year. At Surabaya and Singapore large quantities are manufactured, but it is as soft as ice in ice-cream. When one is accustomed to drinking ice-water, there is no danger of any ill effect; but, on returning from the eastern part of the archipelago where they never have ice, to Surabaya, I suffered severely for a time, and, as I believe, from no other cause. In the frequent cases of fever in the East it is a luxury, and indeed a medicine, which can only be appreciated by one who has himself endured that indescribable burning.

The cook-room, as already noticed, is some distance from the dining-room, but this inconvenience is of little importance in those hot lands. The Malays are the only cooks, and I do not think that cooking as an art is carried to the highest perfection in that part of the world, though I must add, that I soon became quite partial to many of their dishes, which are especially adapted for that climate. The kitchen is not provided with stoves or cooking-ranges, as in the Western world, but on one side of the room there is a raised platform, and on this is a series of small arches, which answer the same purpose. Fires are made in these arches with small pieces of wood, and the food is therefore more commonly fried or boiled, than baked. There is no chimney, and the smoke, after filling the room, finally escapes through a place in the roof which is slightly raised above the parts around it.

As I am often questioned about the mode of living in the East, I may add that always once a day, and generally for dinner, rice and curry appear, and to these are added, for dinner, potatoes, fried and boiled; steak, fried and broiled; fried bananas (the choicest of all delicacies), various kinds of greens, and many sorts of pickles and *sambal*, or vegetables mixed with red peppers. The next course is salad, and then are brought on bananas of three or four kinds, at all seasons; and, at certain times, oranges, pumpelmuses, mangoes, mangostins, and rambutans; and as this is but such a bill of fare as every man of moderate means expects to provide, the people of the West can see that their friends in the East, as well as themselves, believe in the motto, "Carpe diem." A cigar, or pipe, and a small glass of gin, are generally regarded as indispensable things to perfect happiness by my good Dutch friends, and they all seemed to wonder that

JAVANESE AND FAMILY.

I could be a traveller and never touch either. It is generally supposed, in Europe and America, that housekeepers here, in the East, have little care or vexation, where every family employs so many servants; but, on the contrary, their troubles seem to multiply in direct ratio to the number of servants employed. No servant there will do more than one thing. If engaged as a nurse, it is only to care for one child; if as a groom, it is only to care for one horse, or, at most, one span of horses; and as all these Malays are bent on doing every thing in the easiest way, it is almost as much trouble to watch them as to do their work.

The total population of the Residency of Batavia is 517,762. Of these, 5,576 are Europeans; 47,570 Chinese; 463,591 native; 684 Arabs; and 341 of other Eastern nations.

All the natives are remarkably short in stature, the male sex averaging not more than five feet three inches in height, or four inches less than that of Europeans. The face is somewhat lozenge-shaped, the cheek-bones high and prominent, the mouth wide, and the nose short—not flat as in the negroes, or prominent as in Europeans. They are generally of a mild disposition, except the wild tribes in the mountainous parts of Sumatra, Borneo, Celebes, Timor, Ceram, and a few other large islands. The coast people are invariably hospitable and trustworthy. They are usually quiet, and extremely indolent. They all have an insatiable passion for gambling, which no restrictive or prohibitory laws can eradicate.

They are nominally Mohammedans, but have

none of the fanaticism of that sect in Arabia. They still retain many of their previous Hindu notions, and their belief may be properly defined as a mixture of Hinduism and Mohammedanism. A few are "Christians," that is, they attend the service of the Dutch Church, and do not shave their heads or file their teeth. They are cleanly in their habits, and scores of all ages may be seen in the rivers and canals of every city and village, especially in the morning and evening. The *sarong*, their universal dress, is peculiarly fitted for this habit. When they have finished their baths, a dry one is drawn on over the head, and the wet one is slipped off beneath without exposing the person in the least. The females wear the *sarong* long, and generally twist it tightly round the body, just under the arms. Occasionally it is made with sleeves, like a loose gown. A close-fitting jacket or *baju* is worn with it.

The men have but a few straggling hairs for beards, and these they generally pull out with a pair of iron tweezers. The hair of the head in both sexes is lank, coarse, and worn long. Each sex, therefore, resembles the other so closely that nearly every foreigner will, at first, find himself puzzled in many cases to know whether he is looking at a man or a woman. This want of differentiation in the sexes possibly indicates their low rank in the human family, if the law may be applied here that obtains among most other animals.

Every day I went out to collect the peculiar birds and beautiful butterflies of that region, my favorite place for this pleasure being in an old

Chinese cemetery just outside the city, where, as the land was level, the earth had been thrown up into mounds to keep the bones of their inmates from "the wet unfortunate places," just as in China, when far from any mountain or hill. A Malay servant followed, carrying my ammunition and collecting-boxes. At first I supposed he would have many superstitious objections to wandering to and fro with me over the relics of the Celestials, but, to my surprise, I found his people cultivating the spaces between the graves, as if they, at least, did not consider it sacred soil; yet, several times, when we came to the graves of his own ancestors, he was careful to approach with every manifestation of awe and respect.

A small piece of land, a bamboo hut, and a buffalo, comprise all the worldly possessions of most coolies, and yet with these they always seem most enviably contented.

They generally use but a single buffalo in their ploughs and carts. A string passing through his nostrils is tied to his horns, and to this is attached another for a rein, by which he is guided or urged to hasten on his slow motions. This useful animal is distributed over all the large islands of the archipelago, including the Philippines, over India and Ceylon; and during the middle ages was introduced into Egypt, Greece, and Italy. It thrives well only in warm climates. From its peculiar habit of wallowing in pools and mires, and burying itself until only its nose and eyes can be seen, it has been named the "water-ox." This appears to be its mode of resting, as well as escaping the scorching rays of the sun, and the swarms of annoying flies; and in the higher lands the natives make artificial ponds by the roadside, where these animals may stop when on a journey. They are generally of a dark slate-color, and occasionally of a light flesh-color, but rarely or never white. They are so sparsely covered with hair as to be nearly naked. They are larger than our oxen, but less capable of continued labor. They are usually so docile that even the Malay children can drive them, but they dislike the appearance of a European, and have a peculiar mode of manifesting this aversion by breathing heavily through the nose. At such times they become restive and unmanageable, and their owners have frequently requested me to walk away, for fear I should be attacked. When the females are suckling their young, they are specially dangerous. A large male has been found to be more than a match for a full-grown royal tiger.

On most of the islands where the tame buffalo is seen, wild ones are also found among the mountains; but naturalists generally suppose the original home of the species was on the continent, and that the wild ones are merely the descendants of those that have escaped to the forests. The Spaniards found them on the Philippines when they first visited that archipelago.

The plough generally used has both sides alike, and a single handle, which the coolie holds in his right hand while he guides the buffalo with the left.

RAHDEN SALEH.

RAHDEN SALEH'S PALACE.

The lower part of the share is of iron, the other parts of wood. It only scratches the ground to the depth of six or eight inches—a strange contrast to our deep subsoil ploughing. In these shallow furrows are dropped kernels of our own Indian maize and seeds of the sugar-cane. Sometimes the fields are planted with cocoa-nut palms about twenty yards apart, more for their shade, it appears, than for their fruit, which is now hanging in great green and yellow clusters, and will be ripe in a month. Beneath these trees are blighted nuts, and in many places large heaps of them are seen, gathered by the natives for the sake of the husk, from which they make a coarse rope.

Among these trees I was surprised to hear the noise, or more properly words, "Tokay! tokay!" and my servant at once explained that that was the way a kind of lizard "talked" in his land. So snugly do these animals hide away among the green leaves that it was several days before I could satisfy myself that I had secured a specimen of this speaking quadruped.

During my hunting I enjoyed some charming views of the high, dark-blue mountains to the south. One excursion is worthy of especial mention. It was to the palace of Rahden Saleh, a native prince. This palace consisted of a central part and two wings, with broad verandas on all sides. On entering the main building we found ourselves in a spacious hall, with a gallery above. In the centre of the floor rose a sort of table, and around the sides of the room were chairs of an antique pattern. Side-doors opened out of this hall into smaller rooms, each of which was furnished with a straw carpet, and in the centre a small, square Brussels carpet, on which was a table ornamented with carved-work, and surrounded with a row of richly-cushioned chairs. Along the sides were similar chairs and small, gilded tables. On the walls hung large steel engravings, among which I noticed two frequently seen in our own land: "The Mohammedan's Paradise," and one of two female figures personifying the past and the future. In front of the palace the grounds were tastefully laid out as small lawns and flower-plats, bordered with a shrub filled with red leaves. An accurate idea of the harmonious proportions of this beautiful palace is given in the accompanying cut. It is the richest residence owned by any native prince in the whole East Indian Archipelago.

The Rahden at the time was in the adjoining grounds, which he is now forming into large zoological gardens for the government at Batavia. When a youth, he was sent to Holland, and educated at the expense of the Dutch Government. While there, he acquired a good command of the German and French languages, was received as a distinguished guest at all the courts, and associated with the leading literati. In this manner he became acquainted with Eugene Sue, who was then at work on his "Wandering Jew," and—as is generally believed—at once chose the Rahden as a model for his "Eastern prince," one of the most prominent characters in that book. But it is chiefly as a landscape-painter that the Rahden is most famous. A few years ago there was a great flood here at Batavia, which proved a fit subject for his pencil; and the painting was so greatly admired, that he presented it to the King of Holland. When I was introduced to him, he at once, with all a courtier's art, inquired whether I was from the North or the South; and on hearing that I was not only from the North, but had served for a time in the Union army, he insisted on shaking hands again, remarking that he trusted that it would not be long before all the slaves in our land would be free.

I had not been out many times collecting before I found myself seized one night with a severe pain in the back of the neck and small of the back—a sure sign of an approaching fever. The next day found me worse, then I became somewhat better, and then worse again. The sensation was as if some one were repeatedly thrusting a handful of red-hot knitting-needles into the top of my head, which, as they passed in, diverged till they touched the base of the brain. Then came chills, and then again those indescribable darting pains. It seemed as if I could not long retain the command of my mind under such severe torture. At last, after seven days of this suffering, I decided to go to the military hospital, which is open to citizens of all nations on their paying the same price per day as in the best hotels. The hospital consisted of a series of long, low, one-story buildings placed at right angles to each other, and on both sides facing open squares and wide walks or gardens, which were all bordered with large trees and contained some fine flowers. In each of the buildings were two rows of rooms or chambers of convenient size, which opened out on to a wide piazza, where the sick could enjoy all the breezes and yet be sheltered from the sun. Every morning the chief doctor came round to each room with assistants and servants, who carefully noted his directions and prescriptions. He was a German, and appeared very kindly in his manner; but when the time arrived to take medicine, I found he had not only assigned for me huge doses of that most bitter of all bitter things—quinine—but also copious draughts of some fluid villanously sour. The ultimate result of these allopathic doses was, however, decidedly beneficial; and after keeping perfectly quiet for a week, I was well enough to return to my boarding-house, but yet was so weak for some time that I could scarcely walk.

Our consul, who had been kindly visiting me all the while, now came with a letter from His Excellency the governor-general that was amply sufficient to make me wholly forget my unfavorable initiation into tropical life. It was addressed to the "Heads of the Provincial Governments in and out of Java," and read thus: "I have the honor to ask Your Excellency to render to the bearer, Mr. Albert S. Bickmore, who may come into the district under your command in the interest of science, all the assistance in your power, without causing a charge to the public funds or a burden to the native people."

Besides honoring me with this kind letter, His Excellency generously wrote the consul that he would be happy to offer me "post-horses *free* over all Java," if I should like to travel in the interior. But it was with the hope of reaching the Spice Islands that I had come to the East, and, after thanking the governor-general for such great consideration and kindness, I began making preparations for a voyage through the eastern part of the archipelago. I had brought with me a good supply of large copper cans with screw covers. These were filled with arrack, a kind of rum made of molasses and rice. Dip-nets, hooks, lines, and all such other paraphernalia, I had fully provided myself with before I left America. Yet one paper, besides a ticket, was needed before I could go on board the mail-boat, and that was a "permission to travel in the Netherlands India." This paper ought to have been renewed, according to law, once every month; but the governor-general's letter was such an ample passport, that I never troubled myself about the matter again during the year I was journeying in the Dutch possessions.

CHAPTER II.

SAMARANG AND SURABAYA.

On the 7th of June, as the twilight was brightening in the eastern sky, I left my new Batavia home, and was hurriedly driven to the "boom." A small steamer was waiting to take passengers off to the mail-boat that goes to Celebes, Timor, and Amboina, the capital of the Spice Islands.

My baggage all on board, I had time to rest, and realize that once more I was a wanderer; but lonesome thoughts were quickly banished when I began to observe who were to be my companions, there on the eastern side of the world, so far from the centre of civilization and fashion; and just then a real exquisite stepped on board. He was tall, but appeared much taller from wearing a high fur hat, the most uncomfortable covering for the head imaginable in that hot climate. Then his neckcloth! It was spotlessly white, and evidently tied with the greatest care; but what especially attracted my attention were his long, thin hands, carefully protected by white kid gloves. However, we had not been a long time on the steamer, where every place was covered with a thick layer of coal-dust, before Mr. Exquisite changed his elegant apparel for a matter-of-fact suit, and made his second appearance as a *littérateur*, with a copy of the *Cornhill Magazine*. As he evidently did not intend to read, I borrowed it, and found it was already three years old, and the leaves still uncut. It contained a graphic description of the grounds about Isaac Walton's retired home—probably the most like the garden of Eden of any place seen on our earth since man's fall.

The other passengers were mostly officials and merchants going to Samarang, Surabaya, or Macassar, and I found that I was the only one travelling to Amboina. The general commanding the Dutch army in the East was on board. He was a very polite, unassuming gentleman, and manifested much interest in a Sharpe's breech-loader I had brought from America, and regarded it the most effective army rifle of any he had seen up to that time. He was going to the headquarters of the army, which is a strongly-fortified place back of Samarang. It was described to me as located on a mountain or high plateau with steep sides—a perfect Gibraltar, which they boasted a small army could maintain for an indefinite length of time against any force that might be brought against it. About five months later, however, it was nearly destroyed by a violent earthquake, but has since been completely rebuilt.

One genial acquaintance I soon found in a young man who had just come from Sumatra. He had travelled far among the high mountains and deep gorges in the interior of that almost unexplored island, and his vivid descriptions gave me an indescribable longing to behold such magnificent scenery

—a pleasure I did not fancy at that time it would be my good fortune to enjoy before I left the archipelago.

All day the sky was very hazy, but we obtained several grand views of high volcanoes, especially two steep cones that can be seen in the west from the road at Batavia. A light, but steady breeze came from the east, for it was as yet only the early part of the eastern monsoon. When the sun sank in the west, the full moon rose in the east, and spread out a broad band of silver over the sea. The air was so soft and balmy, and the whole sky and sea so enchanting, that to recall it this day seems like fancying anew a part of some fascinating dream.

This word monsoon is only a corruption of the Arabic word *musim*, "season," which the Portuguese learned from the Arabians and their descendants, who were then navigating these seas. It first occurs in the writings of De Barros, where he speaks of a famine that occurred at Malacca, because the usual quantity of rice had not been brought from Java; and "the mução" being adverse, it was not possible to obtain a sufficient supply. The Malays have a peculiar manner of always speaking of any region to the west as being "above the wind," and any region to the east as being "below the wind."

June 8th.—Went on deck early this morning to look at the mountains which we might be passing; and, while I was absorbed in viewing a fine headland, the captain asked me if I had seen that gigantic peak, pointing upward, as he spoke, to a mountain-top, rising out of such high clouds that I had not noticed it. It was Mount Slamat, which attains an elevation of eleven thousand three hundred and thirty English feet above the sea—the highest peak but one among the many lofty mountains on Java, and, like most of them, an active volcano. The upper limit of vegetation on it is three thousand feet below its crest. The northern coast of Java is so low here that this mountain, instead of appearing to rise up, as it does, from the interior of the island, seemed close by the shore—an effect which occurs in viewing nearly all these lofty peaks while the observer is sailing on the Java Sea. M. Zollinger, a Swiss, says that at sunrise the tops of these loftiest peaks are brightened with the same rose-red glow that is seen on Monte Rosa and Mont Blanc when the sun is setting, and once or twice I thought I observed the same charming phenomenon. The lowlands and the lower declivities of all the mountains seen to-day are under the highest state of cultivation. Indeed, this part of Java may be correctly described as one magnificent garden, divided into small lots by lines of thick evergreens, and tall, feathery palm-trees. This afternoon we steamed into the open roadstead of Samarang during a heavy rain-squall; for though the "western monsoon," or "rainy season," is past, yet nearly every afternoon we have a heavy shower, and every one is speaking of the great damage it is likely to do to the rice and sugar crops which are just now ripening. The heavy rain-squall cleared away the thick haze that filled the sky, and the next morning I went on shore to see the city. A few miles directly back of it rises the sharp peak of Ungarung to a height of some five thousand feet, its flanks highly cultivated in fields, and its upper region devoted to coffee-trees. Somewhat west of this, near the shore, I noticed a small naked cone, apparently of brown, volcanic ashes, and of so recent an origin that the vigorous vegetation of these tropical lands had not had time to spread over its surface. Back of Ungarung rise three lofty peaks in a line northwest and southeast. The northernmost and nearest is Mount Prau; the central, Mount Sumbing; and the southern one, Mount Sindoro.

Mount Prau receives its name from its shape, which has been fancied to be like that of a "prau," or native boat, turned upside down. It was the supposed residence of the gods and demigods of the Javanese in ancient times, and now it abounds in the ruins of many temples; some partially covered with lava, showing that earthquakes and eruptions have done their share in causing this destruction. Many images of these ancient gods in metal have been found on this mountain. Ruins of enormous temples of those olden times are yet to be seen at Boro Bodo, in the province of Kedu, and at Brambanan, in the province of Matarem. At Boro Bodo a hill-top has been changed into a low pyramid, one hundred feet high, and having a base of six hundred and twenty feet on a side. Its sides are formed into five terraces, and the perpendicular faces of these terraces contain many niches, in each of which was once an image of Buddha. On the level area at the summit of the pyramid is a large dome-shaped building, surrounded by seventy.

two smaller ones of the same general form. According to the chronology of the Javanese, it was built in A. D. 1344.

At Brambanan are seen extensive ruins of several groups of temples, built of huge blocks of trachyte, carefully hewn and put together without any kind of cement. The most wonderful of those groups is that of "The Thousand Temples." They actually number two hundred and ninety-six, and are situated on a low, rectangular terrace, measuring five hundred and forty by five hundred and ten feet, in five rows, one within another; a large central building, on a second terrace, overlooks the whole. This was elaborately ornamented, and, before it began to decay, probably formed, with those around it, one of the most imposing temples ever reared in all the East. According to the traditions of the Javanese, these buildings were erected between A. D. 1266 and 1296.

These structures were doubtless planned and superintended by natives of India. They were dedicated to Hindu worship, and here the Brahmins and Buddhists appear to have forgotten their bitter hostility, and in some cases to have even worshipped in the same temple. The Indian origin of these works is further proved by images of the zebu, or humped ox, which have been found here and elsewhere in Java, but it does not now exist, and probably never did, in any part of the archipelago.

As two Malays rowed me rapidly along in a narrow, canoe-like boat, I watched the clouds gather and embrace the high head of Mount Prau. Only thin and fibrous cumuli covered the other lofty peaks, but a thick cloud wrapped itself around the crest of this mountain and many small ones gathered on its dark sides, which occasionally could be seen through the partings in its white fleecy shroud. The form of the whole was just that of the mountain, except at its top, where for a time the clouds rose like a gigantic, circular castle, the square openings in their dense mass exactly resembling the windows in such thick walls.

Eastward of Ungarung are seen the lofty summits of Merbabu and Merapi, and east from the anchorage rises Mount Japara, forming, with the low lands at its feet, almost an island, on Java's north coast.

Like Batavia, Samarang is situated on both sides of a small river, in a low morass. The river was much swollen by late rains, and in the short time I passed along it, I saw dead horses, cats, dogs, and monkeys borne on its muddy waters out to the bay, there perhaps to sink and be covered with layers of mud, and, if after long ages those strata should be elevated above the level of the sea and fall under a geologist's eye, to become the subject of some prolix disquisition. This is, in fact, exactly the way that most of the land animals in the marine deposits of former times have come down to us—an extremely fragmentary history at best, yet sufficient to give us some idea of the strange denizens of the earth when few or none of the highest mountains had yet been formed.

Through this low morass they are now digging a canal out to the roads, so that the city may be approached from the anchorage by the canal and the

WATERING THE STREETS, BATAVIA.

A TANDU.

river. This canal is firmly walled in, as at Batavia.
From the landing-place to the city proper the road
was a stream of mud, and the houses are small and
occupied only by Malays and the poorer classes of
Chinese. In such streets two coolies are occasionally
seen carrying one of the native belles in a *tandu*.
The city itself is more compact than Batavia, and the
shops are remarkably fine. It was pleasant to look
again on some of the same engravings exposed for
sale in our own shops. The finest building in the
city, and the best of the kind that I have seen in the
East, is a large one containing the custom and other
bureaus. It is two stories high, and occupies three
sides of a rectangle. I was told that they were
fifteen years in building it, though in our country a
private firm would have put it up in half as many
months. There are several very fine hotels, and I
saw one most richly furnished. Near the river stands
a high watch-tower, where a constant lookout is kept
for all ships approaching the road. From its top a
wide view is obtained over the anchorage, the lowlands,
and the city. Toward the interior rich fields
are seen stretching away to the province of Kedu,
" the garden of Java." A railroad has been begun
here, which will extend to Surakarta and Jokyokarta,
on the east side of Mount Mérapi, and will
open this rich region more fully to the world.*

The church of the city, which is chiefly sustained

---

* The population of the Residency of Samarang, which includes the city, is 1,020,275. Of these 5,162 are Europeans, 1,001,252 are natives, 11,441 are Chinese, 438 are Arabs, and 1,982 are from other Eastern nations. In these figures the military are not included.

here as elsewhere by the Dutch Government, is a large cathedral-like building, finished in the interior in an octagonal form. One side is occupied by the pulpit, another by the organ, and the others are for the congregation. At the time I entered, the pastor was lecturing in a conversational but earnest manner to some twenty Malays and Chinese, gathered around him. At the close of his exhortation he shook hands with each in the most cordial manner.

From this church I went to the Mohammedan mosque, a square pagoda-like structure, with three roofs, one above the other, and each being a little smaller than the one beneath it. It was Friday, the Mohammedan Sabbath, and large numbers were coming to pay their devotions to the false prophet, for his is the prevailing religion in this land. By the gate in the wall enclosing the mosque were a well and a huge stone tank, where all the faithful performed the most scrupulous ablutions before proceeding to repeat the required parts of the Koran. It was pleasant to see that at least they believed and practised the maxim that "cleanliness is next to godliness." From the gate I walked up an inclined terrace to the large doorway, and at once saw, from the troubled expression on the faces of those who were kneeling on their straw mats outside the building, that I had committed some impropriety; and one answered my look of inquiry by pointing to my feet. I had forgotten that I was treading on "holy ground," and had therefore neglected "to put off my shoes." Opposite the entrance is usually a niche, and on one side of this a kind of throne, but what was the origin or signification of either I never could learn, and believe the common people are as ignorant as myself in this respect. Their whole ceremony is to kneel, facing this niche, and repeat in a low, mumbling, nasal tone some parts of the writings of their prophet. Their priests are always Arabs, or their mestizo descendants, the same class of people as those who introduced this faith. Any one who has been to Mecca is regarded as next to a saint, and many go to Singapore or Penang, where they remain a year or two, and then return and declare they have seen the holy city. The first conversions to Mohammedanism in any part of the archipelago occurred at Achin, the western end of Sumatra, in 1204. It was not taught by pure Arabs, but by those descendants of Arabs and Persians who came from the Persian Gulf to Achin to trade. Thence it spread slowly eastward to Java, Celebes, and the Moluccas, and northward to the Philippines, where it was just gaining a foothold when the Spanish arrived. Under their rule it was soon eradicated, and supplanted by Catholic Christianity. Bali is almost the only island where the people can read and write their native tongue, and have not partially adopted this religion. On the continent it spread so rapidly that, within one hundred years after the Hegira, it was established from Persia to Spain; but, as its promulgators were not a maritime people, it did not reach Achin until five hundred and seventy-two years after the Hegira, and then its followers had so little of the fanaticism and energy of the Arabs, that it was more than three hundred years in reaching Celebes, and fully estab lishing itself on that island. The Malay name for this religion is always "Islam."

On our way back to the mail-boat we passed quite a fleet of fishing-boats, at the mouth of the river. They are generally made alike at both ends, and look like huge canoes. Some have high lantern-shaped houses perched on the stern, as if to make them more unsightly. Here they all have decks, but those at Batavia are merely open boats.

The next day we continued on our course to the eastward, around the promontory formed by Mount Japara, whose sides are so completely scored by deep ravines that little or none of the original surface of the mountain can be seen. Dr. Junghuhn, who has spent many years studying in detail the mountains of Java, finds that above a height of ten thousand feet but very few ravines exist. This height is the common cloud-level, and the rains that they pour out, of course, only affect the mountain-sides below that elevation, hence the flanks of a mountain are sometimes deeply scored while its top remains entire. The substances of which these great cones are chiefly composed are mostly volcanic ashes, sand, and small fragments of basalt or lava, just the kind of materials that swift torrents would rapidly carry away.

The volcanoes of Java are mostly in two lines: one, commencing near Cape St. Nicholas, its northwestern extremity, passes diagonally across the island to its southeastern headland on the Strait of Bali. The other is parallel to this, and extends from the middle of the Strait of Sunda to the south coast in the longitude of Cheribon. They stand along two immense fissures in the earth's crust, but the elevating power appears only to have found vent at certain separate points along these fissures. At these points sub-aërial eruptions of volcanic ashes, sand, and scoriæ have occurred, and occasionally streams of basaltic and trachytic lava have poured out, until no less than thirty-eight cones, some of immense size, have been formed on this island. Their peculiar character is, that they are distinct and separate mountains, and not peaks in a continuous chain.

The second characteristic of these mountains is the great quantity of sulphur they produce. White clouds of sulphurous acid gas continually wreath the crests of these high peaks, and betoken the unceasing activity within their gigantic masses. This gas is the one that is formed when a friction-match is lighted, and is, of course, extremely destructive to all animal and vegetable life.

At various localities in the vicinity of active volcanoes and in old craters this gas still escapes, and the famous "Guevo Upas" or Valley of Poison, on the flanks of the volcano Papandayang, is one of these areas of noxious vapors. It is situated at the head of a valley on the outer declivity of the mountain, five hundred or seven hundred feet below the rim of the old crater which contains the "Telaga Bodas" or White Lake. It is a small, bare place, of a pale gray or yellowish color, containing many crevices and openings from which carbonic acid gas pours out from time to time. Here both Mr. Reinwardt and Dr. Junghuhn saw a great number of dead animals of various kinds, as dogs, cats, tigers, rhinoceroses, squirrels, and other rodents, many birds, and even snakes, who had lost their lives in this fatal place. Besides carbonic acid gas, sulphurous acid gas also escapes. This was the only gas present at the time of Dr. Junghuhn's visit, and is probably the one that causes such certain destruction to all the animals that wander into this valley of death. The soft parts of these animals, as the skin, the muscles, and the hair or feathers, were found by both observers quite entire, while the bones had crumbled and mostly disappeared. The reason that so many dead animals are found on this spot, while none exist in the surrounding forests, is because beasts of prey not only cannot consume them, but even they lose their lives in the midst of these poisonous gases.

It was in such a place that the deadly upas was fabled to be found. The first account of this wonderful tree was given by Mr. N. P. Foersch, a surgeon in the service of the Dutch East India Company. His original article was published in the fourth volume of Pennant's "Outlines of the Globe," and repeated in the *London Magazine* for September, 1785. He states that he saw it himself, and describes it as "the sole individual of its species, standing alone, in a scene of solitary horror, on the middle of a naked, blasted plain, surrounded by a circle of mountains, the whole area of which is covered with the skeletons of birds, beasts, and men. Not a vestige of vegetable life is to be seen within the contaminated atmosphere, and even the fishes die in the water!" This, like most fables, has some foundation in fact; and a large forest-tree exists in Java, the *Antiaris toxicaria* of botanists, that has a poisonous sap. When its bark is cut, a sap flows out much resembling milk, but thicker and more viscid. A native prepared some poison from this kind of sap for Dr. Horsfield. He mingled with it about half a drachm of the sap of the following vegetables — arum, kempferia galanga, anomum, a kind of zerumbed, common onion or garlic, and a drachm and a half of black pepper. This poison proved mortal to a dog in one hour; a mouse in ten minutes; a monkey in seven; a cat in fifteen; and a large buffalo died in two hours and ten minutes from the effects of it. A similar poison is prepared from the sap of the *chetek*, a climbing vine.

The deadly anchar is thus pictured in Darwin's "Botanic Garden:"

> "Fierce in dread silence, on the blasted heath,
> Fell Upas sits, the hydra-tree of death!
> So, from one root, the envenomed soil below,
> A thousand vegetative serpents grow!
> In shining rays the steady monster spreads
> O'er *ten square leagues* his far-diverging head,
> Or in one trunk entwists his tangled form,
> Looks o'er the clouds, and hisses at the storm;
> Steeped in fell poison, as his sharp teeth part,
> A thousand tongues in quick vibration dart,
> Snatch the proud eagle towering o'er the heath,
> Or pounce the lion as he stalks beneath;
> Or strew, as martial hosts contend in vain,
> With human skeletons the whitened plain."

All the north coast of Java is very low, often forming a morass, except here and there where some mountain sends out a spur to form a low headland. As we neared Madura this low land spread out beneath the shallow sea and we were obliged to keep eight or ten miles from land. On both sides of the Madura Strait the land is also low, and on the left hand we passed many villages of native fishermen who tend bamboo weirs that extend out a long way from the shore.

Here, for the first time, I saw boats with outriggers. Each had one such float on the leeward side, while, on a kind of rack on the windward side, was placed a canoe and every thing on board that was movable. Each boat carries two triangular sails, made of narrow, white cloths, with occasionally a red or black one in the middle or on the margins by way of ornament.

Just before entering the road of Surabaya we passed Gresik, a small village of Chinese and other foreigners, situated immediately on the beach. It is an old site and famous in the early history of Java, but the houses seemed mostly new, and their red-tiled roofs contrasted prettily with their white ridge-poles and gable-ends. It was here, according to the Javanese historians, that the Mohammedan religion was first established on their soil.

At Surabaya there appears to be much more business than at Batavia, and we found a larger number of vessels at anchor in the roads. At Batavia, the anchorage is somewhat sheltered by the islands at the mouth of the bay. At Samarang, the anchorage is quite exposed during the western monsoon, and the swell and surf are sometimes so great that boats cannot land, but at Surabaya the shipping is perfectly sheltered from all gales. There are, however, strong tidal currents, on account of the size of the bay, at the anchorage, and the narrow straits that connect it with the sea. These straits, though narrow, are not dangerous, and this may be said to be the only good harbor that is frequented on the island of Java. On the south coast, at Chilachap, there is a safe and well-sheltered anchorage, but it has very little trade.

At evening, when the water is ebbing, flocks of white herons range themselves in lines along its retreating edge, and calmly await the approach of some unlucky fish. Then the fishing-boats come up from the east, spreading out their white sails, and forming a counterpart to the lines of white herons along the shore.

The natives, unable to walk to their huts on the banks, have a most novel and rapid mode of navigating these mud-flats. A board about two feet wide, five or six feet long, and curved up at one end like the runner of a sled, is placed on the soft mud, and the fisherman rests the left knee on it while he kicks with the right foot, in just the way that boys push themselves on their sleds over ice or snow. In this way they go as fast as a man would walk on solid ground.

Like Batavia and Samarang, Surabaya* is situated on both sides of a small river, on low land, but not in a morass, like the old city of Batavia, and yet much nearer the shipping. This river has been changed into a canal by walling in its banks. Near its entrance it is lined on one side with nice

---

* The population of the Residency of Surabaya, which also includes that of the city of the same name, is 1,278,600. Of these, 5,124 are Europeans, 1,261,271 are natives, 7,603 are Chinese, 1,477 are Arabs, and 3,125 are from other Eastern nations.

dwelling-houses, and bordered with a row of fine shade-trees. Back of these dwellings is the government dockyard. It is very carefully built, and contains a dry-dock, a place to take up ships like our railways, ample work-shops, and large sheds for storing away lumber. They were then building six small steamers and two or three boats, besides a great dry-dock for the largest ships. Here was the Medusa, the ship that led the allied Dutch, English, French, and American fleet in the attack on Simonosaki, at the entrance of the Inland Sea in Japan. The many scars in her sides showed the dangerous part she had taken in the attack, and I have frequently heard the Dutch officers speak with a just pride of the bravery and skill of her officers in that engagement. Formerly, ships could only be repaired by being "thrown down" at Onrust, an island six miles west of the road at Batavia; but now nearly all such work is done in this yard. It was most enlivening to hear the rapid ringing of hammers on anvils—a sound one can rarely enjoy in those dull Eastern cities.

The government machine-shop is another proof of the determination of the Dutch to make for themselves whatever they need, and to be independent of foreign markets. Here they make many castings, but their chief business is manufacturing steam-boilers for the navy. Nine hundred Javanese were then in this establishment, all laboring voluntarily, and having full liberty to leave whenever they chose. Most of the overseers even are natives, and but few Europeans are employed in the whole works. They all perform their allotted tasks quietly and steadily, without loud talking or any unnecessary noise. Some of them are so skilful that they receive nearly two guilders per day. These facts show the capabilities of the Javanese, and indicate that there may yet be a bright future for this people. Here the standard weights and measures for the government are manufactured; and as an instance of the longevity of this people, when they are correct in their habits, the director told me that one native had worked for fifty-seven years in that department, and for some time had been assisted by both his sons and grandsons. He had just retired, and the director had been able to obtain for him a pension of full pay on account of the long time he had been in the service. There were three others still in the works, who also began fifty-seven years ago. Such cases are the more remarkable, because these natives are usually unable to labor at the age of thirty-five or forty, on account of their dissolute habits. Most of their machinery is not as nicely finished as that imported from Europe, but it appears to be quite as durable. Yet the fact that some Javanese have the capacity to do nice work was proved by one in charge of the engraving-department, whose fine lines would have been creditable to many a European. A merchant also has a similar machine-shop on a still greater scale.

Near by are the government artillery-works, where all the parts of wood and iron and the saddles and harnesses are manufactured, every thing but the guns. The wood used is carefully-seasoned teak. It is extremely durable, and combines in a good degree both lightness and strength. The leather is made by the natives from hides of the *sapi*, or cattle of Madura, the only kind seen here in Surabaya. It is light and flexible, and somewhat spongy compared to that made from our Northern hides. When it is wet it "spots," the wet places taking a darker color, which they retain when the leather again becomes dry. The director of the works thought that these defects might be remedied by adopting some other mode of tanning it. The leather made from the hide of the buffalo is thin, and, at the same time, excessively rigid.

The streets of Surabaya are narrow compared to those of Batavia; but they are far better provided with shade-trees of different species, among which the tamarind, with its highly compound leaves, appears to be the favorite. Here, as in all the other chief cities of the archipelago, the dusty streets are usually sprinkled by coolies, who carry about two large watering-pots. In the centre of the city, on an open square, is the opera-house, a large, well-proportioned building, neatly painted and frescoed within. In the suburbs is the public garden, nicely laid out, and abounding in richly-flowering shrubs. There were a number of birds peculiar to the East: a cassowary from Ceram, a black-swan from Australia, and some beautiful wild pheasants (*Gallus*) from Madura. Of this genus, *Gallus*, there are two wild species on that island and in Java. One of these, *Gallus bankiva*, is also found in Sumatra and the peninsula of Malacca. A third species is found in the Philippines, but none is yet known in the great islands of Borneo and Celebes or in any of the islands eastward. On the peninsula of Malacca, Sumatra, Borneo, and the Spice Islands, the Malay word *ayam* is used, but on the Philippines and Java the Javanese word *manuk* is frequently heard—it has hence been inferred that the Malays and Javanese were the first to domesticate it, and distribute it over the archipelago. Temminck regards the *Gallus bankiva* as the progenitor of our common fowl. If he is right in this conjecture, it was probably brought into Greece by the Persians, for the Greeks sometimes called it the "Persian bird."[*] Its early introduction into Europe is shown by representations of it on the walls of the Etruscan tombs, and Mr. Crawfurd states that it was found in England more than two thousand years ago. The small variety known to us as "the Bantam," is not a native of Java, but received that name because it was first seen by European traders on Japanese junks which came to that city to trade.

All the Malay race, except the Javanese, have the most inordinate thirst for gambling, and their favorite method of gratifying this passion is cock-fighting. This is forbidden by the Dutch Government; but in the Philippines the Spanish only subject the gamblers to a heavy tax, and the extent to which it is indulged in those islands is indicated by a yearly revenue of forty thousand dollars from this source alone.

The passion for this vice among the Malays is also shown in their language; for, according to Mr. Crawfurd, there is one specific name for cock-fighting, one for the natural and one for the artificial spur

---

[*] Crawfurd's Dict. Ind. Arch.

of the cock, two names for the comb, three for crowing, two for a cock-pit, and one for a professional cock-fighter.

But to return to the garden, where, among more interesting objects, were some images of the Brahman or Buddhist gods, worshipped by the ancient Javanese. One, particularly monstrous, appeared to have the body of a man and the head of a beast. A favorite model was to represent a man with the head of an elephant, seated on a throne that rested on a row of human skulls.

Hinduism was undoubtedly introduced into the archipelago in the same way as Mohammedanism—namely, by those who came from the West to trade, first into Sumatra, and afterward into Java and Celebes. This commercial intercourse probably began in the very remotest ages; for, according to Sir Gardner Wilkinson, the Egyptians used tin in manufacturing their implements of bronze two thousand years before the Christian era, and it is more probable that this tin came from the Malay peninsula than from Cornwall, the only two sources of any importance that are yet known for this valuable metal, if we include with the former the islands of Billiton and Banca. In the "Periplus of the Erythræan Sea," written about A. D. 60, it is stated that this mineral was found at two cities on the western coast of India, but that it came from countries farther east. In this same descriptive treatise it is also mentioned that the *malabrathrum*, a kind of odoriferous gum imported from India for the use of the luxurious Romans, was found at Barake, a port on the coast of Malabar,

A KLING.

NATIVE OF BILUCHISTAN.

but that it likewise came from some land farther east; and malabrathrum is supposed by many to be the modern benzoin, a resin obtained from the *Styrax benzoin*, a plant only found in the lands of the Battas, in Sumatra, and on the coast of Brunai, in the northern part of Borneo.

Although we gather from the records of Western nations these indications of products coming from the archipelago in the earliest ages, yet we have no information in regard to the time that the Hindu traders, who sailed eastward from India and purchased these valuable articles, succeeded in planting their own religion among those distant nations. The annals of both the Malay and Javanese are evidently fanciful, and are generally considered unreliable for any date previous to the introduction of Mohammedanism. Simple chronological lists are found in Java, which refer as far back as A. D. 78; but Mr. Crawfurd says that "they are incontestable fabrications, often differing widely from each other, and containing gaps of whole centuries."

The people who came from India on these early voyages were probably of the same Talagu or Telugu nation as those now called by the Malays "Klings" or "Kalings," a word evidently derived from Kalinga, the Sanscrit name for the northern part of the coast of Coromandel. They have always continued to trade with the peninsula, and I met them on the coast of Sumatra. Barbosa, who saw them at Malacca when the Portuguese first arrived at that city, thus describes them:* "There are many great merchants

* Crawfurd's Dict. Ind. Arch., "Hindustan."

here, Moor as well as Gentile strangers, but chiefly of the Chetis, who are of the Coromandel coast, and have large ships, which they call giunchi" (junks). Unlike the irregular winds that must have greatly discouraged the early Greeks and Phœnicians from long voyages over the Euxine and the Mediterranean, the steady monsoons of the Bay of Bengal invited those people out to sea, and by their regular changes promised to bring them within a year safely back to their homes.

The United States steamship Iroquois was then lying in the roads, and our consular agent at this port invited Captain Rodgers, our consul from Batavia, who was there on business, and myself, to take a ride with him out to a sugar-plantation that was under his care. In those hot countries it is the custom to start early on pleasure excursions, in order to avoid the scorching heat of the noonday sun. We were therefore astir at six. Our friend had obtained a large post-coach giving ample room for four persons, but, like all such carriages in Java, it was so heavy and clumsy that both the driver and a footman, who was perched up in a high box behind, had to constantly lash our four little ponies to keep them up to even a moderate rate of speed. Our ride of ten miles was over a well-graded road, beautifully shaded for most of the way with tamarind-trees. Parallel with the carriage-roads, in Java, there is always one for buffaloes and carts, and in this manner the former are almost always kept in prime order. Such a great double highway begins at Angir, on the Strait of Sunda, and extends throughout the whole length of the island to

Banyuwangi, on the Strait of Bali. It passes near Bantam and Batavia, and thence along the low lands near the north coast to Cheribon and Samarang, thence south of Mount Japara and so eastward. This, I was informed, was made by Marshal Daendals, who governed Java under the French rule in 1809. There is also a military road from Samarang to Surakarta and Jokyokarta, where the two native princes now reside. Java also enjoys a very complete system of telegraphic communication. On the 23d of October, 1856, the first line, between Batavia (Weltevreden) and Buitenzorg, was finished. Immediately after, it was so rapidly extended that, in 1859, 1,670 English miles were completed. A telegraphic cable was also laid in that year from Batavia up the Straits of Banca and Rhio to Singapore; but, unfortunately, it was broken in a short time, probably by the anchor of some vessel in those shallow straits. After it had been repaired it was immediately broken a second time, and in 1861 the enterprise was given up, but now they are laying another cable across the Strait of Sunda, from Angir to the district of Lampong; thence it will extend up the west coast to Bencoolen and Padang, and, passing across the Padang plateau, through Fort de Rock and Paya Kombo, come to the Strait of Malacca, and be laid directly across to Singapore.

These Javanese ponies go well on a level or downhill, but when the road becomes steep they frequently stop altogether. In the hilly parts of Java, therefore, the natives are obliged to fasten their buffaloes to your carriage, and you must patiently wait for those sluggish animals to take you up to the crest of the elevation.

Our road that morning led over a low country, which was devoted wholly to rice and sugar-cane. Some of these rice-fields stretched away on either hand as far as the eye could see, and appeared as boundless as the ocean. Numbers of natives were scattered through these wide fields, selecting out the ripened blades, which their religion requires them to cut off *one by one*. It appears an endless task thus to gather in all the blades over a wide plain. These are clipped off near the top, and the rice in this state, with the hull still on, is called "paddy." The remaining part of the stalks is left in the fields to enrich the soil. After each crop the ground is spaded or dug up with a large hoe, or ploughed with a buffalo, and afterward harrowed with a huge rake; and to aid in breaking up the clods, water to the depth of four or five inches is let in. This is retained by dikes which cross the fields at right angles, dividing them up into little beds from fifty to one hundred feet square. The seed is sown thickly in small plats at the beginning of the rainy monsoon. When the plants are four or five inches high they are transferred to the larger beds, which are still kept overflowed for some time. They come to maturity about this time (June 14th), the first part of the eastern monsoon, or dry season. Such low lands that can be thus flooded are called *sawas*. Although the Javanese have built magnificent temples, they have never invented or adopted any apparatus that has come into common use for raising water for their rice-fields, not even the

VISIT TO A SUGAR PLANTATION.

simple means employed by the ancient Egyptians along the hill, and which the slabs from the palaces at Nineveh show us were also used along the Euphrates.

Only one crop is usually taken from the soil each year, unless the fields can be readily irrigated. Manure is rarely or never used, and yet the *sawas* appear as fertile as ever. The sugar-cane, however, quickly exhausts the soil. One cause of this probably is that the whole of every cane is taken from the field except the top and root, while only the upper part of the rice-stalks are carried away, and the rest is burned or allowed to decay on the ground. On this account only one-third of a plantation is devoted to its culture at any one time, the remaining two-thirds being planted with rice, for the sustenance of the natives that work on that plantation. These crops are kept rotating so that the same fields are liable to an extra drain from sugar-cane only once in three years. On each plantation is a village of Javanese, and several of these villages are under the immediate management of a *controleur*. It is his duty to see that a certain number of natives are at work every day, that they prepare the ground, and put in the seed at the proper season, and take due care of it till harvest-time.*

The name of the plantation we were to see was "Seroenie." As we neared it, several long, low, white buildings came into view, and two or three high

---

* For the history of the culture-system and government in the Netherlands India, consult Money's "Java."

chimneys, pouring out dense volumes of black smoke. By the road was a dwelling-house, and the "fabrik" was in the rear. The canes are cut in the field and bound into bundles, each containing twenty-five. They are then hauled to the factory in clumsy, two-wheeled carts called *pedatis*, with a yoke of *sapis*. On this plantation alone there are two hundred such carts. The mode adopted here of obtaining the sugar from the cane is the same as in our country. It is partially clarified by pouring over it, while yet in the earthen pots in which it cools and crystallizes, a quantity of clay, mixed with water, to the consistency of cream. The water, filtering through, washes the crystals and makes the sugar, which up to this time is of a dark brown, almost as white as if it had been refined. This simple process is said to have been introduced by some one who noticed that wherever the birds stepped on the brown sugar with their muddy feet, in those places it became strangely white. After all the sugar has been obtained that is possible, the cheap and impure molasses that drains off is fermented with a small quantity of rice. Palm-wine is then added, and from this mixture is distilled the liquor known as "arrack," which consequently differs little from rum. It is considered, and no doubt rightly, the most destructive stimulant that can be placed in the human stomach, in these hot regions. From Java large quantities are shipped to the cold regions of Sweden and Norway, where, if it is as injurious, its manufacturers are, at least, not obliged to witness its poisonous effects.

After the sugar has been dried in the sun it

is packed in large cylindrical baskets of bamboo, and is ready to be taken to market and shipped abroad.*

Three species of the sugar-cane are recognized by botanists: the *Saccharum sinensis* of China; the *Saccharum officinarum* of India, which was introduced by the Arabs into Southern Europe, and thence transported to our own country † and the West Indies; and the *Saccharum violaceum* of Tahiti, of which the cane of the Malay Archipelago is probably only a variety. This view of the last species is strengthened by the similarity of the names for it in Malaysia and Polynesia. The Malays call it *tabu;* the inhabitants of the Philippines, *tubu;* the Kayans of Borneo, *turo;* the natives of Floris, between Java and Timur, and of Tongatabu, in Polynesia, *tau;* the people of Tahiti and the Marquesas, *to;* and the Sandwich Islanders, *ko*.

It is either a native of the archipelago or was introduced in the remotest times. The Malays used to cultivate it then as they do now, not for the purpose of making sugar, but for its sweet juice, and great quantities of it are seen at this time of year in all the markets, usually cut up into short pieces and the outer layers or rind removed. These people appear also to have been wholly ignorant of the mode of making sugar from it, and all the sugar, or more properly molasses, that was used, was obtained then as it is now in the Eastern islands, namely, by boil-

---

* During 1865 the government sold 250,000 piculs (16,666 tons) of sugar, but the total exported from Java was two million piculs.

† Our word sugar comes from the Arabic *sakar*, and that from the Sanscrit *sarkara*, thus indicating in its name how it first came to be known to Europeans.

ing down the sap of the gomuti-palm (*Borassus gomuti*).*

Sugar from cane was first brought to Europe by the Arabs, who, as we know from the Chinese annals, frequently visited Canpu, a port on Hanchow Bay, a short distance south of Shanghai. Dioscorides, who lived in the early part of the first century, appears to be the earliest writer in the West who has mentioned it. He calls it *saccharon*, and says that "in consistence it was like salt." Pliny, who lived a little later in the same century, thus describes the article seen in the Roman markets in his day: "Saccharon is a honey which forms on reeds, white like gum, which crumbles under the teeth, and of which the largest pieces are of the size of a filbert." (Book xii., chap. 8.)

This is a perfect description of the sugar or rock-candy that I found the Chinese manufacturing over the southern and central parts of China during my long journeyings through that empire, and at the same time it is not in the least applicable to the dark-brown, crushed sugar made in India.

---

* Mr. Crawfurd states that it is a similar product made from the sap of the Palmyra palm (*Borassus flabelliformis*), and not the sugar of the cane, that forms the saccharine consumption of tropical Asia, i. e., among the Cochin-Chinese, the Siamese, the Burmese, and the inhabitants of Southern India, including the Telinga nation who introduced Hinduism and Sanscrit names among these people, and probably were the first to teach them how to obtain sugar from the sap of palm-trees.

CHAPTER III.

THE FLORA AND FAUNA OF THE TROPICAL EAST.

June 15th.—At 8 A. M. we left our anchorage off Surabaya, and steamed down the Madura Strait for Macassar, the capital of Celebes. Along the shores of the strait were many villages of fishermen, and bamboo weirs extending out to a distance of five or six miles from both the Java and Madura shores, and showing well how shallow the water must be so far from land. During the forenoon it was nearly calm, but the motion of the steamer supplied a pleasant air. In the afternoon the wind rose to a light breeze from the east. At noon we passed Pulo Kambing ("Goat Island"), a small, low coral island off the south coast of Madura. Near by was a fleet of small fishing-boats, each containing two men, who were only protected from the broiling sun by a hat and a narrow cloth about the loins. These boats and other larger ones farther out to sea were extremely narrow, and provided with outriggers.

Madura receives its name from a Hindu legend, which makes it the abode of the demigod, Baladewa. It has but one mountain-range, and that crosses it from north to south. It is, therefore, not well watered, and unsuitable for raising rice; and many of its people have been obliged to migrate to the adjoining fertile shores of Java. The coffee-tree is raised on this island, but the land is best adapted for pasturage of the *sapi*, which is similar in its habits to our own neat-cattle, and never wallows in mires and morasses like the buffalo. In the mountains on the western part of Java, a wild species, the *banteng* (*Bos sondaicus*), is still found. It is not regarded as the source of the *sapi*, but a fertile cross is obtained from the two, and this intermediate breed is said to be the one used on Bali and Lombok. The *sapi* is found on all the islands to and including Timur, on Borneo, Celebes, and the Spice Islands, and has been introduced into the Philippines since their discovery, and now lives in a wild state on Luzon, just as the cattle of the pampas in South America, which have also descended from the domesticated breeds imported by the Spaniards.

On the eastern end of the island, which is quite low, great quantities of salt are obtained by evaporating water in "pans," or small areas enclosed with low dikes, like rice-fields. It is also manufactured in a similar manner at several places on the north coast of Java and on the western shore of Luzon, in the province of Pangasinan. Generally the coasts of the islands throughout the archipelago are either too high, or so low as to form merely muddy morasses, which are mostly covered with a dense growth of mangroves.

In some places on the south coast of Java, sea-water is sprinkled over sand. When this water has evaporated, the process is repeated. The sand is then gathered, and water filtered through it and evaporated by artificial heat. In Borneo, and among some of the Philippines, marine plants are burned, and the lye made from their ashes is evaporated for the sake of the salt contained in the residuum. All through the interior, and among the mountains, houses are built for storing it, and officials are appointed to dispose of it to the natives. The quantity yearly manufactured for the government at all the various places is about 40,000 koyangs, or 80,000 tons; but it is not allowed to be shipped and used until it is five years old, and a supply of 200,000 koyangs, or 400,000 tons, is therefore constantly kept on hand. It is deposited in the government storehouses by individuals at one-third of a guilder per picul. It is then transported and sold at a great profit by the government, which monopolizes the traffic in this necessary condiment, and obtains a large portion of its revenue in this manner.*

In the afternoon we were abreast the high Tenger (i. e., wide or spacious) mountains. Here is the famous "Sandy Sea," a strange thing on an island covered with such luxuriant vegetation as everywhere appears in Java. To reach it one has to climb an old volcano to a height of about 7,500 feet above the sea, when he suddenly finds himself on the rim of an old crater of an irregular elliptical form, with a minor

* The prices obtained for it are established as follows: On Madura and the north coast of Java, 6.92 guilders; on the south coast, 5.92 gl.; at Bencoolen, Padang, and Priaman, on the west coast of Sumatra, 6.66¾ gl.; Ayar Bangis and Natal, 6 gl.; Palembang, 5.10 gl.; Banca, 6.72 gl.; Bandyermassin, 6.66 gl.; Sambas and Pontianak, 5.10 gl.

axis of *three and a half* and a major axis of *four and a half miles*. It is the largest crater in Java, and one of the largest in the world. Its bottom is a level floor of sand, which in some places is drifted by the wind like the sea, and is properly named in Malay the Laut Pasar, or "Sandy Sea." From this sandy floor rise four cones, where the eruptive force has successively found vent for a time, the greatest being evidently the oldest, and the smallest the present active Bromo, or Brama, from the Sanscrit Brama, the god of fire. The position and relation of this Bromo, as compared to the surrounding crater, is entirely analogous to those that exist between Vesuvius and Monte Somma. The outer walls of this old mountain are of trachytic lava, and Dr. Junghuhn thinks its history may be summed up thus: first, a period when the trachyte was formed; this was followed by a period of trachytic lavas, then of obsidian; fourth, of obsidian and pumice-stone; fifth, the sand period, during which an enormous quantity of sand was thrown out, and the present sandy floor formed with the cones rising from it; and sixth, the present ash-period, during which only fine ashes are thrown out from time to time, and steam and sulphurous acid gas are constantly emitted.

The earliest descriptions of this crater represent it nearly as it is seen at the present day; but great eruptions, similar to the one supposed to have occurred, have been witnessed by Europeans since they first came to Java. In the year 1772 the volcano Papandayang, which is near the south coast of Java, and about in Long. 108° E., threw out such an immense quantity of scoriæ and ashes, that Dr. Junghuhn thinks a layer nearly fifty feet thick was spread over an area within a radius of seven miles; and yet all this was thrown out during a single night. Forty native villages were buried beneath it, and about three thousand souls are supposed to have perished between this single setting and rising of the sun. Dr. Horsfield, who drew up an account of this terrible phenomenon from the stories of the natives, wrongly supposed that " an extent of ground, of the mountain and its environs, fifteen miles long, and full six broad, was by this commotion swallowed up within the bowels of the earth."

On the 8th of July, 1822, Mount Galunggong, an old volcano, but a few miles northeast of Papandayang, suffered a far more terrible and destructive eruption. At noon on that day not a cloud could be seen in the sky. The wild beasts gladly sought the friendly shades of the dense forest; the hum of myriads of insects was hushed, and not a sound was to be heard over the highly-cultivated declivities of this mountain, or over the rich adjoining plain, but the dull creaking of some native cart drawn by the sluggish buffalo. The natives, under shelter of their rude huts, were giving themselves up to indolent repose, when suddenly a frightful thundering was heard in the earth; and from the top of this old volcano a dark, dense mass was seen rising higher and higher into the air, and spreading itself out over the clear sky with such an appalling rapidity that in a few moments the whole landscape was shrouded in the darkness of night.

Through this thick darkness flashes of lightning gleamed in a hundred lines, and many natives were instantly struck down to the earth by stones falling from the sky. Then a deluge of hot water and flowing mud rose over the rim of the old crater, and poured down the mountain-sides, sweeping away trees and beasts and human bodies in its seething mass. At the same moment, stones and ashes and sand were projected to an enormous height into the air, and, as they fell, destroyed nearly every thing within a radius of more than twenty miles. A few villages, that were situated on high hills on the lower declivities of the mountain, strangely escaped the surrounding destruction by being above the streams of hot water and flowing mud, while most of the stones and ashes and sand that were thrown out passed completely over them, and destroyed many villages that were farther removed from the centre of this great eruption.

The thundering was first heard at half-past one o'clock. At four the extreme violence of the eruption was past; at five the sky began to grow clear once more, and the same sun that at noon had shed his life-giving light over this rich landscape, at evening was casting his rays over the same spot then changed into a scene of utter desolation. A second eruption followed within five days, and by that time more than *twenty thousand* persons had lost their lives.

When the mountain could be ascended, a great valley was found, which Dr. Junghuhn considers analogous to the "Val del Bove" on the flanks of

Ætna, except that a great depression among these movable materials could not have such high, precipitous walls as are seen in that deep gulf. This eruption was quite like that of Papandayang, except that there was a lake in the bottom of this crater which supplied the hot water and the mud, while all the materials thrown out by the former volcano were in a dry state. In a similar way it is supposed the great crater and the "Sandy Sea" of the Tenger Mountains were formed in ancient times. On these Tenger Mountains live a peculiar people, who speak a dialect of the Javanese, and, despite the zealous efforts of the Mohammedan priests, still retain their ancient Hindu religion.

In the evening, fires appeared on the hills near the sea. This was the last we saw of Java, which, though but one-sixth of the area of Borneo, and one-third that of Sumatra, is by far the most important island in the archipelago. It is to the East Indies what Cuba is to the West Indies. In each there is a great central chain of mountains. Both shores of Cuba are opposite small bodies of water, and are continuously low and swampy for miles, but in Java only the north coast borders on a small sea. This shore is low, but the southern coast, on the margin of the wide Indian Ocean that stretches away to the Antarctic lands, is high and bold, an exception which is in accordance with the rule that the higher elevations are opposite the greater oceans, or, more properly, that they stand along the borders of the ocean-beds or greatest depressions on the surface of our globe. In Java, where the coast is rocky, the rocks are hard volcanic basalts and trachytes, which resist the action of the sea, and the shore-line is therefore quite regular; but in Cuba there is a fringing of soft coral rock, which the waves quickly wear away into hundreds of little projecting headlands and bays, and on the map the island has a ragged border. In its geological structure, Cuba, with its central axis of mica slates, granitic rocks, serpentines, and marbles, has a more perfect analogue in Sumatra; for in Java the mountains, instead of being formed by elevations of preëxisting strata, are merely heaps of scoriæ, ashes, sand, and rock, once fluid, which have all been ejected out of separate and distinct vents. The area of Java is estimated at 38,250 square geographical miles; that of Cuba at about 45,000. The length of Java is 575 geographical or 666 statute miles; that of Cuba 750 statute miles. But while the total population of Cuba is estimated only at a million and a half, the total population of Java and Madura is now (1865), according to official statements, 13,917,368.* In 1755, after fifteen years of civil war, the total population of Java and Madura was but 2,001,911. In a single century, therefore, it has increased more than sixfold. This is one of the beneficial effects of a government that can put down rebellions and all internal wars, and encourage industry. In Cuba, of a total area of thirty million acres, it was estimated, in 1857, that only 48,572 were under cultivation, or,

---

* Of this number 27,105 are Europeans; 13,704,535 are natives; 156,192 are Chinese; 6,764 are Arabs; and 22,772 are from other Eastern nations. See Appendix B.

including pasturage, 218,161 acres. In Java and Madura, last year (1864), the cultivated fields and the groves of cocoa-nut palms covered an area of 2,437,037 acres. In Cuba, from 1853 to 1858, the yearly exports were from 27,000,000 to 32,000,000 of dollars, and the imports of about the same value. In Java, last year, the imports amounted to 66,846,412 guilders (26,738,565 dollars); and the exports to the enormous sum of 123,094,798 guilders (49,237,919 dollars). During 1864 twenty-four ships arrived from the United States, of 12,610 tons' capacity, and three sailed for our country, of a united capacity of 2,258 tons.*

Both of these great islands abound in forests, that yield large quantities of valuable timber. Java furnishes the indestructible teak, from which the Malays and Javanese fitted out a fleet of three hundred vessels that besieged Malacca, two years after it had fallen into the hands of the Portuguese. In like manner the Spaniards, between 1724 and 1796, built with timber from the forests of Cuba an armada that numbered one hundred and fourteen vessels, carrying more than four thousand guns. From the Cuban forests come the indestructible *lignum-vitæ*, and the beautiful mahogany. Those jungles shelter no wild animals larger than dogs, but these in Java are the haunts of wild oxen, tigers, one large and two small species of leopard, the rhinoceros, two wild species of hog, and five species of weasel. Two of the latter yield musk; and one, the *Viverra musanga*,

* For a list of the number of ships that arrived during 1864, their tonnage, and the countries from which they came, see Appendix E.

of the size of a cat, is also found in the Philippines. Six species of deer are found on this island, and two of them, the *Cervus rufa* and *Cervus mantjac*, are sometimes domesticated.* The elephant is not found in Java, though it lives in Sumatra, Borneo, and the peninsula. Also the wild horse of Sumatra or Celebes does not exist in Java.

Among the more noticeable birds of Java is a beautiful species of peacock, the *Pavo spicifer*. It was represented to me as quite abundant in some places along the south coast. The natives make very beautiful cigar-holders from fine strips of its quills. In Sumatra it is not found, but is represented by an allied species. Of pigeons, Java has no less than ten species. The web-footed birds are remarkably few in species and numbers. A single duck, a teal, and two pelicans, are said to comprise the whole number. The white heron has already been noticed, and besides this, ten other species have been described. One of the smallest birds in Java, and yet, perhaps, the most important, from its great numbers, is the rice-eater, *Fringilla oryzivora*, a kind of sparrow. Great flocks of these birds are continually annoying the Malays as soon as the rice is nearly grown. The

---

* Albinos are occasionally found among these animals. For a long time previous to 1840 there was a famous "white deer" on the coast at Antju, in the vicinity of Batavia. Many attempts were made to shoot it, and these invariably proved so unsuccessful, that the natives, finding they had an opportunity to give way to their insatiable love for the marvellous, were all fully convinced that this animal was invulnerable. It was, however, shot at last, and proved to be of a gray, rather than a pure white. In 1845 a young one of a pure white color was caught at Macassar.

natives have a very simple and effective mode of driving them away. In the midst of a field a little bamboo house, sufficient to shelter its occupant from the rain and scorching sunshine, is perched high up on poles above the rice-stalks. Around each field are placed rows of tall, flexible stakes, which are connected together by a string. Many radiating lines of such stakes extend from the house to those along the borders, and the child or old person on watch has simply to pull any set of these lines in order to frighten away the birds from any part of the field. There are seven species of owls, and when the hooting of one is heard near any house, many of the natives believe that sickness or some other misfortune will certainly come to the inmates of that dwelling. Of eagles and falcons, or kites, eight species are mentioned. One of the kites is very abundant at all the anchorages, and so tame as to light on the rigging of a ship quite near where the sailors are working. When it has caught any offal in its long talons, it does not fly away at once to a perch to consume the delicious morsel at its leisure, like many birds of prey, but is so extremely greedy that it tears off pieces with its beak and swallows them as it slowly sails along in the air.

When we begin to examine the luxuriant flora of these tropical islands, almost the first tree that we notice by the shore is the tall, graceful cocoa-nut palm. Occasionally it is found in small clumps, far from the abode of man, for instead of being reared by his care, it often comes to maturity alone, and then invites him to take up his abode beneath its shade, by offering him at the same time its fruit for food, and its leaves as ample thatching for the only kind of a hut which he thinks he needs in an unchanging, tropical climate.

As it stands along the shore, it invariably inclines toward its parent, the sea, for borne on the waves came the nut from which it sprang, and now fully grown, it seeks to make a due return to its ancestor by leaning over the shore and dropping into the ocean's bosom rich clusters of its golden fruit. Here, buoyed up by a thick husk which is covered with a water-tight skin, the living kernel safely floats over the calm and the stormy sea, until some friendly wave casts it high up on a distant beach. The hot sun then quickly enables it to thrust out its rootlets into the genial soil of coral sand and fragments of shells, and in a few years it too is seen tossing its crest of plumes high over the white surf, which in these sunny climes everywhere forms the margin of the deep-blue ocean.

When the nut is young, the shell is soft and not separate from the husk. In a short time it turns from a pale green to a light yellow. The shell is now formed, and on its inner side is a thin layer, so soft that it can be cut with a spoon. The natives now call it *klapa muda*, or the young cocoa-nut, and they rarely eat it except in this condition. As it grows older, the exterior becomes of a wood-color, the husk is dry, and the shell hard and surrounded on the inside with a thick, tough, oily, and most indigestible layer, popularly known as "the meat" of the nut. This is the condition in which it is brought to our markets, but the Malays seldom or never think of eating it in this condition, and only value it for its oil. To obtain this the nut is broken, and the meat scraped out with a knife. This pulp is then boiled in a large pan, when the oil separates, floats on the top, and is skimmed off. This oil is almost the only substance used for lighting in the East, where far more lights are kept burning, in proportion to the foreign population, than in our own temperate zone, notwithstanding our long winter evenings, it being the custom there for each man to light his house and veranda very brilliantly every evening; and, if it is a festive occasion, rows of lamps must be placed throughout his grounds.

The natives also are fond of such display. The common lamp which they have for burning cocoa-nut oil is nothing but a glass tumbler. This is partly filled with water, a small quantity of oil is then poured in, and on this float two small splints that support a piece of pith in a vertical position for a wick. When the oil is first made, it has a sweet, rich taste, but in such a hot climate it soon becomes extremely rancid, and that used for cooking should not be more than two or three days old. The cool, clear water which the young nuts contain is a most refreshing drink in those hot climates, far preferable, according to my taste, to the warm, muddy water usually found in all low lands within the tropics. Especially can one appreciate it when, exposed to the burning sun on a low coral island, he longs for a single draught from the cold sparkling streams among his native New-England hills. He looks around him and realizes that he is surrounded by the salt waters of the ocean—then one of his dark attendants, divining his desire, climbs the smooth trunk of a lofty palm, and brings down, apparently from the sky, a nectar delicious enough for the gods.

This tree is of such importance to the natives that the Dutch officials are required to ascertain as nearly as possible the number of them in their several districts. In 1861 there were in Java and Madura nearly twenty millions of these trees, or more than three to every two natives.

Near the cocoa-nut grows the *Pandanus*, or "screw-pine," which may be correctly described as a trunk with branches at both ends. There are two species of it widely distributed over the archipelago. The flowers of one, the *P. odoratissimus*, are very fragrant and highly prized among the Malays. In some places mats and baskets are made from its leaves. Its woody fruit is of a spherical form, from four to six inches in diameter, and its surface is divided with geometrical precision by projections of a pointed pyramidal or diamond shape.

On the low lands, back from the shore, where the soil has been enriched with vegetable mould, the banana thrives. Unlike the cocoa-nut tree, it is seldom seen where it has not been planted by the hand of man. The traveller, therefore, who is worn out with his long wanderings through the thick, almost impassable, jungles, beholds with delight the long, green, drooping leaves of this tree. He knows that he is near some native hut where he can find a shelter from the hot sun, and slake his thirst with the water of the cocoa-nut, and appease his hunger on bananas and boiled rice, a simple and literally a *frugal* meal. Out of the midst of these drooping leaves hangs down the top of the main stem, with its fruit decreasing in size to the end. Some near the base are already changing from a dark green to a bright golden yellow. Those are filled with delicious juices, and they melt in your mouth like a delicately-flavored cream. Such bananas as can be purchased in our markets have been so bruised, and taste so little like this fruit at its home in the tropics, or at least in the East Indian islands, that they scarcely serve to remind one of what he has been accustomed to enjoy. The number of the varieties of bananas and the difference between them is as great as among apples in our own land.

Botanists call this tree the *Musa paradisiaca*, for its fruit is so constantly ripening throughout the year, and is such a common article of food, that it corresponds well to "the tree that yielded her fruit every month," and whose "leaves were for the healing of the nations."

Besides these plants, there are also seen on the low lands *Aroideæ*, *Amaranthaceæ*, papilionaceous or leguminous plants, and poisonous *Euphorbiaceæ*. The papaw (*Carica papaya*) thrives luxuriantly on most soils. The natives are always fond of it, and I found it a most palatable fruit, but the Europeans in the East generally consider it a too coarse or common fruit to be placed on the table. It was evidently introduced by the Portuguese and Spanish from the West Indies, and the Malay name *papaya* comes from the Spanish *papayo*.

At the height of one thousand feet ferns appear in very considerable numbers, and here also the useful bamboo grows in abundance, though it is found all the way down to the level of the sea. Practically this is a tree, but botanically it is grass, though it sometimes attains a height of seventy or eighty feet. It is used by the natives for the walls of their huts. For this purpose it is split open and pressed out flat, and other perpendicular and horizontal pieces hold it in place. It is also used for masts, spear-handles, baskets, vessels of all kinds, and for so many other necessary articles, that it seems almost indispensable to them. Its outer surface becomes so hard when partially burned, that it will take a sharp, almost cutting edge, and the weapons of the natives were probably all made in this manner previous to the introduction of iron. At the present time sharpened stakes, *ranjaus*, of this kind are driven into the ground in the tall grass surrounding a *ladang* or garden, so that any native with naked feet (except the owner) will spear himself in attempting to approach. I saw one man, on the island of Buru, who had received a frightful, ragged wound in this way.

Above one thousand feet the palms, bananas, and papilionaceous plants become fewer, and are replaced by the lofty fig or *waringin*, which, with its high top and long branches, rivals the magnificent palms by the sea-shore. The liquidambar also accompanies the fig. Orchidaceous plants of the most wonderful forms appear on the forest-trees, and are fastened to them so closely, that they seem to be parts of them. Here the ferns also are seen in great variety. *Loranthaceæ* and *Melanostomaceæ* are found in this zone. To this region belongs the beautiful cotton-wood tree Its trunk is seldom more than ten or twelve inches in diameter, and rises up almost perpendicularly thirty feet. The bark is of a light olive-green, and remarkably smooth and fair. The limbs shoot out in whorls at right angles to the trunk, and, as they are separated by a considerable space, their open foliage is in strong contrast to the dark, dense jungle out of which they usually rise. They thrive well also along the banks of rivers. In Java these trees are frequently used as telegraph-posts — a purpose for which they are admirably adapted on account of their regularity. Besides, any thing but a living post would quickly decay in these tropical lands. The fruit is a pod, and the fibrous substance it yields is quite like cotton. I found it very suitable for stuffing birds.

Over this region of the fig comes that of oaks and laurels. Orchidaceous plants and melastomas are more abundant here.

Above five or six thousand feet are *Rubiaceæ*, heaths, and cone-bearing trees; and from this region we pass up into one where small ferns abound, and lichens and mosses cover the rocks and hang from the trees. The tropical world is now beneath us, and we are in the temperate zone.

The tops of all those volcanic mountains that are still in a state of eruption are usually bare; and in others so large a quantity of the sulphur they produce is washed down their sides by the rains that the vegetation is frequently destroyed for some distance below their summits.

One of the great privileges of a residence in the tropics is to enjoy the delicious fruits of those regions in all their perfection. Of all those fruits, in my opinion, the *mangostin* ought unquestionably to be considered the first. This tree, a *Garcinia*, is about the size of a pear-tree. Its Malay name is *manggusta*, whence our own, but it is more generally known in the archipelago by the Javanese name *manggis*. It flourishes in most of the islands from the south coast of Java to Mindanao, the southernmost of the Philippines. On the continent it yields well as far up the Peninsula of Malacca as Bankok, in Siam, and in the interior to 16° N., but on the coast of the Bay of Bengal only to 14° N. The attempts to introduce it into India have failed, but the fruit is sometimes sent from Singapore after it has been carefully coated with wax to exclude the air. In Ceylon they have only partially succeeded in cultivating it. All the trials to raise it in the West Indies have proved unsuccessful, so that this, the best of all tropical fruits, is never seen on our continent. Its limited geographical range is the more remarkable, for it is frequently seen flourishing in the East Indian islands on all kinds of soils, and there is reason to suppose that it has been introduced into the Philippines within a comparatively late period, for in 1685 Dampier did not notice it on Mindanao. The fruit is of a spherical form, and a reddish-brown color. The outer part is a thick, tough

FRUIT MARKET.

covering containing a white, opaque centre an inch or more in diameter. This is divided into four or five parts, each of which usually contains a small seed. This white part has a slightly-sweet taste, and a rich yet delicate flavor, which is entirely peculiar to itself. It tastes perhaps more like the white interior of a checkerberry than any other fruit in our temperate climate. The thick covering is dried by the natives and used for an astringent.

Several fruits claim the second place in this scale. Some Europeans would place the *rambutan* next the *mangostin*, and others would prefer the mango or the *duku*. The *rambutan* (*Nephelium lappaceum*) is nearly as large as an apple-tree. The fruit is globular in form, and an inch or an inch and a half in diameter. The outside is a bright-red rind, ornamented with coarse, scattered bristles. Within is a semi-transparent pulp, of a slightly acid taste, surrounding the seed. This tree, like the *durian* and the *mangostin*, is wholly confined to the archipelago, and its acid fruit is most refreshing in those hot lands. At Batavia it is so abundant in February and March, that great quantities almost line the streets in the market parts of the city, and small boats are seen filled to overflowing with this bright, strawberry-colored fruit.

The mango-tree (*Mangifera indica*) is a large, thickly-branching tree, with bright-green leaves. Its fruit is of an elliptical form, and contains a flat stone of the same shape. Before it is ripe it is so keenly acid, that it needs only to be preserved in salt water to be a nice pickle for the table, especially with the universal curry. As it ripens, the interior changes from green to white, and then to a bright yellow. A tough outer skin being removed, there is seen a soft, almost pulpy, but somewhat fibrous mass within. Some of these fruits are extremely rich, and quite aromatic, while others have a sharp smack of turpentine. They even vary greatly in two localities, which may be but a few miles apart. Rumphius informs us that it was introduced into the moluccas by the Dutch in 1655. It has also been introduced into Zanzibar and Madagascar. When the Spaniards first visited the Philippines it was not noticed, but now it is very common in those islands, and considerable quantities of it are shipped to China, where I was frequently assured it was very delicious; but those who have tasted this or any other tropical fruit from only one locality are by no means competent judges. At Singapore I found some very nice ones that had been brought down from Siam. It also flourishes in India, and Mr. Crawfurd thinks, from the fact that the Malay and Javanese names are evidently only corruptions of the old Sanscrit, that it was originally brought into the archipelago from the continent, and should not be regarded as indigenous.

The *duku* is another highly-esteemed fruit. The tree is tall, and bears a loose foliage. From its trunk and limbs little branchlets grow out, bearing in long clusters the fruit, which is about the size of a robin's egg. The outer coating of this fruit is thin and leathery, and of a dull-yellow color. This contains several long seeds, surrounded by a transparent pulp, which is sweet or pleasantly acid. The seeds themselves are intensely bitter. The natives, however, invariably prefer the *durian* to all other fruits. The *Durio zibethinus* is a very large tree. Its fruit is spherical in form, six or eight inches in diameter, and generally covered with many sharply-pointed tubercles. This exterior is a hard shell. Within it is divided into several parts. On breaking the shell, a seed, as large as a chestnut, is found in each division, surrounded by a pale-yellow substance of the consistency of thick cream, and having an odor of putrid animal matter, so strong that a single fruit is enough to infect the air in a large house. In the season for this fruit the whole atmosphere in the native villages is filled with this detestable odor. The taste of this soft, salvy, half-clotted substance is well described by Mr. Crawfurd as like "fresh cream and filberts." It seems paradoxical to state that the same substance may violate a man's sense of smell, and yet gratify his sense of taste at the same time, but the natives certainly are most passionately fond of it, and I once met a foreigner who assured me that when he had once smelled this fruit he could never be satisfied till he had eaten some of it. Its simple odor is generally quite enough for all Europeans. It thrives well in Sumatra, Java, the Spice Islands, and Celebes, and is found as far north as Mindanao. On the continent forests of it exist on the Malay Peninsula, and it is successfully raised as far north in Siam as the thirteenth or fourteenth parallel. On the coast of the Bay of Bengal it is grown as far north as Tenasserim, in Lat. 14° N. It flourishes well on all the kinds of soils in this area, but all attempts have failed to introduce it into India and also into the West Indies. Its Malay name *durian* comes from *duri*, a thorn, and is thus applied on account of the sharp, thorny points of the pyramidal tubercles that cover its shell. The fact, that the Malay name is the one used wherever the fruit is known, indicates that it originated in a Malay country, and this view is strengthened by the circumstance that, while I was crossing Sumatra, I passed through large forests mostly composed of these trees in the high lands near the sources of the Palembang River.

Another far-famed fruit is the bread-fruit. It grows on a tree, the *Artocarpus incisa*, which attains a height of forty or fifty feet. It will be noticed at once by the stranger, on account of its enormous, sharply-lobed leaves, which are frequently a foot wide and a foot and a half long. The fruit has nearly the form of a melon, and is attached by its stem directly to the trunk or limbs. It is regarded of little value by the Malays, but farther east, in the Society Islands, and other parts of the South Sea, it furnishes the natives with their chief sustenance. Just before it is ripe it is cut into slices and fried, and eaten with a thick, black molasses, obtained by boiling down the sap of the gomuti-palm. When prepared in this manner it tastes somewhat like a potato, except that it is very fibrous. The seeds of this fruit in the South Sea are said, when roasted, to be as nice as chestnuts, but I never saw the Malays make any use of them. From the Pacific Islands it has been introduced into the West Indies and tropical America. Another species of this genus, the *A. integrifolia*, bears the huge "jack-fruit," which very closely resembles the bread-fruit. Sometimes it attains a weight of nearly seventy-five pounds, so that one is a good load for a coolie. The only part which the natives eat is a sweet, pulpy substance enveloping each seed.

June 16th.—This morning the gigantic mountain on Bali, Gunung Agung, or "The Great Mountain," towered up abeam of us against the southern sky. According to Mr. Crawfurd it attains an elevation of twelve thousand three hundred and seventy-nine feet, or four hundred and thirty-three feet higher than the far-famed Peak of Teneriffe.

These mountains are only a continuation of the chain which traverses Java, and Bali may be regarded as almost a part of Java, as it has quite the same flora and fauna, and is only separated from that island by a narrow strait. Here the Asiatic fauna of Sumatra, Borneo, and Java reaches its most eastern boundary. On Lombok, the next island eastward, a wholly different fauna is seen, having well-marked affinities with that of Australia. According to the traditions of the Javanese, Sumatra, Java, Bali, Lombok, and Sumbawa, were all formerly united, and afterward separated into nine different parts, and when three thousand rainy reasons shall have passed away they will be reunited. The dates of these separations are given as follows:

Palembang (the eastern end of Sumatra) from Java, A. D. 1192.

Bali from Balembangan (the eastern end of Java), A. D. 1282.

Lombok from Sumbawa, A. D. 1350.

All these dates are absurdly recent, and besides, the separations, in all probability, did not occur in the order given above. When we compare the fauna of the continent with that of Sumatra, Java, and Borneo, we find that Sumatra has the greatest number of species identical with those of the Peninsula of Malacca; that Borneo has a somewhat less proportion, and that Java has the largest number peculiar to itself. Thence we conclude that Java was the first of these islands that was separated from the continent, that Borneo was next detached, and Sumatra at the latest period. Bali was probably separated from Java at a yet more recent date.

Mr. Sclater was the first to notice the fact that the dividing line between the Asiatic fauna and that of Australia must be drawn down the Strait of Macassar, and this observation has only been confirmed by all who have collected in those regions since. Mr. A. R. Wallace further ascertained that this line should be continued southward, through the Strait of Lombok, between the island of that name and Bali. He visited the latter island, and thus contrasts its birds with those of Lombok: "In Bali we have barbets, fruit-thrushes, and woodpeckers; on passing over to Lombok these are seen no more, but we have an abundance of cockatoos, honeysuckers, and brush-turkeys (*Megapodiidæ*), which are equally unknown in Bali, and every island farther west. The strait here is but fifteen miles wide, so that we may pass in two hours from one great division of the earth to another, differing as essentially in their animal life as Europe does from America."

The royal tiger of Sumatra and Java is also found on that part of Bali nearest Java, but neither this nor any other feline animal exists on Lombok.

Monkeys, squirrels, civets, and others are seen west of this dividing line, but not east of it. Wild hogs are distributed over all the larger islands from Sumatra to New Guinea, and even occur as far eastward as Ceram. The flora of these islands is not divided in this manner, but maintains quite the same character from the northern end of Timur to the eastern end of Java.

In 1845 Mr. Earl pointed out the fact that Java, Sumatra, and Borneo, all stand on a plateau which is only covered by a shallow sea. They therefore not only were formerly connected, as the similarity of their faunæ shows, but are at the present day, and a line on the map, which indicates where the sea reaches a depth of one hundred fathoms, shows exactly where the great basins of the Pacific and Indian Oceans really begin. Northward this line unites the Philippines to Asia, and also proves that Formosa, the Lew-Chew and Japanese Islands, and the Kuriles, are all parts of the same great continent. Judging from what is known of their fauna, Mr. Wallace thinks the separation of the Philippines from the continent occurred before that of Java, and since that epoch they have undergone very considerable changes in their physical geography.

In 1478, when the Hindu religion was driven out of Java, it took refuge in Bali, where it exists to the present day. The natives here, as in India, are divided into four castes. The first and highest includes only the priests; the second, the soldiers; the third, the merchants; and the fourth, and lowest, comprises the common laborers. According to Mr. Crawfurd, who visited the island, the wives of the soldiers frequently sacrifice themselves by stabbing with the *kris*, and the body is afterward burned, and "with the princes, the sacrifice of one or two women is indispensable." The high mountains on Bali contain a number of lakes or tarns, which supply many streams, and the natives are thus enabled to irrigate their land so completely, that about twenty thousand tons of rice are annually exported to other parts of the archipelago, after a population of nearly three-quarters of a million is supplied. In 1861 Java had only a population of three hundred and twenty-five to a square mile, while Bali was supposed to have nearly five hundred, and it is probably the most densely populated island in these seas at the present time.

The Hindu religion also prevails over a part of Lombok. On this island a huge mountain rises up, according to the trigonometrical measurements of Baron van Carnbée, to a height of twelve thousand three hundred and sixty English feet, and probably overtops every other lofty peak in the whole archipelago.

CHAPTER IV.

CELEBES AND TIMUR.

June 18*th*.—We anchored this evening close in to the coast of Celebes on a shallow plateau, which is really only a slightly-submerged part of the island itself. This word Celebes is not of native origin, and was probably introduced by the Portuguese, who were the earliest Europeans that visited this island. It first appears in the historical and descriptive writings of De Barros,* who informs us that it was not discovered until 1525, fourteen years after the Portuguese first came to the Moluccas; but at that time they were only anxious to find the regions where the clove and the nutmeg grew. Afterward they were induced to search for this island from the rumors that came of the gold found here; and, indeed, to this day, gold is obtained in the northern and southwestern peninsulas. At first, Celebes was supposed to

---

* João de Barros, who wrote a classical history of the regions discovered and conquered by the Portuguese in the East, was born in 1496, and died in 1570. He never visited the Indies, but carefully and faithfully compiled his descriptions from the official records, which were all intrusted to his care, in 1532. The first decade of his work was published in 1552, the second in 1553, the third in 1563, and the fourth after his death. He was, therefore, a contemporary of most of the early navigators whose history he narrates.

consist of many islands, and this belief appears to have given it a name in a plural form. It consists of a small, irregular, central area and four long limbs or peninsulas, and De Cauto* very aptly describes it as "resembling in form a huge grasshopper." Two of these peninsulas extend to the south, and are separated from each other by the Gulf of Boni: one takes an easterly direction, and the other stretches away six degrees to the north and northeast. In the southwest peninsula, which is the only one that has been completely explored, two languages are spoken —the Mangkasara, in the native tongue, or Mangkasa, in the Malay (of which word, "Macassar," the name of the Dutch capital, is only a corruption), and the Wugi or Bugi, which was originally more particularly limited to the coast of the Gulf of Boni. North of Macassar, in the most western part of the island, is another people—the Mandhar—who speak another language. On the island of Buton, which ought to be considered a part of the peninsula east of the Gulf of Boni, another language is spoken. The eastern peninsula is unexplored. The northern contains the people speaking the Gorontalo and the Menado languages.

The primitive religion of most of these natives is supposed to have been some form of Hinduism. De

---

* Diogo de Cauto, who wrote the "Asia Portuguesa," was born in Lisbon in 1542, and died at Goa, the Portuguese capital of India, in 1616, at the age of seventy-four. It is believed that he went to India at the age of fourteen, and, after having lived there in the army ten years, returned to Portugal, but soon after went back, and continued there till his death. It is probable that he never visited any part of the archipelago himself, but obtained from others the information he gives us.

Cauto says: "They have no temples, but pray looking up to the skies with their heads raised," which he regards as conclusive evidence that "they had a knowledge of the true God." According to the records of the Macassar people,* the Mohammedan religion was first taught them by a native of Menangkabau, a province on the plateau in the interior of Sumatra, north of the present city of Padang. This occurred just before the arrival of the Portuguese in 1525, and the native annals say that the doctrine of the false Prophet and of Christianity were presented to the prince of Macassar at the same time, and that his advisers pressed him to accept Mohammedanism, because "God would not allow error to arrive before truth."

In the interior live a people called by the coast tribes Turaju, who are represented as head-hunters,

---

* The early kings of Macassar boasted that they descended from the Tormanurong, who, according to their legends, had this miraculous history as given in Pinkerton's "Voyages," vol. ii., p. 216. In the earliest times, it happened that a beautiful woman, adorned with a chain of gold, descended from heaven, and was acknowledged by the Macassars as their queen. Upon hearing of the appearance on earth of this celestial beauty, the King of Bantam made a long voyage to that land, and sought her hand in marriage, though he had before wedded a princess of Bontain. His suit was granted, and a son was begotten in this marriage, who was two or three years old before he was born, so that he could both walk and talk immediately after his birth, but he was very much distorted in shape. When he was grown up, he broke the chain of gold which his mother had brought from heaven into two pieces, after which she, together with her husband, vanished in a moment, taking with her one half the chain, and leaving the other half and the empire to her son. This chain, which the Macassars say is sometimes heavy and sometimes light, at one time dark colored and at another bright, was ever afterward one of the regalia of the kings until it was lost in a great revolution.

and even cannibals. Barbosa * makes a similar statement in regard to all the natives of this island in his time. He says, when they came to the Moluccas to trade, they were accustomed to ask the king of those islands to kindly deliver up to them the persons he had condemned to death, that they might gratify their palates on the bodies of such unfortunates, " as if asking for a hog."

As we steamed up the coast to Macassar, the mountains in the interior came grandly into view. They appear much more connected into chains than in Java. One of them, Lompo-batung, rises to a height of eight thousand two hundred feet above the sea, and is probably the loftiest peak on the whole island.

The harbor of Macassar is formed by a long, curving coral reef, with its convex side from the shore. At a few places this reef rises above the surface of the water and forms low islands; but, in the heavy gales of the western monsoon, the sea frequently breaks over it into the road with such violence as to drive most of the native praus on shore. Near it were fleets of fishing-boats, and this was the first place in these tropical seas where I found a fish that, according to my taste, was as nice as those which come from the cold waters that bathe our New-England shores.

* Odoardo Barbosa (in Spanish, Balbosa) was a gentleman of Lisbon, who travelled in the East during his youth. From his writings it appears probable that he visited Malacca before it was conquered by the Portuguese in 1511. His work appeared in 1516. In 1519 he joined Magellan, and was treacherously murdered by the natives of Zebu, one of the Philippines, in 1521, four days after the great navigator, whom he accompanied, had suffered a like fate.

In the road were many praus of forty or fifty tons' burden, and some even twice as large. In the beginning of the western monsoon they go in great numbers to the Arru Islands, the principal rendezvous* for the people of Ceram, Goram, the Ki Islands, Tenimber, Baba, and the adjacent coast of New Guinea. Mr. Wallace, who was particularly seeking the birds of paradise, went in one of these rude vessels to the Arrus, a distance of one thousand miles. When Mr. Jukes was at Port Essington, in January, 1845, two of these praus were there. One had made the passage from Macassar in ten, and another in fifteen days. But, on these long voyages, many never return. In the last of the month a third came into that port and reported that four others, more than had arrived safely, had just foundered during a heavy gale, and that the crew of only one was saved. Many go every year to the islands off the eastern end of Ceram and to the neighboring coast of Papua, and sometimes along its northern shores to Geelvink Bay. These long voyages indicate that the Bugis are now what the Malays were when the Portuguese first came to the East, namely, the great navigators and traders of the archipelago. They carry to all these localities English calicoes and cotton goods of their own manufacture, also Chinese gongs and large quantities of arrack. They bring in return tortoise-shell, mother-of-pearl shell, pearls, birds of paradise, and *tripang*, which appears to be the common Malay

---

* Mr. Wallace estimated the value of the goods carried there from Macassar alone at 200,000 guilders (80,000 dollars), and those brought from other places at 50,000 guilders (20,000 dollars) more.

name for all kinds of *Holothurians*, or "sea-cucumbers." These latter animals abound on every coral reef throughout the archipelago, just above and below low-water level. As many as twenty different sorts are recognized of perhaps half as many species. That kind is considered the most valuable which is found on the banks of coral sand which are bare, or nearly bare, at low tide, and are covered with a short, green sea-weed. After the animals are collected, the intestines are removed, and they are boiled in sea-water, in some places with the leaves of the papaw, and in others with the bark of a mangrove-tree which gives them a bright-red color. After they have been boiled, they are buried in the ground till the next day, when they are spread out to dry in the sun. Sometimes they are not buried in the ground, but dried at once on a framework of bamboo-splints over a fire. They are now ready to be shipped to China, the only market for this disgusting article. There the Celestials make of them one of their many favorite soups. It is said that the Chinese cooks boil them some time with pieces of sugar-cane to partially neutralize their rank flavor. Many are also gathered in the Gulf of Siam and sent up the China Sea. Mr. Crawfurd has been unable to discover any mention of *tripang* by the Portuguese writers, and this he regards as one proof, among others, "that the Chinese, who chiefly carry on this trade, had not yet settled in the archipelago when the Portuguese first appeared in it." There are yearly shipped from macassar some fourteen thousand piculs of this article, of a value of nearly six hundred thousand dollars! A few cargoes, chiefly of coffee, from Menado and the interior, are exported each year directly to Europe, but ships usually have to go to China for a return-freight. In 1847 Macassar was made a free port, in imitation of Singapore.

Our steamer came alongside a well-built iron pier, the only one of any kind I had yet seen in the East. Though the mail then came but once a month, there seemed to be no great excitement. A small group of soldiers, with red and yellow epaulets, came down and looked on in a most unconcerned manner, while a number of coolies gathered and began carrying the cargo on shore—for trucks and drays are modern innovations that have not yet appeared in these distant regions, not even to any considerable degree in Batavia. The sea-water here is remarkably pure and clear. As we were hauling in to the pier, several boys kept swimming round and round the ship, and shouting out, "*Képing tuan! képing tuan!*" that is, "A small piece of money, sir! a small piece of money, sir!" and I found that when I threw a copper coin as large as a cent, so that it would strike the water edgewise, even at a distance of ten feet from them, some one would invariably catch it before it reached the bottom. This is quite as wonderful skill as is shown by any of the natives in the South Seas.

From the pier a street leads up to a large common, and on the right side is Fort Rotterdam, which was built soon after 1640, when the Dutch first formed a settlement on the island, though they had been trading with the natives since 1607. In 1660 they had driven away their rivals the Portuguese, had conquered the natives of Macassar, and fully established their authority over all this part of the island. Opposite the fort is the "Societeit," or Club-House—for every place of any considerable size in the Netherlands India has one or two of these pleasant resorts, where newspapers and periodicals are received, and all the social Europeans gather in the cool evenings to enjoy a "pijt"—a small glass of gin with bitters—or "a potje van bier," in just the way that Irving pictures the happy moments of Rip van Winkle. Any member may introduce a stranger, who is at once considered one of the fraternity; and I formed many pleasant acquaintances and passed many pleasant hours in this way. Beyond the clubhouse, on a street beautifully shaded with tamarind-trees, are the hotel and residence of the governor. I called on him, for, as I was travelling under the patronage of the government, it was expected that I should present myself before the highest official of each place that I might chance to visit, and thus express my sense of the kindness of the government toward me; and, at the same time, do what the etiquette of the land required. The governor here most kindly offered me post-horses free, if I would stop and travel in the territory under his immediate command. After the heat of the day was passed, two of my merchant-friends gave me a ride through the town, and a mile or two out into the adjoining country, to visit the tombs of the native princes who ruled that region before the arrival of Europeans. These tombs had, originally, been enclosed in a house, but the roof was already gone, and the walls were rapidly crumbling away. At the foot and head of each grave was a square pillar. Near by were the ruins of a building which may have been the residence of one of these princes. It was, like the house enclosing the tombs, about thirty feet square, with an entrance on one side. In the front, and right and left sides, were two ranges of holes, probably designed for windows. The upper ones were small, but the lower ones were a foot and a half in diameter. Its walls were eighteen inches thick, and of the common coral rock. Several steps led up to the entrance, and this and the windows were grotesquely ornamented. De Cauto informs us that these people were accustomed " to burn their dead, and collect the ashes in urns, which they inter in separate fields, where they erect chapels, and for a year the relatives bring food, which they place on their tombs, and which the dogs, cats, and birds carry off."

We then took a delightful walk through the adjoining forest of waringin-trees and cocoa-nut and betel-nut palms, and again and again I wished I could have photographic views of the scenery around us to show to my friends, for words utterly fail to convey any idea of the rich grouping of the palms and shrubbery, and festooning vines about us, as the setting sun shot into the luxuriant foliage long, horizontal pencils of golden light.

Here we found the coffee-tree growing wild, and near by we came to the tomb of a rich native merchant. It was a low, square building, surmounted by a dome, and the whole enclosed by a wall about two feet high, whose outer surface was covered with blue plates of porcelain. As we approached, a monotonous, nasal chanting greeted our ears. It was made by a native priest, who was repeating long prayers from the Koran, by the grave of his departed friends. The notes of his minor, melancholy chant echoed and reëchoed widely through the quiet forest, and were the more impressive because they seemed to come from the abode of the dead. He invited us in, and showed us his books, which were written by hand, and yet all the characters were as neat and regular as copperplate. In the grounds was a papaw-tree with a branch which bore at its summit leaves and fruit like the parent stem.

On the 20th of June we sailed for Kupang, a port near the southern end of the island of Timur. The southern extremity of the southwestern peninsula of Celebes is low, with mountains of moderate height rising in the interior. As we steamed past it on our way southward to Sapi Strait, between Sumbawa on one side and Commodo and Floris* on the other, we found that the eastern monsoon had already freshened to a strong breeze, but it was steady, and the sky and sea reminded one of "the trades." Many flying-fish sprang out of the sea, as if too happy to remain in their more proper element.

On the second morning from Macassar, Gunong Api, "The Burning Mountain," rose up majestically

* The name of this island comes from the Portuguese word *flor*, a flower; plural, *floris*.

before us. Its high top, five thousand eight hundred feet above the level of the sea, was hidden by horizontal clouds, *strati*, which parted while we were observing the mountain, and let down a band of bright sunlight over its dark sides. It is not a single but a double peak—the one to the northwest appearing from the deep valleys and ravines in its sides to be the older. On the eastern flanks of this peak, near the shore, there appears to be an old crater, whose outer wall has been washed away by the sea. For one-third of the distance from the shore to the top of this peak there is some shrubbery in the bottoms of the deep ravines; but the remaining two-thirds are quite bare. At its top, this mountain ends in a small truncated cone. The southwestern peak seems to have recently formed, for, from its top down to the shore, on the southeast side, there is one continuous sheet of fine volcanic materials, scored only by narrow grooves with perpendicular sides. When viewed in profile, the unbroken sweep of its sides, from its summit to the sea, was most majestic. It was so regular, that it was difficult to believe it had not been shaped by the hand of man. By this time we were in the midst of the strait between Sumbawa and Commodo, and soon we passed on the left hand Gilibanta, whose highest point is only twelve hundred feet above the sea. Its name in Javanese means the "one that disputes the way." It is merely the remnant of an old crater, whose northwestern wall has disappeared beneath the sea. The southerly dip of the successive overflows of lava was plainly to be seen.

On our right was Sumbawa, with its high mountains, and near its southeastern end is Sapi, or Cattle Bay, which gives its name to the strait. In a peninsula on the northern side of this island is Mount Tomboro, which suffered such a terrible eruption, and caused so much destruction of human life, in 1815. The first intimation that the people of Java received of this frightful phenomenon was a series of explosions, so closely resembling the reports of cannon, that at Jokyokarta, in Java, a distance of four hundred and eighty miles, troops were marched toward a neighboring post that was supposed to have been attacked. At Surabaya, gunboats were sent out to assist ships that were thought to be trying to defend themselves against pirates in the Madura Strait; and at two places on the coast, boats put off to search for ships that were imagined to be in distress. These reports occurred on the 5th of April, and continued for five days, when the sky over the eastern part of Java began to be darkened by falling ashes, and for four days they could not see the sun. Mr. Crawfurd says that at Surabaya the sky for several months did not become as clear as it usually is in the southeast monsoon. Northward from Sumbawa the reports accompanying this eruption were heard as far as the island of Ternate, near Gilolo, a distance of seven hundred and twenty geographical miles, and so distinctly, that the Resident sent out a boat to look for the ship which was supposed to have been firing signals. To the westward these reports were heard at Moko-moko, a post near Bencoolen, which is no less than nine hundred and seventy geographical miles in a right line—as far as from New York to the Keys off the southern extremity of Florida. The ashes that were poured into the air during this eruption fell to the eastward, or against the prevailing wind, as far as the middle of Floris, about two hundred and ten geographical miles; and westward on Java, in the mountains of Cheribon, about two hundred and seventy miles from the volcano. So great was the quantity of ashes thrown out at this time, that it is estimated that on the island of Lombok, about ninety miles distant, *forty-four thousand* persons perished in the famine that followed. Dr. Junghuhn thinks that, within a circle described by a radius of two hundred and ten miles, the average depth of the ashes was at least two feet; this mountain, therefore, must have ejected several times its own mass, and yet no subsidence has been noticed in the adjoining area, and the only change that has been observed is, that during the eruption Tomboro lost two-thirds of its previous height.* The captain of a ship dispatched

---

* The Rajah of Sangir, a village from twelve to fifteen miles southeast of the volcano, was an eye-witness of this fearful phenomenon, and thus describes it: "About 7 P. M., on the 10th of April, three distinct columns of flame burst forth, near the top of Tomboro Mountain, all of them apparently within the verge of the crater; and, after ascending separately to a very great height, their tops united in the air in a troubled, confused manner. In a short time the whole mountain next Sangir appeared like a body of liquid fire, extending itself in every direction. The fire and columns of flame continued to rage with unabated fury until the darkness, caused by the quantity of falling matter, obscured it at about 8 P. M. Stones at this time fell very thick at Sangir, some of them as large as a man's two fists, but generally not larger than walnuts. Between 9 and 10 P. M. ashes began to fall; and soon after, a violent whirlwind ensued, which blew down nearly every house in the village of Sangir, carrying their tops and light parts along with

from Macassar to the scene of this terrible phenomenon states: "On approaching the coast, I passed through great quantities of pumice-stone floating on the sea, which had at first the appearance of shoals, so much so that I sent a boat to examine one, which, at the distance of less than a mile, I took for a dry sand-bank, upward of three miles in length, with black rocks in several parts of it." This is the kind of stones I saw floating over the sea as we were approaching the Strait of Sunda. Besides the quantities of this porous, foam-like lava, that are thrown directly into the sea by such eruptions, great quantities remain on the sides of the volcano, and on the surrounding mountains, and much of that is conveyed, during the rainy monsoon, by the rivers to the ocean. The land at the southeast extremity of Sumbawa appears to be composed of a light-colored clay, the strata of which have been greatly plicated.

Several ugly rocks rise in this strait. The largest is named, in the native tongue, "The Eye of the Devil," and it winked at us most wickedly out of the white surf as we passed. While in the Java Sea, before entering the strait, we had only light winds; but, as we came into the Indian Ocean, we experienced a strong breeze from the southeast. The current, which had been with us and against the

it. In that part of the district of Sangir adjoining Tomboro, its effects were much more violent, tearing up by the roots the largest trees, and carrying them into the air, together with men, houses, cattle, and whatever else came within its influence. The sea rose nearly twelve feet higher than it had ever been known to do before, and completely spoiled the only small spots of rice-lands in Sangir, sweeping away houses and every thing within its reach."

wind, was met off the southwest promontory of Floris by a current with the wind from the east, and at once the sea rose up into pyramidal masses, or formed waves that rolled over and broke against the wind, like those from the windward quarter of a ship which is sailing "on a wind." High mountains also line the Commodo and Floris side, but the scenery became especially grand as we rounded the southwest promontory of the latter island. It reminded me of the pictures of the precipitous coast of Scotland, except that, while those rocks are all bare, these are all covered with the trailing plants that have gained a foothold in the crevices of these precipices. Floris is also called Endé, from the principal port of that name on its southern coast. The trade of this place is mostly with Sandal-wood Island. It is also called Mangerai, the name of the chief place on its northern shore. The people of the latter port trade mostly with the Bugis and Malays. In the coves and bays on the northern coast near this strait many pirates formerly took shelter. They were merely Malays or Bugis from Bali, Sumbawa, or Celebes. In the interior there is a people whose hair is frizzled. A similar one also live in the interior and mountainous part of Solor, Pintar, Lombata, and Ombay. Those living on the sea-coast belong to the brown or Malay race. On the south coast there is a tribe called Rakka, who are reported to be the worst kind of cannibals, accustomed not only to devour their enemies, but the bodies of their deceased relatives.

At sunset we could just discern the outline of

Sumba or Sandal-wood Island. It appeared uniformly high, as it has always been described. Mr. Jukes passed near its southeast point, while on a voyage in her Britannic Majesty's ship Fly from northern Australia to Surabaya. He describes it as composed of ranges of hills that rise immediately from the sea to a height of two thousand feet. The strata of these hills are nearly level, and appeared to be composed of comminuted coral. This would indicate that the island had undergone a great elevation during the later tertiary period. It is probably composed mostly of volcanic rocks, like the adjacent islands. Its area is about four thousand geographical square miles. The most frequented harbor is near the middle of the northern shore. Vessels go there from Surabaya, in the latter part of the western monsoon, to purchase the active little ponies peculiar to this island, and return in the beginning of the eastern monsoon, after having remained there about three months. These horses are considered more valuable than those from any other part of the archipelago, except the Batta lands, in the interior of Sumatra. When a ship arrives, her crew at once scatter over the whole island, visiting all the various *campongs*, or villages, to make their purchases. A Dutch officer, who has travelled over the island, informs me that these people have quite different features from the natives of the adjoining island of Savu, especially the females, whose faces are much broader. They are said to have a peculiar language, and to be a separate nation; but I judge from all I could learn that they form merely a subdivision of the Malay family. The captain of an American whale-ship, which was wrecked on one of the southern points, complained to me that the natives stole every thing he brought on shore, and threatened him and his crew with violence; but I think it was only because he could not speak Malay, and because each party misunderstood the intentions of the other.

At noon the next day we saw the lofty peak of Mount Romba rising up on Floris. It is said to be only seven thousand feet in height, but it appeared to us as high as Mount Slamat in Java. At the eastern end of the island, opposite Adenara and Solor, is a small Portuguese settlement, called Laruntuka. The extreme length of the island is about two hundred geographical miles, and its area a fraction larger than Sandal-wood Island. It yields much sandal-wood, and the natives state that copper is found there, but gold and iron are not known to occur. While in this part of the Indian Ocean, generally in the morning, we had strong breezes from the southeast, which moderated at noon, and increased again at sunset. They varied considerably in the hour they began, and in their strength and duration, and were quite unlike the steady trades.

At 2 P. M., on our third day from Macassar, we sighted the island of Semao, off the bay of Kupang. Its northern end is only a rock, sparsely covered with trees. It has no mountains, and most of its beaches are composed of coral sand.

After dark that evening we anchored near the village of Kupang, which is situated on the south side of a great bay, some twelve miles wide and twenty long. This is a fine harbor now in the eastern monsoon, but during the western monsoon it is so slightly protected by the northern end of Semao that the sea may be said to roll directly in from the open ocean. At such times the steamer is obliged to seek a partial shelter under the lee of a small island on the north side of the bay. Whalers, and merchant-ships bound to and from China in the western monsoon, however, frequently call here, because it is the only harbor of any kind near the southern end of the island. If the projected line of steamers between northern Australia, Surabaya, Batavia, and Singapore, is established, this port would be one of the places they would visit. The village is situated on a sandy beach, that is terminated on either hand by cliffs of coral rock, which the sea has worn out into caves and small projecting points of the most grotesque forms. It has a population estimated at from six to seven thousand. Its chief exports are tripang, beeswax from the interior, and a sandal-wood, which is said to be the best in the whole archipelago. They raise several kinds of the nicest oranges. The Mandarin orange, probably brought originally from China, is the most delicious of any kind of this fruit that I ever tasted. I doubt very much whether our West India Islands, or Sicily, or any other part of the world, can compete with Timur in the rich flavor of its oranges. The hills around the village are only covered with a scanty vegetation, through which the coral rock outcrops, and in every direction the whole country, except in the valleys, presents a most barren and uninviting aspect, compared to the richly-clothed shores of Java, and most of the other islands we have seen. Indeed, none of the hills and high ridges throughout all the southern half of the island are covered with such dense forests as are seen in the eastern and northern parts of Java, and the middle and northern parts of Celebes, and over all the higher parts of Borneo and Sumatra.

As we passed through Sapi Strait, I noticed that, although both shores were green, yet forests appeared to be wanting both on Sumbawa and Floris, and this is also said to be true of Sandalwood Island. It is also asserted that this is somewhat the condition of the eastern end of Java and the southern end of Celebes. Probably the cause of this partial sterility is chiefly owing to the circumstance that the southeast monsoon, which continues here most of the year, from about March till November, comes over the dry, desert-like interior of Australia, and does not become saturated with moisture on its passage over the Arafura Sea. Most of the precipitation, therefore, that does take place on Timur, must occur on the southeast side of the water-shed, and it is possible that extensive forests may exist on that part of the island. The northern half of the island, which is owned by the Portuguese, is far more fertile, and if it were thickly inhabited, and properly cultivated, might yield large crops of coffee. On landing, the most surprising of all the objects that meet the eye are the natives. At that time there were at least six different kinds in this same village, besides descendants of Malay mothers, and Chinese, Portuguese, Dutch, English, and probably American fathers, of every possible degree of mixture, a perfect Gordian knot for the ablest ethnologist. Each of these varieties of natives had some peculiarity in dress, and one wore the hair long and frizzled; but I doubt whether they could be referred to the true Papuan type. They appeared to be fair specimens of the aborigines, who have been already mentioned as inhabiting the interior of Floris, Solor, Omblata, Pintar, and Ombay. The natives of Savu are described as belonging to this same group, which Mr. Crawfurd calls the Negro-Malayan race. The Rajah of Savu was at Kupang while we were there, and certainly was nearly of pure Malay blood.

Contrary to what would be supposed, from its position, the island of Rotti, off the southern end of Timur, is inhabited by a lank-haired race, who are probably Malays. They were represented to me, by the Resident of Kupang, as a most peaceable people, and very different in this respect from the wild natives of Timur. On the southeast coast of Timur, near Mount Allas, there is said to be a tribe of black people whose hair is frizzled, and, instead of being evenly distributed over the scalp, is collected into little tufts, a characteristic which seems to separate the Papuans from all other people. Mr. Earl says[*] that some of the people on the table-land back of Dilli have "opaque yellow complexions, the exposed parts of the skin being covered with light-brown

---

[*] "Native Races of the East Indian Archipelago, Papuans," by George Windsor Earl, M. R. A. S. London, 1853.

spots or freckles,* and the hair is straight, fine, and of a reddish hue, or dark-auburn color. Every intermediate variety of hair and complexion between this and the black, or deep-chocolate color, and the short tufted hair of the mountain Papuan, is found in Timur." This statement would indicate that all the intermediate shades of difference were the results of a mixture of the Malayan and Papuan blood, and this seems to be the probable origin of the whole Negro-Malayan race. Its position in that part of the archipelago nearest Papua is in entire accordance with this hypothesis.

Tradition says that the Rajah of Kupang formerly sacrificed a young virgin to the sharks and crocodiles once every year, but this was generally regarded as a fable, until a gentleman visited the island of Semao, some twenty years ago, and asserted that a rajah pointed out to him a place on the beach of a bay near the southeast point of that island, where "it was their custom after harvest to bring sugar-cane, rice, fowls, eggs, pigs, dogs, and a *little child*, and offer them to the evil spirits," and the rajah further declared, that he had witnessed this murderous rite himself.

As we were to remain only one day, and I was chiefly interested in collecting shells, I at once en-

---

* Possibly the "spots," of which Mr. Earl speaks, may have been caused by some disease, for spots of a lighter hue than the general color of the body are often seen among all Malays. Both the straight-haired Malaysians and the frizzled-haired Melanesians have the odd custom of rubbing *lime* into their hair, which gives it a dull-yellowish or reddish tinge. Mr. Earl, however, states that he has seen one native whose hair was naturally *red*, a kind of partial albinoism.

gaged a Malay guide to conduct me to a village near the shore, a mile westward toward Semao. Our road was a bridle-path, a few large stones having been removed, but the ragged coral rock everywhere projects so completely through the thin soil, that it was a constant wonder to me how the natives could travel barefoot with such apparent ease. We soon came to half a dozen circular huts, enclosed by a low stone wall. They were the most wretched abodes for human beings that I saw in all my journeys over the archipelago. The walls, instead of being made of boards or flattened bamboos, as in the other islands, are composed of small sticks about three feet high, driven into the ground. These supported a conical roof, thatched with palm-leaves. Ugly-looking pigs, with long bristles on their backs, were rooting about these detestable hovels. Soon after, we passed a burial-place. A low wall enclosed a small irregular plat, that was filled with earth. This contained one or more graves, each of which had for its foot and head stones small square pyramidal blocks of wood, with the apex fixed in the ground. The next village we entered contained only a dozen huts. A pack of wolf-like dogs saluted us with a fierce yelping and barking, and my attendant, after much shouting and bustle, roused the inmates of one of these miserable dwellings. The men were gone to fish, but the women and children came out to gaze at us, and when their dull apprehensions finally allowed them to realize that we had come to purchase shells, and had a good supply of small copper coins, they briskly hunted about, and soon brought me a large number of nautilus-shells of enormous size. The children were nearly all entirely naked, and the women only wore a sarong, fastened at the waist and descending to the knees. This scanty clothing they supplied by coyly folding their arms across their breasts as they approached to sell their shells. Those of the nautilus, they all agreed in saying, did not come from their own shores, but from Rotti; and a gentleman, who had been along all the neighboring shores, assured me that he had seen the natives there dive for them, in about two fathoms at low tide, and bring them up *alive*, and that in this way great numbers are gathered for food.

The latter part of the western monsoon, or the changing of the monsoons, was recommended to me as the most favorable time to collect these rare animals. Besides the nautilus, I obtained many species of *Pteroceras*, *Strombus*, and many beautiful cones and cypræas.

The coral rocks on the hills that we crossed contained specimens apparently of living species, at a height which I judge was five hundred feet above the level of the sea. I marked the whole in my notebook as merely a coral reef of very recent elevation. Since returning, and comparing this observation with the careful description of that region given by Mr. Jukes,[*] in his voyage of the Fly, I find he expresses

---

[*] Mr. Jukes remarks, and I believe, most correctly, that "if the term 'jura kalk' is applied lithologically to these tertiary rocks, it is to a certain extent applicable, as they have a concretionary and oölitic structure. If, however, it is meant to have a chronological meaning, it is either incorrectly applied, or the formation is incorrectly extended on the map to the neighborhood of Kupang."

the same view, having seen this same late formation at an estimated height of six hundred feet above the sea; and a plateau, which rises in the interior to the height of one thousand feet, he also suspects is of the same origin. Mr. Schneider, however, has described a "kalk formatie," about Kupang, which, from its position on the map, would seem to be identical with that seen by Mr. Jukes and myself. This formation Mr. Schneider refers to the age of the "Coral Rag," of the Jura, in England. Other fossiliferous strata he regards as belonging to the old Oölitic period, or the Lias, and underlying all he thinks is a "diorite, or dioritic porphyry and amorphous dioritic porphyry — the last, like that found in Humboldt's Bay, on the north coast of New Guinea, and much like the amorphous dioritic porphyry of Australia." Copper-veins are found more or less wherever the Jurassic beds appear, but in the greatest quantity nearest the diorite.

On the evening of the 24th we steamed out of Kupang Bay, and along the northwest coast of Timur, for Dilli; and all the way to that port we were so completely under the lee of the land, that we had only calms, and light airs from the southeast and east-northeast. With these light winds we always had a very clear sky; but on coming round the southwestern end of Floris, and also on entering Kupang Bay, each time when there was a strong breeze from the east, the sky was remarkably thick and hazy. Our captain, who has made many voyages, at all seasons, in these seas, informs me that the sky is almost always thick when the eastern monsoon has become strong. This coast of Timur is not low, like the north coast of Java, but rises immediately up from the sea, in a succession of hills. No gigantic and lofty peaks can be seen, as in Java, and in all the islands east to and including Ombay; the peaks along the water-shed, on Timur, generally rising to not more than four or five thousand feet, and Lakaan, which is regarded as the highest in that chain, is supposed to be only six thousand. The soil appears to be very infertile, yet when the sun was approaching the western horizon, and the cumuli, floating in the pure air, slowly drew along their changing shadows over the innumerable hills and valleys, the whole scene was nearly as delightful as my first view of the tropics in coming up the Strait of Sunda. There is no road in the interior of the island, and every one who will travel the shortest distance, must go on horseback along the sandy beaches.

This afternoon we passed Pulo Gula Batu, "Sugar-Loaf Island." It is quite high, with steep, almost perpendicular sides, which have a white, chalky appearance, and appear to be composed of strata of coral rock, which would indicate that it had recently been elevated above the sea. At sunset we entered Ombay Passage, the one that ships from England and America usually choose when going to China in the western monsoon, and frequently when returning in the eastern monsoon. One was just then drifting down into the Indian Ocean, on her homeward voyage. This was the first vessel we had seen since we passed down Sapi Strait, and left the

Java Sea. It was then nearly calm, and yet I saw flying-fish come out of the water and go a considerable distance before plunging into it again, thus proving that they must sustain themselves in the air chiefly by a vibrating motion of their great pectoral fins. The sun was now sinking behind the high, dark peaks of the island of Pintar.

At daylight next morning we were steaming into a little bay surrounded by hills of fifteen hundred to two thousand feet. At the head of the bay and around its southern shore extended a narrow strip of level land, bordering the bases of these high hills. On the low land are two miserable forts, and a few houses and native huts. These comprise the city of Dilli, the Portuguese capital in all these waters. Of all the nations in Europe, the Portuguese were the first to discover the way to the Indies by sea. Then, for a time, they enjoyed an undisputed monopoly over the Eastern trade; but now the northern half of this island, the eastern end of Floris, the city of Macao in China, and Goa in Hindustan, are the only places of importance in all the East that continue in their hands. The common, or low Malay language, has been more affected by the Portuguese than any other nation, for the simple reason that those early navigators brought with them many things that were new to the Malays, who therefore adopted the Portuguese names for those articles. The last governor of this place had run away a few months before we arrived, because he had received no pay for half a year, though his salary was only five hundred guilders per month; and a merchant at Macassar told me that, when he arrived at that city, he did not have the means to pay his passage back to Europe. The first inquiry, therefore, that was made, was whether we had brought a new governor. The captain's reply was, that he had but one passenger in the first cabin, and the only place he appeared to care to see in that region was the coral reef at the mouth of the harbor.

The native boats that came off with bananas, cocoa-nuts, oranges, and fowls, were all very narrow, only as wide as a native at the shoulders. Each was merely a canoe, dug out of a single small tree, and built up on the sides with pieces of wood and palm-leaves. They were all provided with outriggers. It was then low water, and the reef was bare. It had not been my privilege to visit a coral reef, and I was most anxious to see one, but I could not make up my mind to risk myself in such a dangerous skiff. The captain, with his usual kindness, however, offered me the use of one of his large boats; and as we neared the reef, and passed over a wide garden richly-tinted with polyps, with here and there vermilion star-fishes scattered about, and bright-hued fishes darting hither and thither like flashes of light, a deep thrill of pleasure ran along my nerves, which I shall never forget to the end of my days. Here in an hour I collected three species of beautiful star-fishes, and sixty-five kinds of shells, almost all of the richest colors. The coral rocks, thus laid bare by the receding tide, were all black, and not white, like the fragments of coral seen on shores. This reef is scarcely covered at high water, and therefore breaks off all swell from the ocean; but, unfortunately, the entrance is narrow, and the harbor is too small for large ships. Only two vessels were there at that time. One was a brig from Amboina, that had come for buffaloes, or for *sapis*, and the other was a small topsail schooner from Macassar, that had come for coffee, which is raised in considerable quantities on the plateau back of Dilli, and is brought down on the backs of horses. Long lines of them were seen ascending and descending the winding paths on the steep hill-sides back of the village. These declivities were sparsely covered with trees, but a thick grove of cocoa-nut palms grew on the low land bordering the bay. The name Dilli, according to Mr. Crawfurd, is identical with that of the Malay state on the northeastern side of Sumatra, which we call Delli, and he suspects from this fact that this area was settled by a colony of Malays from Sumatra in the earliest times. The word Timur, in the Malay, means "East," and this island was probably the limit of their voyages in that direction, hence its name. Immediately off the harbor of Dilli lies Pulo Kambing, or Goat Island, a common name for many islands in the archipelago. On both this island and Pintar the highest peaks are at the southern end. North of Dilli the coast is steep, and the mountains rise abruptly from the sea. The sides of all these elevations are deeply scored with valleys that have been formed by the denuding action of rain.

From Dilli we steamed northward along the southeast coast of Wetta, a high, mountainous island. Its coasts are occupied by Malays, and its interior by a black, frizzled-haired people, allied to the inhabitants of Timur. The bloody practice of "head-hunting" still exists among them. North of Timur is Kissa, the most important island in this part of the archipelago. In the early part of the present century this was the seat of a Dutch residency. It is a low island, and the rice and maize consumed by its inhabitants are chiefly imported from Wetta. Its people, however, carry on a very considerable trade with the surrounding islands, and are said to be far in advance of the natives of Amboina in point of industry. Southeast of Kissa lies Letti, for the most part high and hilly, but level near the sea. Kloff* describes the natives as tall and well formed, and having light-brown complexions. The men wear no other dress than a piece of cloth wrapped around the waist. The women sometimes wear, in addition to this dress, a *kabaya*, open in front. Polygamy is not found, and adultery is punishable with death or slavery. When the Dutch occupied these islands, they induced the natives to change these sentences into exile to the Banda Islands, where men were needed to cultivate the nutmeg-trees. Neither Mohammedanism nor Hinduism has been introduced into these islands; they only pay homage to an image of human shape placed on a heap of stones that has been raised under a large tree near the centre of the village. When a marriage or death, or any remarkable event occurs, a large hog or buffalo, which has been kept and fattened for the purpose, is slaughtered. They are especially anxious

* "Voyage of the Dourga in 1825 and 1826," by Captain Kloff, translated by G. W. Earl.

to obtain elephants' teeth, and hoard them up as the choicest treasures.

The morning after leaving Dilli, Roma appeared on our starboard hand. It is very high and mountainous. In 1823 it suffered very severely from a violent hurricane, which also caused a frightful destruction on Letti. On the latter island the cocoanut trees were levelled to the ground over considerable areas. This disaster was followed by a drought, which destroyed all their crops, and produced great mortality among the cattle, through lack of food. The hurricane also caused the bees to desert the island for a time—a serious loss to the inhabitants, as wax and honey are among their chief exports. These are taken to the Arru Islands, and thence to Macassar and Amboina. When a chief dies, his wife takes his place in the council, a privilege rarely granted to a woman among these Eastern nations. East of Letti is Lakor, a dry coral bank, raised twenty feet above the sea.

Damma soon after came into view. It is also high and mountainous, and has a lofty volcanic peak at its northeastern extremity. In 1825 it was pouring forth great quantities of gas. At its foot is a sulphur-spring, such as exist at many places in Java and Celebes, in the immediate vicinity of existing volcanic action. The doctor of Captain Kloff's ship, the Dourga, sent some of the crew to bathe in this spring, and he states that "though they were so affected with rheumatism as to be not only unfit for duty but in a state of great misery, the use of this water contributed greatly to the improvement of their health."

Springs of this kind are found in the district of Pekalongan, west of Mount Prau, and are frequented by many foreigners, but I never heard that any remarkable cure has ever been effected by the use of their waters. The nutmeg-tree grows wild on Damma, and the *canari* also thrives here. Thirty years after the Dutch deserted this island, the whole population were found to have completely relapsed into barbarism, but some of the natives of Moa, Letti, Roma, and Kissa, continue to be Christians, and five or six native schoolmasters are now located among those islands. Southeast of Damma lies Baba. Its people have the odd custom of rubbing lime into their hair, even from infancy. An English vessel that was trading here was boarded by these wild natives, and all her crew were butchered. Another vessel suffered a like fate at Timur-laut, that is, "Timur lying to seaward," an island about one hundred miles long, and one-third as wide in its broadest part. It is customary here for each family to preserve the head of one of their ancestors in their dwelling, and, as if to remind them all of his valorous deeds and their own mortality, this ghastly skull is placed on a scaffold opposite the entrance. When a young woman marries, each ankle is adorned with heavy copper rings, "to give forth music as she walks." Their war customs are like those of the Ceramese. It is said that among the mountains of this island a black, frizzled-haired people exist. If this should prove true, they will probably be found to be like the inhabitants of Timur and Ombay, and not referable to the Papuan type. The inhabitants of all these islands are constantly separated by petty feuds, or carrying on an open warfare with each other.

We were now fully in the Banda Sea, and on the 28th of June the summit of the Gunong Api, or "Burning Mountain" of that group, appeared above the horizon, but, as I afterward revisited these beautiful islands, a description of them is deferred to a future page. As we steamed away from the Bandas, we passed out of the region of continuous dry weather and began to enter one where the wet and dry seasons are just opposite to what they are in all the wide area extending from the middle part of Sumatra to the eastern end of Timur, including the southern half of Borneo and the southern peninsulas of Celebes. In all that region the eastern monsoon brings dry weather, though occasional showers may occur; but at Amboina, and on the south coast of Ceram and Buru, this same wind bears along clouds that pour down almost incessant floods. At Amboina I was assured that sometimes it rained for two weeks at a time, without apparently stopping for five minutes, and from what I experienced myself I can readily believe that such a phenomenon is not of rare occurrence.

In the northern part of Celebes, at Ternate, and in the northern part of Gillolo, and the islands between it and New Guinea, and also on the shores of the western part of that great island, the wet and dry seasons are not well defined. This exceptional area is mostly included within the parallels of latitude two degrees north and two degrees south of the equator.

North of it the wind at this time of year is from the southwest, instead of from the southeast. This dry southeast monsoon bends round Borneo, and becomes the southwest monsoon of the China Sea, supplying abundant rains to the northern parts of Borneo and the Philippines. It has its origin near Australia, and thence it pushes its way first toward the northwest and then toward the northeast across the whole Philippine group. It appears in Timur in March, and reaches the southern part of the China Sea in May.

9

CHAPTER V.

AMBOINA.

June 29th.—We are this morning approaching Amboina, the goal of my long journey, and the most important of the Spice Islands. Amboina is both the name of the island and its chief city. In form the island is nearly elliptical, and a deep, narrow bay, fourteen miles long, almost divides it longitudinally into two unequal parts. That on the west, which forms the main body of the island, is called Hitu; and that on the east Laitimur, which in Malay means "the eastern leaf." Both are composed of high hills which rise up so abruptly from the sea that, though this bay for one-third of its length is nearly four miles wide, yet it perfectly resembles a frith or broad river. Along the shores are many little bays where praus are seen at anchor, and on the beaches are small groves of the cocoa-nut palm, which furnish food and shade to the natives dwelling in the rude huts beneath them. Higher up the hill-sides, large, open areas are seen covered with a tall, coarse grass; but the richly-cultivated fields on the flanks of the mountains in Java nowhere appear. These grassy hill-sides are the favorite burial-places with the

Chinese, for they rarely or never carry back the bones of their friends to the sacred soil of the Celestial Land from these islands as they do from California. Such graves are always horseshoe-shaped, just as in China, and their white walls make very conspicuous objects on the green hill-sides. Above the open areas, in the wooded regions, we notice a few places filled with small trees that have a peculiar bright-green foliage. Those are the gardens of clove-trees which have made this island so famous throughout the world.

It is now the rainy season here, and thick rain-clouds at first completely enshrouded us; but as we passed up the bay they slowly broke away, and revealed on either hand high hills and mountains, which, on the Hitu side, began to assume a most wonderful appearance. The strong easterly wind pushed away the thick, white clouds from the exposed sides of all these elevations, and caused them to trail off to the west like smoke from hundreds of railroad engines, until every separate peak appeared to have become an active volcano that was continually pouring out dense volumes of white, opaque gas; and as these hills rose tier above tier to high, dark mountains which formed the background, the whole scene was most awe-inspiring, especially in this land where eruptions and earthquakes are frequent, and only a comparatively thin crust separates one from the earth's internal fires.

Near the mouth of the bay the water is very deep, but eight or nine miles within it is sufficiently shallow for an anchorage. Here also the hills on the east or Laitimur side are separated from the beach by a triangular, level area, about a paal * long, and on this has been built the city of "Amboina" or "Ambon," in the native language. Viewed from the anchorage, the city has a pleasing appearance, its streets being broad, straight, and well shaded. About half way from its southern end is Fort Nieuw Victoria. Landing at a quay we passed through this old stronghold out into a pretty lawn, which is surrounded by the Societeit, or Club-House, and the residences of officials and merchants. The total population of the city is about fourteen thousand. Of these, seven hundred are Europeans, three hundred Chinese, and four hundred Arabs. The others are natives. The entire population of the island is about thirty-two thousand. Like all the cities and larger settlements in the Dutch possessions, Amboina is divided into a native *kampong* or quarter, a Chinese *kampong*, and a quarter where foreigners reside. The natives are directly under the control of a rajah or prince, and he, in turn, is responsible to a Dutch assistant resident. In a similar manner the Chinese are subject to a "Captain China," who, in the larger cities, has one or more assistants or "lieutenants." He, likewise, must report himself to the assistant resident. In this way each separate people is immediately ruled by officers chosen from its own nation, and consequently of the same views and prejudices. Justice is thus more perfectly administered, and the hostile feelings which each of these bigoted Eastern nations always entertains against every other are thus completely avoided.

* A paal, the unit of measure on land in the East Indian Archipelago, is fifteen sixteenths of a statute mile.

A PLEASANT HOME.

On leaving Batavia, Cores de Vries & Co., who who then owned all the mail-steamers in the Netherlands India, kindly gave me a letter of credit so that I might draw on their agents from place to place, and wholly avoid the trouble and danger of carrying any considerable sum with me. This letter further recommended me to the kind attention of all their employés, and Mr. Var Marle, their agent at this place, at once said that I must make his house my home while I remained in that part of the archipelago; and this unexpected and very generous invitation was still more acceptable, as both he and his good lady spoke English. A chamber was assigned me, and a large room in an adjoining out-building, where I could store my collections and pack them up for their long transit to America; and thus I was ready to commence my allotted work without the least delay. I then called on His Excellency the Governor of the Spice Islands, who received me in the most cordial manner, and said that boats, coolies, and whatever other assistance I might need, would be immediately ordered whenever I wished.

Amboina has long been famous for its shells, and the Dutch officials have been accustomed for years to purchase very considerable quantities as presents for their friends in Europe. The natives, therefore, are in the habit of gathering them for sale, and a few have become extensive traders in these beautiful objects. It was soon noised abroad that a foreigner had come from a land even farther away than "Ollanda," as they call Holland, solely for the purpose of purchasing shells; and immediately, to my great delight, basketful after basketful of the species that I had always regarded as the rarest and most valuable began to appear, every native being anxious to dispose of his lot before his fellows, and thus obtain a share of the envied shining coin, which I was careful to display to their gloating eyes before I should say I had bought all I desired. Competition, here as elsewhere, had a wonderfully depressing effect on the price of their commodities, judging from what they asked at first and what they were finally willing to take. The trade, however, became more brisk day after day, and some natives came from long distances partly to sell their shells and partly to see whether "that man" could be sane who had come so far and was spending, according to their ideas, so much money for shells. At first I bought them by the basketful, until all the more common species had been obtained, and then I showed the natives the figures in Rumphius's "Rariteit Kamer" of those species I still wished to secure, and at the same time offered them an extra price for others not represented in that comprehensive work. One species I was particularly anxious to secure alive. It was the pearly nautilus. The shell has always been common, but the animal has seldom been described. The first was found at this place, and a description and drawing were given by Rumphius. Afterward a dissection and drawing were given by Professor Owen, of the British Museum, and his monograph probably contains the most complete anatomical description that has ever been made of any animal from a single specimen. He worked, as he himself described it to me, with a dissecting-knife in one hand

and a pencil in the other. So little escaped his pen and pencil, that very little information has been added by later dissections. I was so anxious to secure one of these rare animals, that I felt that, if I should obtain one and a few more common species, I could feel that my long journey had been far from fruitless. Only the second day after my arrival, to my inexpressible delight, a native brought me one still *living*. Seeing how highly I prized it, he began by asking ten guilders (four Mexican dollars) for it, but finally concluded to part with it for two guilders (less than one Mexican dollar), though I should certainly have paid him fifty if I could not have obtained it for a less price. It had been taken in this way: the natives throughout the archipelago rarely fish with a hook and line as we do, but, where the water is too deep to build a weir, they use instead a *bubu*, or barrel of open basket-work of bamboo. Each end of this barrel is an inverted cone, with a small opening at its apex. Pieces of fish and other bait are suspended from within, and the *bubu* is then sunk on the clear patches of sand on a coral reef, or more commonly out where the water is from twenty to fifty fathoms deep. No line is attached to those on the reefs, but they are taken up with a gaff. Those in deep water are buoyed by a cord and a long bamboo, to one end of which a stick is fastened in a vertical position, and to this is attached a piece of palm-leaf for a flag, to make it more conspicuous. In this case it happened that one of these *bubus* was washed off into deeper water than usual, and the nautilus chanced to crawl through the opening in one of the cones to get at the bait within. If the opening had not been much larger than usual, it could not possibly have got in. It was at once placed in a can containing strong arrack. I then offered twice as much for a duplicate specimen, and hundreds of natives tried and tried, but in vain, to procure another during the five months I was in those seas. They are so rare even there, that a gentleman, who had made large collections of shells, assured me that I ought not to expect to obtain another if I were to remain at Amboina three years. Rumphius, who usually is remarkably accurate in his descriptions of the habits of the mollusks he figures, says it sometimes swims on the sea; but this statement he probably received from the natives, who made such a mistake because many empty shells are frequently found floating on the ocean. When the animal dies and becomes separated from the shell, the latter rises to the surface of the sea on account of the air or other gas contained in the chambers. It is then swept away by the wind and tide to the shore of a neighboring island. When the natives are questioned as to where these shells come from, they invariably reply, "The sea;" and as to where the animal lives, they merely answer, "*Dalam*," "In the deep." The dead shells are so abundant on these islands, that they can be purchased in any quantity at from four to ten cents apiece.

My first excursion from the city of Amboina was with a gentleman to a large cocoa-garden, which he had lately planted on the high hills on the Hitu side. A nice boat or *orangbai*—literally, "a good fellow" —took us over the bay to the little village of Ruma

Tiga, or "Three Houses." The boatmen were gayly dressed in white trousers with red trimmings, and had red handkerchiefs tied round their heads. A small gong and a *tifa* or drum, made by tightly stretching a piece of the hide of a wild deer over the end of a short, hollow log, gave forth a rude, wild music, and at least served to aid the boatmen in keeping time as they rowed. Occasionally, to break the monotony of their labor, they sang a low, plaintive song. Instead of steering straight for the point which we wished to arrive at on the opposite side of the bay, our helmsman kept the boat so near the shore that we really passed round the head of the bay, twice as far as it would have been in a right line. This mode of *hassar* steering, or, as the sailors express it in our language, "hugging the shore," I afterward found was the one universally adopted in all this part of the archipelago. When we landed, I had the pleasure to find, just beneath low-water level, hundreds of black sea-urchins, with needle-like spines nearly a foot long, and so extremely sharp and brittle, that it was very difficult to get the animals out of the little cavities in the rocks where they had anchored themselves fast with their many suckers. Near by, the villagers were busy boiling down the sap of the sagaru-palm for the sugar it contains. According to my taste it is much like maple-sugar. Up to the time that Europeans first came to the East, this was the only kind of sugar known to the natives, and large quantities of it are still consumed among the islands here in the eastern part of the archipelago.

From the beach, a narrow footpath led through

a grove of palm-trees into a thick forest, and then
zigzagged up a steep hill-side, until it reached a
small plateau. Here were the young cocoa-trees,
filled with their long, red, cucumber-like fruit. The
original forest had been felled and burned, and these
trees had been planted in its place. Almost the only
difficulty in cultivating the cocoa-tree here is in removing the grass and small shrubs which are continually springing up; yet the natives are all so idle
and untrustworthy that a gentleman must frequently inspect his garden himself, if he expects it to yield
a fair return. This tree,* the *Theobroma cacao*, Lin.,
is not a native of the East. It was discovered by
the Spaniards in Mexico during the conquest of that
country by Cortez. From Mexico they took it to
their provinces in South America and the West India Islands. At present it is cultivated in Trinidad,
and in Guiana and Brazil. It probably thrives as
well here as in Mexico, and is now completely sup-
planting the less profitable clove-tree.

The chief article of food of the natives working
in this garden is our own yellow Indian corn, another exotic, also introduced into the East by Europeans. It is now raised in every part of the archipelago in such quantities as to form one of the chief
articles of food for the natives. The Dutch never
use it, and generally think it strange that it should

---

* The Dutch name for this tree and its fruit is cacao. Our word
chocolate comes from the Spanish "chocolate," which was a mixture
of the fruit of this tree with Indian corn. These were ground up
together, and some honey was usually added. After sugar-cane was
introduced, that was also added to neutralize the bitter qualities of the
cocoa.

be made into bread for the very nicest tables in our land. I never knew the natives to grind it or pound it. They are accustomed to roast it on the ear after the kernels have become quite hard and yellow. Our house in this tropical garden was merely a bamboo hut, with a broad veranda, which afforded us an ample shelter from the pouring rains and scorching sunshine. I had been careful to take along my fowling-piece, and at once I commenced a rambling hunt through the adjoining forest. Large flocks of small birds, much like our blackbird, were hovering about, but they so invariably chose to alight only on the tops of the tallest trees, that I was a long time securing half a dozen specimens, for at every shot they would select another distant tree-top, and give me a long walk over tangled roots and fallen trees in the dense, almost gloomy, jungle. As evening came on, small green parrots uttered their shrill, deafening screams, as they darted to and fro through the thick foliage. A few of these also entered my game-bag.

In these tropical lands, when the sun sets, it is high time for the hunter to forsake his fascinating sport and hurry home. There is no long, fading twilight, but darkness presses closely on the footsteps of retreating day, and at once it is night. On my return, my friend remarked in the coolest manner that I had secured us both a good supper; and before I had recovered from my shock at such a suggestion, the cook had torn out a large handful of rich feathers from the skins, and all were spoiled for my collection; however, I consoled myself with the thought that it did not fall to the good lot of every hunter to live in the midst of such a wondrous vegetation and feast on parrots. In the evening, a full moon shed broad oscillating bands of silver light through the large polished leaves of the bananas around our dwelling, as they slowly waved to and fro in the cool, refreshing breeze. Then the low cooing of doves came up out of the dark forest, and the tree-toads piped out their long, shrill notes. That universal pest, the mosquito, was also there, singing his same bloodthirsty tune in our ears. Our beds were perched on poles, high above the floor of the hut, that we might avoid such unpleasant bedfellows as large snakes, which are very common and most unceremonious visitors. That night we were disturbed but once, and then by a loud rattling of iron pots and a general crashing of crockery; instantly I awoke with an indefinite apprehension that we were experiencing one of the frightful earthquakes which my friend had been vividly picturing before we retired. The natives set up a loud hooting and shouting, and finally the cause of the whole disturbance was found to be a lean, hungry dog that was attempting to satisfy his appetite on what remained of our parrot-stew.

My chief object on this excursion was to collect insects; and among some white-leaved shrubs, near the shore, I found many magnificent specimens of a very large, richly-colored *Papilio*. The general color of the upper surface of its wings was a blue-black, and beneath were large patches of bright red. Another was a blue-black above, with large spots of bright blue. The wings of these butterflies expand five or six inches, and they seem almost like small birds as they flit by.

It was my desire not only to obtain the same shells that Rumphius figures, but to procure them from the same points and bays, so that there could be no doubt about the identity of my specimens with his drawings. I therefore proposed to travel along all the shores of Amboina and the neighboring islands, and trade with the natives of every village, so as to be sure of the localities myself, and, moreover, get specimens of all the species alive, and thus have ample material for studying their anatomy. I now realized the value of the letter with which His Excellency the Governor-General had honored me at Batavia. I had only to apply to the assistant resident, and he at once kindly ordered a boat and coolies for me at the same rate as if they were employed by the government, which was frequently less than half of what I should have been obliged to pay if I had hired them myself; and besides, many times I could not have obtained boats nor coolies at any price; and when the Resident ordered them to come at a certain hour, I always found them ready.

My first excursion along the shores of the island was on the north coast of Hitu. Two servants accompanied me, to aid in arranging the shells, and carrying bottles of alcohol to contain the animals. From the city of Amboina, a boat took us over the bay to Ruma Tiga, where several coolies were waiting with a "chair" to carry me over the high hills to the opposite shore. This "chair," or palanquin, is merely a common arm-chair, with a bamboo fastened on each side. A light roof and curtains on the sides keep out the rain or hot sunshine. Usually eight or more coolies are detailed to each chair, so that one-half may relieve the others every few moments. The motion is much like that on horseback, when the horse is urged into a hurried walk, and is neither extremely unpleasant nor so very delightful as some writers who have visited these islands have described it. In China, where only two coolies carry a chair, the motion is far more regular and agreeable. This is the only mode of travelling in all the islands where horses have not been introduced, and where all the so-called roads are mere narrow footpaths, except in the villages.

From the shore we climbed two hills, and on their crests passed through gardens of cocoa-trees.* The road then was bordered on either side with rows of pine-apples, *Ananassa sativa*, a third exotic from tropical America. It thrives so well in every part of the archipelago, without the slightest care, that it is very difficult to realize that it is not an indigenous plant. The native names all point out its origin. The Malays and Javanese call it *nanas*, which is merely a corruption of the Portuguese *ananassa*. In Celebes it is sometimes called *pandang*, a corruption of *pandanus*, from the marked similarity

* This name must not be confounded with that of the cocoa-nut-tree, or *Cocos nucifera*, which is a palm. The word cocoa is supposed to have been derived from the Portuguese word *macoco* or *macaco*, a monkey, and to have been applied to the cocoa-nut palm, from a fancied resemblance between the end of the shell, where the three black scars occur, and the face of a monkey.

of the two fruits. In the Philippines it is generally called *piña*, the Spanish word for pine-cone, which has the same origin as our name pine-apple. Piña is also the name of a cloth of great strength and durability, made by the natives of the Philippines, from the fibres of its leaves. The Malays, on the contrary, seldom or never make any such use of it, though it grows so abundantly in many places that any quantity of its leaves could be obtained for the simple trouble of gathering them. The fruit raised here is generally regarded as inferior to that grown in the West Indies, and the Dutch consider the variety known as "the West Indian ananas," that is, one that has been recently introduced, as the best. The finest specimens of this fruit are raised in the interior of Sumatra and on the islands about Singapore, and great quantities are exposed for sale in the market at that city.

From the crest of the first range of hills we descended to a deep ravine, and crossed a bridge thrown over a foaming torrent. This bridge, like most the Dutch possessions, was covered with a roof, but left open on the sides. The object of the roof and its projecting eaves is to keep the boards and planks beneath dry, for whenever they are frequently soaked with rain they quickly decay in this tropical climate. The coolies here lunched on smoked fish and sago-cake, their common fare, and quenched their thirst with draughts from the rapid stream. Their ragged clothing and uncombed hair made them appear strangely out of keeping with the luxuriant vegetation surrounding us. Crossing another high range, we caught a view of the blue ocean, and soon descended to the village of Hitu-lama, "Old Hitu." The rajah received me most kindly into his house, and assigned me a chamber. Large numbers of children quickly gathered, and the rajah explained to them that I had come to buy shells, insects, and every curious thing they might bring. As it was high water, and good shells could only be found at low tide, I asked them to search for lizards, and soon I was surprised to see them coming with a number of real "flying-dragons," not such impossible monsters as the Chinese delight to place on their temples and vases, but small lizards, *Draco volans*, each provided with a broad fold in the skin along either side of the body, analogous to that of our flying-squirrel, and for a similar purpose, not really for flying, but to act as a parachute to sustain the animal in the air, while it makes long leaps from branch to branch. Another lizard, of which they brought nearly a dozen specimens in a couple of hours, had a body about six inches long and a tail nearly as much longer. Knowing how impossible it is to capture these agile and wary animals, I tried to ascertain how they succeeded in surprising so many, but they all refused to tell, apparently from superstitious motives, and to this day the mystery is unsolved. When these specimens were brought to me they were always in small joints of bamboo, and when one escaped the natives generally refused to try to catch it in their hands.

As the tide receded, shells began to come in; at first the more common species, and rarer ones as the ebbing ceased. My mode of trading with these people was extremely simple, my stock of Malay being very limited. A small table was placed on the veranda in front of the rajah's house, and I took a seat behind it. The natives then severally came up and placed their shells in a row on the table, and I placed opposite each shell or each lot of shells whatever I was willing to give for them, and then, pointing first to the money and then to the shells, remarked, *Ini atau itu,* "This or that," leaving them to make their own choice. In this way all disputing was avoided, and the purchasing went on rapidly. Whenever one man had a rare shell, and the sum I offered did not meet his expectations, another would be sure to accept it if no more was given; then the first would change his mind, and thus I never failed to obtain both specimens. It was a pleasure that no one but a naturalist can appreciate, to see such rare and beautiful shells coming in alive, spotted cypræas, marbled cones, long *Fusi,* and *Murices,* some spiny and some richly ornamented with varices resembling compound leaves. The rarest shell that I secured that day was a living *Terebellum,* which was picked up on a coral reef before the village, at low-tide level. Afterward I procured another from the same place; but so limited does its distribution appear to be, that I never obtained a live specimen at any other locality.

At sunset I walked out with the rajah along the shore of the bay. Before us lay the great island of Ceram, which the rajah called, in his musical tongue, *Ceram tana biza,* "The great land of Ceram," for indeed, to him, it was a land, that is, a continent, and not in any sense a *pulo* or island. The departing sun was sinking behind the high, jagged peaks of Ceram, and his last golden and purple rays seemed to waver as they shot over the glassy but gently-undulating surface of the bay, and the broad, deeply-fringed leaves of the cocoa-nut palms on the beach took a deeper and richer hue in the glowing sunlight. Then a dull, heavy booming came out of a small Mohammedan mosque, which was picturesquely placed on a little projecting point, almost surrounded by the purple sea. This was the low rolling of a heavy drum, calling all the faithful to assemble and return thanks to their Prophet at the close of the departing day. The rajah then left me to wander along the shore alone, and enjoy the endless variety of the changing tints in the sea and sky while the daylight faded away along the western horizon.

It was in this bay that the Dutch first cast anchor in these seas, and this thought naturally carries us back to the early history of the Moluccas, so famous for their spices, and so coveted by almost every nation of Europe, as soon as enterprise and action began to dispel the dark clouds of ignorance and superstition which had enveloped the whole of the so-called civilized world during the middle ages. Antonio d'Abreu, a Portuguese captain, who came here from Malacca, in 1511, is generally regarded as the discoverer of Amboina and Banda, but Ludovico Barthema (Vartoma), of Bologna, after visiting Malacca and Pedir, in Sumatra, according to his own account, reached this island as early as 1506, yet his description of the Moluccas is so faulty that Valentyn thinks he never came to this region, but obtained his information from the Javanese and Arabs, who, as early at least as 1322, visited these islands to purchase spices.* The Dutch first came to the East in the employment of the Portuguese, and in this manner became acquainted with its geography and its wealth. Their earliest expedition sailed from Holland in 1594, under Houtman. His fleet first visited Bantam and the island of Madura. At the latter place the natives seized some of his crew, and obliged him to pay two thousand rix dollars to ransom them. On the 3d of March, 1599, he arrived here off Hitu-lama. A serious and continual warfare then began between the Spanish, the Portuguese, and the Dutch, for the possession of the Moluccas, which lasted until 1610, when the Dutch became masters of these seas, and monopolized the lucrative trade of the nutmeg and the clove. The English also tried to secure this valuable prize, but the Dutch finally compelled them to

* Francis Valentyn, the author of the most comprehensive and accurate history and description of the Dutch possessions in all the East, was a Lutheran clergyman. He was born at Dordrecht, about the year 1660. In 1686 he arrived at Batavia as a minister, and having resided some time at Japara, near Samarang, he was transferred to Amboina, the future field of his ministry and literary labors. After a residence of twelve years in the Spice Islands, he was obliged to return home on account of ill-health. Having remained in Holland for eleven years, he sailed a second time for India in 1705. Arriving at Java, he remained on that island for two years, and then proceeded to the Spice Islands, where he resided for seven years, and in 1714 he returned again to Holland. Immediately after his arrival he devoted himself to arranging his copious notes for publication. His first volume was published in 1724; this was followed by seven others, all fully illustrated, the last appearing in 1726. They embrace a complete description and history of all the Dutch possessions from the Cape of Good Hope to Japan. The date of the death of this eminent man is not known, but he must have been in his sixty-sixth year when he finished his great work.

leave this part of the archipelago, and have continued to hold it, except for a short time in the early part of the present century.

The guest-chamber of my host, the rajah, was so open at the eaves that a current of damp air blew over me all night, and I had a strong reminder of the Batavia fever the next day. However, I continued along the shore to Hila, where an assistant resident is stationed, whose district also includes a part of the neighboring coast of Ceram. In the days when the clove-tree was extensively cultivated in Amboina, this was an important place, but now it has become almost deserted. It is chiefly famous for its fine mangoes, the fruit of the *Mangifera Indica*.

The Resident here had two fine specimens of an enormous hermit crab, the *Birgos latro*. The habits of this animal are most remarkable. Its food is the cocoa-nut, and, as the ripe nuts fall from the tree, it tears off the dry husks with its powerful claws until the end of the shell where the three black scars are found is laid bare. It then breaks the shell by hammering with one of its heavy claws, and the oily, fattening food within is obtained by means of the pincer-like claws attached to its hinder joints—so perfectly is this animal adapted to its peculiar mode of life. They are esteemed great delicacies after they have been well fed for a time, and these two unfortunates were destined for the table.

A rest of a couple of days stayed the fever, and a boat was ordered to take me to Zyt, the next village, where I reaped another rich harvest of beautiful shells. Here I purchased many *Tritons*, which the natives had brought over from the neighboring coast of Ceram. They are quite similar to the *Tritons* of the Mediterranean, which in mythological times were fancied to be the trumpets used by Neptune's attendants to herald the approach of the grim god, when he came up from the depths of the ocean, and was whirled by foaming steeds over its placid surface. The next village we visited was completely deserted, except by the rajah and his family. The cause of this strange exodus was some misunderstanding between the rajah and his people; and as the Dutch Government claims the right to appoint each native prince, and had refused to remove this rajah, all his people had deserted their homes and moved off to the various neighboring *kampongs*, a quiet and probably an effective mode of remonstrance. Near all these villages the beaches are lined with cocoa-nut palms, and this is frequently the only indication that you are approaching a *kampong*, unless, as occasionally happens, a thin column of smoke is observed slowly rising from out the tall tree-tops. When I wished to take water with me in our canoe, I naturally asked the rajah if he could provide us with a bottle, but he only smiled to think I could be so unaccustomed to tropical life, and ordered a servant to climb one of the cocoa-nut palms above us, and cut off some of its clusters of large green fruit. These we could carry anywhere, and open when we pleased, and a few strokes with a heavy cleaver at once furnished us with a sparkling fountain.

At Assilulu, the next village, I found the rajah

living in such style as I had always fancied a rich Eastern prince enjoyed. His house was in the centre of a large village, and located on the side of a steep hill. It covered three large terraces, and, when viewed from the landing below, appeared like a temple. At this place, besides many rare shells, I purchased several large cassowary-eggs, which had been brought over from Ceram. They are about as long as ostrich-eggs, but somewhat less in diameter, and of a green color. The bird itself belongs to the ostrich family, its feathers being imperfectly developed and separate from each other, and suitable only to aid it to run. One species has a spine on each wing to enable it to defend itself, but the usual mode of attack is by striking with the beak. In size it is twice as large as a full-grown turkey. It is not found wild on any island west of Ceram, and those reported from Java were all undoubtedly carried there from this part of the archipelago. Here also I bought of the rajah a number of superb skulls of the babirusa, *Babirusa alfurus*, literally "the hog-deer," a name well chosen, for its long tusks would at once suggest to these natives the antlers of the deer, the only other wild animal of any considerable size found on these islands. These skulls came from Buru, the eastern limit of this remarkable species of hog.

For some time one of my servants kept alluding to several wonderful and most valuable curiosities which this wealthy rajah was so fortunate as to possess—curiosities indeed, according to his glowing descriptions, compared to the shells I was continually buying. At last I asked him to say to the rajah, that I would be greatly obliged to him if he could show me such rare wonders, being careful not to add, that possibly I should like to purchase one or more; for I had a strong suspicion that the rajah had offered to give him all over a certain sum that I might pay for them, if he could induce me to purchase them. In these Eastern lands, when you send a servant to buy any thing, you have the unpleasant certainty in your mind, that a large part of "the price" will certainly lodge in his pocket; however, if you go to purchase yourself, such exorbitant prices will be demanded, that you will either come away without the article you need, or have the unpleasant reflection afterward that you have been cheated worse than if you had sent your servant and allowed him to levy his black-mail.

As I had anticipated, the rajah was not loath to show me his treasures. They were merely half a dozen glass rings, evidently made by cutting off a piece of a glass rod nine or ten inches long, and half an inch in diameter. This piece, having been heated, was bent into a ring and the two ends united by fusion. Instead of expressing surprise and delight, as all who were looking on seemed to expect, I coolly began explaining to the rajah what they were and how they were made. A look of surprise and incredulity appeared on the faces of all, and the rajah at once, in a most solemn manner, averred that so far from their being the work of man, they had been taken out of the heads of snakes and wild boars! Despite the dignified bearing the occasion was supposed to demand, I could not refrain from a smile as I remarked that I had seen many heads of those animals myself, but never before had I heard that they carried such circular jewels in their brains. "Have you ever seen one of these taken out yourself?" I asked. "Oh, no! They come from *Tana Ceram* (the land or continent of Ceram)." All who were listening, now fearing that their rajah might be worsted in the discussion, and being ready on every occasion to show that they were loyal subjects, abruptly ended the argument by the unqualified assertion that every thing was exactly as the rajah had said; and, as I was his guest, I changed the conversation to another topic. When I returned to the city of Amboina, I looked at once in the "Rariteit Kamer," confident that Rumphius would explain this remarkable and, as I afterward found, common belief; for, though the rajah probably did not believe what he said, his credulous subjects doubtless never thought before of calling in question such a generally-accepted notion; such a query would, in their view, have indicated a weak instead of an inquiring mind. This is one of the obstacles in the way of advancement among these people. Rumphius says that many rings were brought by the Portuguese and sold to the natives, who prize them very highly. This accounted for their origin; and afterward, when I came to travel over the empire of China, and noticed how that people value similar rings of jade (nephrite), and remembered that the coast of Ceram, opposite Assilulu, was once frequented by the people of that empire, who came to purchase cloves and nutmegs, it occurred to me that possibly it was from them that the Amboinese had learned to place so high a value on such simple objects, and had obtained their first specimens. Java is perhaps the only island in the archipelago where such ornaments could have been made by the natives, but I do not find that they are especially prized there, or that they have been dug up with other relics of previous ages.

Off this coast lie three islands, the Three Brothers, and on their shores the natives found a number of rare shells. In the streets of the village considerable quantities of cloves that had been gathered on the neighboring hill-sides were exposed to the sun on mats between the frequent showers, but the culture of that spice has been so neglected of late years, that this was the only place where I saw the fruit in all the Moluccas. The clove-tree (*Carophyllus aromaticus*) belongs to the order of myrtles, which also includes the pomegranate, the guava, and the rose-apple. The trunk of the full-grown tree is from eight to twelve inches in diameter, and occasionally much more. Its topmost branches are usually forty or fifty feet from the ground, though I have seen a tree not larger than a cherry-tree fully loaded with fruit. It was originally confined to the five islands off the west coast of Gilolo, which then comprised the whole group known as "the Moluccas," a name that has since been extended to Buru, Amboina, and the other islands off the south coast of Ceram, where the clove has been introduced and cultivated within a comparatively late period. On those five islands it begins to bear in its seventh or eighth year, and sometimes continues to yield until it has reached an age of nearly one hundred and fifty years; the trees, therefore, are of very different sizes. Here at Amboina it is not expected to bear fruit before its twelfth or fifteenth year, and to cease yielding when it is seventy-five years old. Its limited distribution has always attracted attention, and Rumphius, who describes it as "the most beautiful, the most elegant, and the most precious of all known trees," remarks: "Hence it appears that the Great Disposer of things in His wisdom, allotting His gifts to the several regions of the world, placed cloves in the kingdom of the Moluccas, beyond which, by no human industry, can they be propagated or perfectly cultivated." In the last observation, however, he was mistaken, for since his time it has been successfully introduced into the island of Penang, in the Strait of Malacca, and Sumatra, Bourbon, Zanzibar, and the coast of Guiana and the West India Islands. The clove is the flower-bud, and grows in clusters at the ends of the twigs. The annual yield of a good tree is about four pounds and a half, and the yearly crop on Amboina, Haruku, Saparua, and Nusalaut, the only islands where the tree is now cultivated, is 350,000 Amsterdam pounds.* It is, however, extremely variable and uncertain—for example, in 1846 it was 869,727 Amsterdam pounds, but in 1849 it was only 89,923, or little more than one-tenth of what it was three years before. Pigafetta informs us that, when the Spanish first came to the Moluccas, there were no restrictions on the culture or sale of the clove. The annual crop at that

* According to official statements, the total yield from 1675 to 1854 was 100,034,036 Amsterdam pounds.

time, 1521, according to the same authority, reached the enormous quantity of 6,000 bahars, 3,540,000 pounds of "uncleaned," and 4,000 bahars, 2,360,000 pounds of "cleaned" cloves, about seventeen times the quantity obtained at the present time. Though this statement at first appears incredible, it is strengthened by the fact that the two ships of Magellan's fleet that reached Tidore, one of the Spice Islands, were filled with cloves during a stay of only twenty-four days. When the buds are young they are nearly white, afterward they change to a light green, and finally to a bright red, when they must at once be gathered, which is done by picking them by hand, or beating them off with bamboos on to cloths spread beneath the trees. They are then simply dried in the sun, and are ready for the market. In drying, their color is changed from red to black, the condition in which we see them. They are gathered twice a year, at about this time, in June, and again in the last of December. The leaves, bark, and young twigs also have some peculiar aroma, and at Zanzibar the stems of the buds are also gathered and find a ready sale. The favorite locations of this tree are the high hill-sides, and it is said that it does not thrive well on low lands, where the loam is fine and heavy. The soil best adapted to it appears to be a loose, sandy loam. In its original *habitat* it grows chiefly on volcanic soil, but in Amboina and the other islands, where it is now cultivated, it has been found to flourish well on loams formed by the disintegration of recent sandstone and secondary rocks. The native name for this fruit is *chenki*, perhaps a corrup-

tion of the Chinese *tkeng-ki*, "odoriferous nails."*
The Dutch name for clove is *kruid-nagel*, "herb-nail,"
and for the trees *nagelen-boomen*, "nail-trees." Our
own name clove comes from the Spanish *clavo* (Latin
clavus), a nail, which has also been given them on account of the similarity of these buds to nails.

Although cloves form a favorite condiment among all nations, the natives of these islands where they grow never eat them in any form, and we have no reason to suppose they ever did. The only purpose for which the Amboinese use them, so far as I am aware, is to prepare neat models of their praus and bamboo huts, by running small wire through the buds before they are dried. The Dutch purchase and send to Europe so many of these models, that almost every ethnological museum contains some specimens of this skilful workmanship. The clove probably came into use originally by accident, and I believe the first people who fancied its rich aroma, and warm, pungent taste, were the Chinese. The

* De Canto, who visited these islands in 1540, says: "The Persians call the clove *calafur*, and speaking on this matter, with permission of the physicians, it appears to us that the *carofilum* of the Latin is corrupted from the *calafur* of the Moors (Arabs), for they have some resemblance. And as this drug passed into Europe through the hands of the Moors with the name *calafur*, it appears the Europeans did not change it. The Castilians (Spaniards) called cloves *gilope*, because they came from the island of Gilolo (probably one of the chief sources of this article at that time). The people of the Moluccas call them *chanqué*. The Brahmin physicians first called them *lavanga*, but afterward gave them the Moorish name. Generally all nations give them a name of their own, as we have done; for the first of us (the Portuguese) that reached these islands (the Moluccas), taking them in their hands, and observing their resemblance to iron nails, called them *cravo*, by which they are now so well known in the world."

similarity of the native name to that of the Chinese, and its marked difference, according to De Cauto, from that of the Brahmins or Hindus, lends probability to this view. When the Portuguese first came to these islands, the Chinese, Arabs, Malays, Javanese, and Macassars, were all found here trading in this article. Of the two former nations, the Chinese were probably the first to reach this region, though the Arabs sailed up the China Sea and carried on a large trade with the Chinese at Canpu, a port in Hangchau Bay, south of the present city of Shanghai, in the thirteenth century, or fully two hundred years before the Portuguese and Spaniards arrived in these seas.

The first notice of cloves in Europe occurs in a law passed during the reign of Aurelian the First, between A. D. 175 and 180, where they are mentioned as forming an article of commerce from India to Alexandria; for the Isthmus of Suez and the Red Sea formed at that time the chief highway of Eastern trade. From these islands the cloves were first taken by the Malays and Javanese to the peninsula of Malacca, where they passed into the hands of the Telingas or Klings, who carried them to Calicut, the old Capital of Malabar. Thence they were transported to the western shores of India and shipped across the Arabian Sea, and up the Gulf of Aden and the Red Sea to Cairo. These frequent transfers so increased the original price, that in England, before the discovery of the Cape of Good Hope, thirty shillings were paid for them per pound, or one hundred and sixty-eight pounds sterling per hundred-weight, which was three hundred and sixty times their original price. It was to make this immense profit that the Portuguese, the Spaniards, the Dutch, and the English, were all so anxious to find a passage to the East by sea, and why, when these islands had been discovered, each strove to monopolize the trade itself, and all carried on such a persistent and piratical warfare for many years. So long as cloves were not cultivated elsewhere, and there was no competition in the European markets, the Dutch Government made a handsome profit by means of its monopoly; but when they were raised in other places, the consumption of such a luxury not increasing with the supply, the previous high price began at once to decline, and for many years the income of the government in these islands has not been equal to its expenses in the same region. Some have supposed that a further reduction in the price would be followed with a corresponding greater demand, until its consumption would become as general and as large as that of pepper; but this view is opposed by the common decision of mankind—that pepper is a necessary article of food, and that the clove is only a luxury. If no attempt had been made to keep up the price of this commodity to such a high figure in the European markets, there would have been a less incentive to other nations to introduce it into their own colonies, and thus the market would not have been overstocked so soon, and the price would not have fallen so low as to make the Spice Islands a source of loss instead of profit, except within a recent date.

All the rajahs I met were strict Mohammedans,

and, improving the privileges of their sect, had more than one wife. Soon after arriving at each rajah's house, I was invariably asked whether or not I was married, and for a long time I could not imagine why I was so closely quizzed, until the proverbial jealousy of these people occurred to me. Each wished to know how strict a watch he was to keep over his fascinating harem; and as I was obliged to answer all such queries in the negative, I never even saw one of their wives. At meals only the rajah and myself sat at the table; and as I had two servants, and each of these princes nearly a score, we were always well served, considering our fare. Two articles never failed to appear — chickens and rice — and to these fish was usually added; and for luncheon and dessert always the richest bananas. One kind, the *pisang Ambon*, or "Amboina banana," is very common in that region, but the one I soon learned to prefer, and the one that my servants were always ordered to procure if possible, wherever we chanced to halt, was the *pisang mas*, or "golden banana," a small variety, with a peculiarly rich, honey-like flavor, and a bright golden skin when it is fully ripe. This rajah, I noticed, was particular to seat me at the table so that I could only look out at the front door. The first query he proposed at dinner was, how we are accustomed to eat in our land, adding that, after all, no style suited him so well as dispensing with knives and forks altogether, and adopting the simpler and more natural mode of using one's fingers—a style so common, that each rajah usually keeps a supply of finger-bowls, and frequently these are worth more than all the crockery and other glassware on the table beside. While I was most zealously explaining in reply the superiority of our custom, there arose a suppressed giggle behind me; the secret was out—the rajah's wives had been allowed to leave their close prison and look at me, while I was so placed that I could not, without the greatest rudeness, turn round so as to steal a glance at them. But as this noise was evidently not a part of the proposed programme, I repressed my curiosity, and continued my description. One topic especially they never seemed weary of hearing about, and that was my experience as a soldier. There was something strangely fascinating to their rude imaginations in the scenes of blood through which I have had to pass. At first I had some difficulty in translating my stories into good Malay, but one of my servants fortunately spoke a little Dutch, and supplied me with a word or sentence, as the case demanded.

From Assilulu I set off, during a heavy rainstorm, over a neighboring mountain for the southwest shore, and after a long walk over the rocks, sand, and shingle, we reached Lariki, where there was once a fort with a garrison, but now the ruins of the fort, and a few old, rusty guns are all that remain; and the only official stationed there is an *opziener* or "overseer." In two days, at that place, I so increased my collection, that I had to hire eight coolies to transport it, each carrying two baskets —one on either end of a pole about four feet long. The baskets are made of an open framework of bamboo, covered inside with palm-leaves, and are therefore very light and durable. The most common shell there is the little *cyprœa caput-serpentis*, or "serpent's-head cowry," which has a close resemblance, both in form and color, to the head of a snake.

From Lariki the opziener accompanied me to the neighboring *kampong* of Wakasihu. Our narrow footpath wound along the side of a rugged, projecting crag, and the view from the outer point was very imposing. The stormy monsoon was at its height. The heavy swell rolling in from the open ocean broke and flung its white spray and clotted foam far and wide over the black rocks left bare by the ebbing tide. Thick clouds, heavily freighted with rain, were driven by the strong wind against the rugged coast and adjoining mountains. The cocoa-nut palms that grew just above high-water level, and leaned over toward the sea, twisted and shook their plumy crests in a continual strife with the angry storm, and above them the branches of great evergreens moaned and piped as they lashed to and fro in the fitful gusts of the tempests.

At Wakasihu the old white-bearded rajah, hearing of our approach, came out to welcome us. The opziener explained to him the object of my coming, and immediately he ordered a large *tifa*, that hung under an adjoining shed, to be beaten, as a warning to his people that their rajah required them all to assemble at once before his house. The news quickly spread that a foreigner had come to purchase shells, and the old men, young men, women, and children all came with the treasures that had been accumulating for months, and even years, in their miserable dwellings. Here many perfect specimens of the richly-colored *Cassis flammea* appeared, and also that strangely-marked shell, the *Cyprœa mappa*, or "map cowry," so named from the irregular light-colored line over its back where the two edges of the mantle meet when the animal is fully expanded. They had crawled into the *bubus* that had been sunk for fish at a depth of several fathoms.

The trading was carried on only in Malay, but when I offered a price, which was higher or lower than they had expected, they frequently consulted with each other in their own peculiar dialect or *bahasa*. This the opziener, who was a native of the city of Amboina, was as totally unable to understand as I. He also assured me that even the natives at Lariki, from which we had walked in half an hour, could only understand an occasional word of the *bahasa* of this village, and that the people of neither village could understand a word of the *bahasa* of Assilulu, two or three hours' walk beyond Lariki. In fact, as a rule, every community that is under one rajah, and this is generally but one village, has its own peculiar dialect, which is so different from the dialects of every adjoining village, that all are obliged to learn Malay in order to carry on any trade or hold any communication with their nearest neighbors. The *bahasa* is never a written language, and appears to be constantly changing, for, at the city of Amboina, the natives have completely lost their dialect since the foreigners settled among them, and now can only speak with each other in Malay. The great diversity in the native dialects, and the general adoption of Malay, existed at least as early as when the Spaniards first navigated these waters, for De Barros says: "Two facts give reason to believe that the inhabitants of these islands consist of various and diverse nations. The first is the inconstancy, hatred, and suspicion with which they watch each other; and the second, the great variety of their languages; for it is not the same with them and the Bisayans (the inhabitants of Bisaya, one of the Philippines), where one language prevails with all. The variety, on the contrary, is so great that no two places understand each other's tongue. Even the pronunciation differs widely, for some form their words in the throat, others at the point of the tongue, others between the teeth, and others in the palate. If there be any tongue through which they can understand each other, it is the Malay of Malacca, to which the nobles" (rajahs and capalas) " have lately addicted themselves since the Moors" (Arabs) "have resorted to them for the clove." The Malays and Javanese probably visited these regions long before the Arabs; and they, and not the Arabs, were the people who first taught these natives the Malay language.

From Wakasihu I continued during a violent rain-storm along the south coast to Laha at the mouth of the bay of Amboina, determined to cross the bay and reach home that night, if possible. There were a number of villages along the route, and at each I had to procure a new relay of coolies. This caused much delay, but a foreigner soon learns that he must have an inexhaustible stock of patience to draw on at any unexpected moment if he is going to deal with these people. At one village they all agreed that a neighboring stream, which we could not avoid crossing, had become so swollen by the heavy rains, that it was absolutely impassable; but I simply ordered them to quietly follow me, and where I could not lead the way they might turn back. However, when we came to its banks, we found before us a deep, foaming torrent, far more uninviting and dangerous than I had anticipated, yet by following up its course for half a mile, I came to a place where I made my way to the opposite bank; but here I found myself hemmed in by a precipitous cliff, and there could be nothing done except to beat an inglorious retreat. The natives meantime had been trying the stream farther down, and had found a ford where the strong current was only waist-deep, and here we safely gained the opposite bank. After this came another stream even more difficult to cross, and after that, still a third. Each time I almost expected that the coolies, who were carrying over my shells, would be swept away, but they were all so lightly clad that they succeeded in maintaining their footing, even where the current was perfectly boiling. The streams are changed into rapid torrents in a few hours in these islands, where the water seems to come down from the sky in broad sheets whenever it rains. There are few bridges, and the difficulty of crossing the small rivers is one of the chief obstacles in travelling here during the rainy season. However, as a compensation, there is no sultry, scorching sun. Near the beaches where the streams flow out to the sea, they all widen into deep, oblong pools, which are made very narrow at high-water level by the quantities of sand thrown up by the surf. Near the low-water level they again become broad and shallow, and during ebb-tide the best place to cross them is on the ocean shore as far down as one can go and avoid the danger of being swept away by the heavy surf.

It was nearly night when we reached Laha; we were all thoroughly drenched, and had eaten nothing since morning except some half-ripe bananas. The storm was unabated, but the rajah said it was possible to cross the bay against the wind and waves, and three men were detailed to paddle us six miles to the city. Our boat was a common *leper-leper*, that is, a canoe made from the trunk of a large tree, with pieces of plank placed on the sides to raise them to the proper height. Both ends are sharp, and curve upward. About four feet from the bow a pole is laid across, and another the same distance from the stern. These project outward from the side of the boat six or eight feet, and to them is fastened a bamboo, the whole forming what is known as an "outrigger." The canoes themselves are so narrow, that without these external supports they would be even more crank than the birch-bark canoes of our red Indians. When we launched our *leper-leper*, and placed on board our cargo of shells, and got in ourselves, her sides were only about four inches out of water, but I could not procure a larger boat, so we started. It soon became so dark that all we could discern on the neighboring shores were large fires which the natives had made from place to place to lure the fish by night into their weirs. The wind also increased, and the waves rose higher and began to sparkle brightly, and occasionally a strong gust would seem to change the whole surface of the sea into a sheet of fire. For a time my boatmen felt strong, and encouraged each other with a wild shouting like an Indian warwhoop, and in this way we had made more than a mile from the shore, when the wind became much heavier, and occasionally an ugly wave broke over us. My men still continued to paddle on until we found that we were scarcely holding our own against the storm. Then they became discouraged and proposed to go back, but turning round such a long, narrow boat in the midst of a rough sea was by no means an easy matter. The man forward stopped to rest, and just then a heavy flaw struck the front part of the boat, whirled it round in an instant, and away we flew off before the tempest like a race-horse. It had now become so dark and thick that, though the natives knew every foot of the shore, they could not tell where to steer, and it was only by paddling with all their might that we escaped running into a mass of foaming breakers. Finally we once more reached the shore; the rajah had some rice and fish cooked, and at midnight I took my second meal that day. My bedroom was so open that the wind whistled in on every side and so completely chilled me that I expected to find myself burning with fever the next day, but the excitement counteracted the cold, and I arrived again at Amboina safe and well. After such an excursion several days were passed writing labels, one of which I placed in each individual shell, a wearying and almost an endless task, but the thought continually occurred to me that, if I should not be permitted to return to my native land, such authentic labels in my own handwriting would enable any one into whose hands my collection might fall to fully accomplish the object of my long journey.

July 23d.—This morning, at a quarter-past four, I was suddenly awaked by some cause which, for the moment, I could not understand, but immediately there began a low, heavy rumbling down deep in the earth. It was not a roar, but such a rattling or quick succession of reports as is made when a number of heavily-laden coaches are rapidly driven down a steep street paved with round cobble-stones. At the next instant it seemed as if some huge giant had seized my bed, and had pushed it from him and then pulled it toward him with the greatest violence. The gentleman and lady with whom I was residing shouted out to me: "Run out of the house! run for your life! There is a dreadful earthquake!"

Back of the main house was the dining-room, surrounded by a low wall, and covered with a light roof. This was our place of refuge. The gentleman then explained to me that the shock which had just occurred was the second, and a very severe one, and the first, which was light, was what had so suddenly aroused me from a deep sleep. Of course, no one of us knew but another still heavier might come at the next instant and lay all the buildings near us in a mass of ruins, if indeed the earth should not open and swallow us all alive.

The time that elapsed between hearing the rumbling noise and feeling the shock itself was about five seconds. At this time of the year, in the middle of a monsoon, the wind blows constantly day and night; but after this earthquake there was not the slightest perceptible motion in the air. The tree-toads stopped their steady piping, and the nocturnal insects all ceased their shrill music. It was so absolutely quiet that it seemed as if all nature was waiting in dread anticipation of some coming catastrophe. Such an unnatural stillness was certainly more painful than the howling of the most violent tempest or the roar of the heaviest thunder. Meantime, lights sprang up here and there in the neighboring houses, and all the doors were thrown open, that at the slightest warning everybody might run into the street. The strange words of the Chinese, Malays, and Arabs, sounded yet stranger in the dark, still night, as each called in a subdued but most earnest tone to his or her relatives. The utter helplessness which every one feels at such a time, where even the solid earth groans and trembles beneath his feet, makes the solicitude most keenly painful. It was half an hour—and that half hour seemed an age—before the wind began to blow as before. Then the nocturnal animals, one after another, slowly resumed their nightly cries, and our alarm gradually subsided as the dawn appeared, and once more gave promise of approaching day. I had long been anxious to witness an earthquake; but since that dreadful night there is something in the very sound of the word that makes me almost shudder.

There is usually at least one earthquake—that is, one series of shocks—at Amboina every year, and when eight or ten months have passed without one, a very heavy shock is always expected.

On the 17th of February, 1674, according to Valentyn, Amboina suffered from a heavy earthquake, and Mount Ateti, or Wawanu, on Hitu, west of the village of Zyt, poured out a great quantity of hot mud, which flowed down to the sea. In 1822 Dr. S. Muller visited it and found a considerable quantity of sublimed sulphur, and some sulphurous acid gas rising from it. Again, in 1815, when the volcano of Tomboro, or Sumbawa, was suffering its terrible eruption, an earthquake was felt at several places on this island. Many people described to me a series of shocks of great violence that began on the 1st of November, 1835, and continued three weeks. The whole population of the city were obliged to leave their houses and live for all that time in tents and bamboo huts in the large common back of the forts. Up to that date Amboina had been a remarkably healthy place, but immediately afterward a gastric-bilious fever broke out and continued until March, 1845. On the 20th of July of that year another heavy earthquake was experienced, and this disease at once began again, but had somewhat subsided, when, on the 18th and 20th of March, 1850, another severe shock occurred, and again for the third time it commenced anew. This time both the governor and the assistant resident died. At present Amboina is one of the healthiest islands in these seas. On the 4th and 5th of November, 1699, a series of earthquakes occurred among the mountains where the river that flows through Batavia takes its rise. During these shocks a land-slide occurred, and the water was so filled with mud that the canals and ramifications of the river in the city were silted up, and their currents completely stopped. The immediate consequence was, a large proportion of the population of that city fell victims to a fever engendered by the great quantities of stagnant water. No similar cause could have operated here on the island of Amboina. As the quantity of rain, the strength and direction of the wind, and all other meteorological phenomena, appear to have been the same as in other years, it is evident that the disease was connected in some way with the earthquakes, and the view has been advanced that it was caused by quantities of poisonous gases which are supposed to have risen out of the earth during the violent shocks.

Many fine shells were now brought me from Tulahu, a *kampong* on the northeast coast of Hitu, so I determined to go on my next excursion in that direction. Two miles up the bay from the city of Amboina a tongue of land projects out from either shore, until a passage only five hundred yards wide is left between them. Within this passage the sea again expands into a bay about three miles long and a mile and a half wide. The depth of the water in the passage is sufficient for the largest ships, yet inside it is nowhere more than twenty or twenty-five fathoms. A large navy could anchor here, and be perfectly sheltered from all winds and seas; but vessels rarely

or never enter it, as the road off the city is so far
from the mouth of the bay that it is very seldom any
considerable swell rolls in from the ocean, and moreover, the shores of this bay are considered extremely
unhealthy on account of fevers, while sickness of that
kind is very rare at the outer anchorage. On the
eastern or Laitimur side of the bay there are several
kampongs upon the low land along the shore. Back
from the low land, on the Hitu side, there is a gradual ascent to mountains a mile or two back. One of
them, Salhutu, rises twelve hundred metres above
the sea, and is the highest peak on the island. In
the shallow water around the head of the bay grow
many mangrove-trees (*Rhizophoræ*). A low isthmus
of sand and alluvium, only some thirteen hundred
yards broad, and but a few feet above high-water
level, connects Laitimur with Hitu. Through this a
canal was cut in 1827 to the large bay of Baguala,
in order that the praus bound from Ceram to Amboina might avoid the long route round the dangerous shores of Laitimur; but in twelve years this passage became so filled up with sand as to be impassable, except for small boats, and now they can only
go to and fro during high tide, and thus whatever
there is to be transported must be carried on the
backs of coolies. It is very painful to see such valuable improvements neglected and becoming useless,
for it shows that the whole tendency in this region,
instead of being toward progress, is only toward
decay. Crossing this isthmus, we continued along
the sandy shores on the north side of Baguala Bay,
for this is the only highway between the city of Am-

boina and the populous islands of Haruku, Saparua, and Nusalaut, to the east. Occasionally the path passed over a projecting point, but when it is low water the natives usually prefer to follow along the shore, just as their fathers did for centuries before them, although it is frequently twice as far as by the road. In an hour and a half we came to Suli, a pretty Christian kampong. The road then turned to the north and led us for two or three miles over low hills of coral rock, covered with a thin layer of red soil, to Tulahu, a village on the north coast, which contains a population of about fifteen hundred, and is the largest on the island. Near its centre is a mosque, for the whole community is composed of Mohammedans. As I passed up the main street on my way to the house of the rajah, scores of boys and men kept gathering and following, to learn from my servants who this strange foreigner that headed the procession could be, and what was the object of his coming. The rajah had been notified by the Resident of my proposed visit, and received me with a profound " salaam." In the village was a *ruma négri*, or "house belonging to the village." It had been erected by the villagers, in accordance with orders from the Dutch Government, for the accommodation of all officials and foreigners passing that way. It was built in the usual style of foreign houses in the East, with a broad veranda in front, an admirable place to trade with the people. A comfortable bedroom was fitted up for me, but I dined with the rajah. I was always careful to take a good supply of tea and sugar on such excursions, and my servants. purchased chickens, fish, and whatever else was to be procured; in short, I bought all the food, and the rajah helped me eat it, so that I fulfilled to the letter the order of the governor-general that I should prove "no burden to the native people;" but, on the contrary, as I spent many guilders for shells in each village, my visits, in their eyes, were special blessings. Again and again mothers would come with their children and complain most bitterly that they had so little food and clothing, and beg me to take the shells they had brought, and name my own price. The rajah at first could hardly believe I should collect many shells in his village, but I asked him to beat the *tifa* for his *capalas*, literally "head men," but really a higher class of servants, whose duty it is to convey to the people the rajah's commands, and see them duly enforced. The capalas were ordered to summon all those who probably had shells in their houses, that I might invite them to trade. Meantime supper was prepared. The first object on the table that attracted my attention was an *Octopus*, or "inkfish," an animal much like the squid of our own shores, which fishermen sometimes use for bait, and which whalers know is a favorite morsel for blackfish; but I never heard of men feasting on it before. After this questionable dish and a chicken were disposed of, the fried fruit of the *Artocarpus incisa*, or "bread-fruit tree," was placed on the table. After supper I walked through all the principal streets of the village, supported on either side by a capala, who persistently drove all the natives out of the street before us, and forced them to take their proper place behind us. To give the trade more *éclat*, I took a good quantity of small copper coins and distributed them freely among the small children as I passed along. The result of this manœuvre was most magical; everybody was anxious to make my acquaintance and sell me shells. Even the good Mohammedan priest laid aside his feelings of indifference toward the Christian stranger, and invited me under his roof. He also intimated that he could favor me with a few species, but, as his prices were five times as high as those of the common people, I neglected to make a selection from his treasures.

Each evening that I was in this village the rajah insisted on my passing hour after hour on his veranda, describing to him the foreign countries he could name. Like many other natives who would like to be free from all European rule, it afforded him great comfort to hear that *Tana Ollanda* (Holland) was much smaller in area than France or England. When I came to tell him that *Tana America* was a still greater country, he listened politely, but a half-incredulous smile revealed his belief that I only spoke of it in such an enthusiastic manner because I was an American; yet when I added, that however much other nations might wish to possess these beautiful islands, America would never have such a desire, his knowledge of geography seemed to have become complete at once, and he explained to all who were listening that *Tana America* was admitted by all to be the largest and the most powerful of all nations. He also had an almost endless series of questions to ask about the sovereigns of the lands I had described, and, like a good Mohammedan, expressed his confidence that I should speak well of the Sultan of Turkey, whom he appeared to regard as the next in authority to the Prophet himself.

The next day I went westward to Waai, where I obtained many specimens of the great *Trochus marmoratus*, which lives in abundance a little farther toward the northwestern end of the island, but can only be procured alive during the opposite monsoon. Its beautifully marbled, sea-green surface, and bright, pearly interior have always made it a favorite ornament for the parlor in every land. Many, wishing to improve on Nature, remove the green outer layers either by hydrochloric or nitric acid, so as to give the exterior also a bright nacreous iridescence. Hundreds of the heavy opercula of these animals are found on the neighboring shores, for Nature has provided each with this thick door, which, after it has withdrawn itself into the shell, it can close behind it, and thus be free from all harm.

On my return I found my house besieged with more than two hundred of both sexes and of every age, from infancy to second childhood. Each had a lot of shells to sell, and therefore the prices were very low; but I was careful to pay them more than they could earn in any other way in the same time. The women and children on all these islands are accustomed to gather mollusks at every low tide for food, and whenever any particularly rare or beautiful shell is found, it is always saved; and it was for this reason that I was always confident that I could obtain some valuable specimens in every village. Here I secured one shell, the *Strombus latissimus*, or "thick-lipped strombus," that I had long been hoping to see. It lives in the deep water between these shores and the opposite coast of Ceram, and I could not hear that it is found in any other locality. Many species of long "spindle-shells" (*Fusi*) are found here—some nearly smooth and some richly ornamented with tubercles.

I had now been on the island four weeks, and it was time for the monthly mail to arrive, bringing me letters from home. This exciting thought caused me to forget even my passion for shells, and, promising the natives I would come again and purchase all the specimens they could collect, I returned to the city of Amboina.

CHAPTER VI.

THE ULIASSERS AND CERAM.

THE arrival of the mail here, at Amboina, causes a general rejoicing. Indeed, it is the only thing there is to break the dull monotony of a residence in this enervating climate, unless, as happened this month, there is an earthquake, which affords a grand opportunity for the old residents to describe to all newcomers the fearful shocks they have experienced, and this they invariably do with that peculiar kind of semi-boasting with which a veteran fights over his battles in the presence of raw recruits. The last earthquake, which everybody witnessed, is referred to very much as we at home speak of some violent gale that has swept along the coast. Those who would be weather-wise in our land here discuss the various directions from which the different shocks came—upon which there seems a considerable variance of opinion, but I notice that generally each company agrees with the highest dignitary present. This was a fortunate mail for me. It brought me letters from home, and many American papers from our consul at Batavia, who never failed to send me the latest news all the time I was in any part of the archipelago. Before the next mail my letters were read and re-read. The pages of the Boston papers seemed like the faces of familiar friends, and it was difficult not to peruse the advertisements, column by column, before I could lay them aside. I, in turn, was able to write my friends that already I possessed a full series of nearly all the species of shells I had come to seek.

East of Amboina lie three islands, sometimes called the "Uliassers." The first and nearest to Amboina is Haruku (in Dutch Haroekoe); it is also known to the natives as Oma, or Buwang-bessi, "Ejecting-iron." The second is Saparua (in Dutch Saparoea); but according to Mr. Crawfurd it should be Sapurwa, or Sapurba, from the native numeral *Sa* standing as an article, and the Sanscrit, *purwa*, "source," a name probably given it by the Malay and Javanese traders, who came here to buy cloves long before the Portuguese reached such a remote region, and this is made more probable by the name of the third island Nusalaut (in Dutch Noesalaoet), which is compounded of the Javanese word *nusa*, "an island," and the Malay word *laut*, "the sea." Nusalaut, therefore, means Sea Island, and was evidently so named because it is situated more nearly in the open sea. The Javanese word *nusa*, which is applied, like the Malay word *pulo*, only to small islands, enables us to trace out the early course of the Javanese traders. At the southern end of Laitimur is a kampong named *Nusaniva* (niba), "Fallen Island," perhaps because some island, or a part of Amboina itself, had sunk in that vicinity. Near the Banda group is Nusatelo (better taluh), "Magic

Island." Saparua is also known to the natives as Honimoa, and Liaser, whence probably the old name Uliassers, for this is the most important of the three islands, and would naturally give its name to the whole group. A merchant from Saparua, the chief place on the island of that name, was then visiting Amboina, and kindly invited me to accompany him when he should return—an invitation I was most happy to accept, for Rumphius received many shells from these islands, and I anticipated obtaining some species alive, of which I possessed only shells. A heavy storm delayed us for a week, a frequent occurrence during the southeast monsoon. From Amboina we followed my former route to Tulahu, which we reached at evening, the usual time for commencing a voyage in these seas at this time of year, because the wind generally moderates after sunset, and freshens again the next morning soon after sunrise. We embarked at once on a large prau, manned by eighteen natives of Saparua, and readily distinguished from the people of Amboina by the peculiar custom of clipping the hair short all over the head, except a narrow band along the forehead, which is allowed to hang down over the face, and gives them a remarkably clownish appearance. One of these men, who was coxswain or captain, steered with a large paddle; two others were detailed to keep up the continual, monotonous din, and which these people consider music, and the others rowed. Our musical instruments were a huge *tifa*, that gave out a dull, heavy sound, such as would be caused by beating a hollow log, and not the sharp, quick rap of a drum, which, however monotonous, still has something stirring and lively in it; and two gongs, imported from China, and just harsh and discordant enough to please the musical tympanums of the stupid Celestials. The tifa is beat with a piece of wood of any shape held loosely in the right hand, while the left hand raises the note by pressing against the edge of the vibrating skin. There is, therefore, no such thing as a long roll or a short roll, but one unvaried beating. The two gongs were of different sizes, and were struck alternately, but this was so slight a change that it only made the monotony more wearisome. Each rower had a small wooden box, about a foot long, four inches high, and six wide, where he carried the all-important betel-nut, siri, lime, and tobacco. It also served as a chest for his extra clothing.

The betel-nut is the fruit of a tall, slender, and extremely graceful palm, the *Areca catechu*. The trunk is usually from six to eight inches only in diameter, but the sheaf of green leaves that springs out of its top is thirty or forty feet from the ground. Of all the beautiful palms, this is decidedly the most fascinating to me. Near the house in which I lived, at Batavia, there was a long avenue of these graceful trees, and there in the bright mornings, and cool evenings, I was accustomed to saunter to and fro, and each time it seemed that they were more charming than ever before. This tree grows over all tropical India, and the whole archipelago, including the Philippines. Its Malay name is *pinang*, hence Pulo Pinang is the Betel-nut Island. In nearly all

PINANG, OR BETEL-NUT PALM.

the large islands it has a different name, an indication that it is indigenous. In Javanese it is called *jambi*, and a region on the north coast of Sumatra, where it is very abundant, has therefore received that name. In favorable situations this tree begins to bear when it is six years old, and generally yields about a hundred nuts in a loose, conical cluster. Each nut, when ripe, is about as large as a pullet's egg, and of a bright, ochreous yellow. This yellow skin encloses a husk, the analogue of the thick husk of the cocoa-nut. Within this is a small spherical nut, closely resembling a nutmeg, but very hard and tough, except when taken directly from the tree. It is chewed with a green leaf of the *siri*, *Piper betel*, which is raised only for this purpose, and such great quantities of it are consumed in this way, that large plantations are seen in Java solely devoted to its culture. The mode of preparing this morsel for use is very simple: a small quantity of lime as large as a pea is placed on a piece of the nut, and enclosed in a leaf of siri. The roll is taken between the thumb and forefinger, and rubbed violently against the front gums, while the teeth are closed firmly, and the lips opened widely. It is now chewed for a moment, and then held between the teeth and lips, so as to partly protrude from the mouth. A profusion of red brick-colored saliva now pours out of each corner of the mouth while the man is exerting himself at his oar, or hurrying along under a heavy load. When he is rich enough to enjoy tobacco, a small piece of that luxury is held with the siri between the lips and teeth. The leaf of the tobacco is cut so fine that it exactly resembles the "fine cut" of civilized lands; and long threads of the fibrous, oakum-like substance are always seen hanging out of the mouths of the natives, and completing their disgusting appearance. This revolting habit prevails not only among the men, but also among the women, and whenever a number come together to gossip, as in other countries, a box containing the necessary articles is always seen near by, and a tall, urn-shaped spit-box of brass is either in the midst of the circle or passing from one to another, that each may free her mouth from surplus saliva. Whenever one native calls on another, or a stranger is received from abroad, invariably the first article that is offered him is the siri-box.

From Tulahu we crossed a strait about half a mile broad, and came under the lee of the north side of Haruku, an oblong island, with a long point on the east and southwest. Its extreme length is about two and a quarter geographical miles, its greatest width one and a quarter, and its entire area eight square geographical miles. The surface abounds in hills, but the highest is not a thousand feet above the sea. Its population is upward of seven thousand, and is distributed in eleven villages, and about evenly divided between Christianity and Mohammedanism. Its geological structure is probably like the neighboring parts of Laitimur. It is quite surrounded by a platform of coral, which must be bare in some places at low water. We kept near the shore, so that I could look down deep into the clear water, and distinctly

AFTER THE BATH.

see many round massive heads of brain-coral, *Meandrina*, and other beautiful branching forms, *Astrea*, hundreds of massive and tubular sponges, and broad sea-fans, *Gorgonias*, as we glided over these miniature forests and wide gardens beneath the sea.

A clear sunset gave a good promise of an unusually pleasant night, and the stars twinkled brightly as the evening came on, but the dull vibrations of the tifa and the continual crashings of the gongs, with now and then a wild, prolonged shout from one of the oarsmen, and a similar chorus from the others, kept me awake till late in the night. Finally, just as a troubled sleep was creeping over me, there was a sudden shout from every native, and our round-bottomed prau gave a frightful lurch, first to starboard and then to larboard. All was confusion and uproar, and my first waking thought was that we must have run into the back of some sea-monster, and that, perhaps, the sea-serpent was no myth after all, for when only such savages are seen on the land for men, it is not unreasonable that hideous, antediluvian monsters must be twisting their long, snaky forms beneath in the deep, dark ocean. After awhile the danger was explained: we had struck on a coral reef, though we were at least half a mile from the shore. This indicates the width, at this place, of the platform of coral which encircles the whole island. The heavy swell which had scarcely affected the boat while afloat now made her roll almost over the moment her keel touched the rock. Such rough, projecting coral reefs are very dangerous to the best boats, for in a few moments they will frequently grind a hole through her planks, and immediately she sinks in the surf, while those on board find themselves far from the shore. Pushing off, we stood directly eastward to Saparua, four miles distant, and at half-past three entered a small bay, and were at the kampong Haria. This island has quite the form of the letter H, being nearly divided into two equal parts by a deep bay on the south side and another on the north. The length of the western peninsula, which is a little longer than that of the eastern, is two and a quarter geographical miles, and the narrow isthmus which connects them is about a mile wide. The peninsulas are very mountainous, the highest peaks rising fifteen hundred feet above the sea, but the isthmus is composed of low hills, and is mostly an open prairie. The whole area of the island is ten square geographical miles. Its population numbers more than eleven thousand, making it the most densely peopled of all the islands that now produce cloves. Along its shores are no less than sixteen villages, mostly on the two bays. Of these only three are Mohammedan, the others are Christian. In 1817, when the English restored these islands to the Dutch, a great rebellion broke out in this island, which it took nearly two years to quell, and, what is remarkable, the leaders of this revolt were Christians, that is, members of the Dutch Church.

From Haria we crossed the southern peninsula to the chief town, also called Saparua, at the head of the southern bay. Unlike the narrow footpaths on the island of Amboina, the roads here are broad enough for carts, though none are used, and besides, at the end of every paal from the chief village a small square pillar is set up, indicating the distance from the Resident's house, and the year it was erected. At Saparua, my merchant-friend gave me a nice room, and the Resident, who received me in the politest manner, said he was just planning a tour of inspection to Nusalaut, the most eastern island of the group, and would be happy to have me accompany him, an invitation I most gladly accepted, for the natives had described it to me as abounding in the most beautiful shells, and already I possessed a few rare species that had passed from one native to another until they reached me at Amboina. He also showed me some choice shells that had been sent to him as presents by the various rajahs. Two were magnificent specimens of that costly wentletrap, the *Scalaria preciosa*, for which large sums were once paid in Europe. It was the only kind of shell which I saw or heard of during my long travels among these islands, of which I failed to obtain, at least, one good specimen. He also had many very fine map-cowries, which the natives everywhere regard as rare shells.

That evening the commandant of the "schuterij," or native militia, was to celebrate his birthday by giving a ball at the *ruma négri*. I attended, as a matter of politeness, but not being able to dance myself, withdrew when they had finished the first waltz, for the anticipation of a ramble along the neighboring shores on the morrow would have had a far greater fascination to me than whirling until I was giddy, half embraced in the arms of one of those dark belles, even if I had understood how to take all their odd steps with due grace. The passion of these people for dancing appears to be insatiable, for at eight o'clock the next morning a good proportion of them were still whirling round and round with as much spirit as if the *fête* had just begun. As might naturally be expected, these natives abhor all application and labor, in the same degree that they are fond of excitement.

Saparua Bay is one of the most beautiful inlets of the sea. Near its head is a bold, projecting bluff, and on this rise the white walls of Fort Duurstede. The other parts of the shore form a semicircular, sandy beach, which is bordered with such a thick grove of cocoa-nut palms that no one looking from the bay would imagine that they concealed hundreds of native houses. Here myriads of flat sea-urchins, *Clypeastridæ*, almost covered the flats near low-water level, and completely buried themselves in the calcareous sand as the tide left them. Thousands of little star-fish were also found in the same locality, hiding themselves in a similar manner. Higher up the beach among the *algæ* were many larger starfishes, with the usual five rays; but, as sometimes happens among these low animals, one specimen was provided with one arm more than his companions, and could boast of six. Where ledges of coral rock rose out of the water, countless numbers of the little money cowry, *Cypræa moneta*, filled the excavations formed in this soft rock. They are seldom collected here, as they are too small to be used for food, and these natives never use them as a medium of exchange, as has been the custom from the earliest ages in India.

August 17*th*.—At 5 A. M. started with the Resident for Nusalaut. Our party included the doctor stationed with the garrison, the commandant of militia, whose birthday had been so faithfully observed the day before, my merchant-friend, the " stuurman," or captain, and last, and perhaps I should add least, a little mestizo scribe, whose proper title was " the commissie." A strong head wind, with frequent squalls of rain, made our progress slow till we reached a high point which the natives called Tanjong O, the Headland O. From that point over to Nusalaut was a distance of some two miles. As we left the shore, and pushed out into the open sea, our progress became still slower. Inch by inch we gained till we were half-way across, when the wind freshened, and for a time we could scarcely hold our own, despite the increased jargon from the tifa and the gong, and a wilder whooping from every native, varied by mutterings from each, to the effect that he was the only one who was really working. Almost the moment these people meet with any unexpected difficulty they become disheartened, and want to give up their task at once, exactly like little children.

Nusalaut, like the other Uliassers, is completely surrounded by a shallow platform of coral, which is mostly bare at low water. We therefore entered a small bay, where the deep water would allow our boat to come near the shore. Coolies now waded off with chairs on their shoulders, and landed us dry-footed on the beach, where were a dozen natives, clad in what is supposed to have been the war-costume of their ancestors long before the arrival of

Europeans. They were quite naked, and carried in their right hands large cleavers or swords (some of which I noticed were made of wood). On the left arm was a narrow shield about four feet long, and evidently more for show than use, as it was only three or four inches wide in the middle. On the head was a kind of crown, and, as long plumes are scarce, sticks were covered with white hen-feathers, and stuck in as a substitute. From their shoulders and elbows hung strips of bright-red calico, to make them look gay or fierce (it was difficult to say which). Their war-dance consisted in springing forward and backward, and whirling rapidly round. Forming in two lines, they fiercely brandished their swords, as we advanced between them to a little elevation, where all the rajahs had gathered to receive the Resident.

Nusalaut is oblong in form, less than two miles in length, and in some places only half a mile wide. Its area, therefore, is somewhat less than a single square mile. Its surface is hilly, but the highest point is not more than three hundred meters above the sea. A century and a half ago its population numbered five thousand, but at present it is only three thousand five hundred. The number of villages, and, consequently, of rajahs, is only seven. We first visited Sila, the one nearest our landing. As we entered the kampong, we found the main street ornamented in a most tasteful manner. The young, light-yellow leaves of the cocoa-nut palm had been split in two, and were bent into bows or arcs with the midrib uppermost, and the leaflets hanging beneath. These bows were placed on the top of the fence, so as to form a continued series of arches; a simple arrangement that certainly produced a most charming effect. As we passed along, scores of heavily-loaded flint-locks were discharged in our honor, and these mimic warriors continued their peculiar evolutions. From Sila a short walk brought us to Lainitu, and here our reception took a new phase. In front of the rajah's house was a wide triumphal arch, made of boards, and ornamented with two furious red lions, who held up a shield containing a welcome to the Resident. But just before we passed under that, the crowd in front parted, and lo, before us stood eighteen or twenty young girls, who had been selected from the whole village for their beauty. They were all arrayed in their costliest dresses, which consisted of a bright-red sarong and a low kabaya, over which was another of lace, the latter bespangled with many thin pieces of silver. Their long, black hair was combed backward, and fastened in a knot behind, and in this were stuck many long flexible silver pins, that rapidly vibrated as they danced. Most of them had a narrow strip of the hair over the forehead clipped short, but not shaven, a most unsightly custom, and perhaps originally designed to make their foreheads higher. Their lips were stained to a dull brick-red from constantly indulging in the use of the betel. They were arranged in two rows, and their dance, the *minari*, was nothing more than slowly twisting their body to the right and left, and, at the same time, moving the extended arms and open hands in circles in opposite directions. The only motion of their naked feet was to change the weight of the body from the heel to the toe, and *vice versa*. During the dance they sang a low, plaintive song, which was accompanied by a tifa and a number of small gongs, suspended by means of a cord in a framework of *gaba-gaba*, the dried midribs of palm-leaves. The gongs increased regularly in size from one of five or six inches to one of a foot or fifteen inches in diameter. Each had a round knob or boss in the middle, which was struck with a small stick. When made to reverberate in this manner, their music was very agreeable, and resembled closely that made by small bells. Several gentlemen informed me that this instrument was introduced here from Java by natives of these islands, who were taken there by the Dutch to assist in putting down a rebellion. It is merely a rude copy of the instrument called the *bonang* or *kromo* in Java. The number of gongs composing this instrument varies from six or eight to fourteen. In Java the sticks used in striking the gongs, instead of being made only of wood, are carefully covered with a coating of gum to make the sound softer. Another common instrument in Java is the *gambang*, consisting of wooden or brass bars of different lengths, placed crosswise over a wooden trough. These are struck with small sticks composed of a handle and a round ball of some light substance like pith, as shown in the accompanying photograph of a Javanese and his wife. The instrument in the left hand is a kind of flute, and that in his right is a triangle exactly like those used in negro concerts in our land.

MUSICAL INSTRUMENTS USED BY THE MALAYS AT BATAVIA.

In the Sunda districts of Java very good music is produced by an instrument which consists of a series of small bamboo tubes of different lengths, so placed in a rude framework of wood that they can slightly vibrate, and strike the sides of the frame when it is shaken in the hand.

On the peninsula of Malacca a kind of gigantic Æolian harp is made, by removing the partitions within a bamboo, thirty or forty feet long, and making a row of holes in the side as in a flute. This is placed upright among the dense foliage, and in the varying breeze gives out soft or heavy notes, until the whole surrounding forest seems filled with the harps of fairies.

All these natives are passionately fond of music, and perhaps in nothing has their inventive genius been so well displayed as in their peculiar musical instruments, which have been brought to the greatest perfection in Java, where they are so elaborate that a set of eighteen or twenty pieces, for a complete band, costs from six hundred to one thousand dollars. A number of these were taken to England by Sir Stamford Raffles, and carefully examined by a competent judge, who expressed himself "astonished and delighted with their ingenious fabrication, splendor, beauty, and accurate intonation."

While we were watching the slow, graceful dance, dinner was prepared, and we were summoned from the veranda to an open room in the rear. The wife of the rajah was the only lady at the table, and, as all the princes and notables of the other villages were present, the number of guests who were ready to take seats with us was not small. Our bill of fare was sufficient to satisfy the most fastidious epicure; for substantial diet the neighboring forests had furnished us with an abundance of venison and the meat of the wild boar, and the adjoining bays had yielded several kinds of nice fish. All was prepared in an unexceptional manner, and the rich display of pineapples, mangostins, dukus, and several kinds of bananas was finer than many a European prince could set before his guests. The process of demolishing had fully begun, when the dark beauties, who had been dancing before the house, came in, and ranged themselves round the table. My first impression was, that they had come in to see how Europeans eat, and I only refrained from hinting to that effect to the Resident on my right, because he had already smiled to see my surprise at our novel reception, and besides, I was anxious not to appear to be wholly ignorant of their odd customs. Soon they began to sing, and this, I thought to myself, is probably what is meant by a sumptuous banquet in the East, and, if so, it well deserves the name. As the song continued, one after another took out a handkerchief of spotless white, and folding it into a triangular form, began to fan the gentleman in front of her. This is indeed Eastern luxury, I said to myself, and while I was wondering what would come next, the damsel behind the Resident reached forward and gave him a loud kiss on his cheek. "That was intended as an appetizer I presume?" *Natuurlijk*, "Of course," he replied, and I leaned back in my chair to give way to a hearty laugh, which I had been trying for a long time to restrain, when suddenly I was astonished by a similar salutation on the lips! It was done so quickly that I had no time to recover from my bewildering surprise, and coolly explain that such was not the custom in my land. Instead of my laughing at the Resident's expense, the whole party laughed at mine; but my confusion was dispelled by the assurance of all that even the governor-general himself had to submit to such treatment when he came to inspect these islands. Besides, I was made aware that the fault was largely my own, and that, when I leaned backward to laugh, the fair one behind me had misinterpreted the movement as a challenge (which she certainly seemed not loath to accept). At every village we had to run a similar gantlet, and I must confess that several times it occurred to me that the youngest member of the party certainly received his share of such tender attention, and that many of these beauties, *nona itum*, were determined to improve their present opportunity for fear that they might never again have the privilege of kissing a gentleman with a white face.

The Resident's duties, while on a tour of inspection, consist chiefly in visiting and examining the schools, of which there is one in every village on this island, except at one place where two kampongs, which are near each other, have one in common. On Saparua also thirteen out of the sixteen villages are each provided with a school, and on Haruku eleven villages are supplied with six schools, so distributed over the island as to be accessible to all. The facilities, therefore, afforded by the Dutch Government to these natives to acquire a good common education are far better than they are in many civilized lands. The teachers are all well paid. Those on this island are all natives. They are remarkably awkward, probably because they feel dressed up; for, on such an important occasion as the present, every one who holds a government office must appear in a black suit. Again and again I found it required great self-command to keep from smiling when it was expected I should look very grave and dignified; for here, on the outskirts of civilization, I beheld all the fashions of Europe, apparently for the last two hundred years. All the petty officials wore dress coats, some with tails almost on the ground, and others with sleeves so long that you could scarcely see the ends of the fingers, and still others with the waists so small that they seemed to be in corsets. Some of these coats had narrow collars, and had evidently been worn by the most dainty exquisites, while others had lapels broad enough for the outer coat of a coachman. As soon as the inspection is over these precious articles are carefully rolled up and thoroughly smoked, to prevent their being destroyed by the ants. They are then placed away till the next year, when they are again unrolled and at once put on, entirely filled with wrinkles, and giving out the strongest odors.

On entering the school-house the Resident is greeted with a welcome that has been prepared long before by the teacher and committed to memory by a small boy, who now steps forward, and, stretching out both arms at full length, repeats the oration at the top of his voice, occasionally emphasizing certain sentences by making a low bow, but taking care all the time not to bend his extended arms. This ordeal finished, the children join in singing a psalm, all keeping time by striking the forefinger of the right hand with the palm of the left. It was most amusing to see the little ones perform their part of the ceremony. The four classes, into which the schools are divided, are now successively examined. The two younger classes in reading and spelling the Malay language, written in the Roman alphabet, according to the Dutch rules of pronunciation. The two older classes are likewise examined in these branches, in penmanship, and the simple rules of arithmetic.

As I visited school after school I became more and more surprised at the general proficiency of the children, and I am certainly of the opinion that they would compare very favorably with the children of the same ages in our own country districts. This remarkable promise in childhood is not, however, followed by a corresponding development during youth and manhood.

The population* of these islands is divided into the following kinds: first, that of Europeans, which also includes the mestizoes, or, as they are always called here, "half-castes," who are of all shades of mixture, from those who are as white as Europeans to those who are as brown as the natives. Outside

* In 1855 the population of the islands east of Amboina was thus divided, and so little change has occurred that these figures closely represent the relative numbers of each class at the present time:

Islands.	Mestizoes.	Burgers.	Villagers.		Slaves.	Total.
			Christians.	Mohammedans.		
Haruku...............	88	288	3,204	3,511	64	7,188
Saparua...............	162	2,912	7,840	1,154	97	11,665
Nusalaut...............	4	63	3,386	....	26	3,179

of the city of Amboina nine-tenths of the so-called Europeans are really mestizoes. The second class is composed of those natives who are not required by the government to work in the clove-gardens. They are named by the Dutch "burgers." The third class includes the *negroijvolken* or "villagers," and the fourth comprises those who were slaves, and are mostly natives of Papua. The "villagers," or common people, have paid no direct tax, but have been required instead to work a certain number of days in the clove-gardens belonging to the government, and also sell to the government all they raise themselves at a certain price. Now the Dutch are changing this indirect mode of taxation into a direct mode, and requiring the able-bodied men to pay one guilder each this year, but not obliging them to work so many days in the gardens. Next year they are to pay two guilders and work a less number of days, and so on till the fifth year, when they will pay five guilders, and be entirely free from any other tax.

After the examination of the school has been finished, all the able-bodied men are called together before the rajah's house, and the Resident explains to them this change, and what will be expected of them during the coming year. At present each village is obliged to furnish men at a certain price to carry the chair of every official and of every one who, like myself, has an order for such a privilege from the head government at Batavia. In four years from this time each official will be obliged to make a separate trade at every village with his chair-bearers, and these people are so indolent, and so given to demanding the most extravagant prices, that I fear the chief effect of this change will be to diminish even the little travel and trade there are now, unless the present system shall be continued till large numbers of horses are introduced.

This proposed taxation will certainly be very light, for each man can earn the five guilders required of him by carrying coal or freight for a week at the city of Amboina.

The great obstacle to every reform among these natives is, that only a very few of them, if they have enough for one day, will earn any thing for the morrow. "*Carpe diem*" is a motto more absolutely observed here than in luxurious Rome. The desire of all Europeans to have something reserved for sickness or old age is a feeling which these people appear to never experience, and such innate improvidence is, unfortunately, encouraged from their earliest childhood by the unfailing and unsparing manner in which Nature supplies their limited wants. The possibility of a famine is something they cannot comprehend.

In 1854, 120,283 Amsterdam pounds of cloves were raised on this island from 13,042 trees, each tree yielding the great quantity of nine pounds. In the same year, on Saparua, from 29,732 fruit-trees, 181,137 Amsterdam pounds were gathered, one-third of the whole crop (510,912 pounds) obtained that year in Amboina, Haruku, Saparua, and Nusalaut. On Haruku 38,803 pounds were gathered that year. These three islands, Haruku, Saparua, and Nusalaut, with the neighboring south coast of Ceram, form one residency, over which an assistant resident or resident of the second rank is placed.

From Lainitu we passed along the northern shore to Nullahia, where we remained for the night. Here I purchased many beautiful "harp-shells" and a few large cones, which were formerly so rare that they have been sold in Europe for more than two hundred dollars apiece. The next day we continued on to Amet, the largest *kampong* on the island. Here a good missionary was located, who was indeed like Melchisedek, "both priest and king." From this place he is accustomed to travel to the various villages, preaching, teaching, and keeping a general surveillance over the conduct of his people, and the good results of his labor were well shown in the general spirit of thrift and order which characterizes these villages as compared to the Mohammedan kampongs I had previously visited on the shores of Amboina. Every person in all these villages is nominally a Christian, and this, I believe, is the only island in the archipelago of which that can be said. The missionary, however, informs me that a few of them occasionally steal away to some secret place among the mountains where they practise their ancient rites by making offerings to spirits, possibly those of their ancestors, which they were accustomed to worship before the introduction of Christianity.

The village of Amet is one of the best places in the whole Moluccas to gather shells. The platform of coral which begirts the island extends out here nearly two English miles from high-water level to where the heavy swell breaks along its outer edge;

and all this flat area is either bare at low tide, or only covered to the depth of a few inches by small pools. Here the beautiful "mitre-shells" abound—the *Mitra episcopalis,* or "Bishop's mitre," and the *Mitra papalis,* or "Pope's mitre," and many beautiful cones and cypræas.

From Amet to Abobo, at the southern end of the island, a distance of more than a mile, the coral platform narrows until it is quite near the high-water line. Along the whole length of this reef the heavy swell from the ocean is seen rising again and again into one grand wall, which, slowly curling its high white crest, plunges headlong over the soft polyps, which, despite the utmost efforts of the ocean, slowly but continually advance their wondrous structure seaward. This endless lashing and washing of the waves, which would wear away the most adamantine rocks, only enables those delicate animals to work with a greater vigor, and this is probably the chief reason that the reef here is wider than anywhere else along the shores of the neighboring islands.

Between Amet and Abobo there is sometimes found a very beautiful cone, covered with mottled bands of black and salmon-color, which once commanded fabulous prices in Europe, and is now generally regarded by the natives as the most valuable shell obtained in these seas. Although I travelled along nearly all the shores of the adjacent islands, I was continually assured that this part of Nusalaut was the only place where this shell was ever found, an assertion which I regard as true, so sparing is Nature of her choicest treasures.

Returning from Abobo to Nullahia and Lainitu, I took a small prau for Saparua. The monsoon was light and the sea smooth at first, but when again we approached Tanjong O, which these natives always spoke of with the same respect that our sailors speak of Cape Horn, we found a very strong current setting in one direction, while the wind had freshened from the opposite quarter. The meeting of the wind and current made the waves rise irregularly up in pyramids and tumble over in every direction. The natives, apparently half terrified, stripped off their clothes, as if they expected that the boat would certainly be swamped, and that soon their only chance of escape would be to swim to the shore and attempt to climb up the ragged rocks through the surf; but I encouraged them to paddle with all their might, and though several waves broke over us, we went safely through. As soon as the danger was past, each native frequently looked back and boastfully shook his head, as if to taunt the evil spirit that dwells on this dangerous headland.

When we arrived at Saparua, I found the Resident just on the point of starting for the neighboring coast of Ceram, and only waiting to invite me to accompany him. So again I was in good fortune, for I had not anticipated reaching that almost unknown island. From the southern bay we were taken in chairs across the isthmus, that connects the two main parts of Saparua, to the north bay. It was now night, but we continued along the east side of this bay to the kampong Nollot, at the northern end of the island, the nearest point to the part of Ceram we were to visit. Scores of natives followed us, some to relieve each other as chair-bearers, and others to carry immense torches of dry palm-leaves, which successively blazed brightly for a moment and lighted up the adjoining forests and our strange party. Several villages lay along our route, and, as we entered each, huge piles of leaves were set on fire, and the half-naked natives all whooped and shouted until we really seemed to be in the midst of the infernal regions.

At daylight the next morning we started in two praus for Ceram. As we left the rajah's house the beauties of the villages gathered on the bank, and, while we were embarking, chanted a song of hope that we should have "a pleasant voyage over the sea, and soon return in safety." The tifa and gongs began the monotonous din, the rowers shouted and tugged at their oars, and the high peaks of Saparua slowly sank beneath the horizon. For a time no land was in sight, and I could but note how perfectly we were repeating the experience of the earliest navigators of the Mediterranean along the shores of Phœnicia and Greece.

Ceram is the largest island in the Moluccas. Its length is one hundred and sixty-two geographical miles, but its greatest breadth is only forty. Its area is computed to be about five thousand geographical square miles, which makes it rank next to Celebes in the whole archipelago. It is divided into three peninsulas by two deep bays on its southern coast. The most eastern of these great inlets of the sea is called Elpaputi Bay, which separates the west-

ern end of the island from the eastward. The western third is again divided into two unequal peninsulas by the bay of Tanuno. The westernmost is called Howamowel, or "Little Ceram," and is connected with the middle peninsula, Kaibobo, by an isthmus less than a mile broad. Kaibobo is again connected with the eastern two-thirds of the island by an isthmus about three miles broad. The whole island is really but one great mountain-chain, which sends off many transverse ranges and spurs, and the only low land it contains is east of the bay of Amahai, along its southern shore. In the western peninsula the mountains do not have any considerable height, but in the middle one some peaks attain an elevation of five thousand or six thousand feet, and in the middle part of the eastern peninsula Mount Nusaheli is supposed to rise more than three thousand metres (nine thousand eight hundred and forty-two English feet) above the sea. Over all these elevations stretches one continuous and unbroken forest. So great a part of the whole island is unknown that various and widely-different estimates of its population have been made.*
Some of its peaks now became visible through the mist, and soon we were in Elpaputi Bay, and, changing our course toward the east, entered a small inlet called the bay of Amahai. At the head of this bay is the small village of the same name, containing a population of thirteen hundred souls. The *contro-*

* In 1854 the western part that is included in the residency of Hila was supposed to contain a population of two thousand four hundred and sixty-eight; the middle peninsula and the bay visited on this voyage, twenty-four thousand one hundred and ninety-four; the northern coast

leur stationed here told us of the "Alfura"* who dwelt among the neighboring mountains; and, that I might have the opportunity of seeing these wild savages, the Resident kindly sent a number of the coast people to invite them to come down and perform their war-dance before us. In a few hours a party of about twenty appeared. Only eight or ten were able-bodied men; the others were women, children, and old men. In height and general appearance they closely resemble the Malays, and evidently form merely a subdivision of the Malay race. Their peculiar characteristics are the darker color of their skins and of their hair, which, instead of being lank like that of the Malays, is crisp, but not woolly like that of the Papuans. They wear it so very long, that they may properly be said to have large and bushy

under Wahai, forty thousand nine hundred and twenty-five; and, in the great area east of Elpaputi Bay, it was supposed that there dwelt between twenty-one and twenty-two thousand; making a total of eighty-nine thousand and eighty-seven, about ninety thousand; but Dr. Bleeker, who gives these figures, thinks there are half as many more people among the mountains, and that the whole population of the island should be put down at one hundred and fifty thousand. He gives the population of these islands for 1855 in round numbers as follows:

Amboina	29,500	Amblau	1,000	Manipa	700
Haruku	7,200	Bonoa	1,500	Saparua	11,600
Buru	9,200	Nusalaut	3,500	Ceram	150,000
		Total			214,200

These figures may be regarded as good estimates of the population at the present time.

* This name Alfura, in Dutch Alfoera, is also written Alfora, Alafora, Arafura, and Halafora. Mr. Crawfurd finds that it is composed of the Arabic articles *alor, el,* and the preposition *fora,* without; and was simply a general denomination given by the Portuguese when they were supreme in the Moluccas to all the native inhabitants who were without the pale of their authority.

heads. When in full dress, however, this abundance of hair is confined by a red handkerchief, obtained from the natives on the coast, and ornamented with parts of a small shell, the *Nassa,* in place of beads. Their clothing is a strip of the inner bark of a tree beaten with stones until it becomes white and opaque, and appears much like white, rough paper. This garment is three or four inches wide and about three feet long. It passes round the waist and covers the loins in such a way that one end hangs down in front as far as the knee. On the arm, above the elbow, some wore a large ring, apparently made from the stalk of a sea-fan, *Gorgonia.* To this were fastened bunches of long, narrow green leaves, striped with yellow. Similar ornaments were fastened to the elbows and to the strip of bark at the waist. Each of the warriors was armed with a *parang* or cleaver, which he raised high in the right hand, while on his left arm was a shield three or four feet long but only four or five inches wide, which he held before him as if to ward off an imaginary blow. Their dance was merely a series of short leaps forward and backward, and occasionally whirling quickly round as if to defend themselves from a sudden attack in the rear. Their only musical instrument was a rude tifa, which was accompanied by a monotonous song from the women, children, and old men. At first the time of the music was slow, but by degrees it grew quicker and louder, until all sang as fast and loud as they could. The dancing warriors became more excited, and flourished their cleavers and leaped to and fro with all their might, until, as one of our company remarked, their eyes were like fire. It was easy to understand that in such a state of temporary madness they would no more hesitate to cleave off a head than to cut down a bamboo. They are far-famed "head-hunters." It is a custom that has become a law among them that every young man must at least cut off *one human head before he can marry.* Heads, therefore, are in great demand, and perhaps our realization of this fact made these frenzied savages appear the more shocking specimens of humanity. The head of a child will meet the inexorable demands of this bloody law, but the head of a woman is preferred, because it is supposed she can more easily defend herself or escape; for the same reason the head of a man is held in higher estimation, and the head of a white man is a proof of the greatest bravery, and therefore the most glorious trophy.

On the north coast, near Sawai Bay, the Dutch, a few years ago, had a war with these natives, and when they had driven them to the mountains, they found in their huts between two and three times as many human skulls as it is probable there were people in the whole village, men, women, and children taken together. When a man is afraid to go out on such a hunt alone, he invites or hires two or three others to assist him, and all lie in wait near a neighboring village until some one chances to pass by, when they spring out and dispatch their victim, and escape. This, of course, creates a deadly enmity between each tribe and every other near it; and the whole interior of the eastern half of the island, where this head-hunting prevails, is one unchanging scene of endless, bloody strife. The same custom prevails over the greater part of the interior of Borneo among many tribes known as Dyaks, the Malay word for "savage." There only the heads of men are valued, and new ones must be obtained to celebrate every birth and funeral, as well as marriage. I have seen a necklace of human teeth made in that island by those people. Small holes had been drilled in several scores of them, which were then strung on a wire long enough to pass two or three times round the neck of the hero who wore it. When a head is secured, the brains are taken out, and it is placed over a fire to be smoked and dried. During this process, the muscles of the face contract and change the features until they assume a most ghastly grimace.

The dance being finished, we conversed with them as well as we could about their customs, for none of them could speak but a few words in Malay. On the piece of paper-like bark which hangs down in front, each warrior makes a circle when he cuts off a head. Some had one or two of these circles; but one man had four, and I gave him to understand that I knew what they meant by drawing my hand four times across my throat, and then holding up the fingers of one hand, and instantly he hopped about as delighted as a child, thinking that of course I was regarding him as the bravest of the brave, while I looked at him in mute astonishment, and tried to realize what a hardened villain he was. Our North American savages are civilized men compared to these fiends in human form.

A DYAK OR HEAD-HUNTER OF BORNEO.

From Amahai we sailed westward across Elpaputi Bay to the peninsula already described as rejoicing in the melodious name of Kaibobo. Here, at a small village, a native of Amboina had established himself, and commenced planting cocoa-trees, which we found thriving most satisfactorily, even better than in the gardens I had previously visited on Amboina. At the present prices this is the most profitable product that can be raised in the Moluccas, and the good result of this trial shows what enormous quantities might be shipped yearly from this single great island of Ceram, if foreigners or natives would devote themselves to its culture.

Near by were two villagers of Alfura, who had been induced to abandon their old habits of roaming among the mountains and make for themselves a fixed dwelling-place. The rajah of each place came to the village where we landed, to acknowledge his allegiance to the Dutch Government. From that place we proceeded southward along the eastern shore of the peninsula. While we were in the bay, the opposite shore sheltered us from the heavy southeasterly swell that now rolled in before a driving rain-storm, and made our round-bottomed *praus* roll and pitch so that the rowers could scarcely use their oars. At length, near night, we came to anchor off a village that the Resident was obliged to visit. It was situated on a straight, open beach, which descended so abruptly beneath the sea, that the high swell never once broke before finding itself suddenly stopped in its rapid course; it rose up in one huge wall that reeled forward and fell on the steep shore with a roar like heavy thunder. Although I was born by the shore of the open sea, and had seen boats land in all kinds of weather, I never saw the most daring sailors attempt it through such a surf as was breaking before us. Every few moments the water would rebound from the sand until it rose twice and a half as high as the natives standing near it, at least fifteen feet. One of our number could not conceal his timidity, and declared that every one of us would be drowned if we should attempt to land at that time. The Resident, however, said he should try it, and I assured him he should not go alone; and the others concluded not to allow themselves to be left behind. More than two hundred natives had now gathered on the beach. They soon made a rude skid or wide ladder, with large poles on the sides, and small green ones with the bark torn off for the rounds. This was laid down when the wave was forming, and a heavy prau pushed on to it as the wave broke, and a broad sheet of surf partially buoyed her up. As this wave receded, she was successfully launched. We were now ordered to change from our boat into that one, and at once we ran in toward the shore over the heavy rollers. Other natives now appeared on the beach with a huge coil of rattan an inch or more in diameter, and, two or three of them seizing one end, ran down and plunged headlong into a high wave as coolly and as unhesitatingly as a diver would leap from the side of a boat in a quiet bay. The end of the rattan was fastened firmly to the front part of our boat; the other was carried up a long way on the beach, and the na-

tives ranged themselves in two rows, each grasping it with one hand as if ready to haul in the leviathan himself, when the warning should be given. A number of heavy seas now rolled in and broke, but the natives, by means of their paddles, kept us from being swept forward or backward. A smaller swell is coming in now. Every native gives a wild yell, and those on the shore haul in the rattan with all their might, and away we dart on the crest of a wave with the swiftness of an arrow. We are now in the midst of the surf, and our boat is on the skid, but away we glide at the speed of a locomotive, and already we are high upon the bank before the next wave can come in.

The Resident, who enjoyed surprising me as much as possible, had carefully concealed the urgent business that had compelled him to land in such a difficult place, and my curiosity was not diminished when I noticed his imperative orders for the militia, who accompanied us as a guard, to come on shore immediately. We were evidently near, or already in, an enemy's country. A large gathering of the natives was now ordered at the rajah's house, an examination began, and several men were sentenced to be seized by the guard and brought to Amboina for trial. They had been guilty of participating in a *feest kakian*, or meeting of a secret organization, that was formed as early at least as a few years after the arrival of the Dutch. There are various opinions as to its object, some asserting that it originated as a confederation of many tribes against other tribes, and others supposing its design to be to resist the authority of the Dutch, the view apparently entertained by that government.

But a short time before we arrived they had held one of their drunken revels at a place only half an hour's walk among the neighboring mountains. In these convivials at first each indulges as freely as he chooses in an intoxicating liquor made from the juice of the flowering part of a palm; then all join in a dance, and kick about a human head which has been obtained for this especial occasion, and is tossed into the midst of these human fiends all besmeared with its own clotted blood. The natives whom our soldiers were seizing were present and took part in one of these bloody carousals, as they themselves acknowledged. I must confess that a sickening sensation, akin to fear, crept over me that night before I fell asleep, as I realized the probability that, if it were not for our guard, instead of our taking away those culprits to be punished as they richly deserved, they would sever every one of our heads and have another diabolical revel over their bloody trophies.

All night the wind piped loudly in strong gusts, and the heavy pulsating of the surf came up from the beach beneath us. In the morning the storm had not abated, but I was anxious to go back to Amboina, and no one of the party desired to remain long in that savage place. To embark was more difficult than to land. Again the skid was put down on the sand, the prau placed on it, and as the water receded the natives pushed us off, several waves sweeping over their heads; but they were so completely amphibious, that it did not appear to trouble them in the least. Unfortunately, a strong gust struck us just as we floated, and for some minutes we remained motionless in one spot, the sea rolling up until what Virgil says, with a poet's license, was literally true of us, the naked earth could be seen beneath our keel.

Again all that day we pitched and tossed, and the distance we had to go seemed endless, until, as the sun sank, the high land of Saparua rose before us and we entered a broad bay. The natives saw us coming, and quickly kindled on the shore huge blazing fires, which were repeated in the form of long bands of bright light on the mirror-like surface of the quiet sea, and now we were welcomed with shouts to the same place where the native belles had sung such a plaintive song at our departure.

From Saparua I returned directly to Amboina, for one who has been accustomed to the mail facilities of our land will subject himself to almost any inconvenience in order to reach the place where the mail-boat touches.

Life at Amboina, and at almost every other place in the Dutch possessions, at the best is dull. Once or twice a month, in accordance with an established custom, the governor gives a reception on Sunday evenings, when all the Europeans and most of the mestizoes come and dance till late; and as there are some seven hundred of these people in the city, and the larger portion attend, such parties are quite brilliant affairs. The music is furnished by a small band connected with the detachment of soldiers stationed here.

An occasional wedding also helps to break up the unvarying monotony, and kindly furnishes a topic for general conversation, so that for a time every one does not feel obliged to complain of the abundance of rain, if it is the rainy season, or of the lack of rain if it is the dry monsoon. Whenever an official goes back to Holland, or is transferred from one place to another, which usually occurs once in three years, even when he is not promoted, he sells most of his furniture at auction. His friends always muster in full force, and each one is expected to show his attachment to his departing friend by purchasing a number of articles, or something of little value, at ten or a hundred times its price. Such an occasion also gives a change to the talk among merchants.

An auction here, instead of being a kind of private trade, as with us, is directly under the management of the government. An authorized auctioneer is regularly appointed at each place, and a scribe carefully enters the name of the successful bidder, the article he has purchased, and the price. Three months of grace are allowed before such a bill becomes due, but then the buyer must at once pay the sum due or make some arrangement satisfactory to the seller. When natives, whose assets are always limited, have purchased a number of articles, the scribe frequently takes upon himself the responsibility of ordering them not to bid again.

CHAPTER VII.

BANDA.

Two months had now passed since I arrived at Amboina, and I had not only collected all the shells figured in Rumphius's "Rariteit Kamer," which I had come to seek, but more than twice as many species besides. I was therefore ready to visit some other locality, and turn my attention to a different branch of natural history. During all the time I had been gathering and arranging my collection, Governor Arriens had frequently honored me with a visit, and, as I was finishing my work, he called again, this time to give me a pleasant surprise. He had a fine steam-yacht, of three or four hundred tons. It was necessary that he should go to Banda, and he took it for granted that I would accompany him. If I had planned for myself, what could I have desired more; but he added that, when his yacht, the Telegraph, returned, there would be an item of business for her to do on the north coast of Ceram, which I should also visit, though alone, and that, when she returned to Amboina a second time, we would go together to Ternate, and, taking the Resident stationed there, proceed to the north coast of Papua—a royal programme.

Sept. 7th.—At 5 P. M. steamed down the beautiful bay of Amboina for Banda. Our company is composed of the governor, who is going on a tour of inspection, our captain, myself, an "officer of justice," and a lieutenant with a detachment of soldiers in charge of a native of Java, who is sentenced to be hanged as soon as we reach our port. The worst of the rainy season is now over, and this evening is cool, clear, and delightful.

Early the next morning Banda appeared on the horizon, or more correctly the Bandas—for they are ten in number. The largest, Lontar, or Great Banda, is a crescent-shaped island, about six miles long and a mile and a half wide in the broadest parts. The eastern horn of its crescent turns toward the north and the other points toward the west. In a prolongation of the former lie Pulo Pisang, "Banana Island," and Pulo Kapal, "Ship Island." The first is about two-thirds of a mile long, and half as wide; the last is merely a rock about three hundred feet high, and somewhat resembling the poop of a ship, hence its name. Within the circle of which these islands form an arc, lie three other islands. The highest and most remarkable is the Gunong Api,* or "Burning Mountain," a conical, active volcano, about two thousand three hundred feet high. Between Gunong Api and the northern end of Lontar lies Banda Neira, about two miles long and less than a mile

---

* This Gunong Api must not be confounded with another similar volcano of the same name north of Wetta, and still another near the western end of Sumbawa, at the northern entrance to the Sapi Strait.

broad. Northeast of the latter is a small rock called Pulo Krakka, or "Women's Island."

The centre of the circle of which Lontar is an arc falls in a narrow passage called Sun Strait, which separates Gunong Api from Banda Neira. The diameter of this circle is about six miles. Without it, another concentric circle may be drawn, which will pass through Pulo Ai, "Water Island," on the west, and Rosengain in the southwest; and outside of this a third concentric circle, which will pass through Swangi, "Sorcery or Spirit Island," on the northwest, Pulo Run (Rung), "Chamber Island," on the west, and the reef of Rosengain on the southwest. The total area of the whole group is seventeen and six-tenths geographical square miles.

The first European who reached these beautiful and long-sought islands was D'Abreu, a Portuguese, but he cannot correctly be styled their discoverer, for the Arabs and Chinese, and probably the Hindus, had been trading here for years before his arrival, as De Barros informs us D'Abreu, while on his way, touched at Gresik, in Java, to procure "Javanese and Malay pilots who had made this voyage," and he further adds: "Every year there repair to Lutatam" (Lontar) "Javanese and Malays to load cloves, nutmegs, and mace; for this place is in the latitudes most easily navigated, and where ships are most safe, and as the cloves of the Moluccas are brought to it by vessels of the country, it is not necessary to go to the latter in search of them. In the *five* islands now named" (Lontar, Rosengain, Ai, Run, and Neira), "grow all the nutmegs consumed in every part of the world." A proof of the correctness of a part of De Barros's statements is seen in the names of the different islands, which are all of Malay or Javanese origin. The population at that time was given at fifteen thousand, which, if correct, would have made this group far more densely peopled than any island or number of islands in the whole archipelago is at the present day. Their personal appearance and form of government are thus minutely described by De Barros: "The people of these islands are robust, with a tawny complexion and lank hair, and are of the worst repute in'these parts. They follow the sect of Mohammed, and are much addicted to trade, their women performing the labors of the field. They have neither king nor lord, and all their government depends on the advice of their elders; and as these are often at variance, they quarrel among themselves. The land has no other export than the nutmeg. This tree is in such abundance that the land is full of it, without its being planted by any one, for the earth yields without culture. The forests which produce it belong to no one by inheritance, but to the people in common. When June and September come, which are the months for gathering the crop, the nutmegs are allotted, and he who gathers most has most profit." * The fact that the natives were Mohammedans may be regarded as a proof that they were in advance of the other nations, who continued in heathenism, and their daring and determination are well shown in their long contest with the Dutch.

For nearly a hundred years the Portuguese monop-

* De Barros, in Crawfurd's "Dictionary of the India Islands."

olized the trade of these islands, and appear to have generally kept on good terms with the natives, but in 1609 the Dutch appeared with seven hundred troops, as large a force—Mr. Crawfurd pointedly remarks—as Cortez had with which to subjugate all Mexico. The admiral commanding this expedition, and forty-five of his companions, were taken by an ambuscade, and all slain. The Dutch then began a war of extermination, which lasted eighteen years, and was only brought to an end by a large expedition from Java, conducted by the governor-general in person. During this long contest the natives are said to have lost three thousand killed and a thousand prisoners, or more than a fourth part of what has been stated as their whole number when the Dutch arrived. All who were left alive fled to the neighboring islands, and not a vestige of their language or peculiar customs is known to exist at the present time.

The Dutch were thus left sole possessors of the coveted prize, but there were no natives to cultivate the nutmeg-trees, and they were therefore obliged to import slaves to do their labor. When slavery was abolished in the Dutch possessions, convicts were sent from Java to make up the deficiency, and at this time there are about three thousand of them in all these islands. Most of them are in Lontar and Neira. They are a most villanous-looking set, and have nearly all been guilty of the bloodiest crimes. They are obliged to wear around the neck a large iron ring, weighing a pound or a pound and a half. It is bent round, and then welded, so that it can only be taken off by means of a file. It is not so heavy that it is difficult for them to carry, but is designed, like the State-prison dress in our country, to show that they are common felons. The one on board our ship, who will be executed on our arrival, killed a secretary of the government—a European—in cold blood, at Banda, where he had already been banished for murder, like most of his fellows. The secretary, having occasion to arrange some papers in a box at the farther end of his room, noticed this common coolie disturbing some letters on his desk, and naturally ordered him to let them alone, and then leaned forward to continue his work. Instantly the Javanese, without further provocation, sprang forward, and, striking him on the back of the head with a heavy cleaver, killed him on the spot. Afterward, when this villain was seized and tried, he could assign no other reason for his committing the murder than the order from his superior to attend to his own business. When he heard that he was sentenced to death, he coolly remarked that he cared very little, as they would hang him, and not take off his head, so that what he had done would in no way affect his entering Paradise!

In 1852 some natives came from Timur, Timurlaut, and the neighboring islands, to work on the nutmeg-plantations, or, as the Dutch prefer to call them, "parks." In two years these people numbered two hundred and thirteen, but they have not increased since to such a degree as to form a large fraction of the whole population.

But while we have been glancing back over the eventful history of the Bandas, our fast yacht has rapidly brought us nearer to them over the quiet, glassy sea. This is Pulo Ai on our right. It is only from three hundred to five hundred feet high, and, as we see from the low cliffs on its shores, is mostly composed of coral rock. This is also said to be the case with the other islands outside of the first circle we have already described, and we notice that, like it, they are all comparatively low. Now changing our course to the east, we steam up under the high, steep Gunong Api. On its north-northwest side, about one-fourth of the distance from its summit down to the sea, is a deep, wide gulf, out of which rise thick, opaque clouds of white gas, that now, in the still, clear air, are seen rolling grandly upward in one gigantic, expanding column to the sky. On its top also thin, veil-like clouds occasionally gather, and then slowly float away like cumuli dissolving in the pure ether. These cloud-masses are chiefly composed of steam and sulphurous acid gas, and, as they pour out, indicate what an active laboratory Nature has established deep within the bowels of this old volcano.

The western horn of crescent-shaped Lontar is before us. Its shore is composed of a series of nearly perpendicular crags from two to three hundred feet high, but particularly on the northern or inner side the luxuriant vegetation of these tropical islands does not allow the rocks to remain naked, and from their crevices and upper edges hang down broad sheets of a bright-green, unfading verdure. The western entrance to the road, the one through which we are now passing, is between the abrupt,

magnificent coast of Lontar on the right, and the
high, overhanging peak of Gunong Api on the left;
and, as we advance, they separate, and disclose to our
view the steep and lofty wall that forms Lontar's
northern shore. This is covered with a dense, matted
mass of vegetation, out of which rise the erect, col-
umnar trunks of palms, from the crests of which, as
from sheaves, long, feathery leaves hang over, slowly
and gracefully oscillating in the light air, which we can
just perceive fanning our faces. Now Banda Neira is
in full view. It is composed of hills which gradually
descend to the shore of this little bay. On the top
of one near us is Fort Belgica, in form a regular
pentagon. At the corners are bastions surmounted
by small circular towers, so that the whole exactly
resembles an old feudal castle. Its walls are white,
and almost dazzling in the bright sunlight; and
beneath is a broad, neatly-clipped glacis, forming
a beautiful, green, descending lawn. Below this
defence is Fort Nassau, which was built by the
Dutch when they first arrived in 1609, only two
years before the foundations of Belgica were laid,
and both fortifications have existed nearly as they
are now for more than two and a half centuries. On
either hand along the shore extends the chief village,
Neira, with rows of pretty shade-trees on the bund,
or front street, bordering the bay. Its population is
about two thousand. In the road are a number of
praus from Ceram, strange-looking vessels, high at
stern, and low at the bow, and having, instead of a
single mast, a tall tripod, which can be raised and
lowered at pleasure. They are all poorly built, and

THE LONTAR PALM.

it seems a wonder that such awkward boats can live any time in a rough sea. A number of Bugis traders are also at anchor near by. They are mostly hermaphrodite schooners, carrying a square-sail or foresail, a fore-topsail, and fore-royal, and evidently designed, like the praus, to sail only before the wind. They visit the eastern end of Ceram, the southwestern and western parts of Papua or New Guinea, the Arus, and most of the thousand islands between Banda, Timur, and Australia. When the mail-steamer that took me to Amboina touched here, a merchant of this place, who joined us, brought on board four large living specimens of the *Paradisea apoda* or "Great Bird of Paradise," which he had purchased a short time before from one of these traders, and was taking with him to Europe.* They were all sprightly, and their colors had a bright, lively hue, incomparably richer than the most magnificent specimens I have ever seen in any museum.

At our main truck a small flag slowly unfolds and displays a red ball. This indicates that the governor is on board, and immediately a boat comes to take us to the village; but as business is not pressing—as is usually the case in the East—we prefer to conform to the established custom in these hot lands, and enjoy a *siesta*, instead of obliging our good friends on shore to come out in full dress and parade in the scorching sunshine.

At 5 P. M. we landed, and the Resident politely conducted us to his residence. Our first excursion

* Subsequently I learned that two of them were still living when he reached France.

was to the western end of the opposite island, Lontar, the Malay name of the Palmyra palm, *Borassus flabelliformis*. Its leaves were used as parchment over all the archipelago before the introduction of paper by the Arabs or Chinese, and in some places even at the present time. Lontar, as already noticed, has the form of a crescent. Its inner side is a steep wall, bordered at the base with a narrow band of low land. On the outer side from the crest of the wall many radiating ridges descend to the sea, so that its southwestern shore is a continued series of little points separated by small bays. The whole island is covered with one continuous forest of nutmeg and *canari* trees. The nutmeg-tree, *Myristica moschata*, belongs to the order *Myristicaceæ*. A foot above the ground the trunk is from six to ten inches in diameter. It branches like the laurel, and its loftiest sprays are frequently fifty feet high. It is diœcious, that is, the pistils and the stamens are borne on different trees, and of course some of them are unproductive. The fruit, before it is fully ripe, closely resembles a peach that has not yet been tinged with red; but this is only a fleshy outer rind, *epicarp*, which soon opens into two equal parts, and within is seen a spherical, black, polished nut, surrounded by a fine branching *aril*—the "mace"—of a bright vermilion. In this condition it is probably by far the most beautiful fruit in the whole vegetable kingdom. It is now picked by means of a small basket fastened to the end of a long bamboo. The outer part being removed, the mace is carefully taken off and dried on large, shallow bamboo baskets in the sun. During this process its bright color changes to a dull yellow. It is now ready to be packed in nice casks and shipped to market. The black, shining part, seen between the ramifications of the vermilion mace, is really a shell, and the nutmeg is within. As soon as the mace is removed, the nuts are taken to a room and spread on shallow trays of open basket-work. A slow fire is then made beneath, and here they remain for three months. By the end of that time the nutmeg has shrunk so much that it rattles in its black shell. The shell is then broken, and the nutmegs are sorted and packed in large casks of teak-wood, and a brand is placed on the head of the cask, giving the year the fruit was gathered and the name of the plantation or "park" where it grew.

From Neira a large cutter took us swiftly over the bay to Selam, a small village containing the ruins of the old capital of the Portuguese during the sixteenth and early part of the seventeenth centuries, while their rights remained undisputed by the Dutch. This western end of Lontar is about four hundred feet high, and is composed of coral rock of a very recent date. Walking eastward, we next came to a conglomerate containing angular fragments of lava. This rock was succeeded on the shore of the bay by a fine-grained, compact lava, somewhat stratified, and this again by trachytic and basaltic lavas. Indeed, the whole island, except the parts described above, consists of these eruptive rocks, and Lontar may be regarded as merely a part of the walls of an immense crater about *six miles* in diameter, if it were circular, though its form may have been more nearly elliptical. Pulo Pisang and Pulo Kapal, already noticed as falling in the first circle, are two other fragments of the old crater wall. All the remaining parts have disappeared beneath the sea. Here, then, is another immense crater, greater even than the famous one in the Tenger Mountains in the eastern part of Java, the bottom of which is covered with shifting, naked sand, and has been appropriately named by the Malays the Laut Pasar or "Sandy Sea." That crater is elliptical in outline, its major axis measuring *four and a half miles*, and its minor axis *three and a half miles*, and, though of such dimensions, its bottom is nearly a level floor of sand. Out of this rise four truncated cones, each containing a small crater. One of these, the "Bromo" (so named from Brama, the Hindu god, whose emblem is fire), is still active. In this old crater the island Banda Neira represents the extinct cones rising in the "Sandy Sea," and Gunong Api has a perfect analogue in the active Bromo. The enclosed bay or road, where vessels now anchor in eight or nine fathoms, is the bottom of this old crater, and, like that in the Tenger Mountains, is composed of volcanic sand. The radiating ridges on the outer side of Lontar represent the similar ridges on the sides of every volcano that is not building up its cone by frequent eruptions at its summit. Again, the islands crossed by the second and third circles are only so many cones on the flanks of this great volcano. True, those parts of them now above the sea are largely composed of coral rock like the west end of Lontar, but undoubtedly the polyps began to build their high walls on the shores of islands of lava. They are doing this at the present moment. Every island in the group is now belted with a fringing reef, except at a few places where the shore is a perpendicular precipice and the water of great depth. The western entrance, through which we came to the road, is already quite closed up by a broad reef of living coral.

A stroll through these beautiful groves would be one of the richest treats a traveller could enjoy, even if he took no interest in the rocks beneath his feet. All the nutmeg-trees were loaded down with fruit, which is chiefly gathered during this month (September), and again in June, though some is obtained from time to time throughout the year. It seemed surprising that the trees could bear so abundantly season after season, but the official reports show that there has been little variation in the annual yield for the last thirty years. An average crop for the last twenty years has been about 580,000 Amsterdam pounds of nuts and 137,000 pounds of mace. The trees may be estimated, in round numbers, at 450,000, of which only two-thirds bear. As the governor remarked to me, while I was expressing my wonder at the abundance of fruit on every side, it is, indeed, strange that the income of the government does not equal its expense. For this cause it now, for the first time, proposes to give up its long-continued monopoly. Beneath the trees is spread a carpet of green grass, while high above them the gigantic *canari* trees stretch out their gnarled arms and shield the valuable trees intrusted to their care from the strong winds which strive in vain to make them cast off their fruit before it is ripe. Such good service do the tall *canaris* render in this way, that they are planted everywhere, and when the island is seen from a distance, their tops quite hide the nutmeg-trees from view. The roots of this *canari* are most remarkable. They spring off from the trunk above the ground in great vertical sheets, which are frequently four feet broad where they leave the tree, and wind back and forth for some distance before they disappear beneath the soil, so that the lower part of one of these old trees might well be fancied to be a huge bundle of enormous snakes struggling to free themselves from a Titanic hand that held them firmly forever.

As we leisurely strolled along the crest of Lontar, with a thick foliage over our heads that effectually shut out the direct rays of the sun, we occasionally caught distant views under the trees of the blue sea breaking into white, sparkling surf on the black rocks far, far beneath us.

Soon we came to the "Lookout," known here, however, by the Malay name *Orang Datang*, "The people come," for it is a peculiarity of that language, instead of naming a place like this *subjectively*, as we do, that is from one's own action, to name it *objectively*, that is, from the result of that action. The lookout is placed on the edge of the interior wall, and is about six hundred feet above the sea. From this point most of the Bandas are distinctly seen in a single glance, and the view is undoubtedly one of the most charming to be enjoyed among all the isles of the sea. Before us was Banda Neira, with Neira its pretty village, and to the left of this the dark, smoking volcano; and beyond both, on the right, Banana Island, where the lepers live in solitary banishment; and still farther seaward, Ship Rock, with the swell chafing its abrupt sides, while, on our left, in the distance, were Pulo Ai and Pulo Run, all rising out of the blue sea, which was only ruffled here and there by light breezes or flecked by shadows of the fleecy clouds that slowly crossed the sky.

The next day we again went over to Lontar, and followed along the narrow band of low land between the base of the old crater-wall and the bay, visiting a number of the residences of the "Perkenniers," as the proprietors of the parks are styled. Each of these consisted of a rectangular area of a eighth or a quarter of an acre, enclosed by a high wall. The side next the sea is formed by the park-keeper's house, and on the other three sides of the great open yard are rows of store-houses, and the houses of the natives who work on that plantation. Near the place where we landed was a small area where all the mace is *white* when the fruit is ripe and not *red*. From the west end of the island we followed most of the distance round its outer shore, and then crossed to our landing. In the early morning, while we were leaving on our excursion, preparations were made in Fort Nassau for the execution of the Javanese we had brought the day before from Amboina, whither he had been taken to be tried for his capital crime. Long lines of natives, most of them women, were seen hurrying along to witness the shocking sight, apparently with exactly the same feelings they would have if they were on their way to some theatrical show.

As the governor had now finished his duties as inspector, he proposed that we try to reach the top of the volcano! As we looked up toward its high, dark summit, then but partially lighted by the fading sunset, the thought of such a dangerous undertaking was enough to make one shudder, and, indeed, even while we were sitting on the broad veranda, and discussing the dangers we must incur on the morrow, there was a sudden jar—everybody darted instantly down the steps—it was an *earthquake*, and no one knew that a shock might not come the next instant so severe as to lay the whole house in ruins. These frightful phenomena occur here, on an average, once a month, but, of course, no one can tell what moment they may occur or what destruction they may cause. Such is the unceasing solicitude that all the inhabitants of these beautiful islands have to suffer. The governor had ascended fifteen volcanoes on Java, some of them with the famous Dr. Junghuhn, and such a slight earthquake could not shake his decision. But our party had to be made up anew. I promised the governor he should not go alone, though I could not anticipate the ascent without some solicitude. The captain of our yacht then volunteered, also a lieutenant, and finally, as no other shock disturbed us, the excursion became as popular as before, and a number asked permission "to go with His Excellency," a favor the governor was quite ready to grant, though I noticed a good-natured smile on his countenance to see such devotion and such bravery.

There was only one man, a native, who had ever been to the top and "knew the way," though from a distance one part of the mountain seemed as dangerous as another. That man was engaged as our "guide," and also some ten others whose duty it was to carry a good supply of water in long bamboos. Early next morning the coolies were ready, but only the four of us before mentioned appeared at the appointed hour; the daring of the others had evidently been dispelled by portentous dreams. From the western end of the village we crossed "the Strait of the Sun" to the foot of the mountain. Some coolies had preceded us, and cleared away a path up the steep acclivity; but soon our only road was the narrow bands where large masses of rocks and sand, which had been loosened from some place high up the mountain, and shot down in a series of small landslides, ploughing up the low shrubbery in their thundering descent. As long as we climbed up among the small trees, although it was difficult and tiring, it was not particularly dangerous until we came out on the naked sides of the mountain, for this great elevation is not covered with vegetation more than two-thirds of the distance from its base to its summit. This lack of vegetation is caused by the frequent and wide landslides and by the great quantity of sulphur brought up to its top by sublimation and washed down its sides by the heavy rains. Here we were obliged to crawl up on all fours among small, rough blocks of porous lava, and all spread out until our party formed a horizontal line on the mountain-side, so that when one loosened several rocks, as constantly happened, they might not come down upon some one beneath him. Our ascent now was extremely slow and difficult, but we kept on, though sometimes the top of the mountain seemed as far off as the stars, until we were within about five hundred feet of the summit, when we came to a horizontal band of loose, angular fragments of lava from two to six inches in diameter. The mountain-side in that place rose at least at an angle of thirty-five degrees, but to us, in either looking up or down, it seemed almost perpendicular. The band of stones was about two hundred feet wide, and so loose that, when one was touched, frequently half a dozen would go rattling down the mountain. I had got about half-way across this dangerous place, when the stones on which my feet were placed gave way. This, of course, threw my whole weight on my hands, and at once the rocks, which I was holding with the clinched grasp of death, also gave way, and I began to slide downward. The natives on either side of me cried out, but no one dared to catch me for fear that I should carry him down also. Among the loose rocks, a few ferns grew up and spread out their leaves to the sunlight. As I felt myself going down, I chanced to roll to my right side and notice one of them, and, quick as a flash of light, the thought crossed my mind that my only hope was to seize *that fern*. This I did with my right hand, burying my elbow among the loose stones with the same motion, and that, thanks to a kind Providence, was sufficient to stop me; if it had broken, in less than a minute—probably in thirty or forty seconds—I should have been dashed to pieces on the rough rocks beneath. The whole certainly occurred in a less space of time than it takes to read two lines on this page. I found myself safe—drew a long breath of relief—thanked God it was well with me—and, kicking away the loose stones with my heels, turned round and kept on climbing. Above this band of loose stones the surface of the mountain was covered with a crust formed chiefly of the sulphur washed down by the rains, which have also formed many small grooves. Here we made better progress, though it seemed the next thing to climbing the side of a brick house; and I thought I should certainly be eligible to the "Alpine Club"—if I ever got down alive. At this moment the natives above us gave a loud shout, and I supposed of course that some one had lost his footing and was going down to certain death. "*Look out! Look out!—Great rocks are coming!*" was the order they gave us; and the next instant several small blocks, and one great flake of lava two feet in diameter, bounded by us with the speed of lightning. "*Here is another!*" It is coming straight for us, and it will take out one of our number to a certainty, I thought. I had stood up in the front of battle when shot and shell were flying, and men were falling; but now to see the danger coming, and to feel that I was perfectly helpless, I must confess, made me shudder, and I crouched down in the groove where I was, hoping it might bound over me: and at that instant, a fragment of lava, a foot square, leaped up from the mountain and passed directly over the head of a coolie a few feet to my right, clearing him by not more than

five or six inches. I took it for granted that the
mountain was undergoing another eruption, and that
in a moment we should all be shaken down its almost
vertical sides; but as the rocks ceased coming down
we continued our ascent, and soon stood on the
rim of the crater. The mystery concerning the falling rocks was now solved. One of our number had
reached the summit before the rest of us, and, with
the aid of a native, had been tumbling off rocks for
the sport of seeing them bound down the mountain,
having stupidly forgotten that we all had to wind
part way round the peak before we could get up on
the edge of the summit, and that those of the party
who were not on the top must be directly beneath
him.

The whole mountain is a great cone of small angular blocks of trachytic lava and volcanic sand, and
the crater at its summit is only a conical cavity in
the mass. It is about eighty feet deep and one hundred or one hundred and fifty yards in diameter.
The area on the top is elliptical in form, about three
hundred yards long and two hundred wide. This,
on the eastern side, is composed of heaps of small
lava-blocks, which are whitened on the exterior,
and, in many places, quite incrusted with sulphur.
Through the heaps of stones steam and sulphurous
acid gas are continually rising, and we soon hurried
around to the windward side to escape their suffo-
cating fumes, and in a number of places we were
glad to run, to prevent our shoes from being scorched
by the hot rocks. On the western side of the crater
the rim is largely composed of sand, and in one place

rises one hundred and twenty feet higher than on the eastern side. The top, therefore, partly opens toward the east, and from some of the higher parts of Lontar most of the area on the summit of this truncated cone can be seen. In the western part were many fissures, out of which rose sheets and jets of gas. When we had reached the highest point on the northwest side, we leaned over and looked directly down into the great active crater, a quarter of the distance from the summit to the sea. Dense volumes of steam and other gases were rolling up, and only now and then could we distinguish the edges of the deep, yawning abyss. Here we rested and lunched, enjoying meanwhile a magnificent view over the whole of the Banda group when the strangling gas was not blown into our faces. Again we continued around the northern side, and came down into an old crater, where was a large rock with "Ætna," the name of a Dutch man-of-war, carved on one of its sides, and our captain busied himself for some time cutting "Telegraph," the name of our yacht, beneath it. Great quantities of sulphur were seen here, more, the governor said, than he had noticed on any mountain in Java, for the abundance of sulphur they all yield is one of the characteristics of the volcanoes of this archipelago. It was now time to descend, and we called our guide, to whom some one had given the classical prænomen of Apollo (a more appropriate title at least than Mercury, for he never moved with winged feet); but he could not tell where we ought to go, every thing appeared so very different when we looked downward. I chose a place where the vegetation was nearest the top, and asked him if I could go down there, to which, of course, he answered yes, as most people do when they do not know what to say, and must give some reply.

I had brought up with me an alpen-stock, or long stick, slightly curved at one end, and with this I reached down and broke places for my heels in the crust that covered the sand and loose stones. For hundreds of feet beneath me the descent seemed perpendicular, but I slowly worked my way downward for more than ninety feet, and had begun to congratulate myself on the good progress I was making. Soon, I thought, I shall be down there, where I can lay hold of that bush and feel that the worst is past, when I was suddenly startled by a shout from my companions, who were at some distance on my right. "Stop! Don't go a step farther, but climb directly up just as you went down." I now looked round for the first time, and found, to my astonishment, that I was on a tongue of land between two deep, long holes or fissures, where great land-slides had recently occurred. I had kept my attention so fixed on the bush before me that I had never looked to the right or left—generally a good rule in such trying situations. To go on was to increase my peril, so I turned, climbed up again, and passed round the head of one of these frightful holes. If at any time the crust had been weak, and had broken beneath my heels, no earthly power could have saved me from instant death. As I broke place after place for my feet with the staff, I thought of Professor Tyndal's dangerous ascent and descent of Monte Rosa. At last I joined

ASCENT OF BURNING MOUNTAIN; BANDA.

my companions, who had found the way we had come up, and after some slips and sprains, and considerable bruising, we all reached the bottom safely, and were glad to be off the volcano, and, landing on Banda Neira, feel ourselves on *terra firma* once more.

For a few days I could scarcely walk or move my arms, but this lameness soon passed away; not so with the impressions made on my mind by those dangers: and even now, when I am suddenly aroused from sleep, for a moment the past becomes the present, and I am once more on the tongue of land, with a frightful gulf on either hand, or I am saving myself by grasping *that* fern.

According to the statements of the officials, many years ago a gentleman had the hardihood to attempt to ascend this mountain alone. As he did not return at the expected time, a party of natives was sent to search for him, and his dead body was found some distance beneath the summit. The rocks to which he had intrusted himself had probably given way, and the only sensation that could have followed was one of falling and a quick succession of stunning blows, and life was gone. Governor Arriens assured me that the band of loose stones was the most dangerous place he had ever crossed, though he had climbed many nearly perpendicular walls, but always where the rocks were fixed and could be relied on for a footing and a hold. If the ascent and descent were not so difficult, sulphur might be gathered in such quantities at the summit crater that it would form an important article of export. The authorities informed me that much was obtained in former times.

and that the natives who undertook this perilous climbing were always careful to array themselves in *white* before setting out, so that if they did lose their lives in the attempt they would be dressed in the robes required by their creed, and at once be taken to Paradise. The first European who reached its summit, so far as I am aware, was Professor Reinwardt, in 1821; the second was Dr. S. Müller, in 1828; and from that time till the 13th of September, 1865, when we ascended it, only one party had attempted this difficult undertaking, and that was from the steamer Ætna, whose name we had found on a large rock in the old crater.

The height of this volcano we found to be only two thousand three hundred and twenty-one English feet. Its spreading base is considerably less than two miles square. In size, therefore, it is insignificant compared to the gigantic mountains on Lombok, Java, and Sumatra; but when we consider the great amount of suffering and the immense destruction of property that has been caused by its repeated eruptions, it becomes one of the most important volcanoes in the archipelago.* In 1615 an eruption occurred in March, just as the Governor-General, Gerard Reynst, arrived from Java with a large fleet to complete the war of extermination that the Dutch had been waging with the aborigines for nearly twenty years.

For some time previous to 1820, many people

* From Valentyn and later writers we learn that eruptions have occurred in the following years: 1586, 1598, 1609, 1615, 1632, 1690, 1696, 1712, 1765, 1775, 1778, 1820, and 1824.

lived on the lower flanks of Gunong Api, and had succeeded in forming large groves of nutmeg-trees. On the 11th of June of that year, just before twelve o'clock, in an instant, without the slightest warning, an eruption began which was so violent that all the people at once fled to the shore and crossed over in boats to Banda Neira. Out of the summit rose perpendicularly great masses of ashes, sand, and stones, heated until they gave out light like living coals. The latter hailed down on every side, and, as the accounts say, "set fire to the woods and soon changed the whole mountain into one immense cone of flame." This happened, unfortunately, during the western monsoon; and so great a quantity of sand and ashes was brought over to Banda Neira, that the branches of the nutmeg-trees were loaded down until they broke beneath its weight, and all the parks on the island were totally destroyed. Even the water became undrinkable, from the light ashes that filled the air and settled down in every crevice. The eruption continued incessantly for thirteen days, and did not wholly cease at the end of six weeks. During this convulsion the mountain was apparently split through in a north-northwest and south-southeast direction. The large, active crater which we saw beneath us on the northwestern flanks of the mountain, from the spot where we stopped to lunch, was formed at that time, and another was reported higher up between that new crater and the older one on the top of the mountain. A stream of lava poured down the western side into a small bay, and built up a tongue of land one hundred and eighty feet long. The fluid rock heated the sea within a radius of more than half a mile, and nearer the shore eggs were cooked in it. This stream of lava is the more remarkable, because it is a characteristic of the volcanoes throughout the archipelago, that, instead of pouring out molten rock, they only eject hot stones, sand, and ashes, and such materials as are thrown up where the eruptive force has already reached its maximum and is growing weaker and weaker.

On the 22d of April, 1824, while Governor-General Van der Capellen was entering the road, an eruption commenced, just as had happened two hundred and nine years before, on the arrival of Governor-General Reynst. A great quantity of ashes again suddenly rose from its summit, accompanied by clouds of "black smoke," in which lightnings darted, while a heavy thundering rolled forth that completely drowned the salute from the forts on Neira. This was followed, on the 9th of June, by a second eruption, which was succeeded by a rest of fourteen days, when the volcano again seemed to have regained its strength, and once more ashes and glowing stones were hurled into the air and fell in showers on its sides.

But the people of Banda have suffered quite as much from earthquakes as from eruptions, though the latter are usually attended by slight shocks.*
Almost the first objects that attract one's attention on landing at the village are the ruins caused by

---

* Heavy earthquakes, without eruptions, have occurred in 1629, 1683, 1710, 1767, 1816, and 1852.

the last of these destructive phenomena. Many houses were levelled to the ground, but others that were built with special care suffered little injury. Their walls are made of coral rock or bricks. They are two or three feet thick and covered with layers of plaster. At short distances, along their outer side, sloping buttresses are placed against them, so that many of the Banda residences look almost as much like fortifications as dwelling-houses. The first warning any one had of the destruction that was coming was a sudden streaming out of the water from the enclosed bay, until the war-brig Haai, which was lying at anchor in eight or nine fathoms, touched the bottom. Then came in a great wave from the ocean which rose at least to a height of twenty-five or thirty feet over the low, western part of the village, which is only separated from Gunong Api by the narrow Sun Strait. The praus lying near this shore were swept up against Fort Nassau, which was then so completely engulfed, as it was stated to me on the spot, that one of these native boats remained inside the fort when the water had receded to its usual level. The part of the village over which the flood swept contained many small houses, and nearly every one in them was carried away. The rapid outflowing of the water of this enclosed bay (which is really only an old crater) was probably caused either by the elevation of the bottom at that spot, or else by such a sinking of the floor of the sea outside, that the water was drained off into some depression which had suddenly been formed. We have no reason to suppose that there was any great commotion in the open ocean, and certainly there was no high wave or bore, or it would have risen on the shores of the neighboring islands. There are three entrances or straits which lead from the road out to the open sea. Two of these are wide and one is narrow. When the whole top of the old volcano, that is, Banda Neira, Gunong Api, Lontar, and the area they enclose, was raised for a moment, the water steamed out from the crater through these straits, causing only strong currents, but as the land instantly sank to its former level, the water poured in, and the streams of the two wider straits, meeting and uniting, rolled on toward the inner end of the narrow strait. Here they all met, and, piling up, spread out over the adjoining low village, causing a great destruction of life. At the Resident's house, a few hundred yards east of Fort Nassau, the water only rose some ten or fifteen feet above high-water level, and farther east still less. The cause assigned above, though the principal one, may therefore not have been sufficient in itself to have made the sea rise so high over the southwestern part of Banda Neira and the opposite part of Gunong Api, and I suspect that an additional cause was that the land there sank for a moment below its proper level. Valentyn thus describes another less destructive earthquake wave: "In the year 1629 there was a great earthquake, and half an hour afterward a flood which was very great, and came in calm weather. The sea between Neira and Selam" (on the western part of Lontar) "rose up like a high mountain and struck on the right side of Fort Nassau, where the water rose nine feet higher than in common spring floods. Several houses near the sea were broken into pieces and washed away, and the ship Briel, lying near by, was whirled round three times."*

However, all these events are but as yesterday when we glance over the early history of this ancient volcano; for, if we can judge by analogy, taking as our guide the great crater already referred to as this day existing among the lofty Tenger Mountains on Java, we see in our mind's eye an immense volcanic mountain before us. From its high crater during the lapse of time pour out successive overflows of lava which has solidified into the trachyte of Lontar. That period is succeeded by one in which ashes, sand, and hot stones are ejected, and which insensibly passes into recent times. During one of these mighty throes the western half of the crater-wall disappeared beneath the sea, if the process of subsidence had gone on so far at that time. Slowly it sinks until it is at least four feet lower than at the present day, for we found on the western end of Lontar a large bank of coral rock at that height. The outer islands are now wholly submerged. This period of subsidence is followed by one of upheaval, but not till the slow-building coral polyps had made great reefs, which have become white, chalky cliffs, and attained their present elevation above the sea. A tropical vegetation by degrees

---

* In this case the facts that the water in the roads did not pour out into the sea, and that the "flood" did not come until half an hour after the shock had occurred, indicate that this wave had its origin elsewhere, and that there is no need of supposing, as in accounting for the great wave of 1852, that any part of the group was raised or depressed.

spreads downward, closely pursuing the retreating sea, and the islands become exactly what they are at the present day.

The Banda group form but a point in the wide area of the residency of Banda. All the eastern part of Ceram is included in it, the southwest coast of New Guinea, and the many islands south and southwest to the northern part of Timur. Southeast of Ceram are the Ceram-laut, that is, "Ceram lying to seaward," or Keffing group, numbering seventeen islands. Their inhabitants are like those I saw on the south coast of Ceram, and do not belong to the Papuan or negro race. They are great traders, and constantly visit the adjoining coast of New Guinea, where they purchase birds of paradise, many *luris* or parrots of various genera, "crown pigeons," *Megapodiideæ*, scented woods, and very considerable quantities of wild nutmegs, which they sell to the Bugis traders, who usually touch here at Banda on their outward and homeward passages. I saw many of the wild nutmegs that had been brought in this way from New Guinea. Instead of being spherical, like those cultivated here at Banda, they are elliptical in outline, frequently an inch or an inch and a quarter long, and about three-fourths of an inch in diameter. They do not, however, have the rich, pungent aroma of the Banda nutmegs, and this, I am assured, is also the case with all wild ones wherever found, and even with those raised on Sumatra and Pinang from seeds and plants originally carried from these islands. Wild nutmegs are also found on Damma southwest of Banda, and on Amboina, Ceram,

Buru, Batchian, the Obi Islands, and Gilolo, also on the islands east of the latter, and on the northern coast of the western part of New Guinea. This fruit is widely planted by the "nut-crackers," two large species of doves, *Columba ænea*, Tem., and *Columba perspicillata*, Tem., which swallow the nuts covered with the mace, the only part digested. The kernel enclosed in its hard, polished shell is soon voided, while it yet retains the germinating power, and a young tree springs up far from its parent.

East of this group is that of Goram, composed of three islands, inhabited by natives who are Mohammedans. Southeast of Goram is the Matabella group. Indeed, these groups are so united that they form but one archipelago. The Ceram-laut Islands are low, but those of Goram and Matabella are high. On the island Teor, or Tewer, in the last group, there is a volcano which suffered a great eruption in 1659. Mr. Wallace describes the Matabellas as partly composed of coral reefs raised from three to four hundred feet. Sometimes these people go as far west as Sumbawa and Bali. The "Southeastern Islands" begin on the north with the Ki group, ten in number, south of the former archipelago. Three of the Kis are large islands and two are high, a peak on one being estimated at about three thousand feet. They are so well peopled that they are supposed to contain over twenty thousand souls. The natives are very industrious, and famous as boat-builders. The wood they use comes from their own hill-sides, and they need no iron to complete boats of considerable size, which they sell to the inhabitants of all that part of the archipelago. Farther to the east are the Aru (in Dutch, Aroe) Islands, that is, "the islands of the casuarina-trees." They number about eighty, and are very low, forming a chain about a hundred miles long and half as broad. When seen on the west they appear as one continuous, low island; but on coming nearer, intricate channels are found winding among them, through which set strong tidal currents. The people are said to closely resemble those of Haruku, Saparua, and Nusalaut. The total population is given at only fourteen thousand. A few are Christians, and two or three native schoolmasters from Amboina are employed there. Papuans are said to live on the most eastern island. Large quantities of tripang are gathered on the shallow coral banks of these low islands, and in the sea the dugong, *Halicore dugong*, Cuv., is seen. The great bird of paradise, *P. apoda*, is found here, and also the red bird of paradise, *P. regia*. The skins of these beautiful birds were probably brought here to Banda and sold to the Chinese traders for many ages, but the first account we have of them is by Pigafetta, who accompanied Magellan's fleet. He says that the king of Bachian, an island west of the southern end of Gilolo, gave his companions a slave and nearly two hundred pounds of cloves as a present for their Emperor, Charles V., and also "two most beautiful dead birds. These are about the size of a thrush, have small heads, long bills, legs a palm in length and as slender as a writing-quill. In lieu of proper wings, they have long feathers of different colors, like great ornamental plumes. The tail resembles that of a thrush. All the feathers except those of the wings are of a dark color. It never flies except when the wind blows. We were informed these birds came from the terrestrial Paradise, and they called them *bolondinata*,* that is, 'birds of God.'" This word the Portuguese translated into their language as "ave de paraiso," and hence our name "birds of paradise," a name well chosen, for in some species the feathers have all the appearance of the most brilliant jewels. Southwest of the Ki Islands lies Timur-laut, and passing on toward Timur we come to the "Southwestern Islands," composed of the Baba, Sermatta, Letti, Roma, Wetta, and Lamma groups, which we noticed as we steamed away from Dilli.

Returning northward from Wetta, we come to Gunong Api, an uninhabited volcano, rising between six and seven thousand feet above the sea. It is a well-known landmark for the ships bound to China that have passed up the Ombay Passage, or those coming down the Floris Sea, intending to pass out through that strait into the Indian Ocean. Northeast of Gunong Api are the Lucipara and Turtle (in Dutch Schilpad) Islands, which praus from Amboina frequently visit for tortoise-shell. East of Gunong Api is Nila, an active volcano, about seventeen hundred feet in height, and north of it is Serua, which is merely a volcanic cone rising abruptly from the sea. In 1694 a great eruption took place in this volcano. A part of the crater wall fell in, and the lava overflowed until the whole island is repre-

* Mr. Crawfurd thinks this is a corruption of *burungdewata*, which in Malay means "birds of God."

sented as having become one "sea of fire," and all the inhabitants were obliged to flee to Banda. Again, in September, 1844, after a rest of a hundred and fifty years, another eruption began, which compelled every one to leave its inhospitable shores once more. Since that time it has been settled again, and here in Banda are many of the boats its people bring in the latter part of this month, when continuously for days not a breeze ripples the glassy sea—halcyon days indeed. As the natives have no iron, the whole boat is built of wood. The central part is low, but the bow and stern curve up high, quite different from all I have seen in any other part of the archipelago, and reminding one of the representations usually given of those used in some parts of the South Sea.

While I had been turning my attention to geology, the native who was assisting me to collect shells was searching for a "hunter," that is, one who can skin birds. He soon had the good fortune to find one, who was also a native of Amboina, for all these natives dislike those of another village, and only associate with them when they can find none of their own people. During the few days we were at the Bandas they collected several species of most beautiful kingfishers; indeed, those who have seen only our sombre-colored specimens can scarcely conceive of the rich plumage these birds assume in the tropical East. They were also so fortunate as to find a few superb specimens of a very rare and valuable bird, with scarcely any tail, and having eight very different colors, the *Pitta vigorsi*. An allied species is found on the Arru Islands, and another on

Buru, a third on Gilolo, and a fourth on Celebes, but none is yet known on the great island of Ceram.

We now steamed back to Amboina, and while the yacht was taking in coal and preparing to go to Ceram, I crossed over Laitimur with the governor. Our procession was headed by a native carrying a large Dutch flag, and after him came a "head man," supported on the right by a man beating a *tifa*, and on the left by another beating a gong. Then came the governor, borne in a large chair by a dozen coolies, and I, in a similar chair, carried by the same number. From the city we at once ascended a series of hills, sparsely covered with shrubbery, and composed of a soft red sandstone, which is rapidly disintegrating, and is evidently of very recent origin. It is found on the highest elevation we crossed, which is from fifteen to eighteen hundred feet above the sea. Near this point we descended into a small ravine, where the soft sandstone had been washed away, and the underlying rocks were exposed to view. Here we found feldspathic porphyry and serpentine. Thence we crossed other hills of sandstone and came down to the sea-shore at the village of Rutong. We were hoping to find a small hill of granite that Dr. Schneider had discovered, but we were not able to identify the places he describes. Dr. Bleeker, who crossed over to Ema in 1856, remarks that the first hills he ascended were composed of coral rock, and that he came on to it again when he descended toward the sea-shore. We did not notice it at this time, but, on my first excursion to the cocoa plantation on Hitu, I found a long coral reef, fully five hundred feet above the sea. It was a perfect repetition of the reef I visited in the bay of the Portuguese village of Dilli, at the northern end of Timur. A small place had been cleared on its crest, and there I found several pairs of the huge valves of the *Tridacna gigas*, which appeared from their relative position to have been once partially surrounded by the soft coral rock, which, having been washed away, allowed the valves to fall apart. They were much decayed, but had not lost more than half their weight. They had evidently never been brought there by men; because the natives rarely or never use them for food. There is no need that they should take the trouble to gather such enormous bivalves when they have a plenty of sago-palms, and all that it is necessary for them to do to obtain an abundance of food is to cut down these trees and dig out the pith. If, in former times, they did collect the *Tridacna* for food, they never would have carried these great shells, each of which originally weighed a hundred pounds or more, a mile back among the hills, but would have taken out the animal and left them on the shore. Governor Arriens, who had carefully studied these recent reefs, stated to me that he had found them as high up as eight hundred feet above the sea, but at that elevation they seem to disappear.

When returning we stopped for some time on the hills back of the city to enjoy a magnificent view of the bay and the high hills rising on the opposite side. Just then the broad strati, floating in the west, parted, and rays of bright sunlight, darting through their fissures, lighted up the dark water beneath us. There were not many vessels and praus at anchor off the city at that time, but I was informed that in about a month later many would arrive, for the dry season, with its clear sky and light winds, had set in about the 15th of September, when we arrived from Banda.

About two hundred vessels and praus of all kinds come to Amboina in a year. The praus are owned and commanded by the natives themselves, but most of the vessels are commanded by mestizoes and owned by Arabs and Chinese, who carry on the larger part of the trade in the eastern part of the archipelago. Since a line of steamers has been established, these Arabs and Chinese avail themselves of that means of importing their goods from Batavia and Surabaya, where they are received directly from Europe. The total value of the imports is from a half to three-quarters of a million of guilders. The chief article is cotton fabrics, and the next rice, which is shipped here all the way from Java and Sumatra for the sustenance of the troops. Very little rice is raised on any of these islands, because there are no low, level lands suitable for its cultivation. In the Bandas the whole attention of the population is so devoted to cultivating the nutmeg that they are entirely dependent on other islands for a supply of food. The most important exports from this island are cloves, cocoa, kayu-puti oil, nutmegs, various kinds of woods, and mace. Formerly the inhabitants of Ceram-laut, Goram, and the Arru Islands were accustomed to bring their tripang, tortoise-shell, paradise birds, and massoi-bark to this port to sell to the

Bugis, but for the last forty or fifty years the Bugis have gone from Macassar directly to those islands and traded with the people at their own villages. In 1854, Amboina, Banda, Ternate, and Kayéli, were made free ports, but this has not materially increased the trade at any of those places.

The period when the trade at Amboina was most flourishing was when it was last held by the English, from 1814 to 1816. The port was then free, but, when it once more passed into the hands of the Dutch, duties were again demanded, which forced the trade into other channels, where it still remains, notwithstanding there are now no duties. The proper remedy has been applied, but applied too late. This is also the history of the trade at Batavia, where the heavy duties have induced the traders of the eastern part of the archipelago to sail directly to the free port of Singapore.

I had been at Amboina a long time before I could ascertain where the grave of Rumphius is located, and even then I found it only by chance—so rarely is this great man spoken of at the present time. From the common, back of the fort, a beautifully-shaded street leads up to the east; and the stranger, while walking in this quiet retreat, has his attention drawn to a small, square pillar in a garden. A thick group of coffee-trees almost embrace it in their drooping branches, as if trying to protect it from wind and rain and the consuming hand of Time. Under that plain monument rest the mortal remains of the great naturalist.

The inscription, which explains itself, and shows

how nearly this sacred spot came to be entirely neglected and forgotten forever, reads as follows:

MEMORIÆ SACRUM GEORGII EVERARDI RUMPHII,
de re botanica et historica naturali optime merita
TUMULUM
dira temporis calamitate et sacrilegia manufere
DIRUTUM,
Manibus placatis restitui jussit
et
pietatem reverentiamque publicam testificans
HOC MONUMENTUM
IPSE CONSECRAVIT
Godarus Alexander Grardus Phillipus
Liber Baro A. Capellen
Totius Indiæ Belgicæque
PREFECTUS REGIUS.
Amboinæ Mensis Aprilis,
Anno Domini M.DCCC.XXIV.

GEORGE EVERARD RUMPF, whose name has been latinized into Rumphius, as an acknowledgment of the great service he has rendered to the scientific world, was a German, a native of a small town in Hesse-Cassel. He was born about the year 1626, and, having studied medicine, at the age of twenty-eight went to Batavia, entered the mercantile service of the Dutch East India Company, and thence proceeded to Amboina, where he passed the remainder of his life. At the age of forty-two, while contemplating a voyage back to his native land, he suddenly became blind, and therefore never left his adopted island home; yet he continued to prosecute his favorite studies in natural history till his death, which occurred in 1693, when he had attained the ripe age of sixty-seven.

His great work on the shells of Amboina, which

was not published till 1705, twelve years after his death, was for a long time the acknowledged standard to which all conchological writers referred. His most extensive work, however, was the "Hortus Amboinense," which was only rescued from the Dutch archives and published at the late date of forty-eight years after his death. It contains the names and careful descriptions of the plants of this region, their flowering seasons, their *habitats*, their uses, and the modes of caring for those that are cultivated. When we consider that, in his time, neither botany nor zoology had become a science, and consider, moreover, the amount and the accuracy of the information he gives us, we agree with his contemporaries in giving him the high but well-merited title of "the Indian Pliny."

CHAPTER VIII.

BURU.

Sept. 25*th.*—Steamed down the bay from Amboina, this time not without a slight feeling of sadness as I recalled the many happy hours I had passed gathering shells on its shores and rambling over its high hills, and as I realized that it would probably never be my privilege to enjoy those pleasures again. Only three months had elapsed since my arrival at Batavia, but I had passed through so many and such different scenes, that Amboina appeared to have been my home for a year—and so it seems to this day.

As we came out of the mouth of the bay, we changed our course to the west, and kept so near the land, that I had a fine opportunity to reëxamine the places I had visited during a heavy storm, when the sea was rolling into white surf and thundering along the shore.

Off the western end of Ceram lie three islands, Bonoa, Kilang, and Manipa. Bonoa, the most easterly, is a hilly island about twelve miles long and half as broad. Its population is divided into Christians and Mohammedans, and each has such a bitter hatred against the other, that the Christians at last determined to expatriate themselves, and accordingly, in 1837, migrated to Bachian. The clove-gardens in Bonoa were thus in danger of being neglected, and the man who was governor of the Moluccas at that time therefore sent messengers to induce them to return; but, when this measure proved unavailing, he went himself in a war-ship, and brought them back.

From Amboina we passed up the strait between Kilang and Manipa, which is less than a mile wide, and made much narrower by long tongue-shaped reefs of coral which project from several points. A fresh breeze had sprung up from the south, and, under a full head of steam and a good press of canvas, we ploughed through the waves which rolled up against the wind. In all these straits the tidal currents are very strong, and in many places so swift that a good boat cannot make headway against them with oars, and this makes many of these narrow channels very dangerous for the native boats.

That evening the bright fires built by the fishermen on the shores of Bonoa were seen on our larboard side, and the next morning we were near the Seven Brothers, a group of islands on the west side of Sawai Bay. Here are three dangerous reefs not laid down on the charts, a mile or more from the shore. As we passed, mountains three or four thousand feet in height were seen standing by the sea near the head of the bay. At noon we came to anchor in the little harbor of Wahai, which is formed by coral reefs that are bare at low tide. Unfortunately, it is too small for sailing-ships to enter safely, or it would be visited occasionally by those of our whalers who frequent these seas. The whole village consists of a small fort, a house for the commandant, who has the rank of captain, a house for the doctor, and a few native huts on either hand. The only communication the inhabitants of this isolated post have with the rest of the world is by means of coolies, who cross over from the head of Elpaputi Bay to the head of Sawai Bay, and then come along the shore. All the natives in the interior are entirely independent of the Dutch Government, and the coast natives, who carry the mail, are liable to be robbed or killed at any moment while on their journey.

My hunter at once began collecting birds, while I searched the shores for shells, and bought what the natives chanced to have in their miserable dwellings. The most common shell here is an *Auricula*. Its peculiar aperture, as its name implies, is like that of the human ear. It lives on the soft, muddy flats, where the many-rooted mangrove thrives. The rarest and most valuable shell found here, and indeed one of the rarest living in all these seas, is the *Rostellaria rectirostris*. It is so seldom found that a pair is frequently sold here for ten guilders, four Mexican dollars. My hunter soon returned with two large white doves, the *Carpophaga luctuosa*, and a very perfect specimen of that famous bird, the *Platycercus hypophonius*, G. R. Gray, called by the Malays the *castori rajah*, or "prince parrot," from its being the most beautiful of all that brilliantly-plumaged family. It is a small bird for a parrot. The head, neck, and under parts are of a bright scarlet; the wings a dark, rich green, and the back and rump a bright lapis-lazuli blue, that shades off into a deeper blue in the tail, which is nearly as long as the body. These birds generally fly in pairs, and as they dart through the evergreen foliage, and you catch a glimpse of their graceful forms and brilliant plumage, it seems like the momentary recollection of some dream of Paradise. Large flocks of red luris, *Eos rubra*, Gml., other species of parrakeets, and many sorts of doves, frequent the surrounding woods, and several species of kingfishers and snipes live by the shore. For three days I enjoyed this rare hunting. We then steamed out of the little bay of Wahai for the island of Buru. While passing Bonoa we kept near the shore, and saw a large white monument which was erected by the Portuguese, and is probably one of the *padroes*, or "pillars of discovery," placed there by D'Abreu when he first reached these long-sought isles. Soon we passed Swangi, "Spirit Island," a lonely rock near Manipa, supposed by these superstitious natives to be haunted by some evil spirit.

Buru, the island to which we were bound, lies a few miles west of Manipa. Its area is estimated at about twenty-six hundred geographical square miles, so that it is one-half larger than Bali or Lombok. Its form is oval, with the greatest axis east and west. Its shores, instead of being deeply indented, like those of all the larger islands in that region, are entire, except on the northwest corner, where they recede and form the great bay of Kayéli. The entrance to this bay is between two high capes, three or four miles apart, so that on the northeast it is quite open to the sea. Within these capes the shores become low, forming on the southwest a large morass; and the bay expands to the east and west until it is about seven miles long. In the low lands bordering the south side of this bay is the Dutch "bezitting," or post, also named Kayéli. Here is a small, well-built fort, in which are stationed a lieutenant and doctor, and a company of militia from Java or Madura. A *controleur* has charge of the civil department, and the governor had kindly given me a note to him, and he and his good lady at once received me kindly, and, as it proved, I made my home with them and the doctor for a long time. The plan the governor proposed was that we should leave for Ternate and New Guinea in five days after the steamer landed me at Kayéli. Those five days passed, but no steamer appeared. Again and again I watched by the hour, hoping, almost expecting, to be able to discern smoke on the horizon, and soon see the Telegraph coming into the harbor. Thus a week passed, then ten days, and by this time all, like myself, had come to the conviction that some unexpected and unfortunate event must have happened. But what was it? No one could tell. Fifteen days of such uncertainty and solicitude passed, when a large prau was seen coming in from the sea. It brought me a letter from Governor Arriens, stating that just as he was on the point of coming to take me, as proposed, news came that a great revolt had broken out in Ceram. Immediately he accompanied the captain of a large man-of-war, whose duty it was to put down all insurrections. When they arrived off the village, the captain, contrary to the advice of all, landed with a small force, hoping to be able to treat with the rebels, but he had scarcely touched the shore when a party of them in ambush poured a volley into his boat, wounding him twice severely, but not fatally. I now found myself really banished, for the yacht was needed too much to come and take me away. I therefore resigned myself quietly to my fate, and determined to profit by the opportunity to make a collection of the beautiful birds of the island. My first excursion was to a cliff on the southeast side of the bay, near its mouth, which I found was composed of metamorphic schists, that were very much fissured by joints and seams, and fell apart in cubical blocks. Another place I frequently visited was the low morass on the southwest side of the bay, through which flows out a stream of such size that a large canoe can ascend it for three days. Along the canals in this morass is a thick forest, the high branches of which meet above, forming for a considerable distance grand covered avenues. Here the kingfishers delight to gather, and, perching on the lower boughs, occasionally dart downward, like falling arrows, into the quiet water. It was most delightful, during the heat of the day, to glide along in these cool and shady canals, which wind to and fro, and in such an endless series of curves and angles, that no one could weary of the rich, almost oppressive, vegetation that continually surrounds him. At the mouth of this small river are long shallow banks of sand, which are bare at low tide, and on these are many large snags and logs that have come down the streams and grounded while on their way to the sea. On these wide banks, as the ebbing ceases and the tide begins to flow, long lines of gulls, sandpipers, plovers, and curlews, gather, and, as the water advances, they are forced to approach the shore until the only resting-places left them are the logs and snags that raise their crooked limbs and roots above the surface of the water. At such times these perching-places are one living, fluttering mass of birds. Again and again I came to this spot, and always returned with as many specimens as my native hunter could skin on the following day.

A few minutes' walk back of the *controleur's* house took me into the surrounding forest, where I was accustomed to ramble to and fro hour after hour until I knew all the favorite haunts of most of the birds; yet nearly every day, till the time I left, I secured specimens of a species that had not been represented in my collection. Still others were seen, and one or more specimens of them must be obtained; and thus, the more I collected, the more interesting became my work. My regular daily routine was to hunt in the morning till ten or eleven o'clock, return to the house to avoid the heat, and then go out again about four, and remain till the setting sun warned me to return or grope my way back as best I could through the dark woods. Soon after I arrived, a tree, as large as our oak, became filled with great scarlet flowers, and in the early morning flocks of red luris (*Eos rubra*, Gml.) and other parrakeets, with blue heads, red and green breasts, and the feathers on the under side of the wings of a light red and brilliant yellow (*Trichoglossus cyanogrammus*, Wagl.), would come to feed on them. It was easy to know where those birds had begun their morning feast by their loud, unceasing screeching and chattering; and, after stealthily creeping through dense shrubbery for hundreds of yards, I would suddenly behold one of these great trees filled with scores of such brilliantly-plumaged birds, flying about or climbing out to the ends of the branches, and using their wings to aid in poising themselves while they made a dainty breakfast on the rich flowers. These are indeed the birds that Moore describes as—

> "Gay, sparkling loories, such as gleam between
> The crimson flowers of the coral-tree
> In the warm isles of India's sunny sea."

Soon after sunset huge bats always came out, in pairs, and sailed about on their leathery wings, searching for those trees that chanced to be in fruit. The wings of a male that I shot measured four feet and four inches from tip to tip, and the wings of the female, which accompanied him, expanded four feet eight inches. They are very properly named by the Dutch, "flying foxes," and almost seem to be antediluvian monsters, which ought to have disappeared from the face of the earth long ago, like the formidable *Pterodactyles*. During the day they hide away in the thick foliage, and one afternoon I found one hanging, as they delight to do when they rest or sleep, with its head downward, from the limb of a tree. They are very tenacious of life, and will receive charge after charge of large shot in the head before they will let go of the limbs with their crooked claws and allow themselves to fall. They are said to be good for food, but I never saw the natives eat them, and certainly had

A JUNGLE.

no desire myself to try the flavor of such questionable meat. A small path, leading a mile through the forest, brought me out on to a large open field or prairie, covered with a coarse grass as high as a man's shoulders. Beyond this was another forest, and there I was informed was a settlement of two or three houses, the farthest place inland inhabited by any of the coast people or common Malays. Beyond that point there is not the slightest footpath. All the hills and high mountains, which I could see toward the interior of the island, are covered with one dense, unbroken forest, and only on some of the lower hills, bordering the bay, are there open areas of grass. What a nice thing it would be to live out there for a week in the midst of that forest! My mind was made up to do it. I returned and explained my plan to the *controleur*, and the next day we set off to hire one of the distant huts. The farthest one from Kayéli, and exactly the one I wanted, chanced to be unoccupied, for the native who owned it had found the place so lonely that he had deserted it and taken up his abode in the village. The rent for a week was agreed to without much parleying. The owner further agreed to send his son to bring water and keep house while I and my hunter were away, and to be generally useful, which he interpreted to mean that he would only do what he could not avoid. Another man was engaged as cook, and my domestic arrangements were complete, for I purposed not only to live in a native house, but to conform entirely to the Malay *cuisine*. Our cooking-apparatus consisted of a couple of shallow kettles and a small frying-pan; and the little teapot that accompanied me on my Amboina excursions was not left behind.

October 16*th*.—This morning we came out to our forest home. Our house is about eight feet wide, twelve feet long, and perched upon large posts four feet from the ground. It is divided by a transverse partition into a front room or parlor, and a back room or kitchen. In one corner of the latter is a square framework filled with ashes, in which are inserted three long stones, whose tops slightly incline toward each other. These are to support the kettles, for no Malay has ever conceived of a machine for cooking so complicated as a crane. As to a chimney, there is none whatever, but the smoke is allowed to escape under the eaves or through a hole in the side of the house that also serves for a window. The frame of the house is made from small trees. For a flooring, broad sheets of bark are used. The walls are made of *gaba-gaba*, the dry midribs of large palm-leaves, and the roof is of *atap*. The front door is in one of the gable ends, and is reached by a rickety ladder of two rounds. This part is transformed into a rude piazza by a shed-roof, beneath which we have made a seat and a kind of table for the hunter to use in skinning birds.

My daily routine here is the same as before—hunting every morning and evening, with a native to carry my ammunition and to pick up the birds—a very difficult task whenever we are in the thick jungle or among the tall grass. Near our house is the stony bed of a torrent, which is now perfectly dry. It is the only cleared way there is through the dense forest around us, and I avail myself of it to travel up toward the mountains and down toward the sea. Indeed, I feel proud of our grand highway. True, it is not paved with blocks all carefully cut down to one precise model, and so exactly uniform as to be absolutely painful to the eye, but Nature herself has paved it in her own inimitable way—notice how all the stones have been rounded by the boiling torrent which pours down here from the mountains during the rainy season. Some are almost perfect ellipsoides or spheres, but most are diskshaped, for they are made from thin fragments of slate that had sharp corners when they broke away from their parent mountain. To prevent a dull uniformity of color, she has scattered here and there rounded boulders of opaque milk-white quartz, fragments, undoubtedly, from beds of that rock which, at this place at least, are interstratified with the slate. Here and there are deeper places, where the troubled stream was accustomed to rest before it went on again in a foaming torrent to empty its sparkling waters into the wide sea, the original source of all streams. By this way I visit my nearest neighbors and procure chickens, which our cook roasts on sticks over the fire, after having carefully rubbed them with salt and a liberal allowance of red pepper, the two universal condiments among the Malays. For ages all the salt these people have had has been brought from Java. The red pepper thrives well everywhere without the slightest care, and it is almost always found growing near every hut. A large bush

of it at one corner of our house is now filled with
fruit of all sizes; some small and green, and some
fully grown and showing it is already ripe by its
bright-pink color. In this condition the Malays
gather and dry it, and always carry a good supply
wherever they go. Its Malay name is *lombok*, but
the one more generally used is the Javanese name
chabé. Besides chickens, we have paddy, that is, rice
in the husk. A large elliptical hole is made in a log
for a mortar, a small quantity of paddy is then poured
in and pounded with a stick five or six feet long, and
as large round as a man's arm. This is raised vertically, and, when the hole is nearly even full, a native
will usually pound off all the husks without scattering more than a few grains on the ground; but, if a
foreigner attempts it, he will be surprised to see how
the rice will fly off in all directions at every blow.
When the husks are pounded off they are separated
from the kernels by being tossed up from a shallow
basket and carried away by the wind, as our farmers
used to winnow grain. This is the only mode of preparing rice practised by the Malays, and the process
is the same in every part of the archipelago. From
one corner of our piazza hangs a large bunch of green
bananas to ripen in the sunshine. I find it very
agreeable to pluck off a nice ripe one myself when I
come in weary and thirsty from a long hunt. From
the other corner hangs a cluster of cocoa-nuts filled
with clear, cool, refreshing water.

Not far from us is a hut inhabited by two natives, who are engaged in cultivating tobacco. Their
ladangs, or gardens, are merely places of an acre or

less, where the thick forest has been partially destroyed by fire, and the seed is sown in the regular spaces between the stumps. As soon as the leaves are fully grown they are plucked off, and the petiole and a part of the midrib are cut away. Each leaf is then cut transversely into strips about a sixteenth of an inch wide, and these are dried in the sun until a mass of them looks like a bunch of oakum. It is then ready for use, and at once carried to market. This cosmopolite, *Nicotiana tabacum*, is a native of our own country. Las Casas says that the Spaniards on Columbus's first voyage saw the natives in Cuba smoking it in tubes called *tabacos*, hence its name. Mr. Crawfurd states that, according to a Javanese chronicle, it was introduced into Java in the year 1601, ninety years after the conquest of Malacca by the Portuguese, who were probably the first Europeans that furnished it to the Javanese, as the Dutch had not yet formed an establishment on the island. It is now cultivated in every part of the archipelago. The fact that this narcotic was originally found only in America leads us to infer, without raising the questions whether our continent received her aboriginal population from some other part of the globe, or whether they were created here, that there never has been any extensive migration of our Indians or red-men to the islands in the Pacific, or to any distant part of the world; for if they had colonized any area, in that place at least, its use would undoubtedly continue to exist at the present day, since it is probable that they would never have thought of going to a new land without taking with them this plant, which they valued more even than food, and which they had been accustomed to cultivate. If, after establishing themselves in their new colony, they had been overpowered and completely destroyed by some more powerful tribe, their conquerors would probably have become addicted to the same habit as readily as the people of every clime and every stage of civilization do now, and thus the practice would have been perpetuated, though the people who introduced it perished ages ago, and all the idols, and temples, and fortifications they might have made, have long since crumbled into dust. This inference is greatly strengthened, if we consider the past and present geographical distribution of maize, or Indian corn, which is also a native of our continent only, and, like tobacco, is now raised in every part of the archipelago. Unlike rice, this plant thrives on hillsides and elevated lands, and can therefore be raised on all the larger islands in those seas, where there are few level areas that can be readily inundated for the cultivation of rice. It was also probably introduced by the Portuguese, for Juan Gaetano, a Spanish pilot, who visited Mindanao in 1642, twenty-one years after the discovery of the Philippines by Magellan, states* that "in a certain part of that island ruled by the Moors" (Arabs), "there are some small artillery, and hogs, deer, buffaloes, and other animals of the chase, with Castilian" (or common) " fowls, rice, palms, and cocoa-nuts. There is no maize in that

* Vide Ramusio, vol. i., p. 376, in Crawfurd's "Dictionary of the India Islands."

island, but for bread they use rice and a bark which they call sagu, from which also they extract oil in like manner as they do from palms."

As maize is not difficult to be transported on account of its bulk or liability to any injury, and formed the chief article of food among most of our red-men, it would be the very provision they would take with them on their migrations; and as the part eaten is the fruit, they would have plenty of seed, and would know from their previous experience precisely how to cultivate it.

One part of the surrounding forest is a grove of *jati*, or teak-trees, *Tectona grandis*, Linn. Those found here are only a foot or fifteen inches in diameter and forty feet high, a size they attain in Java in twenty-five or thirty years, where they do not reach their full growth in less than a century. The native name *jati* is a word of Javanese origin, signifying true, or genuine, and was probably applied to these trees on account of the well-known durability of the wood they yield. Now, near the end of the dry monsoon, they have lost nearly all their foliage; for, though it is sometimes asserted that in the tropics the leaves fall imperceptibly one by one, that is not true, in this region, where there are well-defined wet and dry seasons. The teak also thrives in a few places on the continent, and is found in the central and eastern provinces of Java, in Madura, Bali, and particularly in Sumbawa, where the wood is considered better than that of Java, but it is said to be unknown in Sumatra, Borneo, and in the peninsula of Malacca. It exists in some places in Celebes, but the natives assert that the seed was brought there from Java by one of the sovereigns of Tanéte. It is therefore uncertain whether the teak is a native of this island. In the early morning, and again soon after sunset, flocks of large green parrots, *Tanygnathus macrorynchus*, Wagl., come to these trees to feed on the fruit which is now ripe. They are so wary that it is extremely difficult to get near them, especially as the large dry leaves of this tree cover the ground and continually crack and rustle beneath one's feet. To see these magnificent birds flying back and forth in the highest glee, while they remain unconscious of danger, is a grand sight, and it seems little less than absolute wickedness to shoot one, even when it is to be made the subject, not of idle gazing, but of careful study, and it requires still greater resolution to put an end to one's admiration and pull the fatal trigger. When one of these birds has been wounded, its mate, and sometimes the whole flock, hearing its cries, at once comes back, as if hoping to relieve its misery.

In many places in this vicinity the tall canari-tree is seen raising its high crest, and there flocks of cream-colored doves, *Carpophaga luctuosa*, gather to feed on its fruit. Their loud, continuous cooing leads the hunter a long way through the jungle. Among the limbs of the lower trees are seen the long-tailed doves, *Carpophaga perspiclata*. On the banks of the dry brook, near our house, are bunches of bamboos, through which flit fly-catchers, *Muscicapidæ*, and the beautiful *Monarcha loricata*, a slender bird about as large as a martin, of a blue above, and a pure, almost silvery white beneath, except on the throat, which is covered with scale-like feathers, of a rich metallic blue-black. So far as is known, this beautiful bird is only found on this island. In the bushes and shrubbery is constantly heard the cheerful note of a bird, the *Trobidorynchus bouruensis*, somewhat larger than our robin. By day I enjoyed this Robinson Crusoe life very much, but the mosquitoes proved such a torment by night that we could scarcely sleep. A great smouldering fire was made under our hut, but its only effect was to increase our misery, and make the mosquitoes more bloodthirsty. We were frequently disturbed also by several yellow dogs, which came to crunch what chicken-bones the cook had thrown away, and to upset every thing around the house that was not already in a state of stable equilibrium. Afterward, when all was still, occasionally a heavy crash sighed through the deep woods, caused by the falling of some old tree, whose roots had been slowly consumed by the fires that prevail in the neighborhood during the dry season.

At the end of a week my hunter had preserved the skins of sixty-three beautiful birds, including specimens of six species that I had not secured before. We now returned to Kayéli; and though there were only eight white persons in the whole place, I could nevertheless feel that I was returning to civilization, and that I could speak some other language than Malay.

The village of Kayéli is really composed of eleven separate parts, or *kampongs*, all situated on a low, marshy place, a couple of hundred yards back from the sand-beach. They are separated from each other by a little stream, or *kali*, and each has its own rajah, and formerly had its own little square mosque, for all these eleven tribes are Mohammedans, and keep separate from each other, because they lived in different parts of the island when the Dutch arrived. In the centre of this village is a large, square lawn, formed by the fort, the residence of a *controleur*, and a few other houses. Back of the lawn is the Christian kampong; for in every village where there are Mohammedans and Christians, each has a separate part to itself. Occasionally, instead of a healthful spirit of rivalry, a more bitter hostility springs up than existed between the Jews and the Samaritans, and finally the weaker party is obliged to migrate, as in the case mentioned in regard to the inhabitants of Bonoa.

From Valentyn we learn that, according to native accounts, as early as A. D. 1511, ten years before the arrival of the Portuguese, the Sultan of Ternate sent out expeditions which subjected all the tribes of this island. In 1652 a treaty was made between the sultan and the Dutch, that all the clove-trees on the island should be uprooted. The natives opposed this measure to the best of their ability, but after a resistance which lasted five years, they were completely subjected, all their clove-trees were destroyed, and they were obliged to remove to Kayéli Bay, and live under the range of the Dutch cannon. Since that time (1657), the clove-tree has never been introduced again. Previous to the expedition of the Sultan of

Ternate in 1511, the shores of the island were occupied by the Malays, who had already subjected the earliest inhabitants of the island of which we have any knowledge. During my stay at Kayéli I saw several of them, though they are always shy about entering the village. Like the Alfura of Ceram, they resemble the Malays in stature and general appearance, but are distinguished from them by their darker color, and by their hair, which is frizzly, not lank like that of the Malays, and not woolly, like that of the Papuans. As in Ceram, many of them suffer from that unsightly disease, icthyosis, in which the skin becomes dry and comes off in scales. Their houses are described as the most miserable hovels, consisting of little more than a roof of palm-leaves resting on four poles, with a kind of platform a foot or two above the ground, where they sit and sleep. They are all free, and slavery is wholly unknown. Mr. T. J. Miller, who was formerly resident here, took much pains to gather all the information possible in regard to them. He states that they have divided the island into *Fennas* or tribes, each of which has a chief. Instead of living together in villages, like the Malays, they are scattered over their whole territory. Several of these chiefs continue to acknowledge one of the Mohammedan rajahs, or, as they are named by the Dutch, "regents," in the village of Kayéli, as their superior. Formerly, each was obliged to send one young girl to its regent for a bride every year, but the Dutch have long since relieved them from such an unwelcome exaction. In former times also they were compelled to pay their regent a certain part of their rice and sago, and provide men to row his prau or to carry his chair, if he proceeded by land, but they have been freed from this onerous service, and the Malays who live in the village with the rajah are obliged to perform such offices for him. In regard to marriage, each man buys his wife, her price, according to their laws, depending on the rank of her father, as in Ceram, but a man is not, however, required to cut off a human head before he can be allowed to marry, as is the custom in that island. Instead, therefore, of being fierce head-hunters, as the Alfura of Ceram, they are mild and inoffensive. They believe, according to Mr. Miller, in one Supreme Being, who made every thing, and is the source of all good and all evil. They believe in evil spirits. Prayer leads to prosperity; the negligence of this duty to adversity. Through the love that this Supreme Being had for man, whom He had created, He sent him a teacher, Nabiata, who lived among the mountains. He gave the will of his Master in seven commandments, namely: 1. Thou shalt not kill nor wound. 2. Thou shalt not steal. 3. Thou shalt not commit adultery. 4. Thou shalt not set thyself against thy *fenna*. 5. A man shall not set himself up against the chief of his tribe. 6. The chief shall not set himself up against him that is over his or other tribes. 7. The chief over more than one tribe shall not set himself up against him who is placed over all the tribes. Nabiata also taught that, though the body perishes, the soul shall still continue to exist. They who have kept the foregoing commandments—for all the acts of men are recorded by this Supreme Being—shall dwell far above the clouds near the Omniscient One. They who have done wickedly shall never rise to the abode of the happy nor remain on earth, but continually, in solitude and sorrow, wander about on the clouds, longing in vain to join their brothers who are above or beneath them. Nabiata also instituted circumcision, which was performed on both sexes when they attained the age of eight or ten years. From the introduction of this rite we may infer that this Nabiata was a Mohammedan teacher, probably an Arab, who had found his way to this region on a Javanese or Malay prau, that had come to purchase cloves. Finally, according to their legend, Nabiata made men of birth his disciples and teachers, and ascended to the abode of the good from whence he came.

One day, while at Kayéli, I received a most polite invitation to attend a feast at one of the rajah's houses. The occasion was the shaving of a young child's head. An Arab priest began the rite by repeating a prayer in a monotonous nasal chant, five others joining in from time to time by way of a chorus. After the long prayer was ended, a servant brought in the child, and another servant followed carrying a large plate partly filled with water, in which were two parts of the blossom of a cocoa-nut-palm, a razor, and a pair of shears. The child was first carried to the chief priest, who dipped his fingers in the water, placed them on the child's head, and then cut off a lock of hair with the large shears. The lock of hair was then carefully thrown into the water along with a guilder. We all did the same. Tea and small cakes made of rice were then served, and "the feast" was ended. The child was one year old; when it becomes eight or nine it will have to submit to that abominable custom prevailing among both sexes of all ranks of Mohammedans, filing the teeth. This, I was informed, was done with a flat stone, or a fragment of slate, and sometimes even with a piece of bamboo. The object is to make the teeth short, and the front ones concave on the outer side, so as to hold the black dye. The Christians never file theirs, and the Mohammedans always ridicule the teeth of such natives by calling them "dogs' teeth," because they are "so white and so long."

At another time I received an invitation to attend a wedding-feast, but, when I reached the house, it proved to be a feast that the married couple give to their friends a few days after the wedding. As on all such festive occasions, the house and veranda were brilliantly lighted, and on either side from the house out to the street were a number of posts made of the large soft trunks of bananas. On their tops large lumps of gum were burned. Between them were arches made of young leaves of the cocoa-nut palm, arranged as I had previously seen in Nusalaut. The bride (who, of course, is to be spoken of first), to our surprise, did not prove to be a young and blooming lass, but already in middle life, yet a suitable helpmeet at least for the bridegroom, who was an Arab, and had married this, his second wife, since he came to Buru, only four months ago. The former wife he had sent back to her parents, much against her wishes. When a wife desires to leave her husband, she cannot do so without his consent, which the husband generally grants, choosing the less of two evils, and, moreover, it is regarded as very ungallant to retain an unwilling mate; but, while travelling in Sumatra, I saw one husband who would not allow his wife another choice, but his was a very peculiar case. His father was a Chinaman, and therefore, as the descendants of the Chinese do, he had shaved his head and wore a cue, and was a Chinaman also; but, becoming desperately enamoured of a Mohammedan lass, he concluded to yield to her unusual demand, that he too must become a Mohammedan before he could be accepted. She soon repented of her proposal, but he replied that he had suffered so much for her sake, he would not release her from her vows—such are the unlimited privileges granted the husband by the laws of the false Prophet.

While at Amboina I was surprised one day, just before dinner, to see a strange servant appear with a large platter containing fifteen or twenty kinds of fishes, fruit, and the various inimitable mixtures made by the Chinese, in whose quarter of the city we were residing. The gentleman with whom I was living, however, explained the mystery. There was to be a wedding in a house near by, and the father of the bride was one of his hired men, and those nice preparations were intended as a present, that is, in form, it being expected that only two or three of them would be taken—and that was quite all a European palate would desire. This was repeated for three or four days. Meantime the father of the bride had hired a house where other friends were received and feasted, and the father of the bridegroom also received and entertained his friends in like manner. At length came an invitation to attend the *finale* of this long ceremonial. We first walked to the house of the bridegroom. Large Chinese lanterns brilliantly lighted the veranda and the adjoining narrow lane, which was thronged with men and boys. We then visited the house where the bride was waiting to receive her lord. The piazza opened into a large room, and on one side of it was a smaller one, closed by a red curtain instead of a door. No one but the lady-guests were allowed to enter where the bride was sitting. The larger room contained many small tables loaded with delicacies, mostly of Chinese manufacture. Not to be unsocial, we sat down and sipped a cup of boiling tea, and observed the assembled guests while all were waiting for the coming of the bridegroom as in good Scripture times. In the opposite corner was a table surrounded with Malay ladies. It also was covered with sweetmeats, but room was soon made for the more necessary siri-box; a liberal quid of lime, pepper-leaves, and betel-nut was taken by each one, and, to complete the disgusting sight, an urn-shaped spittoon, an inseparable companion of the siri-box, was produced, and handed round from one to another as the occasion demanded. A shrill piping was now heard down the street, and every one rushed out on the veranda to see the approaching procession. First came boys with wax-candles, and near them others carrying the presents that the bride and the bridegroom had received. Then came the bridegroom himself, supported by his friends, and surrounded by candles arranged at different heights on rude triangular frames. He was dressed in a Malay suit of light red, and wore a gilded chain. I had been told that, when he should attempt to enter the room where the bride sat waiting, the women would gather and persistently dispute his right to proceed, and here, in the distant East, I thought to myself, I shall see an illustration of the maxim, " None but the brave deserve the fair." On the contrary, so far from manifesting any disposition to oppose him and prolong the ceremony, they only made way for him to enter the bridal-chamber as quickly as possible. As my friend and I were the only white persons present, we were allowed the especial favor of entering also. On one side of the room was a small table covered with a red cloth, and on this were two gigantic red wax-candles. Behind the table sat the bride, arrayed in a scarlet dress, with a white opaque veil concealing her face, and fastened to her hair. As the bridegroom approached, she slowly rose. Placing his hands with the palms together, he bowed three times in the same manner as the Chinese address the images in their temples. She returned the salutation by also bowing three times, but without raising her hands. Now came the exciting moment. She remained standing while he stepped forward and commenced pulling out the pins that held fast the opaque veil which hid her beauty from his longing eyes. Not being very skilful in this operation, a couple of the maids-in-waiting assisted him, and, by degrees, was revealed a face that was at least one shade darker than most of the ladies near her, and I could but think, if that really was the first time her husband had ever seen her, he must feel not a little disappointed. However, his countenance remained unchanged, whether such a saddening reflection crossed his mind or one of delightful surprise. He then passed round the table to the side of his bashful bride, and both sat down together and were stupidly gazed at. In the opposite end of the room was the bridal-bed. The four posts rose above the bed nearly to the ceiling, and supported a mosquito-curtain which was bespangled with many little pieces of tinsel and paper flowers. Both the bride and bridegroom were Mohammedans, and this marriage was nominally according to the Mohammedan usage, but it should perhaps be more properly regarded, like most of the Malay customs at the present day, as combining parts of the rite in China and Arabia with that which existed among these nations while they observed the Hindu religion, or continued to remain in heathenism. The boys usually marry for the first time when about sixteen, and the girls at the age of thirteen or fourteen, though I was once shown a child of nine years that was already a wife, and mothers eleven or twelve years old are occasionally seen. The great obstacle to marriage in all civilized lands—the difficulty of supporting a family—is unknown here. Children, instead of being a source of expense, are a source of income. Until four or five years old, the boys do not usually wear any clothing. Their food costs very little, and all the education they receive still less, or nothing at all. The average number of persons in one family in Java, where it is perhaps as large, if not larger, than elsewhere, is estimated at only four or four and a half. The fact that children help support their parents secures for them such attention that they are never entirely neglected. Polygamy is allowed here as in other Mohammedan lands, but only the wealthier natives and the princes are guilty of it. The facility with which marriages are made, and divorces obtained, is one cause why it is not more general. In regard to the evil effects of polygamy, and the ideas of this people in respect to the sacred rite of marriage, Sir Stamford Raffles, who was Governor-General of Java, most truthfully remarks: "Of the causes which have tended to lower the character of the Asiatics in comparison with Europeans, none has had a more decided influence than polygamy. To all those noble and generous feelings, all that delicacy of sentiment, that romantic and poetical spirit, which virtuous love inspires in the breast of a European, the Javan is a stranger; and in the communication between the sexes he seeks only convenience and little more than a gratification of an appetite. But the evil does not stop here: education is neglected, and family attachments are weakened. A Javan chief has been known to have sixty acknowledged children, and it too often happens that in such cases sons having been neglected in their infancy become dissipated, idle, and worthless, and spring up like rank grass and overrun the country."

In the little village of Kayéli there were only three Chinamen, but one of them was an opium-seller. He was agent for another Chinaman at Amboina, who had bought the privilege of selling it from

the Dutch Government, who "farm out" or grant
this privilege in every district to the highest bidder
From this article alone, the government obtains in
this way an income of four or five million dollars.
Opium, as is well known, is the inspissated juice obtained from the capsule of the white poppy, *Papaver
somniferum*. Its Malay name is *apyun*, which, coming from the Arabic *afyun*, shows at once by whom
it was introduced into the archipelago; the same
people, as Mr. Crawfurd remarks, who made them
acquainted with ardent spirits, and at the same time
gave them a religion forbidding both. It is imported
from India, and the poppy is not cultivated in any
part of the archipelago. Barbosa mentions it in a
list of articles brought from Arabia to Calicut in
Malabar, and in his time its price was about one-third
what it is now. The man who sells it is obliged to
keep a daily account of the quantity he disposes of,
and this account is open to the inspection of the
government officers at all times. So large is the sum
demanded by the government for this farming privilege, and so great are the profits obtained by the
Chinese, who are the people that carry on most of
this nefarious traffic, that the price the Malays are
obliged to pay for this luxury limits its consumption
very considerably. When imported, it is usually in
balls five or six inches in diameter. It is then soft
and of a reddish-brown color, but becomes blacker
and harder the longer it is kept. It is slightly elastic, and has a waxy lustre, a strong, unpleasant odor,
and to the taste is bitter, nauseous, and persistent.
To prepare it for smoking, it is boiled down to the

A MALAY OPIUM SMOKER.

consistency of thick tar. While it is boiling, tobacco and siri are sometimes added. A lamp is then lighted, and a small quantity is taken up on a piece of wire as large as a knitting-needle. This is held in the flame of the lamp until it melts and swells up as a piece of spruce-gum would do under similar circumstances. During this process it is frequently taken out of the flame and rolled between the thumb and forefinger. It is then placed in a small hole in the large bowl of the pipe, and the wire being withdrawn, a hole is left for inhaling the air. The bowl of the pipe is now placed against the lamp and the smoke inhaled with two or three long breaths, which carry the fumes down deep into the lungs. By this time the small quantity of opium in the bowl of the pipe is consumed. It is then filled as before, and this process is repeated until the eyelids become heavy and an irresistible desire to sleep possesses the whole body. Its immediate effect is to produce a passive, dreamy state. This is followed by a loss of appetite, severe constipation, and kindred ills. When a man has once contracted the habit of using it, it is impossible to reform. Greater and greater doses are required to produce the desired lethargic effect. The evil results of this vice are well shown in the accompanying photograph of a Malay, where the victim, although only in middle life, has already become so emaciated that he is little more than a living skeleton. The rude platform of planks covered with a straw mat, on which he is sitting, is his bed, while stupified with his favorite drug. A pipe, of the customary form, is seen in his right hand. Being too poor to own a lamp, he has instead a small fire of charcoal raised on the top of an urn-shaped vessel of earthen-ware. By his side are seen vessels for making tea, and by copious draughts of that stimulant he will try to revive his dead limbs by and by, when he awakes from his contemplated debauch, and finds his whole energy gone, and, as it were, his very life on the point of leaving the body.

My next excursion, after a week in the woods, was with the commandant of the fort to a high bluff on the eastern side of the entrance of the bay of Kayéli. The fires which rage here year after year destroy much of the thick forest, and a tall, coarse grass takes its place. In these prairies grow many *kayu-puti*, or whitewood-trees, so called from their bark, which makes them resemble our white birches. Their branches are very scattering, and bear long, narrow leaves, somewhat like those of our willow, which are gathered about this time of year, for the sake of their "oil." It is obtained in the following manner: the leaves are plucked off by hand and placed in baskets which are carried to sheds, where they are emptied into large kettles, that are partly filled with water, and carefully closed. From the centre of the cover of the kettle rises a wooden tube, to which is joined another of cloth, that is coiled up in a barrel containing cold water. A fire being made beneath the kettle, the volatile "oil" is carried over and condensed in the tube. About eight thousand bottles of this article are manufactured here every year. Indeed, it forms almost the only export from this large island. The price here is about a guilder per bottle. It is sent to Java and other parts of the archipelago, and is used as a sudorific. The tree, *Melaleuca cajeputi*, is also found in Amboina, Ceram, Celebes, and Sumatra, but the best oil comes from this island.

After we had wandered over a number of hills, we came down into a basin, in the bottom of which was a little lake, where we found a flock of brown ducks. The borders of the lake, however, were so marshy that I could get no fair shot at this rare game. In a small lake near by I had the privilege of seeing a pair of those beautiful birds, the *Anas rajah*, or "prince duck." Around the borders of the lake was a broad band of dead trees. My hunter spied a nice flock of the brown ducks on the opposite side, and for nearly a mile we carefully crept along through the sharp-edged grass, until we were just opposite the flock. If we went down to the margin of the pond they would be completely shielded from our shot by the trees. I therefore ordered my hunter, whose gun was loaded with a ball for deer, to lie down, while I sprang upon my feet and tried the effect of one barrel of my fowling-piece, which, by-the-by, was loaded with small shot for doves. Shy as they were, we had evidently taken them by surprise. There was a click, a report, and four out of the eight remained where they were. The next thing was to get them. We had no dog nor boat, and I proposed to my hunter, as he was a good swimmer, that he swim for them, but he only shrugged his shoulders and declared the whole pool was so full of crocodiles that a man could not get out where the birds were before he would be devoured. It evidently was just such a place as those monsters delight to frequent, but I determined to go after them myself; and as I proceeded to carry out my resolution, my hunter, ashamed to remain on the banks, joined me, and after an ugly scramble through the bushes and sticks, and much wallowing in the soft mud, we got into the water and out to the flock, and as soon as possible were back again on the bank. The commandant now came up, and I recounted to him what we had been doing. He was horrified! That a man could go into that pond and escape the crocodiles for ten minutes he regarded as next to a miracle. A number of natives, who had frequently visited the place, assured me that nothing could have induced them to run such a risk of losing their lives. Our whole party then continued on over the grassy hills, and came down to Roban, a place of two native huts, and one of those was empty. Here, I thought to myself, will be another good locality to find new species, and I determined to return and occupy the vacant house for a few days.

It was already late in the afternoon before we thought of returning, and pushed off from the shore in a boat that had come round the cape at the mouth of the bay to take us home. Soon the wind sprang up ahead, our little sail was taken in, and our men used their oars; but the sun set and the moon arose, and yet we were slowly toiling on, and occasionally our boat grated on the top of a coral head that rose higher than those around it. At last we passed the cape, and reached the smooth water of the bay, yet the helmsman kept near the shore, and took us between two little islands on the east side of the bay, called by the natives Crocodile Islands. As we passed the low point of one of them, within a boat's length from the shore, an enormous crocodile crawled out of the jungle and clumsily hurried down the narrow bank into the water, as if he had come out expecting to make a meal of us. The thought of the danger I had incurred that very day of being devoured by such monsters made me shudder and seize an oar, but the amphibious beast was already out of my reach.

Along the eastern side of Kayéli Bay there is an extensive coral reef, and farther out around the cape is another, a quarter of a mile wide, that is bare at low tide. Along the outer edges of this I floated the next day, while on my way back to Roban. The water was still, and as clear as crystal, and we could see distinctly far down into the deep, deep sea. Now, as we come near the reef, its outer wall suddenly rises up, apparently from the unfathomable abyss of the ocean. Among the first forms we notice are the hemispherical *Meandrinas*, or "brain corals," named, because, when the soft polyps are removed, small fissure-like depressions are found winding to and fro over its surface, making the raised parts between them closely resemble the convolutions of the brain. Near by are some sending out many branches, like a thick bush, and others with only a few, resembling deer-antlers of abnormal growth. Some, which do not attach themselves to their neighbors, are circular, as we see them from above. Their under surfaces are horizontal and their upper sides slightly convex. When the soft parts are removed, a number of radiating partitions are seen, so that the whole resembles a gigantic mushroom turned upside down; and this family of polyps is hence called *Fungidæ*. Scattered among the stone corals are many *Gorgonias*. Some are much like broad sheets of foliage and similar to those known to us as "sea-fans," which generally come from the tropical waters among our West Indies. Others resemble bundles of rattans; and, when the soft polyps are taken off, a black horn-like axis stick is left. Others, when taken out of the sea and dried, look like limbs cut from a small spruce-tree after it has been dried, and lost hundreds of its small needle-like leaves. Numbers of sponges are also seen, mostly of a spherical form, with many ramifying ducts or tubes. But the most accurate description possible must fail to convey any proper idea of the beauty and richness of these gardens beneath the sea, because, in reading or hearing a description, the various forms that are distinctly seen at a single glance have to be mentioned one after another, and thus they pass along in a series or line before our mental vision, instead of being grouped into circular areas, where the charm consists not so much in the wonderful perfection of a few separate parts, as in the harmonious relations, or, as architects say, the effect of the whole. The pleasure of viewing coral reefs never becomes wearisome, because the grouping is always new. No two places are just alike beneath all the wide sea, and no one can fail to be thrilled with pleasure, when, after a few strong strokes of the oars, his canoe is left to glide on by her own momentum, and the coral gardens pass in review below with a magical effect like a panorama.

At Roban I remained with my men three days, and, as we were nearer the shore, the mosquitoes did not torment us as badly as previously at our hut near the mountains. This proved to be a favorite locality of the *castori rajah*, or "prince parrot," which I had already seen in Ceram, and I secured two or three pairs of them here, but I was specially anxious to get a specimen of the *malayu*, as the Malays strangely name a bird, the *Megapodius Forsteni*, which is allied to the hen. The common name for these birds is "mound-builders," from their peculiar habit of scratching together great heaps of sand and sticks, which are frequently twenty or twenty-five feet in diameter, and five feet high. These great hillocks are their nests, and here they deposit their eggs. There is also another species here, the *M. Wallacei*, which burrows deeply in the sand. The natives brought me one specimen, which they caught while she was crawling up from her hidden nest. I kept her alive for some time, but, after laying an egg more than one-third as large as her whole body, she died. Two eggs of the same dimensions were found at the bottom of the tunnel she had made in the loose sand. This bird usually comes down from the hills in the early part of the evening to deposit its eggs, and then its wailing cry is occasionally heard, but it is so extremely shy, that it is one of the most difficult of all the birds on the island to procure.

I usually shot the birds, and my hunter always skinned them, noting the locality of each, its sex, and as nearly as possible the color of its eyes. The greatest annoyance that troubles the collector of birds in the tropics is caused by the swarms of small ants that fill every conceivable place. If a bird is shot and laid down on the ground for half an hour, it will almost surely be injured so much by these insects that it will not be worth skinning. There is no certain means of keeping them away altogether, except by completely isolating a place with water, which is usually done by putting small basins under each leg of a table, but before one is aware of it, something is sure to be placed so as to touch the table, and thus form a bridge for these omnivorous pests to cross over and continue their work of destruction. As soon as the birds are brought in they are hung up by a thread or piece of small twine. After the skins are taken off, they are thoroughly poisoned with arsenic and camphor, mixed with water to the consistency of cream. Each is then filled with the cotton from the cotton-wood tree, until it has exactly the size of the bird. They are then spread in the sun on a bamboo frame, which is suspended by twines fastened at its corners. After they have become thoroughly dried, they are kept in a tight tin box with large pieces of gum-camphor, and even then they must be looked after every day or two, for they are still liable to be injured by the ants, which are particularly fond of gnawing at the base of the bill and around the eyes. During the rainy season it is extremely difficult to dry the skins properly, there is so little sunshine. No one who has not lived in the tropics can have any idea what a source of constant vexation the ants are. Bread, sugar, and every thing eatable, they are sure to devour, unless it is kept in glass-stoppered bottles; and this is the greater annoyance, because, when a quantity of provisions is lost, as is constantly happening, it is so difficult to procure another supply in every part of the archipelago, except in the immediate vicinity of the few chief cities. They are sure, in some way or other, to find their way into every little nook or corner; and though a table be set with the greatest care, in nine cases out of ten some will be seen running on the white cloth before dinner is over. The floors of the houses occupied by Europeans are usually made of large, square pieces of earthen-ware, and through the cracks that chance to occur in the cement between them ants are sure to appear. It is this, probably, that has given rise to the saying, that "the ants will eat through a brick in a single night." In all parts of the archipelago it is an established custom either to whitewash the walls inside and outside, or else paint them white, except a narrow strip along the floor, which is covered with a black paint chiefly composed of tar, the only common substance to which these pests show any aversion. All these troubles are caused by the "black ants," but their ravages do not compare with those caused by the "white ants," which actually eat up solid wood. The frames of many of the smaller buildings and outhouses in the East are not mortised, but are fastened together with pieces of *coir* rope, and, of course, when they are eaten off, the whole structure comes to the ground. A large L attached to the *controleur's* house, which we have been using for a dining-room, fell down from this cause the other day. Afterward, when I came to Macassar, a fine war-steamer of eight hundred or one thousand tons was pointed out to me, which the white ants had succeeded in establishing themselves in, and several gentlemen, who ought to have known, said that she was so badly eaten by them that she was almost unseaworthy.

On another occasion the commandant and I went to the west end of the bay to hunt deer. We started early, and at eight o'clock were already at the mouth of a small stream, which we ascended for a short distance, and a guide then led us through a strip of woods that lined the banks. Our party in all consisted of more than twenty, half of whom were soldiers, armed with rifles; the others came to start up the game. When we passed out into a level, open prairie, all that had guns were posted about twenty yards apart, in a line parallel to the woods. The others made a long circuit round, and finally entered the forest before us. Then forming into a line, they began to drive toward us, shouting with all their might, and making a din horrid enough to frighten other animals less timid than deer. Packs of dogs, that the natives had brought, were meantime yelping and howling. Soon there was a cracking in the bushes near me, and at the next instant came a female and her fawn, with high, flying leaps through the tall grass. I carried a heavy government rifle, for, unfortunately, my light breech-loading Spencer was not on the island. I aimed at the foremost and fired; she fell, and I ran, shouting out to the others that I had one, when, to my surprise, at the next instant she sprang up again and with one leap disappeared into the dense jungle. That was the only good shot I had that day. Again and again we drove, but when we stood in the tall grass, which was as high as our heads, we could not see our game, and when we perched on stumps, or climbed into the trees, we could not turn round quickly enough to fire suddenly in an unexpected quarter with any certain aim. However, when the horn was sounded for all to assemble, one fine deer and one large wild hog were brought in. Once a large male came out about five hundred yards from where I was standing. At the crack of the rifle he only raised his head high and darted away, almost with the speed of a bullet. His antlers were very large and branching, and the gracefulness and speed with which he flew over the plain made the sight one of the finest I ever enjoyed. The natives are accustomed now, during the dry monsoon, to burn the prairie-lands, partly in order that new, sweet grass may spring up, and that when the deer come out of the forests to eat it they will be fully exposed to the rifles, and partly, as they say, to induce them to come out in order to lick up the ashes. The usual method, besides driving, is to lie in wait near a newly-burnt place by night, when there is moonlight enough to enable the hunters to see every thing within a rifle-shot plainly. After the deer is secured its flesh is cut up into thin slices and smoked, and now, in many places on the hills around the bay of Kayéli, columns of smoke are seen rising every day, where the natives are busy changing venison into *dinding*, the only kind of meat they have except that of wild boars, which are very abundant on this island, though seldom taken. They are accustomed to come out into the prairie-lands in great droves, and frequently an area of a quarter of an acre is so completely rooted up by them that it looks as if it had been ploughed. They even come by night to the gardens, or cultivated places, at a little distance from the village, and in a short time destroy almost every thing growing in them. One time, seeing a rare bird perched high on the top of a lone tree that stood in the tall grass, I cautiously approached within range and fired, when suddenly there was a rattling of hoofs on the dry ground, caused by the stampede of a large herd within pistol-shot of where we were, but entirely hidden from our view by the thick grass. The natives are usually afraid of them, and the one who was crawling along behind me to pick up the bird fled at the top of his speed when he heard the thundering tread of more than a hundred hoofs, while I stood wondering what sort of beasts had so suddenly sprung out of the earth, and half querying whether my shot, as they fell on the ground, had not been changed into quadrupeds in the same miraculous way that the dragon teeth, sown by Cadmus, were transformed into men. The hog-deer, or *babirusa*, is also found among these mountains. While I was at Kayéli a young one was caught by some of the natives.

During this day's hunt I came to a wide field of recently-elevated coral, about one hundred feet above the sea. The natives, who were surprised that I should stop to look at such common rocks, asserted that the same kind of *batu puti*, "white stone," was found among the hills, and I have no doubt that recent coral reefs will be found in the mountainous parts of all the adjacent islands as high up as Governor Arriens has already traced them on Amboina.

While these days were passing by, we all wondered what the authorities were doing to put down the great insurrection in Ceram. All the boats that came brought us only the vaguest tidings, sometimes of entire success, and sometimes of entire failure. We had good cause to be solicitous, for at two or three posts on that island there were only about a dozen Dutch soldiers, and if any numbers of the head-hunting Alfuras made an attack in concert, all would inevitably be butchered. While we were in this state of suspense, six large praus were seen coming in round one of the capes and entering our bay. As the foremost hove to and waited for the others, that all might reach the anchorage together, they appeared to be coming with some evil design, and immediately there was no little bustle in our settlement of nine Europeans, four of whom were ladies. The commandant summoned all his troops into the fort, sergeants were posted in the four corners by the four cannon, the men once more put through the routine of loading, so that if anybody was killed by the discharge of their pieces, which, by the by, were only six-pounders, it might be some one outside of the fort.

In short, every thing was made ready to do battle. Meantime the six praus came to anchor off the beach. One of them had the required pass from the Dutch authorities at Ceram, allowing his boat to come to Kayéli, but the others had no such papers, and, according to their own story, had become frightened at the great guns in Ceram, and had also deserted their homes. This seemed to me so probable that I went down on the beach, and, if the authorities had allowed it, I would have taken half a dozen natives in a canoe and boarded every one of the praus myself, and found out what they contained. I was importuned to come back from the shore, but as I had been in battle myself, I did not purpose to get frightened and hide in the fort until I could see some cause for it. After a long consultation, it was decided that I should not be permitted to inspect the praus, and a number of Malays were sent off to carefully examine each of the dangerous vessels. This was done, and the report brought back that there were only three or four natives in each, and that as to weapons, not one of them had even an old flint-lock. Thus ended the alarm, and once more the usual dull routine set in, but this time to be broken by a circumstance as romantic as it was peculiar.

In our little community of nine persons there was a young officer. He was affable, energetic, and withal a good military man for one of his years, but, unfortunately, his mind had been fed on novels until this world appeared to him little more than half real. He was engaged to a young lady, who lived also in our little village. Besides his romantic notions, another of his faults was that he was exceedingly irritable, so much so, that he and the lady's father fell into a serious dispute, in which he became so enraged that he ordered his servant to saddle his horse forthwith, while he pulled on his long-spurred riding-boots, and stuck a large Colt's revolver (navy size) into his belt. He now declared his intention to put an end to all his ills with his own hand, and, disregarding the screams of his affianced, and the prayers and entreaties of all, he sprang into the saddle, and, dashing by the house where I was living, disappeared up the road into the forest. The gentleman with whom I was residing saw him as he passed, and at once surmised his intent, but I assured my host that it took a brave man to commit suicide, and in due time we should certainly see our friend safely return. The sequel proved the correctness of my judgment, for in a couple of hours he came back, his horse reeking with perspiration, and he himself as crestfallen as Don Quixote after his most heart-breaking misfortunes. The only one who suffered from this event was the young lady, who had so much confidence in her gallant friend as to foolishly believe he would carry out his desperate resolve to the bitter end.

Instead of remaining only a few days as I had planned, I had now lived more than three months in exile here at Buru, when one morning it was announced that the governor's yacht, the Telegraph, had arrived, to my great delight, for I had already engaged a prau to call in for me while on her way from Amboina to Ternate. The Telegraph came from Ceram to afford me an opportunity of going to

Ternate, the very place I was anxious to reach, and at the same time to leave an order for *sapis*, which she would take to Ceram on her return. The sapi or Madura cattle have been introduced into all these islands by the government to be used as food for the soldiers, but only in cases of emergency. I immediately prepared to continue my travels to other islands, and that day, September 6th, we steamed out of Kayéli Bay. For two months I had wandered over hills and mountains, penetrating the densest jungles, and picking my way through bogs filled with thorny vines. Again and again the natives entertained me with descriptions of the great pythons with which the whole island abounds, but whenever I saw a bird that I wanted, I always followed it as long as I could see it. The result was, that I had collected eighty-one species,* which were represented by over four hundred specimens, nine-tenths of which I had shot myself.

This bay is a good harbor for our whalers, and, before the war, several came here every year. It is a free port, and there is a safe anchorage, plenty of good water and wood, and vegetables can be obtained at cheap rates.

For the last time I looked back on the mountains rising behind in the interior of the village. Many and many an hour, as the sun was setting, I used to stand by the shore of the bay where a large cannon was planted erect in the sand, and, leaning against its dumb, rusty mouth, watch the changing of beautiful

---

* In the same length of time Mr. A. R. Wallace collected sixty-six species on this island.

colors in the clouds that rested on the high peaks in the south, while the day was fading into twilight, and the twilight into a pure, starlight night. Near this spot the sand-pipers came and tripped to and fro on the beach when the tide was full, and many long-winged night-hawks swooped back and forth, feasting on multitudes of insects that came out as evening approached. Far back of those mountains, near the centre of the island, there is a lake, and on its shores, according to the ancient belief of the natives, grows a plant which possesses the wondrous power of making every one who holds it in his hand *young again*, even when his locks have grown white with years, and his hand is already palsied with old age. This must be the fountain of youth, which, according to Mohammedan tradition, is situated in some dark region in the distant East, and which Moore in his "Lalla Rookh" refers to as—

>"—— youth's radiant fountain,
> Springing in some desolate mountain."

CHAPTER IX.

TERNATE, TIDORE, AND GILOLO.

As we steamed out of the bay of Kayéli a heavy rain came on, for the rainy season, which had been prevailing on the south side of Buru, was now beginning on the north side.

The same alternation of seasons is seen in Ceram. When I was on the south side of that island, there was one continuous rain; but when I came soon after to Wahai on the north coast, the grass was dry, and in many places completely parched. The cause of this interchange of seasons is, that the clouds which come up from the southeast are heavily charged with moisture, and when they strike against the high mountain-chain which extends from the eastern to the western end of that island, the larger part of their moisture is condensed and falls in heavy torrents, so that when they pass over the water-shed they pour out few or no showers.* When the wind changes and comes from the northeast, the north sides of Ceram and Buru are deluged, while it is dry weather on their southern coasts.

* A similar cause produces the rainless district of Peru, but there the prevailing wind throughout the year, at least in the upper strata of the atmosphere, is from the southeast.

When we were three miles from the northern end of Buru, we struck into a series of tide-rips, exactly like those seen in the middle of the South Atlantic Ocean, hundreds and hundreds of miles from any shore. Night now came on, and it was so dark and thick that we could not see fifty yards in any direction. It is especially at such a time, when there is no moon, no stars, no light in the whole heavens, except the lightning which fitfully darts and flashes anywhere and everywhere over the sky, that one can feel the inestimable value of the mariner's compass. That night we had much rough sea, and I was thankful that I was on a good steamer instead of the old prau on which I had been expecting to make this voyage. In the afternoon of the next day we passed the islands of Bachian and Tawali, which are heaved up into ridges about a thousand feet in height, and are separated by a long, narrow strait, abounding in the grandest scenery. On Bachian the clove-tree grows wild. The northern part of the island is of sedimentary origin of various ages, and there some coal and copper have been found, and gold has been washed since 1774. The southern part of the island is chiefly of volcanic origin. North of Bachian lies a small group of islands, and north of these Makian, an old volcano. In 1646 it underwent a fearful eruption, and all the villages on its flanks were destroyed. They were said to contain a population of some seven thousand. At that time the whole mountain was so completely split in two in a northeast and southwest direction, that when viewed from either of those points two peaks were seen. After this destruction it was again settled, and in 1855 its population numbered six thousand. In 1862 it again burst forth, destroying nearly every one on the whole island. So great a quantity of ashes was thrown out, that at Ternate, about forty miles distant, they covered the ground to the depth of from three to four inches, and nearly all the vegetation, except the large trees, was destroyed. A similar devastation caused the severest suffering within all that radius. But this eruption, fearful as it was, could not be compared to that of Mount Tomboro, already described.

North of Makian is Motir, a deep cone of trachytic lava, about one thousand feet in height. During the next night we passed between the high, sharp peak of Tidore on the right and that of Ternate on the left, and, entering a large, well-sheltered bay, anchored off the village, situated on the eastern declivity of the latter mountain. This morning as the sun rose the scene was both charming and imposing —imposing, while we looked upward to the lofty summit of this old volcano and watched the clouds of white gas rising in a perpendicular column high into the sky, until they came up to a level where the air was moving, and at once spread out into a broad, horizontal band, while the sun was pouring down a perfect flood of bright light over the high crest of the ancient peak and the city on its flanks; charming as we looked below the level water-line on the shore, and beheld the whole grand sight above, perfectly mirrored beneath in the quiet sea. This was the first mountain, whose flanks are cultivated, that I had seen since leaving Java. Many small ridges extend from its crest part way down its sides, and then spread out into little plateau-like areas; and there the natives have cleared away the luxuriant shrubbery and formed their gardens, and from them were rising small columns of smoke as if from sacrificial altars. The whole island is merely a high volcano, whose base is beneath the ocean. Its circumference at the shore line is about six miles, and its height five thousand four hundred feet. From Valentyn, Reinwardt, Bleeker, and Junghuhn, we learn that severe and destructive eruptions took place in 1608, 1635, and 1653. In 1673 another occurred, and a considerable quantity of ashes was carried even to Amboina. Then, for one hundred and sixty-five years, only small clouds of gas rose from the summit—not even hot stones were thrown out, and the mountain seemed to have undergone its last labor, when, on the 26th of February, 1838, another but not a severe eruption took place. This, however, came suddenly—so suddenly that, of a party of six natives who chanced to be on the summit collecting sulphur, four who had gone down into the crater did not have time to escape, and the two who remained on its edge only saved themselves by hastening down the mountain; and even they were badly burned and lacerated by the showers of hot stones. On the 25th of March, of the next year, a more violent eruption occurred. A heavy thundering roared in the earth, thick clouds of ashes enveloped the whole island, and streams of glowing lava flowed down the mountain. Again, the next year, on the 2d of February, at nine o'clock in the forenoon, a third eruption, yet more severe, began. Heavier thundering was heard, smoke and ashes poured out, and hot stones rose from the crater, and fell like hail on the sides of the volcano, setting fire to the dense wood which had completely spread over it during its long rest, and causing it to assume the appearance by night of a mountain of flame. At the same time much lava poured out over the crater on the north side, and flowed down to the sea between Fort Toluko and Batu Angus, "the Hot Stone." This destruction continued for twenty-four hours, and at four o'clock the next day all was still. During the next ten days clouds of black smoke continued to pour out, but all trusted that the worst had passed, when, on the 14th, at half-past twelve or almost exactly at midnight, a "frightful, unearthly thundering" began again, and the shocks became heavier and more frequent until half-past three (before it would have been light if the sky had been clear), when the last house in the whole place had been laid in ruins. The earth split open with a cracking that could be distinctly heard above the awful thundering of the mountain. Out of the fissures jets of hot water rose for a moment, and then the earth closed again, to open in another place. An educated gentleman, who, from his great wealth, generosity, and liberality, is justly known as the "Prince of the Moluccas," assured me that when two men were about one thousand yards apart, one would see the other rise until his feet seemed as high as the head of the observer, then immediately he would sink and the observer rise until he seemed as much above his fellow as he had been below him before. The published accounts entirely agree with this statement. For fifteen hours the solid ground thus rolled like the sea, but the heaviest wave did not occur till ten o'clock on the 15th of February. Fort Orange, which had withstood all the shocks of two hundred and thirty years, was partly thrown down, and wholly buried under a mass of pumice-stone and the *débris* of the forests above it. The people, as soon as this last day of destruction commenced, betook themselves to their boats, for, while the land was heaving like a troubled ocean, the sea continued quiet; no great wave came in to complete the work of destruction on the shore. It seemed, indeed, as if the laws that govern these two great elements had been suddenly exchanged, and the fixed land had become the mobile sea. The whole loss caused by this devastating phenomenon was estimated at four hundred thousand Mexican dollars; and yet, after all this experience, so great was the attachment of both foreigners and natives to this particular spot, that they would not select some one less dangerous on the neighboring shores, but all returned and once more began to build their houses for another earthquake to lay in the dust, proving that the common remark in regard to them is literally true, that "they are less afraid of fire than the Hollanders are of water." The present city, however, judging by the area of the ruins, is not more than two-thirds the size of the former one. Its total population is about 9,000. Of these, 100 are Europeans, 300 mestizoes, 200 Arabs, 400 Chinese, and the others natives of this and the adjoining islands. It is divided into two parts, the southern or European quarter, known by the peculiar name Malayu, and north of this the Chinese and Arab quarter. Near the latter is Fort Orange, which was built in 1607, as early as the settlement of Jamestown. In 1824 this fort was pronounced by the governor-general the best in all the Netherlands India. Beyond the fort is "the palace" of the Sultan of Ternate, and north of this is the native village. The palace is a small residence, built in the European style, and stands on a terrace, facing a wide, beautiful lawn, that descends to the sea. Near it is a flag-staff, which leans over as if soon to fall, a fit emblem of the decaying power of its owner, whose ancestors were once so mighty as to make the Dutch regard them with fear as well as with respect.

According to Valentyn, who gathered his information from the native records, there were formerly in Gilolo a number of independent states, each with its "kolano" or chief. In about A. D. 1250, two hundred and seventy years before any European sailed in these seas, a great migration took place to the neighboring islands, and a village named Tabona was formed on the top of this mountain, which has been an active volcano ever since it was known to Europeans. In A. D. 1322, many Javanese and Arabs came here to buy cloves. This is the first historical record we have of the spice-trade. The inhabitants of Obi and Bachian now united to counteract the growing power of the prince of Ternate, but this union effected little, for, in A. D. 1350, Molomateya, who was then reigning at Ternate, learned from the Arabs how to build vessels, and, having prepared a fleet, conquered the Sula Islands. The Arabs and Javanese meantime made great exertions to convert these people to Mohammedanism, and in A. D. 1460,[*] a little more than two centuries after it had been introduced into Java, Mahum, the prince of Ternate, became a Mohammedan "through the influence of the Javanese." About this time Malays and Chinese came from Banda to purchase cloves, which they sold to Indian traders at Malacca. In 1512 Francisco Serano, whose vessel struck on the Turtle Islands, when returning with D'Abreu from Amboina and Banda, induced the natives to assist him in getting his ship afloat while the rest of the fleet were returning to Malacca, and to pilot him to Ternate; and thus he was the first European who reached the great centre of the clove-trade. In 1521 the fleet of Magellan anchored off Tidore, an island separated from Ternate by only a narrow strait.

Ferdinand Magellan, who organized this fleet, was a Portuguese nobleman. He sailed, however, under the patronage of Charles V. of Spain. On the 20th of September, 1519, he left the port of St. Lucas with "five small ships of from sixty to one hundred and thirty tons," his object being to find a *western* passage to the Indies, particularly the Spice Islands. Coast-

---

[*] This date is corroborated by Pigafetta, who wrote in 1521, and remarks in regard to this point: "Hardly fifty years have elapsed since the Moors (Arabs) conquered (converted) Maluco (the Moluccas), and dwelt there. Previously these islands were peopled with Gentiles (i. e., heathen) only."

ing southward along the shores of Brazil, he found the strait which still continues to bear his name. This he passed through with three ships, one having been wrecked, and one having turned back. For one hundred and sixteen days he continued sailing in a northwest direction, over (as it seemed to them) an endless ocean. Their food became exhausted, but they yet kept on the same course until at last their eyes were blessed with the sight of land. Pigafetta, a member of this expedition, thus pictures their sufferings: "On Wednesday, the 28th day of November, 1520, we issued from the strait, engulfing ourselves in the ocean, in which, without comfort or consolation of any kind, we sailed for three months and twenty days. We ate biscuit which was biscuit no longer, but a wormy powder, for the worms had eaten the substance, what remained being fetid with the urine of rats and mice. The dearth was such that we were compelled to eat the leathers with which the yards of the ships were protected from the friction of the ropes. This leather, too, having been long exposed to the sun, rain, and wind, had become so hard that it was necessary to soften it by immersion in the sea for four or five days, after which it was broiled on the embers and eaten. We had to sustain ourselves by eating sawdust, and a rat was in such request that one was sold for half a ducat."

The first islands Magellan saw were those he named the Ladrones or "Islands of Thieves."* From those he came to the Philippines, and on one of these (Mactan, near Zebu) he was murdered by the na-

---

* Vide Pigafetta in Crawfurd's "Dict. India Islands."

tives, as was also Barbosa, a gentleman of Lisbon, who had previously visited and described India, and from whose writings we have frequently had occasion to quote. From Zebu, Magellan's companions sailed to the northern part of Borneo and Tidore. Thence they continued southward, touching at Bachian and Timur, in 1522, and finally arrived safely back in Spain, having completed the first circumnavigation of our globe. This great voyage was accomplished nearly a century before the Pilgrims landed on our New-England shores. Soon after the Portuguese had established themselves at Ternate, they began to teach the natives their Catholic creed, and in 1535 the native king, who had accepted that religion and been christened at Goa, returned to Ternate and began his reign. Other native princes then proposed to the Portuguese to become Catholics, if they would take them under their protection, and thus Catholicism began to spread rapidly, but the same year all the native converts were destroyed by Mohammedans, headed by Cantalino, who was styled "the Moluccan Vesper." In 1546, Francis Xavier,[*] a Catholic priest, visited Ternate. He afterward went back to Malacca and proceeded to China and Japan, and returning from the latter country died on an island off Macao, near Canton. The Dutch first came to Ternate under Admiral Houtman, in 1578. In 1605, under Stephen van der Hagen, they stormed and took Ternate, and thus drove the Portuguese out of the Moluccas, and the island, since that date, has

---

[*] He has since been canonized, and is worthily considered by his people a model of piety and devotion to the missionary cause.

continued in their hands, the English not being able to capture it during the early part of this century, when they took Amboina and the neighboring islands. They now continued their strenuous attempts to dislodge the Spaniards from their stronghold on Tidore, until the besieged, finding themselves constantly in danger, deserted the whole Moluccas to the Dutch in 1664.

As the Portuguese and Spaniards had been anxious to convert the natives to Catholicism, so the Dutch were anxious to convert them to Protestantism, but they did not, however, labor in the same manner as the former. Pigafetta informs us that in eight days "all the inhabitants of this island" (Zebu, one of the Philippines) "were baptized, and also some of the other neighboring islands. In one of the latter we set fire to a village" (because the inhabitants would neither obey the king of Zebu nor Magellan). "Here we planted a wooden cross, as the people were Gentiles. Had they been Moors" (Arabs), "we should have erected a stone column, in token of their hardness of heart, for the Moors were more difficult of conversion than the Gentiles." In three days after this conversion, these very natives murdered Magellan, and in twelve days more they waylaid and butchered twenty-four of his companions. The natives were first instructed in Protestant doctrines by teachers in 1621, and in 1623 the first Protestant clergyman came into the Moluccas. This faith has made little progress, however, and, except the inhabitants of Haruku, Saparua, and Nusalaut, and small communities at the chief places of Amboina and Ternate, the whole native population east of Celebes is either Mohammedan or heathen.

The islands on which the clove-tree grew spontaneously, and the ones originally known as "the Moluccas," are Ternate, Tidore, Motir, Makian, and Bachian, which are situated in a row off the west coast of the southern half of Gilolo. Of this group Tidore and Bachian, only, belong to the prince of Ternate, and the Dutch East India Company, in order to make the monopoly they already enjoyed more perfect, offered this prince a yearly sum of seventeen thousand four hundred guilders, nearly seven thousand dollars, for the privilege of destroying all the clove and nutmeg trees they could find in his wide territory; for besides these five islands and other smaller ones near them, and also the adjoining coast of Gilolo, where the clove-tree was indigenous, it had been introduced by the natives themselves into Ceram, Buru, and Amboina, before the arrival of the Portuguese. This offer the prince accepted in 1652, perhaps because he could not refuse longer. From that date his power began to decline, and in 1848 he was unable to make the people of the little island of Makian acknowledge his sovereignty, which once extended from north of Gilolo to Buton and Muna south of Celebes, a distance of six hundred geographical miles. His empire also included the western coast of Celebes; and the islands that lie between it and Bachian, Buru, and a large part of Ceram, and one-half the area of Gilolo, were within its limits. For a long time expeditions were fitted out every year by the Dutch, to search each island anew, and destroy all the trees which had sprung up from seed planted by birds. Another such piece of selfishness it would be difficult to find in all history. The result of this agreement and this policy has been that, for a considerable number of years, the income of the government in the Moluccas and Bandas, taken together, has not been nearly equal to its expenses in these islands; and it is now evident to all that very much has been lost by this ungenerous and exclusive mode of trade.

On landing at this village I found a pleasant residence with a good English lady, the second it had been my good fortune to meet since I left Java. After living so long among a people speaking another language, it is a privilege indeed to hear one's native tongue spoken without a foreign accent, and to converse with a person whose religion, education, and views of life accord with one's own. On these outer borders of civilization, Americans and Englishmen are—as we ought to be everywhere—members of the same family.

The same afternoon, as it was clear, I rode with an officer up the mountain to a summer-house, two thousand four hundred feet above the sea. From this high position we had a fine view over the wide bay of Dodinga, formed by the opposite retreating coast of Gilolo. High mountains are seen to rise in the interior, and several of these are said to be volcanoes, either active or extinct. In the northern part of the island, opposite the island of Morti, the Resident informed me that there was a crater which, according to the accounts given him by the officials who had visited it, must be nearly as large as the famous one in the Tenger Mountains on Java. On Morti itself is Mount Tolo, which suffered a severe eruption in the previous century. Before that time Morti was said to be well peopled, but now only the natives of the adjoining coast of Gilolo, who are most notorious pirates, stay there from time to time.

A large number of the natives of Gilolo were then here at Ternate. Though frequently called "Alfura," they are strictly of the Malay type, and have not the dark skin and frizzly hair of the Alfura of Ceram and Buru, though representatives of that people may exist in other parts of Gilolo. Of the whole population of Gilolo, which is supposed to be about twenty-seven thousand, all but five thousand are under the Sultan of Ternate. During the war in Java, from 1825 to 1830, the sultan sent a considerable force of his subjects to assist the Dutch, and those who were then at Ternate had been ordered to come over to hold themselves in readiness to aid in suppressing the revolt in Ceram, for the Dutch believe in the motto "cut diamond with diamond." These natives appear to be quite as mild as most Malays, but the foreigners here say that they fought so persistently while in Java, that soon they were styled "the bloodhounds of Gilolo." A small number of Papuans are also seen in the village. They were mostly brought here from Papua by the fleet that collects the yearly tribute for the Sultan of Tidore. While I was at Amboina a very unfavorable account of them was given by a native captain of

Macassar, who had been taken prisoner near this place. According to his report to the government, when he returned, all his crew was seized and eaten one after another, and the only thing that saved him from a like fate was that he read parts of the Koran. This led them to believe him a priest, and finally induced them to allow him to depart on the next vessel that came to their shores. East of Geelvink Bay two Dutch expeditions have found that the whole population, men, women, and children, always go absolutely naked.

On our right, as we looked toward the east from our lofty position, the steep, conical peak of Tidore was seen rising about six thousand feet above the sea. It is one of the sharpest peaks in all this part of the archipelago. As it has no crater either at the summit or on its sides, there is no vent by which the gases beneath it can find a ready escape. They must therefore remain confined until they have accumulated sufficient power to hurl high into the air the whole mass of ashes, sand, and rock which presses them down. This is exactly what happened at Makian. Professor Reinwardt, who examined this peak in 1821, declared that it would be blown up in twenty years, and, strange to say, it was nineteen years afterward that the terrific eruption of Makian, already described, occurred. As the islands Ternate, Tidore, Motir, and Makian, are only cones standing on the same great fissure in the earth's crust, Professor Reinwardt's prediction was fulfilled almost to the very letter.

The village of Tidore is situated on its southern

side, and is the residence of the sultan, whose territory is no less extensive than that of the Sultan of Ternate. It includes Tidore, Mari, the two eastern peninsulas of Gilolo, Gebi, Misol, Salwatti, Battanta, and the adjacent islands, the western and northern shores of the western peninsula of New Guinea, and the islands in Geelvink Bay. The population of Tidore and Mari is about seven thousand five hundred. The former cultivate the flanks of the mountain up to a height of about three thousand feet. Above this line is a dense wood, but the pointed summit is quite bare. The income of this sultan consists in his share of the produce obtained on Gilolo, in the sago, massoi-bark, tortoise-shell, tripang, and paradise-birds, which are yearly brought from Papua, and the islands between it and Celebes, and in twelve thousand eight hundred guilders (over five thousand dollars) paid him by the Dutch Government, in accordance with the promise made by the East India Company, when they destroyed the spice-trees in his territory. The extension of the empire of Tidore eastward was probably effected by Malays, who migrated in that direction; for it is stated in regard to Misol that the Papuans, who are now driven back into the interior, occupied the whole island when it was first visited by Europeans. This tendency to push on toward the coast is the more interesting, because it is generally supposed that, ages and ages ago, the ancestors of the present Polynesian race passed out from this part of the Malay Archipelago into Micronesia, and thence into the wide area they now occupy. From the northern end of Gilolo, and the adjacent island of Morti (which is really but a part of the northern peninsula), the voyage to Lord North's Island, and thence to the Pelew group, would not be more difficult to accomplish than the piratical expeditions which even the Papuans, an inferior race, are known to have made since the Dutch possessed the Moluccas.

The taxes on paradise-birds* and other articles, levied on Papua and the islands near it, are obtained by a fleet which is sent out each year from the port of Tidore, and which, according to the official reports of the Dutch, carries out the sultan's orders in such a manner that it is little better than a great marauding expedition.

But while we have been engaged in viewing the scene before us, and recalling its history, the hours have been gliding by, and we are admonished to hasten down the mountain by the approaching night. When we reached the village, I was shown a remarkable case of birth-mark on a young child, whose father owned the summer-house we had just visited high up on the mountain. A short time pre-

* Mr. A. R. Wallace, who has travelled more widely than any other naturalist over the region where these magnificent birds are found, gives the following complete list of the species now known, and the places they inhabit: Arru Islands, *P. apoda* and *P. regia;* Misol, *P. regia* and *P. magnifica;* Wagiu, *P. rubra;* Salwatti, *P. regia, P. magnifica, Epimachus albus,* and *Sericulus aureus;* coast regions of New Guinea generally, *Epimachus albus,* and *Sericulus aureus;* central and mountainous regions of the northern peninsula of New Guinea, *Lophorina superba, Parotia sexsetacea, Astrapia nigra, Epimachus magnus, Craspedophora magnifica,* and probably *Diphylloides Wilsonii* and *Paradigalla carunculata.*

vious to the birth of the child, the family were living there. One night a heavy earthquake occurred, and a brilliant cloud was seen rising out of the top of the mountain. Immediately they began to prepare to hasten down, and the mother, being greatly frightened, attempted to run before, but fell heavily on her right arm, bruising it severely in one place. Soon afterward the child was born, and on its right arm, and exactly in the same relative position as where the mother had received the injury from her fall, was found a red spot, or mark, which all agreed had exactly the outline of the bright cloud seen by them on the mountain-top.

The chief articles of export from this place are those brought from the islands to the east, namely, tortoise-shell, tripang, paradise-birds, massoi-bark, and wax. Up to 1837, paradise-birds formed a very important article of export from Ternate. In 1836 over 10,000 guilders' worth were exported, chiefly to China. In 1844 over 10,000 guilders' worth of massoi-bark was exported from this small emporium. It comes from the interior of New Guinea, and is sent to Java, where its aromatic oil is used by the natives in rheumatic diseases. Until 1844, from 14,000 to nearly 70,000 guilders' worth of tortoise-shell was annually exported, chiefly to China; but since that time it has frequently not exceeded 4,000. The chief imports are rice, salt, and cotton goods. A merchant who sends a small vessel each year to Misol, and along the northern coast of Papua, kindly offered me an opportunity to take passage on her; but as it would be about six months before she

would come back to Surabaya, in Java, I was in
doubt whether I ought to go farther east, especially
as Mr. Wallace had obtained little at Dorey, the
only port on the north coast, and besides, it has the
unfavorable reputation of being one of the most
sickly places in the whole archipelago. The two
missionaries stationed at that place are now here,
having been obliged to return on account of repeated and severe attacks of fever. I was told that
the residents of Dorey are only free from this disease when they have a running sore on some part
of the body. While I was thus doubting whither to
direct my course, the man-of-war stationed to watch
for pirates in the Molucca Passage, between this
island and the northern end of Celebes, came into
port. She would return immediately to Kema, a
port on the eastern shore of the northern peninsula
of Celebes, and her commander kindly offered to
take me over to the "Minahassa," as the Dutch call
the northern extremity of that island. I had long
heard this spoken of as decidedly the most charming
part of the archipelago, and probably the most beautiful spot in the world. But a moment was needed,
therefore, to decide whether I would go to the sickly
coast of Papua, or visit that beautiful land, and I accepted the commander's invitation with many thanks.
I had been on this island four days, and we had had
four earthquakes. Indeed, the mountain seemed
preparing for another grand eruption, and I was not
loath to leave its shores. So great is the danger of
its inhabitants being entombed alive by night in the
ruins of their own dwellings, that all the foreigners

have a small sleeping-house in the rear of the one occupied by day. The walls of the larger one are usually of brick or stone, but those of the sleeping-house are always made of *gaba-gaba*, the dried mid-ribs of large palm-leaves, which, when placed on end, will support a considerable weight, and yet are almost as light as cork. The roof is of *atap*, a thatching of dry palm-leaves, and the whole structure is therefore so light that no one would be seriously injured should it fall on its sleeping occupants. Such continual, torturing solicitude changes this place, fitted, by its fine climate, luxuriant vegetation, and beautiful scenery, for a paradise, into a perfect purgatory.

On the morning of the 12th of December we steamed out of the roads for Kema. Soon we passed near the southeast end of Ternate, and the commander pointed out to me a small lake only separated from the sea by a narrow wall, and informed me that when the Portuguese held the island they attempted to cut a canal through the wall or dike, and use this lake as a dock—certainly a very feasible plan; but for some reason, probably because they were so continually at war with their rivals, the Spaniards, they did not carry it out. This lake is said to be deep enough to float the largest ships, and is, I believe, nothing more than an old, extinct crater. On our larboard hand now was Mitarra, a steep volcanic cone as high as the Gunong Api at Banda, but appearing much smaller from being, as it were, beneath the lofty peak of Tidore. It also is of volcanic formation. We now came out into the Molucca Passage, and were steering west, and I could feel that at least my face was turned homeward, a thought sufficient to give any one a deep thrill of pleasure who had wandered so far.

The wind being ahead, and our vessel steaming slowly, we did not expect to see the opposite shore until the next day, much to my satisfaction, for it gave me a good opportunity to learn from the officers many particulars about the pirates in these seas. Piracy has probably existed among these islands ever since they were first peopled. It was undoubtedly plunder, and not trade, that stimulated the natives to attempt the first expedition that was ever made over these waters. Piracy is described in the earliest Malay romances, and spoken of by these natives, not as a failing of their ancestors, but as an occasion for glorying in their brave deeds. Such has also been the case in the most enlightened parts of the earth, when civilization and Christianity had made no further progress in those regions than it has here among the Malays. It has also been prevalent along the northern shores of Europe and the British Isles. The only reason that it was not a common practice among our Indians was because they had not made sufficient progress in the arts to construct large boats, and were obliged to confine their plundering expeditions to rivers and lakes, and could not sail on the stormy ocean.

Pirates have been as numerous on the coasts of China for centuries as they are now. Sometimes they have come to the Philippines and the northern parts of Borneo, but rarely or never among these islands. When the Europeans first came to the East, pirates abounded in every part of the archipelago, particularly in the Straits of Malacca, in the Sulu archipelago, between Borneo and Mindanao, and especially on the southern shores of the latter island. The establishment of a large port at Singapore by the English, and a settlement on Rhio by the Dutch, have quite scattered them from the former region, but they continue to infest the Sulu Sea and the southern part of the Philippines. They come down here in the middle of the western monsoon, that is, in January and February, and return in the beginning of the eastern monsoon, so as to have fair wind both ways, and be here during the calms that prevail in these seas in the changing of the monsoons, when the large number of oars they use enables them to attack their prey as they please. They appear to come mostly from the shores of Lanun Bay, on the south coast of Mindanao. From Dampier we learn that in 1686 they were an inland people. "The Hilanoones," he says, " live in the heart of the country" (Mindanao). "They have little or no commerce by sea, yet they have praus that row with twelve or fourteen oars apiece. They enjoy the benefit of the gold-mines, and, with their gold, buy foreign commodities of the Mindanao people." They are now the most daring pirates in these seas. Last year the man-of-war on this station had the good fortune to surprise five boats, one of them carrying as many as sixty men. At first they attempted to escape by means of their oars, but her shot and shell soon began to tear them to pieces.

They then pulled in toward the shore and jumped overboard, but, by this time, they had come near a village, and the natives at once all turned out with their spears, the only weapons they had, and scoured the woods for these murderers until, as far as could be ascertained, not one of them was left alive. They seldom attack a European vessel, but, when they do and succeed, they take revenge for the severe punishment their countrymen receive from the Dutch war-ships, and not one white man is left to tell the tale of capture and massacre. The vessels that they prey on chiefly are the small schooners commanded by mestizoes and manned by Malays, which carry on most of the trade between the Dutch ports in these islands. One of those vessels was taken and destroyed by these murderers last year while sailing down the coast from Kema. The whites and mestizoes are always murdered, and the Malay crews are kept as slaves. While I was at Kema two Malays appeared at the house of the officer with whom I was residing, and said they were natives of a small village on the bay of Gorontalo; and that, while they were fishing, they had been captured by a fleet of pirates, who soon after set out on their homeward voyage; and, while the fleet was passing Sangir, a small island between the northern end of Celebes and Mindanao, they succeeded in escaping by jumping overboard and swimming a long distance to the shore. They had now reached Kema, on their voyage toward Gorontalo, and they came to the officer to apply for food, clothing, and some means of reaching their homes once more. Such cases are specially provided for by the Dutch Government, and their request was immediately granted. A few years ago these pirates sent a challenge to the Dutch fleet at Batavia to come and meet them in the Strait of Macassar, and several officers assured me that five ships were sent. When they arrived there no pirates were to be seen, but to this day all believe the challenge was a *bona fide* one, and that the only reason that the pirates were not ready to carry out their part was because more men-of-war appeared than they had anticipated. A short time after I arrived back at Batavia, a fleet of these plunderers was destroyed in that very strait. One chief, who was taken on the opposite coast of Borneo a few years ago, acknowledged that he had previously commanded two expeditions to the Macassar Strait, and that, though the Dutch war-ships had destroyed his fleet both times, he had been able to escape by swimming to the shore. At Kema I saw one of the five praus that were taken in that vicinity last year. It was an open boat about fifty feet long, twelve wide, and four deep. There were places for five oars on each side. At the bow and stern was a kind of deck or platform, and in the middle of each a small vertical post, on which was placed a long swivel, throwing a pound-ball. They do not, however, depend on these small cannon, but always get alongside a vessel as soon as possible, and then board her at the same moment on all sides in overpowering numbers. It is almost impossible to catch them unless it is done by surprise, and this they carefully guard against by means of spies on the shore. Our captain informed me that several times when he has suddenly appeared on some part of the adjacent coasts, fires have been instantly lighted on the tops of the neighboring hills, evidently as signals to pirates in the immediate vicinity. As soon as they receive this alarm they hide away in the shallow creeks and bays among the mangrove-trees, so that a war-vessel might steam past them again and again without discovering the slightest indication of where they are concealed. To the Dutch almost exclusively belongs the honor of having rendered the navigation of these seas so comparatively safe as it now is. The English have assisted in the western part of the archipelago, but the Spaniards, from whose territory these marauders now come, have effected little toward removing this pest from the Philippines, where it is as rife as it was two hundred years ago.

CHAPTER X.

THE NORTHERN PENINSULA OF CELEBES.

On the morning of the 13th of December Mount Klabat, a conical volcanic mountain attaining an elevation of six thousand five hundred feet, appeared on the horizon; and soon after, north of Klabat, was seen Mount Sudara, "The Sisters," a twin cone whose highest peak is about four thousand four hundred feet above the sea. North of this again is Batu angus, two thousand three hundred feet in height. Its name in Malay means "the hot rock," but it is really a large volcano, whose top has been blown off and a great crater thus formed; and this shows the fearful fate that awaits each of the other two cones, as soon as the gases pent up beneath their mighty masses have acquired the necessary power. We now approached Limbi, a high, uninhabited island with abrupt shores extending in a northwest and southeast direction, and soon after came to anchor in the road off Kema, the coast here curving inward so as to form a small bay. This is the port used now in the western monsoon. During the eastern monsoon, steamers and ships go round the northern end of Celebes to Menado, in the Strait of Macassar. Kema is a village of two thousand inhabitants. Its streets are very broad, and cross each other at right angles. The houses are well built, and placed on piles twelve or eighteen inches in diameter and six feet high—a remnant of the old custom of placing their huts on high posts to avoid attacks of enemies, which was practised by these people previous to the arrival of Europeans. It is certainly a good custom, not only because all such unwelcome intruders as the large snakes, which are very numerous here, are thus avoided, but also to keep the house dry and cool, by allowing a free circulation of air beneath. Each house has a small plot of ground, and this is separated from that of its neighbor by hedges, which also border the streets, and give the whole village a charming air compared to the irregular, unsightly appearance of those I had been visiting. Most of the streets are also lined with shade-trees, and in the gardens, behind the hedges, are rows of orange-trees, some of their branches bearing flowers, some green fruit, and some drooping under the abundance of their golden-yellow loads.

The *controleur* here kindly received me into his house. He was just going to Limbi, an island five or six miles north of Kema, to try to take some living *babirusa* for the governor-general's garden at Buitenzorg, back of Batavia. That was exactly such an excursion as suited my fancy, and I was very willing to accept his invitation to join him before I began a journey I had been planning over to Menado, and thence up into the interior. While we were preparing for our excursion, another gentleman, Mr. K., decided to join us.

December 20th.—A bright, clear day, and just suitable for starting on our hunt. We have a ship's long-boat and a small prau, both containing about twenty natives, and a large pack of dogs to start up the game. The *controleur* is the captain of our boat, and an old, gray Malay, who has been a seaman and a whaler for most of his days, is the coxswain of the other, and pilot for both. For ballast we have a full load of rice, our two boats carrying only half the whole party, the other portion—twenty-five natives and half as many dogs—went yesterday, under the charge of the second native chief of the village, who rejoices in the euphonious title of *Hukom kadua*, but the Dutch call him the "Second Head." From Kema up to the strait, between Limbi and Celebes, we had a light air off the shore. A thin cloud, like a veil of gauze, gathered on the heads of the twin-peaks known as "The Sisters," and fell down in rich graceful folds over their green shoulders. From the crests of all these peaks, down to the high-water line on the shore, is one dense, unbroken forest. There dwells the *sapi utung* or "wild ox," probably not indigenous, but descended from the tame sapi introduced from Java and Madura. The natives describe them as being exceedingly fierce, both the cows and the bulls. Here that peculiar antelope, the *Anoa depressicornis*, H. Smith, abounds. In these same dense, undisturbed forests the babirusa (*Babirusa alfurus*, Less.) is found in large numbers; and a species of *Sus*, much like the lean hog that lives in the forests of our Southern States, is very abundant. As soon as we entered the strait we found a strong current against us, and landed on the south side in a small bay to take our lunch. Again we rowed and beat until we came to the narrowest part of the strait, where high, perpendicular walls of rock rise on either hand. The tide which sets toward the east, that is before the wind, now changed, and away we shot between the overhanging crags with the speed of an arrow. Outside of these narrows the shores open on both sides, so that almost at once we were exposed to the full strength of the stormy monsoon. The strong tide running against the wind rolled up a high, irregular sea; in fact, the ocean seemed to boil. "Have you any idea that we can land on that exposed shore in the midst of such a surf?" I asked the *controleur*. "Well, it is getting dreadfully rough," was his indefinite reply. The old Malay pilot, who had kept his boat ahead, now stood up, and seeing the combing waves, into which the strong current was rapidly driving us, shouted out to the *controleur*, "*Dra bisa Tuan!*" "It is impossible, sir! It is impossible, sir!" Instantly we tacked and stood over toward the Celebes side, and, under the guidance of the old whaler, soon entered a small, well-sheltered bay. Near its middle part the island of Limbi is very narrow, and across that place had been stretched a series of strong nets made of rope a quarter of an inch in diameter, the meshes being about six inches square. Our plan was to commence driving at the northern end of the island and force the wild babirusas into this trap; but it was already quite dark, and the place where the *hukom* had landed was a long way to windward, and we therefore concluded to camp here to-night. For a tent we cut poles from the neighboring bunches of bamboo and covered them with the boat's sail and an old tarpaulin. Our friend K., who was extremely careful not to boast of being a good sailor, became exceedingly frightened while we were in the midst of the combing waves, and asked me, half a dozen times during the evening, if the tide would not rise so high as to wash us off this steep shore before morning, but I tried to quiet his nerves by assuring him that such a thing could not happen unless the earth should sink, a very possible thing now that I come to think of it, for that very beach was composed of black volcanic sand, and we were almost beneath a cone, which rose on the flanks of *Batu angus*, and had been formed so recently that even the luxuriant vegetation of these tropics had not yet had time to gain a footing on its dark sides. In order to get a partial shelter from the heavy showers we expected before morning, we pitched our camp beneath the sturdy branches of an old tree. There we slept while the wind, in heavy gusts, sighed through the dense foliage over our heads, and at our feet rose the heavy, pulsating roar of the ocean-surf.

December 21st. — After passing a comfortable night, notwithstanding the fears of our companion that we should awake before morning, and find ourselves in the midst of the sea, we again attempted to reach the northern end of Limbi, but, as soon as we got out of the bay, we struck into such a heavy sea that our men could not take us to windward, and were therefore obliged to put back once more. This time, to vary the scenery, we passed through the narrows, and encamped on a charming little beach on the island side of the strait, between two high, precipitous crags. Our first care was, of course, to construct a tent, a work soon finished by our large crew. At 11 A. M. we all felt a heavy earthquake-shock, which lasted, apparently, thirty seconds; but these are frequent phenomena in this part of Celebes. On the 25th of last month, not four weeks ago, there was a very heavy earthquake over the whole Minahassa. At Kema we could still see great rents in the ground, three or four inches wide, which could be traced for several rods. The shock was so severe that nearly every article of glass or earthen-ware in the *controleur's* house was broken into fragments. Indeed, as I look up now toward the west, I do not wonder the earth heaves beneath us like a troubled sea; for there rises the old volcano known in olden times as Mount Tonkoko. It has a great yawning crater, six hundred feet deep, out of which are rising thick, white clouds of gas. On the northwest side a deep ravine cuts through its flanks, and opens out into the crater. Farther down this same side is the new cone, beneath which we pitched our camp last night. In 1806 a great eruption began in this old volcano, and ashes, sand, and pumice-stone were thrown out in great quantities. At Ayar-madidi the ashes were fine and of a gray color, and covered the ground with a layer an inch thick. For two days the heavens were darkened by the great quantity of these light materials floating in the air. So many stones were ejected, that at a distance of nearly three miles a new cone was formed, from which a long tongue of land stretched itself into the sea. This point the natives called *Batu angus*, "the Hot Rock," and since that time the whole volcano has been known by that name. Some of the pumice-stones were said to have been as large as the native huts, but so changed into a kind of foam by the action of heat, that they readily floated on the sea.

Soon after sunset I went out to fish in a small canoe with the *controleur* and his old pilot. The place we chose was under a high, perpendicular precipice that rose up out of the dark water like an artificial wall. Here we remained while the rocks grew higher and higher and more and more overhanging as the daylight faded, and the approaching night blended the sharp outlines and increased the magnitude of every object around us. Near by was a deep ravine, and from its farthermost recesses rolled out the reverberating, moaning cries of monkeys, who all night long keep up a piteous calling, each answering his fellow in the same mournful tones.

Our lines were just about as large as a mackerel-line. The hooks each native makes for himself, from brass wire, and about a fathom of wire is attached to each hook before the line is fastened to it, in order to prevent the fish from severing the cord with their sharp teeth. For bait, small fish are taken. In fishing at anchor, no leads are used, but, instead of them, a kind of sling of palm-leaf is fastened to each hook. This sling contains a small stone, so fixed that it will carry down the line, but drop out as soon as it touches the bottom. After we had obtained a good supply of fine fish, we slowly passed along the high, well-sheltered shore, while the heavy wind sighed through the lofty branches over our heads. Now a gleam of light comes over the dark water, just beyond that high bluff; we are near the camp, and in a few moments stand again on the beach. This day is done, and yet the storm continues, but we hope we may be more favored to-morrow.

December 22*d.*—Last night I soon fell asleep after such vigorous use of the paddle, though the storm wailed, and my couch was any thing but a bed of down. At midnight a troubled dream disturbed my brain. An indefinite horror thrilled along my veins as I fancied for a moment that I was whirling round such a deep yawning maelstrom as Poe has pictured, and then literally "a change came o'er the spirit of my dream," but scarcely a change for the better, for I was fixed in the midst of a water-spout, and, in my struggles to escape, awoke and found a great stream of water pouring down on me from the tarpaulin that formed the roof of our tent. A heavy shower had come on, and the water was all running into a depression in the sail over me, in which, of course, there was a hole, so that the whole formed one big tunnel. Of course, both K. and the *controleur* enjoyed my discomfiture greatly, but I consoled myself with the thought that long before daylight they would find themselves in the same plight; and the next morning, apparently, the thing that was farthest from their thoughts was to inquire of me in regard to the water-spout.

That portion of the party that had left Kema in

advance of us had taken little rice. The *controleur*, therefore, thought we must make a third attempt to reach the northern end of the island, notwithstanding K.'s earnest entreaties to be only taken back to Kema once more. We had not reached the narrows, however, before we met the hukom with all his men and dogs. They had found the surf so high that the only way most of his men had been able to reach their boats, was to run down the steep rocks and plunge head foremost into the combing waves. We now landed a few natives to scour the woods, and finally come to the southern end of the island, while we went round in the boats. In order to make their way through the dense forest, instead of putting on more clothing as a protection against the sticks and stones and thorny vines, they stripped off what little they wore, except a narrow band over the loins. At the southern end of the island was a small, deep bay, and here we encamped for the third time. Soon the natives came in, but they had secured only two wild hogs. I preserved the skull of one, a female, in which the canine teeth were not as long as those of a male. The hukom declared that in the babirusa only the males have the long curved teeth, which the Malays have fancied resemble the antlers of a deer. While waiting for us, he had been hunting in the vicinity of his camp, and had taken one female by driving her to the end of a high point. As soon as she saw there was no chance for her to escape, she leaped down the precipice and was killed by the fall. Such suicide, he says, is frequently resorted to by that animal when it finds it can retreat no farther.

The wild hogs plunge into the water to avoid the dogs, and the natives then pursue them in boats and kill them with spears. As soon as the hunters return to camp, they cut up the hogs, and smoke the pieces over a smouldering fire. The dogs now skulk about to seize a piece if possible, and while the natives are crouching round the fire transforming the lean pork into tough bacon, you are frequently startled by a sharp yelping as some one finds his portion disappearing beneath the jaws of one of these hungry brutes, and a liberal chastisement is at once administered to the thief with the first stick or club at hand.

December 23d.—Last night there was another heavy shower. The water poured down in torrents through our thatching of palm-leaves, for we had already found that both the boat's sail and the old tarpaulin afforded little protection here where the water appears to fall in broad sheets. Late in the evening the *controleur* came back from fishing. We could hear the Malays that were pulling his boat singing in an unusually loud and merry style, and all gathered on the beach to see what wonderful monster of the deep they had secured. It proved to be a fish as large as a horse-mackerel, and weighing fully two hundred pounds, which the *controleur* had succeeded in taking with a small line by chancing to get it alongside the boat and securing it by gaffs. As our stock of rice was getting low, we decided to return, though I could scarcely feel satisfied, for I had hoped to get a complete skeleton of the rare babirusa; however, the *controleur* more than made up the loss by giving me half a dozen skulls of the equally rare antelope of this region. We now crossed over to the Celebes side to a village of four or five huts, to be sheltered from the heavy rains that have drenched us every night but one since we left Kema. A few natives have moved here from Kema because they take many fish off this part of the coast, and there is a small stream emptying into the sea in the vicinity. They live almost wholly by fishing, and have cleared only a small place near their houses for a garden of Indian corn. This evening they have shown me one of the monsters of these forests. It was an enormous python. Its head has been taken off, but by careful measurement I find it must have been at least fifteen feet long. It was killed here the day before yesterday by one of the natives living in the house where we are now sheltered from the rain. Missing his dog, he chanced to go to the brook where they get water, and there he found this monstrous reptile trying to swallow his favorite. As quietly as possible he stole back to the village and gave the alarm, and at once all went out and succeeded in cutting off its head before it could disgorge its prey and attack them. The natives are now taking off the skin to make rude moccasins, which they frequently use when hunting in the woods, or more especially when travelling through the tall, sharp-edged prairie-grass. They all agree that this tough, scaly skin is much more durable for such a purpose than the best kind of leather. Our old boatman tells me that he once killed one of those great reptiles on Limbi, while it was trying to swallow a wild pig. All the natives assert that this monster sometimes attacks the wild ox, *sapi utung*, though none of them have ever seen such a dreadful combat. The *controleur* states to me that when he was stationed at Bachian, near the southern end of Gilolo, he was once out hunting deer, at a place called Patola, with a large party of natives. They had succeeded in starting up several, and he himself saw one of them pass under a tree and at the same instant a great snake came down from one of the lower limbs and caught the flying deer with his jaws. Unfolding his tail from the limb, he instantly wound round his victim, crushing its bones as if they were straw. An alarm was given, and the natives gathered with their spears and killed the great reptile on the spot. It was not as large round as this one, but longer. Many of our men tell me that they once assisted in killing a larger snake than this at the bathing-place back of Kema. It had seized a hog, whose squealing soon gave all the inhabitants a warning of what had happened. They also say (and this remarkable story has since been repeated to me by several other persons at Kema) that a few years ago a native boy went out as usual to work in his *ladang*, or garden, some distance from the village. At night he did not return, and the next morning a native chanced to pass the garden and saw one of these great monsters trying to swallow the boy head first, having already crushed the bones of its victim. He at once returned to the village, and a large party of natives went out and found the snake and its prey exactly as had been reported, and immediately killed it with such weapons as they had, and gave the body of their young friend a decent burial.

While they were telling me these stories I thought of the danger to which I must often have been unconsciously exposed while wandering mile after mile through the jungles on Buru, never suspecting that, before I left the archipelago, I myself should be forced into a deadful combat with one of these monsters, and in such a place that one or the other must die on the spot.

The next day we returned to Kema, and I began my journey over the peninsula to Menado, and thence up to the plateau in the interior.

December 26th.—At 9 A. M. started on horseback, the only mode of travelling in the Minahassa, for Menado, the largest village in this peninsula of Celebes, and the place where the Resident of this region is located. I went there first, in order to see the Resident and obtain letters to the officials of the interior. The distance from Kema to Menado is about twenty miles. The road is made only for carts, but nearly all the way it is lined with shade-trees, and in several places, for long distances, they meet overhead so as to form a continuous covered way, thus affording to those who travel to and fro an admirable shelter from the hot sunshine and heavy showers. Among these trees were many crows, *Corvus enka*, not shy as they always are in our country, but so tame that I frequently rode within ten yards of where they were sitting without causing them to move. Numbers of a bright-yellow bird, about as large as our robin, were seen among the branches, and on the ground another somewhat larger than a blackbird, *Dicrurus*, with a long, lyre-shaped tail, and a plumage of shining blue-black.

These birds rarely or never hear the report of a gun, and therefore have not learned to look on man as a universal destroyer, and the tameness they manifest is perfectly charming. Even the black crow, with its hoarse caw, becomes an attractive bird when you find he no longer tries to shun your company, but makes all the overtures he can to be social.

The road runs along the southern flanks of Mount Klabat, and is slowly ascending from Kema to Ayar-madidi, which is about half-way across, and then slowly descends again to the western shore of the peninsula. On my right hand was a deep valley, and fine scenery was occasionally revealed through the foliage of the trees that covered the way. On the opposite side of the valley were many small projecting ridges that have been formed by denuding torrents, and extend down to the level of the stream that flows out from the lake of Tondano to the ocean at Kema.

By noon I came to the village of Ayar-madidi, "Hot Water," a name it receives from a neighboring spring, which in former times was hot. As it comes out of Mount Klabat, it was probably heated by the volcanic action that raised that great mountain, which is only an extinct volcano. As the volcanic action decreased, the heat passed off, until now, the water is as cool as that of any other stream in the vicinity. Even as late as the 12th of November, 1848, this water was described as "cooking hot." According to Valentyn, in the year 1683, a great eruption took place in a mountain near Menado, which he calls "Kemaas," and all the surrounding country was laid waste. "Kemaas" Dr. Junghuhn has supposed to be Klabat, but he never visited this region, and the conical summit of Klabat shows its destruction by heavy eruptions has not yet begun. It is far more probable that Kemaas was the mountain now known as Sudara, whose two peaks are only the fragments of the upper part of the cone that were left standing when the eruptive force blew off the other parts, or so weakened their foundations, that they have long since fallen, and the materials of which they were composed have been brought down, and spread out by the rains over the flanks of the mountain. Natives, who have been to the top of Klabat, inform me that there is a small lake on the northwest side. Its basin is, no doubt, that part of the old crater which has not yet been filled so as to make the whole elevation a perfect cone. If this lake was of any considerable size, then, as occurred on Mount Papandayang, in Java, mud and hot water will certainly pour down the sides of this mountain, if it is again convulsed by the mighty forces that are now slumbering beneath it. Ayar-madidi is a large *kampong*, or *negri*, as the Malays sometimes call their villages. It is beautifully situated on the southern flanks of Mount Klabat. Its streets all cross each other at right angles, and are well shaded. So far as we are aware, the Malays and Javanese had no word for village previous to the arrival of the Telingas, and it has been conjectured, from this fact, that they were scattered everywhere over their particular territories exactly as we have seen is the custom of the aborigines of Buru, the Alfura, who have been beyond the influence of both Hindus and Arabs, and even of those natives who have adopted any foreign religion or custom. Ayar-madidi is a prettier village than Kema. Indeed, the more I travelled in the Minahassa, the more I admired the kampongs, they are so incomparably superior to those of every other part of the archipelago in the regularity of their streets and the beautiful hedges with which they are lined, and, above all, in the neatness and evidence of thrift that everywhere appear.

The chief native of this village is also the chief of the district, which contains several villages. His title in the native language is *Hukom Biza*, or "Great Chief," though he prefers to be addressed by the Dutch title of major. The native official next in rank is the chief of one of the smaller villages, as at Kema. His title is *Hukom Kadua*. At smaller villages than Kema the chief is called *Hukom Tua*, or "Old Hukom," and beneath him is the *Hukom Kachil*, or Little Hukom. These officers are nominally elected by the natives, but the choice is generally confined to the sons of the deceased.

The Majors and Second Heads receive a percentage on all the coffee raised and delivered to the government. This amounts to about twenty thousand guilders per year for the seventeen districts in the whole Minahassa. Besides this income, the Major receives one guilder, and the Second Head half a guilder from each family in their respective districts and sub-districts, and the *Hukom Tua* five days' labor from each able-bodied man yearly.

The natives themselves are divided by the Dutch

into burgers or "free citizens," and inlanders or "natives," who are obliged to work a certain number of days in the coffee-gardens belonging to the government. The total population of the Minahassa in this year (1866), as furnished me by the Resident from the official documents, is 104,418,* and the marked degree of variation in the population of this country, where the natives have never been a maritime people, is worth more than a passing notice, because it shows in some degree the beneficial effect of a stable government, and how the natives are sometimes swept away by disease. In 1800, according to Valentyn, the population was 24,000, though he gives the number of able men at only 3,990. In 1825 it was 73,000; in 1842, 93,332; in 1853, 99,588. In 1854 a great mortality appeared, and the population was diminished to 92,546, no less than 12,821 persons, or about one-seventh of the population, having died in a single year. In the district of Amurang the loss was as high as 22¼ per cent. The principal diseases are fevers and dysentery. The population of the Minahassa, as compared to its area, 14,000 English square miles, is by no means large. The island of Madura, which is of about the same extent, has more than five times as large a population; and the residency of Surabaya, also of about the same extent, contains more than ten times as many people. The natives directed me to the major's residence, which I found to be a small but neat and well-painted house, built in European

* This number is divided according to nationalities as follows: Europeans, 550; natives, 102,423; Chinese, 1,434; Arabs, 11.

style. It is situated in the middle of a large, oblong lawn, that is surrounded with a row of trees much like our locust-trees, and which are now in full bloom. Near the gate are a guard-house and long series of stables. Dismounting here, I walked up to the broad piazza, where the major sat smoking his pipe in the Dutch style, and discussing in the Dutch language the state of the weather, the crops, and such things as interested the Dutchmen of those lands. His manners were polished, and he received me in a most stately way. His friends were going to Menado, so that I should have companions the rest of the way. Our dinner was in European style, which seemed the more remarkable to me because it differed so much from the way I had been entertained by the rajahs of the Moluccas. In our dining-room was a fine series of pictures representing scenes in that most charming tale, "Paul and Virginia." We were just at the foot of Mount Klabat, but we could not see its summit on account of thick rain-clouds that covered its sides, and now and then rolled down and poured out heavy showers over the village. As one of these floated away to the east, the sun came out brightly and changed the falling drops into a remarkably broad and brilliant rainbow, which seemed suspended from the cloud, and floated along with it in a most magical manner.

Here I saw for the first time the plant from which "manilla hemp" is manufactured. It is a species of banana, *Musa textilis*, and grows to a height of twelve or fifteen feet. It appears to be indigenous, and can be raised here from the seed.

The fibres are taken from the large, succulent leaves. Though it resembles the banana so closely that at first most people would mistake it for that plant, its fruit is small, disagreeable to the taste, and not edible. Several residents have made strenuous efforts to extend its cultivation, but the result has shown that the natives can be more profitably employed in raising coffee. The rain-clouds having cleared away, we all started for Menado. The horse that had been kindly furnished me by an officer was not fast nor sure-footed; and, finally, as we were going down a gentle declivity at a quick canter, he fell headlong. As I am, at least, a much better sailor than horseman, I went off over his head with a most surprising momentum, my feet, unfortunately, passing so far into the stirrups that I could not extricate either of them. This so frightened the horse that he reared and plunged fearfully, but I had no idea of being dragged off like Mazeppa, and held on to the reins until my feet were once more clear, when, with one leap, I was again in the saddle, and ready for further experience in this mode of travelling. Though I was aware my position was somewhat dangerous, I could not help feeling amused at the alarm manifested by my companions. They all seemed delighted to know that I had escaped with only such inconvenience as one clad in a summer suit of white would necessarily experience in coming down in such an unceremonious manner into the midst of a muddy stream. Late in the evening we came to the Resident's house, where a cordial welcome awaited me, and I had the pleasure to find myself once more in the midst of a pleasant family after so long and lonely an exile.

The next morning I walked through the village. Its total population is only about 2,500, of which 300 are Europeans and mestizoes; about 600 Chinamen, and 1,200 natives, half of whom are Christians and the other half Mohammedans. The Resident's house is surrounded by large grounds, abounding in the choicest of tropical plants. Not far from it is the market, a house without walls, the roof resting on pillars of wood and masonry. This is the universal style of the markets in all parts of the archipelago. Here various kinds of fruits, gambier, betel-nuts, and siri are sold by the natives, and salt, cotton fabrics, and cutlery, by Chinese. The salt used here is not imported from Java, as that used on the other islands I have visited, but is made by the natives themselves in the following manner: Littoral-plants are gathered and burned. The ashes are then placed in a bamboo, which is filled with water. After this has remained for some time, the water is strained off and evaporated. The residuum is a dark, impure salt, but the natives prefer it to any that can be imported. This custom seems to have been introduced lately, for in 1841 the government sold three hundred and twelve thousand pounds of imported salt, but in 1853 only two thousand. From the village of Menado I walked northward parallel to the bay, and, crossing the little stream Menado, came to the village of the Bantiks, a peculiar people, numbering about two thousand five hundred, who refuse to become Mohammedans or Christians, and continue to retain the heathen belief of their forefathers. Many of them are taller than the other people I saw in the Minahassa. Their houses are not placed on higher posts than those of other natives, but they are frequently long, and occupied by several families—a custom which appears to have been general throughout the archipelago in ancient times, and is still practised at Dorey, on the north coast of New Guinea, and again by the people of the Tenger Mountains in Java, who pride themselves on retaining the customs of their ancestors. The view has been advanced that the Bantiks are descendants of Chinamen, who established themselves here when they first came to the Moluccas to purchase spices. This may have been the case, but their features, though somewhat different from the other natives, did not appear to me to be so unlike them as to necessitate such a theory. As they have kept themselves more away from the influence of all foreigners than most Malays, they give us a good idea of what the aborigines of this region were before the arrival of the Portuguese.

About three miles round the northern side bay, we came to Temumpa, where all the lepers of this residency are obliged to live, banished forever from all communication with other natives, except such of their friends as come to see them. The little village consists of twelve small houses, regularly arranged on either side of a street. They were all neatly whitewashed, and each has a small plot of ground, where its unfortunate occupants can busy themselves, and forget their incurable sufferings and their ban ishment. A native who lives near by has charge of them, and my opinion was very decided that they were well cared for by the government. As we passed from house to house, the officer called them out, and I gave each a small piece of silver, for which they appeared very grateful. There are now nineteen here afflicted with this loathsome malady. The part that appears to be the first attacked is the nose, the next is the hands, and the last the feet, though in some it only appears in one of these organs. In one case the nose had wholly disappeared—even the partition between the nostrils—so that I could look directly into the chamber over the mouth. At the same time the muscles on one side of the face were so contracted that the features presented a most sickening sight. In another case, the nose and all the upper lip were gone, and even the outer part of the upper jaw, so that the front teeth only stuck fast on one side, and were completely exposed to view throughout their entire length. These, however, were the older cases, in which the disease had made greater progress. Many had lost their fingers and toes. One little girl had her ankles and feet so swollen that her ankle-bones could not be seen, and yet I could not but notice how cheerful she appeared. Two men had the disease in their feet, which had swollen until they were three times their proper size, and all broken open and fissured in the most shocking manner. No one who has not seen such lepers as these can have any idea of what forms human flesh can assume, and life yet remain in the body. Suffering from such an incurable, loathsome malady is literally a living death. I found it so sickening, even to look at them, that I was glad when I came to the last house. Here I was shown a young child, a few weeks old. No marks of the disease could be detected, unless it might be that it was very much lighter colored than either of its parents. The father was one of the worst cases I saw, but the disease had not appeared in the mother, except as a great swelling in the ankles. This child must certainly die a leper, and probably will never leave the village where it was born. For this reason, if for no other, the government certainly acts wisely in compelling all who have this disease to come and live here together, where, at all events, it cannot be widely spread. When it does not appear in a very malignant form in the parents, it has been known to fail to appear in the children, but to appear again in the grandchildren. Governor Arriens told me of such a case in Java. It was evident that the man was a leper, though only a considerable swelling could be detected on one ear, yet he was able to prove that neither of his parents was a leper, but, on further inquiry, the governor found that the man's grandfather was a leper. This disease is regarded here as an endemic, that is, chiefly confined to the Minahassa and the Moluccas. Much discussion has arisen whether leprosy is contagious. The doctor with whom I resided while at Buru had been previously stationed at Amboina, and while there a soldier who was born in Holland was taken, and died with this disease. In that case it was evident that the disease was not hereditary, and, after the most careful inquiry, the doctor was not able to learn that he had ever been near a leper, or that he might have taken the disease from any one; for all afflicted with this loathsome malady in Amboina and the neighboring islands are banished to Molano, a small island southwest of Saparua. This is the only case that I heard of, during my travels among these islands, where a foreigner had suffered from this disease. It may be remarked that this is not the leprosy spoken of in the sacred Scriptures, where the sufferers are described as being "white as snow."

From the shore near Temumpa we had a delightful view over the bay of Menado. The sea was as smooth as glass, and scarcely a ripple broke on the sandy beach, which was shaded by graceful, overhanging palms. Before me to the south rose the high mountains which form the great buttresses to the plateau they enclose, and on my right was the sharp volcanic peak called Old Menado because foreigners first established themselves on that island, and then moved over to Celebes.

In the evening the Resident showed me the large wooden store-houses where the coffee is received from the interior, and kept for exportation. As we entered the building, I was surprised at the rich aromatic fragrance that filled the air. It differed much more from the fragrance given out by the coffee seen in our land than any one will readily believe. Here it is stored in bags, just as it comes in from the plantations. In order that I might see what superior coffee the Minahassa produces, the Resident had several bags opened. I found the kernels, instead of being opaque, and having, as when we usually see them, a tinge of bronze, were translucent, and of a greenish-blue color. The best are those which have these characters, and at the same time are very hard. This coffee commands a much higher price than that of Java, and is superior to any raised in the archipelago, unless it may be some that comes from the highlands in the interior of Sumatra.

The coffee crop is subject to some variation, but the Resident informs me that the average yield of the government gardens during the last few years has been no less than 37,000 piculs (5,000,000 pounds). The whole number of trees belonging to the government is 5,949,616, but a large proportion of these are young, and therefore bear little or no fruit. Several private individuals also own large plantations, that yield as well in proportion to the number of trees they contain. The trees are found to thrive best above an elevation of one thousand feet.

The native name of this plant and its fruit is *kopi*, a corruption of the name in Dutch, the people who introduced it into this archipelago. The tree, *Coffea Arabica*, is a native of Africa, between the tenth and fifteenth degrees of north latitude,[*] but it thrives anywhere within the tropics on the hundreds of high islands in the archipelago, as well as in the dry lands where it is indigenous. It was as late as 1450, about half a century before the discovery of our continent, that it was brought over from Abyssinia to the mountainous parts of Arabia. In this way it happened that the Arabians were the people who introduced it

[*] Crawfurd's "Dictionary of the India Islands."

into Europe. In 1690, forty years after, the people of Europe had learned to use it as a beverage. Governor-General Van Hoorne had some of the seeds brought to him from ports on the Arabian Gulf, by the vessels of the Dutch East India Company, who then carried on some trade between those places and Java. The seeds were planted in a garden near Batavia, where the plants flourished well and bore so much fruit that their culture was at once begun, and since that time has spread to many parts of the archipelago, but the chief islands from which coffee is now exported are Celebes, Bali, Java, and Sumatra. It is also raised to some extent in the Philippines, and these and the Malay Islands furnish one-fourth or more of all that is used. One of the first plants raised at Batavia was sent to Holland, to Nicholas Witsen, the head of the East India Company, where it arrived safely and bore fruit, and the plants from its seeds were sent to Surinam, where they flourished, and in 1718 coffee began to be an article of export from that part. Ten years later, in 1728, it was introduced from Surinam into the French and English islands of the West Indies, having previously been successively introduced into Arabia, Java, and Holland. I am told that it was first brought here from Java by a native prince, and, the remarkable manner in which it thrived having attracted the attention of the officials, more trees were introduced. In 1822 only eighty piculs were produced; in 1834. a remarkably favorable year, 10,000, but in the next year only 4,000 were obtained. In 1853 the crop was 13,000 piculs, and in 1854, 23,000. This indicates how remarkably this crop varies in the same locality—in that year the total number of trees was 4,600,000—and that there has been a steady increase since, both in the number of trees and in the quantity of fruit they have yielded; but yet not more than one-half the number are planted that might be if the population was sufficiently great to take proper care of them. With such an enormous yield a large surplus is left in the hands of the government after it has paid the natives who cultivate it, the percentage to the chiefs, and the cost of transportation from the small store-houses in the interior to the large ones at Menado, from which it is put on board of vessels either directly for foreign ports or to be taken to Macassar and thence be reshipped to Europe. Though the government wishes to give up its monopoly in the cultivation of spices in the Bandas and Moluccas, I did not hear that it is particularly anxious to do so here with the profitable cultivation of coffee.

From the store-houses we walked to the hospital, where I was shown a patient whose case was most remarkable. He was a native of Kema, and was bathing in one of the streams that flow through the village, when suddenly he found his head between the teeth of an enormous crocodile. Fortunately, the great reptile did not close his jaws, nor settle down with his prey as usual, and another native, hearing the cries of his friend, caught a large stick, and beat the brute until he let go. The man was at once brought here to the hospital, and has now nearly recovered. On his left jaw-bone there was one continuous incision from the ear to the chin, and on the right side of his face the muscles near the cheek-bone and on the temple were dreadfully lacerated. That a man should ever escape alive after his head had once been between a crocodile's jaws is certainly the next thing to a miracle. I asked him what he thought when he found his head in such a vice. "Well," said he, coolly, "I thought my time had come, but that I had better sing out while I could, and that's what saved me, you see."

December 28th.—At 6 A. M. bade the Resident good-by, and started for the highlands in the interior with an *opas* or official servant as a guide and attendant. It was a lovely morning. The cuckoos were pouring out their early songs, and the gurgling of the brook by the wayside was almost the only other sound that disturbed the stillness of the morning. A few cirri were floating high in the sky, and also a number of cumuli, whose perpendicular sides reflected the bright sunlight like pearly, opaque crystals. Along the way we met natives of both sexes carrying tobacco and vegetables to market, the men having their loads in a sled-shaped frame on their backs, and the women carrying theirs in shallow baskets on their heads. Our road, which led to the south, was—like all in the Minahassa—broad and well graded, and where it ascended an acclivity coarse fibres from the leaves of the *gomuti* palm were laid across it from place to place to cause the water to drain off into the ditches by its sides. When the road came to a village it always divided, that all the carts may go round the village, and not through it. This arrangement enables the natives to keep the street through their village neat and smooth. Such streets usually consist of a narrow road, bordered on either side by a band of green turf, and outside of these are sidewalks of naked soil like the road. Six miles out we came to Lotta, a village of about four hundred souls, and soon after began to rapidly ascend by a well-built road, that zigzags up the sides of Mount Empung, which forms one of the northern buttresses of the plateau situated to the south and east. Nine *paals* from Menado, when we were about twelve hundred feet above the sea, I wheeled round my horse and enjoyed a magnificent view over the bay of Menado and the adjacent shore. Out in the bay rose several high islands, among them the volcanic peak of Menado Tua, its head raised high in the blue sky, and its feet bathed in the blue sea. Near the shore the land is very low, and abounds in various species of palms. Farther back it begins to rise, and soon curves up toward the lofty peak of Klabat.

The beautiful cirri which we had noticed in the early morning now began to change into rain-clouds, and roll down the mountain, and soon the beautiful landscape beneath us was entirely hidden from our view. The road here passes through deep cuts that show well the various kinds of rocks, which are trachytic sand, pumice-stone, and a conglomerate of these materials. As we ascended we passed many places on the mountain-side where the natives were cultivating maize, and from far above us and beneath us came the echoing and reëchoing songs of the natives, who were busy cultivating this exotic but most useful plant. The custom of these people to sing while working in the field is the more noticeable, because the Javanese and Malays usually toil without thinking of thus lightening their monotonous labor. Upward and upward we climbed until we were about three thousand feet above the sea, when we came to two small villages. Beyond, the road again became level, and soon we reached Tomohon, where I met the *controleur* from Tondano, a large village to the east, who had come at the Resident's request to accompany me for the rest of that day's journey. Another horse was brought and saddled for me, and we continued on toward the south, our party now numbering six or eight, for the chief of each village and one or two servants are obliged by law to accompany the *controleur* from their own village to the next one he comes to, in whatever direction he may choose to travel. We soon after entered the charming village of Saronsong. In the centre of it and on one side of the street is the chief's house, and opposite to it but back from the street is the *ruma négri*, and the space between the two is a pretty garden abounding in roses. This reminder of home gave me a thrill of pleasure that I shall remember as long as I love to look on this, the most beautiful of all flowers. As we galloped out of this village the thick rain-clouds and fog cleared away, and only cumuli and cirri were again to be seen in the sky. I now had a magnificent view, on the left, of the high range along the west side of lake Tondano, toward the northwest of the sharp volcanic cone of Lohon, about five thousand feet in height, west of that of Empung, attaining nearly that height, and in the northeast Gunong Api with its three peaks. Somewhat farther on we rode down into a little valley, where the road ran along the side of a small lake, whose muddy water was of a dirty-white color, and from which strong, almost strangling, fumes of sulphur were rising—a most unearthly place, and one that would remind the traveller of Bunyan's picture of "the Valley of the Shadow of Death," where the way was narrow, and on either hand " ever and anon came up flame and smoke in great abundance with sparks and hideous noises." In one place a flock of ducks was swimming in this sulphurous pool, and on its margin I noticed a few waders running to and fro seeking food. Its banks were mostly covered with ferns, the leaves of which were of a bright red, reminding one of the brilliantly-colored leaves of our maples in autumn.

Near the next village, Lahendong, we made a short excursion to the left, up a high but not a steep hill, to see the remarkable lake Linu. The hill is the top of an old volcano, and soon, as we descended and turned a sharp point, we found before us the lake now filling the bottom of the crater. On our way down to a house near its edge, we passed a place where much sulphurous gas was escaping. It looked indeed much like the top of a great half-slaked lime-kiln. The lake is about half a mile in diameter, and has an outlet on the southwest, through a former split in the old crater-wall. In most parts the water has a blue color, but in some it has a whitish tinge from gases that rise up through the bottom of its basin. On the northeast end there is a large solfatara, like the one we passed in coming down to the lake, but larger. Here it was that the Italian count, Carlo de Vidua, who had travelled over a large part of the globe, met with a misfortune that caused his untimely death. He ventured too far on the soft, hot clay, and sank in, and before the natives, who had cautioned him against going there, could take him out, he was burned so badly that he died in a short time afterward at Amboina, whither he was taken, that he might be cared for in the best possible manner. He had travelled over a considerable portion of our own continent, and, after escaping many imminent dangers, ventured in this spot too far. Such is the history of many a daring traveller, and no one who comes out here, where on the sea there are pirates, and on the land earthquakes and savage beasts, and in some places still more savage men, can know at what moment he is planning a fatal voyage, or when he is taking the step that may be his last. Yet some one must take this risk if the limited boundaries of our knowledge of these remote lands are ever to be extended.

Although the water of this lake is largely impregnated with sulphur and other substances that rise up through its bottom, yet Dr. Bleeker found two kinds of fish here, *Ophiocephalus striatus*, Bl., and *Arrabas scandens*, Cuv., and an eel, *Anguilla Elphinstonei*, Syk., which are also found in the fresh waters of Java and Sumatra, and in India. Returning to the main road, we continued on to Sonder, and, passing through a part of the village, came to the *ruma négri*, a public-house for any officer who chances to come to that place. This house is said to be far better even than any of the same kind in Java. It stands at the end of a long, beautifully-shaded avenue. The road is bordered with a narrow band of grass, neatly clipped, and the sidewalks are of a white earth, which has been brought from some distance. A fine grove surrounds the house, and here are many *casuarina* or cassowary-trees, the long, needle-like leaves of which closely resemble the downy plumage of that strange bird. This evening, as the full moon shines through the foliage, the whole grove is transformed into an enchanted place.

CHAPTER XI.

THE MINAHASSA.

December 29*th*.—Early this morning rode about two miles from Sonder in a northwest direction, down over the edge of the plateau on which that village is situated. The road was nothing but a narrow path, and led along a deep ravine, whose sides in several places were high precipices. A short distance beyond the native village of Tinchep is the beautiful waterfall Munte, nine hundred and sixty-four feet above the sea, but six hundred and fifty below Sonder. The height of the fall is about sixty feet, and the width of the stream at this time is nearly twenty. The rock over which it pours is a perpendicular wall of trachytic lava. The place from which travellers view the fall is some two hundred feet above it, where the road runs along the side of a mountain-chain, that curves in the form of a horseshoe around it, and makes a magnificent background for this charming picture. Luxuriant foliage hangs over the stream above the cataract, and vines and small trees have found a foothold in the crevices and on the projecting ledges of the steep wall beneath; and as the showers of falling drops strike the ends of their branches, they continually wave to and fro, though where the beholder stands, not the slightest breeze is moving in the air. We had come at just the right time to see it when it is most charming, for the early sun was then shooting oblique bands of bright light across the falling water, and as the stream is divided into millions of drops the moment it curves over the edge of the cliff, those pearly spheres were now lighted up and now darkened, as repeatedly they shot out of the shaded parts into the bands of golden light.

Returning to Sonder, I proceeded along the main route in the southeast direction to Sonder Tua, "Old Sonder," and Kawangtoan, and thence to the lovely négri of Tompasso. During this distance, of about eight miles, we had slowly ascended until we were about five hundred and seventy-five feet above Sonder. The view here is open on all sides. In the southwest is Mount Tompasso, which attains an elevation of over thirty-eight hundred feet. In the southeast the high, steep mountains are seen that border this elevated plain on the south. Great landslides appear on their sides; and the people at Tompasso said that, not long before, three natives, who had cleared and planted large gardens on the steep declivities, went one morning to continue their labor, as usual, when to their great surprise their gardens had disappeared, and all that was left of them was a huge heap of sandstones and fragments of trees piled up on the edge of the plain.

This village is laid out with a large, square pond in the middle, and on a broad dike which crosses it is the highway. A well-graded street borders this pond, and the houses on its four sides are all placed facing its centre. The hedges that border the house-lots are mostly composed of rose-bushes, and the pond itself is nearly filled with the richly-colored and fragrant lotus, *Nymphæa lotus*, a large water-lily, held sacred in Egypt and India as the symbol of creation. It is the beautiful flower upon which Buddha is represented as sitting in each of the great images, where he is supposed to personify the Past, the Present, and the Future, three immense statues, to be seen in any of the thousand temples in the East dedicated to that heathen god. The "lotus" or "lotos" of northern Africa, the fruit of which was supposed to possess the wonderful power of making all who tasted it forget their "homes and friends and native shores," is a tree, the *Celtis Australis*. If the ancients, who delighted so much in fables and myths, had only known of this charming place, they would have located their lotus-land here in the distant East, where the air is so pure and balmy, and the scenery so enchanting.

About a mile and a half beyond Tompasso we came to a number of "mud-wells," and I began to examine them; but, as a heavy shower was now seen coming up, my attendant and I again leaped into our saddles and dashed off at a fast canter to Langowan, where the chief very politely insisted on my remaining with him instead of going to the next village—an invitation I was happy to accept, for I was determined not to leave this wonderful region until I had visited all the hot-springs in the vicinity, especially as the missionary here offered to go with me on the morrow, so that I should not fail to see those that were most interesting.

December 30*th*.—Early this morning, in company with the missionary, the *hukom tua*, and a number of natives rode back nearly to Tompasso to reëxamine the mud-wells seen yesterday. The area in which most of them are found is about half a mile square, on the side of a gentle declivity. Some time before we came to them, we could tell where they were by the quantities of steam and gas rising from them, and, as we came nearer, we could hear the heavy bubbling of the principal one. It is of a triangular form, and measures about thirty feet on a side, one of the angles lying toward the top of the hill. The mud is generally of a lead color, and varies in consistency from the centre, where it is nearly as thin as muddy water, to the edges, where in some places it is as thick as cream, and in others like putty. It boils up like pitch—that is, rises up in small masses, which take a spherical form, and then burst. The distance between the centres of these ebullitions varies from six inches to two feet or more, so that the whole surface is covered with as many sets of concentric rings as there are separate boiling points. Near each of the centres the rings have a circular form; but, as they are pressed outward by the successive bubbling up of the material within them, they are pressed against each other, and become more or less irregular, the corners always remaining round until they are pressed out against those which originated from another point. By that time the rings have expanded from small circles into irregular polygons. They, therefore, exactly represent the lines of concretionary structure frequently seen in schists, and represented in nearly every treatise on geology.* If this bubbling action should cease, and in the course of time the clay become changed by heat and pressure into slates, the similarity of the two would perhaps be very close. Have, therefore, the particles now forming the old schists which show this structure been subjected to such mechanical changing in their relative position to each other, before they were hardened into the schists they now form, as the particles of clay in this pool are undergoing at the present time?

Near this large well was a hot-spring about three feet in diameter, and two feet deep. Its temperature was as high as 98° Celsius, 208.4° Fahrenheit, and of course much steam rose from its surface. We boiled some eggs here hard in a few minutes. The water was pure and the natives living in the vicinity frequently come and wash their clothing in this natural boiler. No trace of vegetation could be detected beneath the surface nor on its edges where the bubbling water splashed. At the foot of the hill we visited a considerable lake which was strongly impregnated with sulphur, and near it a pond of thick, muddy water which in several places boiled up at intervals. About twenty of these boiling pools are found on this hill-side, and in the low, marshy land at its feet. Up the hill above the mud-well first described was a naked spot several yards in diameter.

* For an accurate representation of these rings, see the drawings of concretionary structure in Dana's "Manual of Geology," p. 99, fig. 85.

It is composed of *tana puti*, white earth; that is, decomposed lavas. Considerable steam was escaping from two or three holes where the natives had been taking out this white earth or clay, which they mix with rice-water and use in whitewashing their houses, a common practice throughout the Minahassa. We now rode west to Tompasso, and turning to the north came to a small village called Nolok. Thence the natives guided us a short distance in a northeasterly direction to a brook, and following up this for some distance, we came to a large bowl-shaped basin about seventy-five feet in diameter and twenty feet deep. Its sides were of soft clay, and so steep that we had much difficulty in getting near enough to its edge to obtain such a view as I desired, and the only way we accomplished it was by selecting a place where the intertwining roots of many small trees made a kind of turf. The coolies cleared away the shrubbery with their cleavers, and then by taking the left hand of one native while he held fast to another with his right, I was enabled to lean over its soft edge and obtain a complete view of the boiling water which partly covered its miry bottom. The stream which flows down into this basin rises on higher land to the north, and is cool until it comes into this basin. Here it is heated and strongly impregnated with sulphur, and changed to a whitish color. This circular basin I suppose has been wholly formed by the motion of the water that boils with the heat beneath it. One object in visiting these hot springs was to ascertain at what degree of temperature vegetation first began to appear. We therefore went down the stream, and began following its course upward toward this basin. At a place where the temperature was 48° Celsius, 118.4° Fahrenheit, the rocks and sticks in the water were thickly covered with darkgreen algæ. A little higher up the temperature was 51° Celsius, 123.8° Fahrenheit, and algæ were still present, though the fumes of sulphur that rose choked me as I stooped to examine the temperature. We had now come to a thick jungle where the ground was so soft and miry it was both difficult and dangerous to get nearer the boiling pool. At last one of the natives was induced by the promise of a large piece of silver to cut away the bamboos and small shrubbery, if I would keep close behind him. Thus we slowly worked our way several yards higher up, when I ordered him to turn toward the stream. This hot-bog was certainly the next place to Tartarus. In several places between the clumps of small trees and bamboos the water was boiling and bubbling furiously, and pouring out great volumes of stifling gases, but I followed my coolie so closely that he had no time to regret his agreement, and at last we reached the bank of the stream, a place was cleared, and fastening my thermometer to the end of a long bamboo, I placed it in the hot, opaque water. Three times I repeated the observation, and each time the mercury stood at 50° Celsius, 122° Fahrenheit, but I judged from the rate it fell after the first reading that it stood at 52°, certainly not higher, before it was raised into the air. In this spot we had unfortunately come among hundreds of ants, that came out and bit me until my ankles seemed to be surrounded with live coals, and at the end of the third reading I dropped the bamboo and ran back with all my might to escape these pests and end my misery. While I held the thermometer in the bubbling (not boiling) water, I ordered the coolie to raise the sticks that were floating in it, but could not discern the slightest appearance of any vegetable growth, though it was very noticeable a little farther down the stream where the temperature of the water was not more than one degree lower, but where the quantity of sulphur in the water must have been much less, judging by the proportionate strength of the fumes that rise in the two places. All the other readings given here were made while the mercury remained in the water, and as the thermometer had been carefully marked the observations are liable to but little error. If some other observer should go to the same places and find a greater or less quantity of water, no doubt the temperature also would be found to have slightly changed. The missionary in our party, who had visited this place several times, assured me that frequently, when the cold stream that flows into this basin is much swollen by heavy rains, the water is thrown up at short intervals as high as a common palm-tree, about fifty feet. The natives also told me they had all often seen it in such violent action. The basin is therefore nothing but the upper, expanding part of a deep geyser-like tube.

We now returned toward Langowan, and visited a large basin of hot water to the left of the road, and about a mile from that village. Its basin is bowl-shaped, nearly circular in form, forty-eight feet in diameter. The water does not boil up except in one or two places, and almost the only gas that escapes is steam. Its temperature is 78° Celsius, 172.4° Fahrenheit. On one side is a small brook which carries off the surplus water, for this is truly a spring, that is, a place where water flows up from the ground. A short distance to the west and north are a number of hills, from which this water no doubt comes. As stifling gases were not pouring out, I had a better opportunity for examining the banks of the brook, which flowed off sixty feet, and was then conducted across the road by a causeway. Tracing it with the current several times, I invariably came to the first indication of vegetable life in the same place. It was a small quantity of algæ on the bottom of the brook, each plant being about as large round as a pin, and an eighth of an inch in length, and resembling the *Vaucheria*, or brook silk, the green threads of which are seen in the fresh-water ponds by our roadsides in summer. Here the temperature was $76\frac{3}{4}$° Celsius, 170.15° Fahrenheit. As the water flowed out through this shallow brook, a large part of all the sulphurous gas it contained of course passed off, and I believe the vegetation began at that point, not so much because the water was $1\frac{1}{4}$° Celsius cooler than in the basin, as because it was much purer, for at a short distance nearer the basin, where the temperature was $77\frac{1}{8}$° Celsius, 172.82° Fahrenheit, no kind of vegetation could be detected, and yet the difference in the temperature of the water in the two places was only three-eighths of a degree in Celsius's scale.

THE ANCIENT APPEARANCE OF OUR EARTH. 365

Geologists suppose that our earth was once a molten, liquid mass, which cooled by degrees until a crust was formed, that slowly thickened until condensation began in the surrounding atmosphere, and thus the water of the primeval ocean was formed. At first this water must have been just below the boiling point, and the query has arisen, How cool did the sea become before vegetation began to appear in it, and on the land then above the sea? The partial answer indicated by the few observations above is, that the presence of vegetable life depended more on the chemical composition of the water than on its temperature. If it was as pure then as the larger pool described above, the whole ocean was yet one great steaming caldron when these very simple aquatic plants, each apparently consisting of only a single branching cell, began to grow in the shallow places along its shores. Before this time, however, other algæ, like those which now grow in moist terrestrial places, may have been thriving on the land in the steamy atmosphere.

Sunday, December 31*st.*—At 8 A. M. attended the native church, where the missionary preaches. It was well filled, and the attention manifested by all was highly commendable. At the close of the service four or five couples were married; the pastor, after performing the ceremony, explaining to the husbands that they must support their wives, and not, like the Alfura, who are heathens, live in idleness, and expect their wives to support them. A *controleur*, who had been stationed in the interior, back of Gorontalo, now arrived at Langowan, on his way to Kema, having been transferred, at his request, to Sumatra. We should therefore be companions on the steamer all the way to Java, which was especially agreeable to me, as he spoke English well, and no one not born in Holland can ever learn to pronounce the harsh gutturals of the Dutch language with perfect ease and accuracy. From Langowan we rode four miles in a northerly direction to Kakas, a village at the southern end of the lake of Tondano. The *ruma négri* here is one of the most pleasantly-situated buildings in the Minahassa. It is large and carefully built, and has broad verandas both toward the lake and the village. It is surrounded with plots of green grass, neatly bordered with gravelled walks, and rose-bushes covered with large crimson flowers. In the evening, when the moon rose over the sharp peaks a short distance to the east, and spread a broad band of silver light over the lake, the effect was charming; and now, while we inhale the balmy air, and recall to mind the ponds of beautiful lotus we have been passing, we may feel that we are indeed in the enchanted lotus-land that Tennyson thus pictures:

> In the afternoon they came unto a land
> In which it seemed always afternoon;
> At noon the coast with languid air did swoon,
> Breathing like one that hath a weary dream.
> Full-faced above the valley stood the moon;
> And like a downward smoke the slender stream
> Along the cliff to fall, and pause, and fall, did seem.

January 1, 1866.—Walked with the *controleur* and chief through the village, and saw the mode of pounding out rice by water-power. The axle of the water-wheel is made very long, and filled with a number of small sticks, which, as they turn over, raise poles fixed in a perpendicular position, that fall again when the revolving stick is drawn away from them. A large boat, manned by seven natives, was made ready for me to go to any part of the lake of Tondano and ascertain its depth. It occupies the lower portion of a high plateau, and its surface, as measured by S. H. De Lange, is two thousand two hundred and seventy-two English feet above the sea. It is about seventeen miles long in a northerly and southerly direction, and varies in width from two to seven miles. It is nearly divided into two equal parts by high capes that project from either shore. On the south and southwest and on the north, its shores are low, and the land slowly ascends from one to five miles, and then curves upward to the jagged mountain-crest that bounds the horizon on all sides. In the other parts of its shores it rises up from the water in steep acclivities. All the lowlands and the lower flanks of the mountains are under a high state of cultivation, and the air is cool and pure, while it is excessively hot and sultry on the ocean-shore below. Some writers have regarded this lake-basin as an old extinct crater; and some, as only a depression in the surrounding plain, or, in other words, the lower part of the plateau. To settle this question beyond a doubt, it was necessary to ascertain its form. I therefore asked the Resident if he could furnish me with a line to sound with as I crossed it. He replied that he had but one of two hundred fathoms, and that I could not expect to reach the bottom with that, for all the fishermen who live on its shores declare that it "has no bottom," that is, is unfathomable. It would be something to know that it was more than twelve hundred feet deep—so a coolie was ordered to carry the line. From Kakas we rowed over a short distance toward the high shore opposite, that being said to be one of the unmeasurable places. A heavy sinker was put on, and the whole line cleared, so that it would run out freely to the last foot. I gave the man at the bow the command, and the cord began to rattle over the boat's side, when suddenly it stopped short. "Is the sinker off?" "No, it's on the bottom." "How many fathoms are out." "Eleven fathoms and five feet." After this we sounded eight times, and the deepest water, which was near the middle, between the two high capes, is only twelve fathoms and two feet. The water not only proved shallow, but the bottom was found to be as even as the lowland at the northern and southern ends of the lake. The basin is therefore only a slight depression in the lower part of the plateau. The only fishes known in this lake are the same three species already mentioned as existing in the sulphurous waters of Lake Linu. Reaching the large village of Tondano, at the northern end of the lake, I was kindly received by the *controleur*, who had accompanied me already from Tomohon to Sonder. A heavy rain set in, and I was obliged to defer the rest of my journey till the next day.

January 2d.—The thick rain-clouds of yesterday

broke away this morning as the sun rose, and the sky is now perfectly clear. The *controleur* provided me with a horse, and a *hukom tua* accompanied me as a guide. Our course was nearly west, and soon the road became very steep, and extremely slippery from the late rain. As we rose, the view over the plateau beneath us widened, until we wound round the mountain to the little village of Rurukan, the highest *négri* in this land. The head of this village guided us to the top of a neighboring peak, where I found a large part of the Minahassa spread out before me like a great map. From the point where I stood, there stretched to the south a high mountain-chain, forming the western border of the lake of Tondano. A little more to the east were seen the lake far below, and the level land along a part of its shores, while on the opposite side of the lake rose the mountains that form the other end of the chain on which I was standing. This chain curves like a horseshoe, the open part being turned toward the north. At the same point where all the details of this plateau were comprised in a single view, by turning a little toward the north, I could look down the outer flanks of this elevated region away to the low, distant ocean-shore, where the blue sea was breaking into white, sparkling surf. A little farther toward the north rose the lofty peak of Mount Klabat, covered with a thick mantle of fleecy clouds, which had a hue of ermine in the bright light. This mantle was slowly raised and lowered by the invisible hand of the strong west wind. Beneath it, low on the sides of the mountain, was seen a line of trees marking the shady way I had taken from Kema to Menado. This is considered, and I believe rightly, the finest view in the archipelago, and one of the most charming in the world, because the other famous views, like that of Damascus, do not include that great emblem of infinity, the open ocean.

Rice is raised at even as great an elevation as the place we had reached, about four thousand five hundred feet, in what are called *kebon kring*, " dry gardens." These are known as *tegal* lands in Java. The yield is said not to be as large as on the low lands, *sawas*, by the margin of the lake which are overflowed in the usual manner. The yearly crop in the Minahassa is from one hundred and fifty to two hundred thousand piculs, of which ten to eighteen thousand are exported chiefly to Ternate and Amboina. Tobacco is also cultivated, but only for home consumption. Cocoa is also raised; and this year (1865) forty-four and three-fourth piculs were exported. Like that at Amboina, it is all bought by Chinamen, who send it to Manilla. Cocoa-nuts are also exported to the chief islands eastward. The yield this year is estimated by the officials at four million. There is a great abundance here of the gomuti or sagaru palm-tree, the large petioles of which spread out at the base into broad fibrous sheets that enclose the trunk. Some of the fibres resemble horsehair, but are much stiffer and very brittle, and are gathered by the natives and manufactured into *coir*, a kind of coarse rope. As the fibres soon break, they project in every direction until the rope becomes extremely rough and difficult to handle. It has the valuable

THE GOMUTI PALM.

property, however, of being nearly indestructible in water, and the Resident tells me that this coir will probably prove of much value in manufacturing telegraph-cable. The quantity of fibres that could be gathered yearly would be very considerable if there should be any demand for them. Among the flexible, horsehair-like fibres are coarser ones, which the natives use for pens and arrows for their blowpipes, and interwoven with them is a mass of small fibres nearly as soft as cotton, which are used as tinder. The flowering part is cut off with a knife, and the sap which exudes is gathered in a piece of bamboo. In this condition it has a slightly acid and very bitter taste, resembles the thin part of buttermilk, and is a very agreeable and refreshing beverage in such a hot climate. As soon as it is allowed to ferment it becomes *tuak*, a highly-intoxicating drink, of which the natives are very fond. This palm prefers higher lands than the cocoa-nut, which flourishes well only on the low areas near the level of the sea. It will be readily distinguished from all the other palms of this land by its large leaves and the rough appearance of its trunk. Gomuti is the Malay name for the coir only, the tree itself they call *anau*. In Amboina the native name for it is *nawa*, and in other parts of the archipelago it has local names, showing that it is probably an indigenous plant. The soft envelopes of the seeds, which are so numerous that, when ripe, one bunch will frequently be a load for two men, contain a poisonous juice which the natives were accustomed to use on their arrows, and which the Dutch have named "hell-water."

Besides the fruits already mentioned, there are durians, mangostins, jambus or rose-apples, lansiums, pompelmuses, limes, bread-fruits, bananas, pine-apples, and oranges. The latter are particularly nice, and in one of the kinds the leathery rind is not yellow when the fruit, which is merely a berry, is ripe, but still remains as green as when only half-grown. It is the custom here at the table to peel this fruit with a knife, exactly as we peel an apple.

From Tondano to Kema the road is built in a deep, zigzag ravine, and commences to descend a mile north of the lake. Through the ravine flows a stream which is the outlet of the lake. On the northern side of the plateau where the road begins to descend, this stream is changed into a waterfall, which is known as the waterfall of Tondano. It consists of three falls, but, when seen from the usual point, a short distance north of the lower fall, the upper and middle ones form a boiling rapid, and only the lowest one presents a grand appearance. Where the first and second occur the water shoots down through a deep canal, which has been apparently formed in the rock by the strong current. Having rolled in a foaming mass through this deep canal, the water takes a flying leap down seventy feet into a deep, circular pool, the outer edges of this falling stream breaking up into myriads of sparkling drops, which fall in showers into the dark pool, where they disappear forever.

Here a strange tragedy occurred in the year 1855, when the governor-general from Java was journeying through this land. One of the highest officers on his staff, a gentleman who had previously been governor of the Moluccas, came to this place while the others were resting at Tondano, and committed suicide by plunging headlong into the deep canal above the high fall. Only a short time before, he had dined with the whole company and seemed very cheerful, but here, probably in a moment of unusual despondency, he made the fatal leap.

Continuing in the way that followed this crooked stream, I occasionally beheld the high top of Mount Klabat before me. Several large butterflies flitted to and fro, their rich, velvety blue and green colors seeming almost too bright to be real. At the eighth paal we came to the native village Sawangan, and the chief showed me the burial-place of his people previous to the arrival of Europeans. Most of the monuments consist of three separate stones placed one on another. The lowest is square or oblong, and partly buried in the earth. Its upper surface has been squared off that the second might rest on it more firmly. This is a rectangular-parallelopipedon, one or two feet wide and two-thirds as thick, and from two to three feet high. It is placed on end on the first stone. In its upper end a deep hole has been made, and in this the body of the deceased is placed. It was covered by the third stone of a triangular form when viewed at the end, and made to represent that part of a house above the eaves. It projects a little beyond the perpendicular stone beneath it. On the sides of the roof rude figures of men, women, and children were carved, all with the knees drawn up against the chin and clasped by the arms, the hands being locked together in front below the knees. In many of these the faces of the figures were flat, and holes and lines were cut representing the eyes, nose, and mouth; in others rude busts were placed on the eaves. This burial-place contains the finest monuments of olden times now existing in the Minahassa. Others can be seen at Tomohon, and especially at Kakas, but they are not as highly ornamented as these. At Kakas they are mostly composed of but two stones, one long one set upright in the ground, and another placed over this as a cover to the hole containing the body. At each of these places they are entirely neglected, and many of the images here have already fallen or been broken off. Noticing that a very good one was loose and ready to fall, I remarked to the chief that, if I did not take it, it would certainly soon be lost, and, before he had time to give his assent, I had it under my arm. The missionary at Langowan informed me that originally these graves were beset with such obscene ornaments that one of the Residents felt it his duty to order that they should all be broken off. This fact, and the rude form of the images, led me to think that they ought to be classed with the remarkable temple found near Dorey, on the north coast of New Guinea, and with the nude statues used by the Battas to ornament the graves of their deceased friends.

When the Portuguese first arrived in the Moluccas, this region was tributary to the prince of Ternate. All the natives were heathen then, and many of them yet retain the superstitious belief of their ancestors. Mohammedanism had not gained a foot-

THE BAMBOO.

hold among them, nor has it since, and the only Mohammedans now in the land are the immigrants at Menado, who have come from other parts of the archipelago, and a few natives banished from Java. Even as late as 1833, but little more than thirty years ago, Pietermaat, who was then Resident, in his official report, says of these people: "They are wholly ignorant of reading, writing, and arithmetic. They reckon by means of notches in a piece of bamboo, or by knots made in a cord." Formerly they were guilty of practising the bloody custom of cutting off human heads at every great celebration, and the missionary at Langowan showed me a rude drawing of one of their principal feasts, made for him by one of the natives themselves. In front of a house where the chief was supposed to reside, was a short, circular paling of bamboos placed upright, the upper ends of all were sharpened, and on each was stuck a human head. Between thirty and forty of these heads were represented as having been taken off for this single festive occasion, and the missionary regarded the drawing as no exaggeration, from what he knew of their bloody rites.

The remarkable quantities of coffee, cocoa-nuts, and other articles yearly exported from the Minahassa show that a wonderful change has come over this land, even since 1833; and the question at once arises, What is it that has transferred these people from barbarism to civilization? The answer and the only answer is, Christianity and education. The Bible, in the hands of the missionaries, has been the chief cause that has induced these people to lay aside their bloody rites. As soon as a few natives had been taught to read and write, they were employed as teachers, and schools were established from place to place, and from these centres a spirit of industry and self-respect has diffused itself among the people and supplanted in a great measure their previous predisposition to idleness and self-neglect. In 1840, seven years after Pietermaat gave the description of these people mentioned above, the number of Christians compared to that of heathen was as one to sixteen, now it is about as two to five; and exactly as this ratio continues to increase, in the same degree will the prosperity of this land become greater.

The rocks seen on this journey through the Minahassa, as noted above, are trachytic lavas, volcanic sand and ashes, pumice-stone, and conglomerates composed of these materials and clay formed by their decomposition. They all appear to be of a late formation, and, as Dr. Bleeker remarks, the Minahassa seems to be only a recent prolongation of the older sedimentary rocks in the residency of Gorontalo. In this small part of the peninsula, there are no less than eleven volcanoes. North of Menado is a chain of volcanic islands, which form a prolongation of this peninsula. On the island Siao there is an active volcano. North of it is the large island of Sangir. According to Valentyn, the highest mountain on the island underwent an eruption in December, 1711. A great quantity of ashes and lava was ejected, and the air was so heated for some distance around, that many of the natives lost their lives. North of the Sangir islands are the Talaut group. These are the most northern islands under the Dutch, and the boundary of their possessions in this part of the archipelago.

The steamer Menado, on which I had previously taken passage from Batavia all the way to Amboina, now arrived at Kema. She had brought my collection from Amboina, Buru, and Ternate, and I was ready to return to Java, for some months had passed since I accomplished the object of my journey to the Spice Islands, and during that time I had travelled many hundred miles and had reached several regions which I had not dared to expect to see, even when I left Batavia. A whale-ship from New Bedford was also in the road, and when I visited her and heard every one, even the cabin-boy, speaking English, it seemed almost as strange as it did to hear nothing but Malay and Dutch when I first arrived in Java. Many whales are usually found east of the Sangir Islands, and north of Gilolo and New Guinea.

January 10th.—At noon steamed out of the bay of Kema and down the eastern coast of Celebes for Macassar. When the sun was setting, we were just off Tanjong Flasco, which forms the northern limit of the bay of Gorontalo or Tomini. As the sun sank behind the end of this high promontory, its jagged outline received a broad margin of gold. Bands of strati stretched across the sky from north to south and successively changed from gold to a bright crimson, and then to a deep, dark red as the sunlight faded. All this bright coloring of the sky was repeated in the sea, and the air between them assumed a rich, scintillating appearance, as if filled with millions of minute crystals of gold.

The *controleur*, on board, who travelled with me from Langowan, has been farther into the interior, south of Gorontalo, than any foreigner previously. He found the whole country divided up among many petty tribes, who are waging a continual warfare with each other; and the immediate object of his dangerous journey was to conciliate two powerful tribes near the borders of the territory which the Dutch claim as being under their command. He found that all these people are excessively addicted to the use of opium, which is brought from Singapore to the western coast, near Palos, by Mandharese and Macassars.

The dress of the people consists of a sarong, made from the inner layers of the bark of a tree. They have large parangs, and value them in proportion to the number and minuteness of the damascene lines on their blades. Twenty guilders is a common price for them. The *controleur* gave me a very fine one, which was remarkably well tempered. The most valuable export from this bay is gold, which is found in great quantities, at least over the whole northern peninsula, from the Minahassa south to the isthmus of Palos. The amount exported is not known, for, though the Dutch Government has a contract with the princes to deliver all the gold obtained in their territory to it at a certain rate, they are offered a much higher price by the Bugis, and consequently sell it to them. No extensive survey has yet been made in this territory, by the mining engineers employed by the government, and the extent and richness of these mines are therefore wholly matters of the most uncertain speculation. The fact, however, that gold was carried from this region before the arrival of Europeans, more than three hundred and forty years ago, and that the amount now exported appears to be larger than it was then, indicates that the supply must be very great. The government has not yet granted to private individuals the privilege of importing machinery and laborers, and proving whether or not mining can be carried on profitably on a large scale. A fragment of rock from this region was shown me at Kema by a gentleman, who said he knew where there were large quantities of it; and that specimen certainly was very rich in the precious metal. Gold is also found in the southwestern peninsula of Celebes, south of Macassar. The geological age of these auriferous rocks is not known, but I was assured that, back of Gorontalo, an outcropping of granite had been seen. Buffaloes and horses are plenty and cheap at Gorontalo, and many are sent by sea to the Minahassa. The horses are very fine, and from the earliest times the Bugis have been accustomed to buy and kill them to eat, having learned that such flesh is a most delectable food, centuries before this was ascertained by the enlightened Parisians.

January 11*th*.—Last night and to-day the sea has been smooth, almost as smooth as glass, while we know that on the opposite or western side of Celebes there has been one continuous storm. This is why we have come down the eastern side of the island. Here the seasons on the east and west coasts alternate, as we have already noticed in Ceram and Buru, though those islands extend east and west, while Celebes extends north and south. To-day we passed through the Bangai group, lying between the Sula Islands and Celebes. From the appearance of the water, and from such soundings as are given, there appears to be only a depth of some thirty fathoms in the straits. These islands, therefore, not only have formed a part of the adjacent peninsula of Celebes, but do at the present day.

A remarkable similarity has been noticed between the fauna of Bachian, near the southern end of Gilolo, and that of Celebes, and in the Bangai and the Sula Islands we probably behold the remnants of an old peninsula that once completely joined those two lands. When we compare Celebes and Gilolo, we notice that the Bangai and Sula groups, stretching off to the east and southeast from one of the eastern peninsulas of Celebes, are analogous in position to Gebi, Waigiu, and Battanta, and the adjacent islands which are but the remnants of a peninsula that in former times connected Gilolo to the old continent of New Guinea and Australia.

Now, at sunset, we were approaching the Buton Passage, which separates the large island of Buton from Wangi-wangi, "The Sweet-scented Island." This is a great highway for ships bound from Singapore to China in the west monsoon, and several are now here, drifting over the calm sea.

Buton is a hilly island, but no mountains appear. Its geological formation is said to consist of "recent limestone, containing madrepores and shells." Here, again, we find indications of the wide upheaval that appears to be occurring in the whole archipelago, but especially in its eastern part. It is quite famous for the valuable cotton it produces, which, in the fineness and length of its fibres, is said to excel that raised in any other part of the archipelago, and is therefore highly valued by the Bugis and Macassars.

January 13th.—This morning we passed a large American man-of-war coming down grandly from the west, under steam and a full press of canvas. It is a most agreeable and unexpected pleasure to see such a representation of our powerful navy in these remote seas.*

The next day we passed through Salayar Strait, which separates the southern end of the peninsula of Celebes from the Salayar Islands, and may be regarded as the boundary between the alternating wet and dry seasons on the opposite sides of Celebes.

January 15th.—Arrived back at Macassar. There is nothing but one continuous series of heavy, pouring showers, with sharp lightning and heavy thunder.

---

* I had little idea, when the above was written, that this ship was no other than the Hartford, made so famous by Admiral Farragut's brave and successful assault on the forts below Mobile, and that Rear-Admiral H. H. Bell, then commanding our Asiatic squadron, was on board; and that during that same year (1866) it would be my privilege to meet him, and receive from him and the other officers of our United States ships so much kind assistance in making long voyages on the coasts of China, Corea, and Japan.

January 16th. — Sailed for Surabaya in Java. This morning there is only such a wind as sailors would call a fresh, but not a heavy gale. In all the wide area between Java and the line of islands east to Timur on the south, and the tenth degree of north latitude, none of those frightful gales known in the Bay of Bengal as cyclones, and in the China Sea as "typhoons," have ever been experienced. The chief sources of solicitude to the navigator of the Java and the Banda Seas are the strong currents and many reefs of coral.

Our large steamer is little else than a great floating menagerie. We have, as usual, many native soldiers on board, and each has with him two or three pet parrots or cockatoos. Several of our passengers have dozens of large cages, containing crested pigeons from New Guinea, and representatives of nearly every species of parrot in that part of the archipelago. We have also more than a dozen different kinds of odd-looking monkeys, two or three of which are continually getting loose and upsetting the parrot-cages, and, before the sluggish Malays can approach them with a "rope's end" unawares, they spring up the shrouds, and escape the punishment which they know their mischief deserves. These birds and monkeys are mostly purchased in the Spice Islands; and if all now on board this ship could be safely transported to New York or London, they would far excel the collection on exhibition in the Zoological Gardens of the latter city.

Besides the Chinese, Arabs, Malays, and other passengers forward, there is a Buginese woman, a raving maniac. She is securely shackled by an iron band around the ankle to a ring-bolt in the deck. One moment she is swaying to and fro, and moaning as if in the greatest mental agony and despair, and, the next moment, stamping and screeching in a perfect rage, her long hair streaming in the wind, her eyes bloodshot, and flashing fire like a tigress which has been robbed of her young. It would be difficult to fancy a more frightful picture. They are taking her to the mad-house near Samarang, where all such unfortunates are kindly cared for by the government. Her nation, the Bugis or Buginese, are famous for "running a muck." *Amuk*, which was written by the early navigators "a muck," is a common term in all parts of the archipelago for any reckless, bloody onset, whether made by one or more. It is, however, generally used by foreigners for those insane attacks which the Malays sometimes make on any one, generally to satisfy a feeling of revenge. When they have decided to commit a murder of this kind, they usually take opium, and, when partially under its influence, rush out into the street with a large knife and try to butcher the first person they may chance to meet. Many years ago such *émeutes* were of frequent occurrence, and even at the present time most of the natives who stand guard in the city of Batavia are each armed with a long staff, on the end of which is a Y-shaped fork, provided on the inner side with barbs pointing backward. This is thrust against the neck of the murderer, and he is thus secured without danger to the policeman.

CHAPTER XII.

SUMATRA.

On the third day from Macassar we arrived safely at Surabaya, and thence proceeded westward to Samarang, and, on the first of February, 1866, I was again in Batavia, having been absent in the eastern part of the archipelago eight months. Through the courtesy of Messrs. Dümmler & Co., of that city, who obligingly offered to receive and store my collections and forward them to America, I was left entirely free to commence a new journey.

The generous offer of the governor-general to give me an order for post-horses free over all parts of Java was duly considered; but as many naturalists and travellers have described it already, I determined to proceed to Sumatra, and, if possible, travel in the interior of that unexplored island, and, accordingly, on the 12th of February, I took passage for Padang on the Menado, the same steamer in which I had already travelled so many hundred miles.

From Batavia we soon steamed away to the Strait of Sunda, and once more it was my privilege to behold the lofty peaks in the southern end of Sumatra. From that point as far north as Cape Indrapura

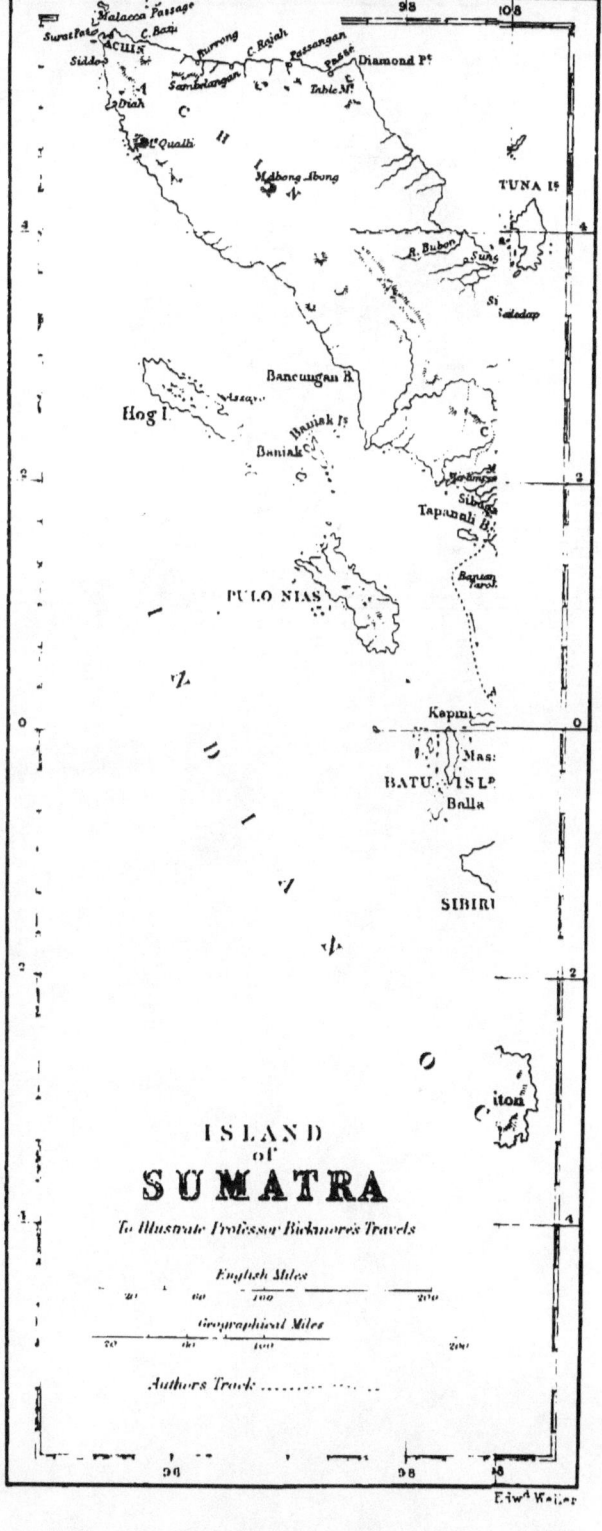

the coast is generally bordered with a narrow band of low land, from which rises a high and almost continuous chain of mountains extending parallel with the southwest, or, as the Dutch always call it, the "west" coast, all the way north to Achin.

The next morning, after passing the lofty peak of Indrapura, found us steaming in under the hills and high mountains that stand by the sea at Padang and rise tier above tier until they reach the crest of the Barizan chain, producing one of the grandest effects to be enjoyed on the shores of any island in the whole archipelago. Padang, unfortunately, has no harbor, and the place where ships are obliged to anchor is an open, exposed roadstead. There is a sheltered harbor farther to the south, but it would cost a large sum to build a good road from Padang to it by cutting down the hills and bridging the ravines. The distance from the anchorage to the city is some three miles, and all the products exported must be taken out to the ships on barges.

The city of Padang is situated on a small plain, whence its name; *padang* in Malay, meaning an open field or plain. Its population numbers about twelve thousand, and is composed of emigrants from Nias, Java, some Chinese and Arabs, and their mestizo descendants, besides the natives and Dutch. The streets are well shaded and neat. Near the centre of the city is a large, beautiful lawn, on one side of which is the residence of the governor. On the opposite side is the Club-House, a large and well-proportioned building. On the south side is a small stream where the natives haul up their boats, and here the barges take in their cargoes. This part of the city is chiefly filled with the storehouses and offices of the merchants. In front of the governor's residence is a large common. Two of its sides are occupied by private residences and the church, the roof of which has fallen in, and indeed the whole structure is in a most dilapidated condition compared to the rich Club-House on the other side of the green. Having landed and taken up my quarters at a hotel, I called on Governor Van den Bosche, who received me politely, and said that the inspector of posts, Mr. Theben Terville, whose duty it is not only to care for transporting the mails, but also to supervise and lay out the post-roads, had just arrived from Java, and must make an overland journey to Siboga, in order to examine a route that had been proposed for a post-road to that place.

He had promised the inspector, who was an old gentleman, the use of his "American," a light four-wheeled carriage made in Boston. There was room for two in it, and he would propose to the inspector to take me with him, and further provide me with letters to the chief officials along the way; but as it would be two or three days before Mr. Terville, who was then in the interior, would be ready to start, he proposed that I should leave the hotel and make my home with him as long as I might remain in Padang. "Besides," he added, "I have eight good carriage-horses in the stable, and I have so much writing to do that they are spoiling for want of exercise; now, if you will come, you can ride whenever you please." So again I found myself in the full tide of fortune. It is scarcely necessary to add that I did not fail to avail myself of such a generous offer. In the evenings, when it became cool, the governor was accustomed to ride through the city, and occasionally out a short distance into the country. Our roads were usually shaded with tall trees, frequently with palms, and to fly along beneath them in a nice carriage, drawn by a span of fleet ponies, was a royal pleasure, and one never to be forgotten. One pleasant day we drove out a few miles to a large garden where the governor formerly resided. The palace had been taken down, but a fine garden and a richly-furnished bathing-house yet remain. The road out from Padang to this place led through a series of low rice-lands, and just then the young blades were six or eight inches high, and waved charmingly in the morning breeze. The road, for a long distance, was perfectly straight and bordered by large shade-trees. It was one of the finest avenues I ever saw. Here I was reminded of the region from which I had so lately come, the Spice Islands, by a small clove-tree, well filled with fruit. Much attention was formerly given here to the culture of the clove, but for some years raising coffee has proved the most profitable mode of employing native labor. There were also some fine animals in various parts of the garden, among which was a pair of the spotted deer, *Axis maculata*. Thus several days glided by, and the time for me to go up into the interior and meet the inspector came almost before I was aware of it.

February 21*st*, 1866.—At 8 A. M. we started from

Padang for Fort de Kock, sixty miles from this city. A heavy shower during the night has purified the air, and we have a clear, cool, and in its fullest sense a lovely morning. This "American" is generally drawn by two horses, but the governor has had thills put on so that one may be used, for he says, between Fort de Kock, where the present post-road ends, and Siboga, a distance of about one hundred and ninety miles, by the crooked route that we must travel, that we shall find it difficult to get one horse for a part of the way. Behind the carriage a small seat is fastened where my footman sits or stands. His duty is to help change the horses at the various stations, which are about five miles apart. When the horses are harnessed his next duty is to get them started, which is by far the most difficult, for most of those we have used to-day have been trained for the saddle, and we have not dared to put on any breeching for fear of losing our fender, these brutes are so ready to use their heels, though fortunately we have not needed any hold-back but once or twice, and then, by having the footman act as hold-back himself with a long line, I have urged on the horse, and in every case we have come down to the bottom of the hill safely. With only a weak coolie tugging behind, of course I have not been able to make these wild horses resist the temptation to go down the hill at a trot, and, after running and holding back until he was out of breath, the coolie has always let go, generally when I was half-way down; nothing of course then remained to be done but to keep the horse galloping so fast that the carriage cannot run on to him, and by the time we have come to the bottom of the hill we have been moving at a break-neck rate, which has been the more solicitous for me, as I had never been on the road, and did not know what unexpected rocks or holes there would be found round the next sharp turn.

From Padang the road led to the northwest, over the low lands between the sea and the foot of the Barizan, or coast chain of mountains. In this low region we have crossed two large streams, which come down from these elevations on the right, and are now quite swollen from the recent rains. A long and large rattan is stretched across from one bank to the other, and a path made to slip over it is fastened to one end of a rude raft. This rattan prevents us from being swept down the boiling stream, while the natives push over the raft with long poles. I began to realize what an advantage it was to ride in the carriage of the *Tuan Biza*, or "Great Man," as the Malays all call the governor. As soon as those on the opposite side of the stream saw the carriage they recognized it, and at once came over by holding on to the rattan with one hand and swimming with the other. In their struggles to hasten and kindly assist, several times the heads of a number of them were beneath the water when they came to the middle of the stream, where the current was strongest and the rattan very slack; but there was very little danger of their being drowned, for they are as amphibious as alligators. I had not been riding long over these low lands before I experienced a new and unexpected pleasure in beholding by the roadside numbers of beautiful tree-ferns, which, unlike their humbler representatives in our temperate regions, grow up into trees fifteen to eighteen feet high. They are interesting, not only on account of their graceful forms and limited distribution, but because they are the living representatives of a large family of trees that flourished during the coal period.

As we proceeded, our road approached the base of the Barizan chain until we were quite near them, and then curved again around some spur that projected toward the sea-shore. Late in the afternoon we came to the opening of a broad, triangular valley, and beheld on our right, and near the head of the valley, the towering peak of Singalang, whose summit is nine thousand eight hundred and eighty feet above the sea. Large numbers of natives were seen here travelling in company, returning homeward from the market at Kayu Tanam, the next village. Their holiday dress here as elsewhere is a bright red. Beyond Kayu Tanam the road ran along the side of a deep ravine, having in fact been cut in the soft rock, a narrow wall of it being left on the outer side to prevent carriages from sliding off into the deep chasm. Suddenly, as we whirled round the sharp corners while dashing through this place, we came into a deep cañon extending to the right and left, called by the Dutch the Kloof, or "Cleft," a very proper name, for it is a great cleft in the Barizan chain. Up this cleft has been built a road by which all the rich products of the *Padangsche Bovenlanden*, or "Padang plateau," are brought down to the coast. Opposite to us was a torrent pouring over the perpendicular side

APPROACH TO THE "CLEFT," NEAR PADANG.

of the cleft, which I judge to be about seventy-five feet in height. Where it curved over the side of the precipice it was confined, but, as soon as it began to fall, it spread out and came down, not in one continuous, unvarying sheet of water, but in a series of wavelets, until the whole resembled a huge comet trying, as it were, to escape from earth up to its proper place in the pure sky above it. On either side of this pulsating fall is a sheet of green vegetation, which has gained a foothold in every crevice and on every projecting ledge in the precipice. Behind the falling water there is a wall of black, volcanic rock, and at its foot is a mass of angular *débris* which has broken off from the cliff above. Now we turned sharply round to the north, and began ascending to the plateau. The cleft has not been formed in a straight but in a zigzag line, so that, in looking up or down, its sides seem to meet a short distance before you and prevent any farther advance in either direction; but, as you proceed, the road suddenly opens to the right or left, and thus the effect is never wearying. It resembles some of the dark cañons in our own country between the Rocky Mountains and Sierra Nevada, except that while their dark sides are of naked rock, the sides of this ravine are covered with a dense growth of vines, shrubs, and large trees, according to the steepness of the acclivities. Here were many trees and shrubs with very brilliantly-colored leaves. The whole scenery is so grand that no description, or even photograph, could convey an accurate idea of its magnificence. For four miles we rode up and up this chasm, and at last came on to the edge of the plateau at the village of Padang Panjang. We were then more than two thousand four hundred feet above the plain, having ascended about two thousand feet in four miles. Here the inspector left word for me to wait a couple of days for him, as he was still away to the south. Heavy showers continued the next day, so that I had little opportunity of travelling far; besides, it was very cool after coming up from the low, hot land by the shore. There is almost always a current of air either up or down this cleft, and the warm air of the coast region is brought into contact with the cool air of the plateau, and condensation and precipitation seems to occur here more abundantly than at any other place in the vicinity, the number of rainy days numbering two hundred and five. This is no doubt due to the local causes already explained. The average temperature here is 49.28° Fahrenheit. In the cleft, at one or two places, are a few houses made by the people who have moved down from the plateau. They are placed on posts two or three feet above the ground. Their walls are low, only three or four feet high, and made of a rude kind of panel-work, and painted red. Large open places are left for windows, which allow any one passing to look in. There are no partitions and no chairs nor benches, and the natives squat down on the rough floor. It requires no careful scrutiny of these hovels to see that they are vastly more filthy than the bamboo huts of the Malays who live on the low land.

In all the villages I have passed to-day, both on the low land and here on the plateau, there is a *pasar*, or market, and, where they have been erected by the natives, they are the most remarkable buildings I have seen in the archipelago. They are perched upon posts like the houses. The ridge-pole, instead of being horizontal, curves up so high at each end, that the roof comes to have the form of a crescent with the horns pointing upward. Sometimes a shorter roof is placed in the middle of the longer, and then the two look like a small crescent within a large one. Long before Europeans came to this land these people were accustomed to meet to barter their products, and this was their only kind of internal commerce. The next morning I rode part way down the cleft to near the place where the post-horses are changed, and found a marble that was soft, but so crystalline as to contain no fossils. I understand, however, that Mr. Van Dijk, one of the government mining engineers, discovered some pieces of this limestone which had not been crystallized, and that he considered the species of corals seen in them to be entirely of the recent period. Limestone again appears in the cleft of Paningahan, a short distance to the south. The rocks with which it is interstratified are chloritic schists, that is, layers of clay changed into hard schists by the action of heat and pressure.

February 23*d*.—The inspector arrived this morning, and we set out together for Fort de Kock, about twelve miles distant. From Padang Panjang the road continues to rise to the crest of a ridge or *col*, which crossed our road in an easterly and westerly direction, and connects Mount Singalang with Mount Mérapi. This acclivity is very nicely terraced, and the water is retained in the little plats by dikes. When any excess is poured into the uppermost in the series, it runs over into those beneath it, and thus a constant supply of water is kept over all. On looking upward we saw only the vertical sides of the little terraces covered with turf, and, in looking down, only the rice-fields. Near the crest of the col we could look down the flanks of the Mérapi to Lake Sinkara away to the south. The earth here is a tenacious red clay formed by the decomposition of the underlying volcanic rocks and volcanic ashes and sand. These are arranged in layers which have an inclination nearly parallel to the surface. The layers of ashes and sand may have been partly formed in their present position by successive eruptions in the summits of the neighboring peaks, but those of clay show that the col has been elevated somewhat since they were formed. The height of this col is three thousand seven hundred feet, and this is the highest place crossed by the road from Padang to Siboga. We now began slowly to descend, passing wide, beautifully-cultivated sawas on either hand to Fort de Kock. Here on a pretty terrace is located the house of the Resident, who has command of the adjoining elevated lands, so famous in the history of this island as the kingdom of Menangkabau, whence the Malays originally migrated, whom we have found on the shores of all the islands we have visited, and who are very distinct from the aborigines of these islands, as we have particularly noticed at Buru.

The dress of the men here is not very different from that of the Malays of Java, but the costume

WOMAN OF THE PADANG PLATEAU.

of the women is remarkable. On the head is worn a long scarf, wound round like a turban, one end being allowed to hang down, sometimes over the forehead, and sometimes on one side, or on the back of the head. The upper part of the body is clothed in a baju of the common pattern, and passing over one shoulder, across the breast, and under the opposite arm is a long, bright-colored scarf. The ends of this, as well as that worn on the head, are ornamented with imitations of leaves and fruit, very tastefully wrought with gold thread. At the waist is fastened the sarong, which is not sewn up at the ends as in other parts of the archipelago. It is therefore nothing but a piece of calico, about a yard long, wound round the body, and the two ends gathered on the right hip, where they are twisted together, and tucked under, so as to form a rude knot. As the sarong is thus open on the right side, it is thrown apart higher than the knee at every step, like the statues representing the goddess Diana in hunting-costume. Their most remarkable custom, however, is distending the lobe of the ear, as seen in the accompanying cut from a photograph of one of the women at the kampong here at Fort de Kock. When young, an incision is made in the lobe, and a stiff leaf is rolled up, and thrust into it, in such a way that the tendency of the leaf to unroll will stretch the incision. When one leaf has lost its elasticity it is exchanged for another, and, in this way, the opening increases until it is an inch in diameter. This must be a very painful process, judging from the degree to which the ears of the young girls are inflamed and swollen. A saucer-shaped ornament, with a groove in its rim, is then put into the ear, exactly as a stud is put into a gentleman's shirt-bosom. It is generally made of gold, and the central part consists of a very fine open work, so that it is very light, yet the opening in the ear continues to increase until it is frequently an inch and a half in diameter, and almost large enough for the wearer to pass one of her hands through. The front part of the loop is then only attached to the head by a round bundle of muscles, smaller than a pipe-stem, and the individual is obliged to lay aside her ornaments or have the lower part of her ears changed into long, dangling strings. While these ornaments (for it is not proper to call such a saucer-shaped article a ring) can be worn in the ear, the appearance of the native women, as seen in the cut, is like that of the other Malay women; but as soon as these ornaments are taken out, and the lobes of their ears are seen to be nothing but long loops, their appearance then becomes very repulsive. The men are never guilty of this loathsome practice. A similar habit of distending the lobe of the ear prevails in Borneo, among the Dyak women. It is also seen in all the Chinese and Japanese images of Buddha. The native women of India are accustomed to wear several small rings, not only all round in the edge of the ear, but in the nostrils. A large number of rings are shown in the ear of the cut of a Dyak or head-hunter of Borneo. Even in the most civilized lands this same barbaric idea—that a lady is made more prepossessing by having some foreign substance thrust through, and dangling from, each ear—still prevails.

After we had rested from our ride, the Resident took us through the adjoining kampong. The houses were like those already described in the Cleft. Our attention was particularly drawn to the magnificent bamboos by the roadside, many of which attain a height of forty or fifty feet.

February 24th.—The inspector, having travelled for some time, prefers to rest to-day, and as I am anxious to see the lake of Manindyu, which is some distance off our route, I avail myself of the opportunity. The Resident kindly gave me a very fine saddle-horse, and early this morning we started in a northwesterly direction for Matua. Our path at once led down from the high plateau into a series of deep valleys with perpendicular sides, composed of stratified sand and clay, formed by the disintegration and decomposition of pumice-stone. These deep valleys have been wholly formed by the action of the rapid streams which flow in their bottoms, and which, by changing their courses from one side of the valley to the other, have carried away the talus that has formed at the bases of the cliffs. These cliffs, therefore, are perpendicular, whether the valleys be wide or narrow. The strata of the sand and clay are so horizontal that we are warranted in considering them deposited in a lake of fresh or salt water. No fossils of any kind, so far as I can learn, have ever been seen in these late deposits, to determine whether they are of lacustrine or marine origin. The upper edges of the sides of these deep valleys are so sharply defined that the buffaloes, feeding on the grass-lands above, unconsciously venture too far, and of course are instantly killed by such a high fall, and, for this reason, the Dutch call them "buffalo holes."

At several places small tributaries come in as branches to the main stream, which here flows to the northwest, and the tongue of land in the acute angle of such branches rises up like a perpendicular wall with a sharp edge. These deep valleys resemble the cañons of the Colorado, which were also formed by the erosive action of running water; but here the scenery is on a small scale compared to those deep, dark, gloomy chasms. Two or three times we climbed the zigzag path that led up the sides of one valley, and then went down again into the next valley. The bottoms of these cañons, being well watered, are admirably suited for the cultivation of rice, and here were some plats still overflowed where the rice was only a few inches high, and not far from them others, where the natives were collecting the ripe, golden blades. Such a mingling of planting the seed, and gathering in the ripe grain, appeared the more strange when I thought of our temperate climate, where we are obliged to sow at a certain time in the year or reap no harvest. The higher lands between these valleys form a plateau, which, from Fort de Kock to Matua, is very sterile when compared to the high land farther south.

From Matua our course changed to the west and lay through broad sawas filled with half-grown rice. It slowly ascended, until we found ourselves on the edge of a crater of most enormous dimensions. Thick rain-clouds gathered and began pouring down heavy showers, which obscured every thing about us, and I could only see that we stood on the edge of a vast yawning gulf. Our way now rapidly descended first to the right and then to the left, and, as I looked down into the deep abyss which we were descending, such thick vapors enveloped us that every thing was hidden from our view at the distance of a hundred yards, and it seemed as if we must be going down into the Bottomless Pit. Down and down we went, until at last I became quite discouraged, and seriously began to think of explaining to my native guide that the wisest heads which lived in my land believe that the centre of the earth is nothing but a mass of molten rock, and to inquire of him whether he was sure we should stop short of such an uncomfortable place, when the thick mist which enshrouded us cleared away, and I beheld far, far beneath me a large lake, and above me the steep, overhanging crater-wall which I had descended; but I was only halfway down, yet I had the satisfaction of knowing there was an end to the way, and, besides, the road was not so steep, and consequently not so slippery as the half we had already come. So we slipped and plodded on, and early in the afternoon I came to the residence of the *controleur* of that region, at the village of Manindyu, on the east side of the lake.

The height of the edge of the crater where we began to descend is thirty-six hundred feet, and that of the lake fifteen hundred and forty above the sea. The perpendicular distance that we had come down, therefore, was over two thousand feet; but to come that distance, our road had zigzagged so continually to the right and left, that we had travelled five miles. Toward evening the rain ceased, and the *controleur* conducted me a short distance north of the kampong to a hot spring, where the natives have a square pool for bathing, and covered it with a small house, for they ascribe all sorts of healing virtues to this warm water. I found the water to be perfectly pure to the eye, and free from any sensible escape of gas. Its temperature was $102\frac{1}{2}°$ Fahrenheit, and an abundance of algæ was seen on the rocks beneath its surface.

At sunset, the heavy clouds that had filled the crater during the day slowly rose upward, but not so high at first as to allow us to see the tops of the peaks in the serrated crest of the crater-wall opposite. The bright sunlight, therefore, shone in through the triangular openings between the lower surface of the level clouds, and the bottoms of the sharp valleys, and these oblique bands of golden light fell on the water at some distance from the opposite shore, and then came over the lake and illuminated the place where we sat watching this unique and magnificent view.

After the sunlight had faded, the clouds rose higher, and I could look round and behold all sides of the largest crater it has been my privilege to see, and indeed one of the largest in the world. The general height of the wall does not vary much from that point where I crossed it coming down, and is very steep, except at that place, and in many parts nearly perpendicular. It is not circular, but composed of two circles of unequal diameter, which unite on one side, and leave a tongue of land projecting from the east and west sides. Each of these circles is a crater, and the tongues of land that project from either side of the lake mark the boundaries between them. The width of the larger crater at the level of the lake, as given on the best maps I have been able to consult, is three geographical miles; that of the smaller crater, at the same level, two and a quarter miles; and the length of the lake, which lies in a northerly and southerly direction, and is approximately parallel to the great Barizan chain in which it is found, is no less than six geographical miles. These two craters, I believe, were not formed at the same time. The larger crater, which is on the north, is older, and the smaller one to the south is the later, the eruptive force which formed the larger having lost some of its power, as well as having slightly changed its position when it formed the smaller. This gigantic crater is the more interesting to us, because it is as large as the one we supposed formerly existed in the Banda Islands, when we regarded Great Banda, Pulo Pisang, and Pulo Kapal, as parts of the walls of that crater, if, as was then suggested, that crater was not circular, but nearly elliptical, like this great one of Manindyu. Even the famous crater of the Tenger Mountains becomes of moderate dimensions, when compared to this.

In the western side of the larger crater is a cleft or deep ravine that conducts the superfluous waters to the sea. This split, it may be noticed, has occurred on the side toward the sea, where, of course, the wall of the crater was thinnest and weakest. This region is considered quite valuable, because coffee-trees flourish here remarkably well. The coffee obtained is brought over the lake in boats to the mouth of the outlet, and thence transported to the village of Tiku, on the coast.

The *controleur* also showed me a quantity of the edible birds'-nests obtained in the neighboring cliffs, that were considered of a superior quality, that is, by Chinese palates, for, if the Celestials had not taken a fancy that these should be regarded as dainties, I do not believe that Europeans would have ever thought of tasting them.

February 25th.—At eight o'clock rode back with the *controleur* up the crater wall, by the way I came down yesterday. The road is built on the spur or projecting ridge that forms the boundary between the two craters on the east side, and zigzags to the right and left in such a manner that, when viewed from beneath, it reminds one of the way, usually pictured, that the people of Babel climbed their lofty tower. To shorten the distance, we went over a number of steep places, instead of going round by the road. The clay and wet grass, however, were so slippery that such climbing was exceedingly dangerous; but the rider had the satisfaction of knowing that, if his horse did lose his footing altogether, they would both go down so many hundred feet that neither would suffer pain for many moments after their descent was ended.

The heavy rain of yesterday had wholly cleared away, and when we reached the crater rim we enjoyed a perfect view of this enormous gulf, six miles long and four miles broad, and more than two thousand feet deep. Apparently the crater had ceased its action a long time ago, and now the hot springs on the borders of the lake are the only reminders of the causes that formed it ages and ages ago. As we looked down from our high point, clouds were seen floating beneath us, and on the opposite wall of the crater long, narrow, vertical strips of naked earth marked the places where land-slides had come down its precipitous declivities.

Soon after we reached Matua, the inspector arrived from Fort de Kock, and we went on together toward the northwest. The road was exceedingly rough, and, after riding five miles, our little pony became so worn out that I got out and walked to Palimbayang, the next station, a distance of nine miles, in the scorching, tropical sun. The road from Matua is built on the side of the Barizan chain, and we had on our right a deep valley, in the bottom of which coursed the stream that we had previously crossed in the deep cañons near Fort de Kock. Several small streams came down from the mountains on our left, and in the side valleys, where those streams entered the main one, the natives had formed many terraces.

A number of these smaller valleys had the form of an ellipse, cut in two at its minor axis. In the distance they looked like immense amphitheatres, the horizontal terraces forming the seats for the imaginary spectators—amphitheatres of such ample dimensions that, in comparison with them, even the great Coliseum at Rome dwindles into insignificance.

The height of this point is a little less than that at Matua, and all the way from Fort de Kock to this place I have been able to keep in sight the remains of the plateau which begins on the south with the *col* between the Singalang and Mérapi. The horizontal layers, that once filled the whole valley west of us, have been carried away by the streams until only a narrow margin is left on the Barizan, and its parallel chain; it forcibly reminds me of the terraces seen along the upper part of some of our own New-England rivers—for instance, those in the upper part of the Connecticut Valley.

Here, at Palimbayang, I have had the first opportunity of enjoying a view of that magnificent mountain, Ophir, nine thousand seven hundred and seventy feet in height. Its truncated summit indicates that its highest parts are the ruins of an old crater, and this thought reminds us of the volcanic action to which the mountain owes its birth. The name of this mountain is not of native origin, but was given it by the Portuguese, because they fancied that at last they had found the place where the ships of Solomon obtained the enormous quantities of gold that he used in adorning the magnificent temple of Jerusalem. The same name they also gave to another, but a much smaller mountain, on the Malay Peninsula, forty miles north of the city of Malacca.

In the vicinity of both of these mountains much gold had been obtained for centuries before Europeans ever came to this region. The idea entertained by the Portuguese, that a part of the gold which reached Jerusalem came from this island and

A SCENE IN THE INTERIOR OF SUMATRA.

the peninsula, has been the subject of much ridicule, but, nevertheless, there may be considerable evidence in favor of such an hypothesis.

No one region is known in that part of the east that could have furnished all the different articles brought by Solomon's fleet; and Ophir has therefore been considered the name of an emporium, situated near the entrance of the Red Sea, or, more probably, near the head of the Arabian Sea, at the mouth of the Indus. The names in the Hebrew of the articles thus brought, show that they are all of foreign origin, having been evidently adopted from some other language, and probably from the Sanscrit.* The name for peacock appears to have been derived from the word in Tamil, a language spoken on the Malabar coast by the Telingas, or "Klings," who visited this island and the Malay Peninsula long before the time of Solomon, 1015 to 975 B. C., for the tin used by the Egyptians in making their implements of bronze, as early as 2000 B. C., doubtless came from the Malacca, and the Klings were the people who took it as far toward Egypt as the eastern shore of India. Tin and gold are both obtained in the same manner, namely, by washing alluvial deposits.

Gold is found in small quantities over a very considerable part of the Malay Peninsula. It has always been more highly valued than tin, and it is, therefore, by all means probable that it was an article of commerce, and was exported to India

---

* Vide Max Müller's "Lectures on the Science of Language," First Course. p. 224.

as early as tin, or at least five hundred years before Solomon commenced building his splendid temple.

Gold is also found in the western and southern parts of Borneo, and in some places on Luzon and Magindanao, in the Philippine Archipelago. As we have already noticed, it is found on Bachian, and, in the northern and southern peninsulas of Celebes. It is indeed one of the most widely-distributed metals obtained in the archipelago. It is not only found on many of the islands that are not wholly of volcanic origin, between Asia and Australia, but also from place to place over both of those continents. The quantity obtained here, on Sumatra, is wholly unknown, but, judging from what is used in ornaments, it must be very considerable. It is always bought and sold in the form of "dust," and has never been coined for money in any part of the archipelago, except at Achin.

CHAPTER XIII.

TO THE LAND OF THE CANNIBALS.

February 26th.—At 7 A. M. rode down the edge of the plateau to the bottom of a deep ravine, and then climbed up the opposite ridge. Here we met all the rajahs and their attendants in the vicinity, and again descended to the bottom of a second ravine to the little village of Pisang. As the way was exceedingly rough, I preferred to ride a nice horse the *controleur* had given me, to being jolted in the carriage. Beyond Pisang our road lay in a narrow valley, and, as the sky was clear and the neighboring hills prevented any breeze from reaching us, we seemed to be at the focus of a great burning lens. In the thick woods on either hand troops of large, black monkeys kept up a hooting or trumpeting, their prolonged cries sounding exactly like a score of amateurs practising on trombones. In some places the din they made was quite deafening. In one place the road passed through a deep cut through strata, composed of sand and conglomerate, which probably once filled the whole valley. From Pisang, which is at an elevation of seventeen hundred feet, we continued to descend until we came to the small valley of Bondyol, which is only seven hundred and forty feet above the sea. On the way we met the *controleur* superintending the construction of a bridge, for the officials in these small places have to plan buildings and bridges and be at the same time judges, architects, and masons. The residence of this officer was located on a hill rising on one side of the small valley. It was nicely shaded, and commanded a view over the adjoining lowlands, which were all sawas. At this place I saw some of the beautiful little musk-deer of this region—a deer that is only about a foot and a half high, without antlers, and weighs less than a rabbit.

There were more than a dozen monkeys in the backyard. Some of them were of the dog-like species, others with long tails and long limbs. Some of them were extremely restless, while others sat still and looked so grave and dignified as to be more comical than their mischievous companions. There are ten species on this island, none of which are found in Java, while the four species of Java are never seen here, such a limit does the Strait of Sunda form to the faunæ of these two islands, although it is only fifteen miles wide in some places, and islands are nearly midway from either shore. The most remarkable of the apes found on the island is the orang-utan, which lives in the lowlands in the northern and eastern parts of the island. The governor at Padang had a live one that had been sent him from that region. She was more than three feet high and very strong. Escaping one time from the box where she was fastened, she climbed a neighboring shade-tree and commenced breaking off large limbs and placing them in a fork of the tree until she had made herself a nice resting-place. That, however, not being high enough, she climbed up nearly to the top of the tree and then broke all the twigs near her, and thus formed a second couch. She did not sway to and fro continually, as many monkeys do, but used to sit quietly picking off all the foliage within her reach, and then took up another position and demolished the foliage there in the same manner. It is very singular this animal is found on Sumatra and Borneo, and has never been seen on the Malay Peninsula, which almost lies between them.

February 27th. — At 7.30 A. M. started on horseback for Lubu Siképing. At first the road led through the lowland near Bondyol, and then crossing a rapid stream began to ascend a narrow winding valley. My little pony took me up the steep places apparently with as little exertion as if we were ascending a gentle acclivity. Like all the saddle and carriage horses used in the archipelago, he was a stallion, it being considered among all these islands as disgraceful for a man to ride or drive a mare as it would be in our land for a farmer to plough with a yoke of cows. Even geldings are never seen, and, as would naturally be expected, the stallions, unless remarkably well-trained, are very vicious, and, worse than all, extremely capricious, springing, or kicking, or halting, without any provocation, and without giving their rider the slightest warning; but, when they are perfectly trained, they are among the finest saddle-horses in the world, they are so fleet and so sure-footed. In a short time the narrow valley changed into a deep ravine, and the road continued to ascend along one of its steep sides, and became so narrow that I was afraid my horse would lose his footing in the soft clay, and that we should both go down to certain destruction on the rocks that raised their ragged jaws above the spray of the foaming torrent below. A dark forest of primeval, gigantic trees covered the sides of the mountains above us, and crossing a rickety bridge we found many of their huge trunks lying across our path. They had lived to their allotted age and had not fallen by the hand of man. This road has been lately made, and already great fissures in its outer edge show that it is quite ready to slide down the mountain.

Large troops of monkeys have established themselves in this dark gorge, and just when I was in the most dangerous place they made a frightful noise, some trumpeting, some screeching, and some making a prolonged shrill whistling, yet I could only see one or two, though the natives who were building the road assured me that the tops of the trees were full of them. While in this deep ravine I crossed the equator for the third time since I entered the archipelago.

I had now climbed up one thousand four hundred feet during my short ride, and was therefore two thousand one hundred feet above the sea. To the northwest there now opened out before me a long, narrow, gently descending valley, like the one I had left behind; in fact, this water-shed is merely a transverse ridge which unites the Barizan chain with the chain parallel to it, in the same way as it is done by the transverse ranges in which the Mérapi and the Sago rise. This appears to be naturally as fruitful a region as the Menangkabau country proper, and was undoubtedly included within the limits of that empire during its most flourishing period. This valley is generally very poorly cultivated, on account of the small numbers of its population. By the wayside were a number of coffee-gardens. The trees were well filled with fruit, but they had been greatly neglected, and the tall grass was rapidly choking them.

A few miles farther on I came to Lubu Siképing, where we were to rest until the next day. A native *opziener*, or "overseer," was stationed here to receive the coffee from the adjoining plantations. He had not heard of our coming, and was quite surprised to see a stranger here in such a remote spot among the mountains, and not the less so when I informed him that the inspector was just behind me, and that I only chanced to be in advance because, from what I had heard of the road in the gorge, I had no fancy to ride through it in a wide carriage. He received us, however, like all the other officials, in the most polite manner, and was evidently glad that something had occurred to break up the dull routine of such a life of exile. It was market-day here, and, as soon as I met some of the natives returning to their homes, I saw that they were a different people from those of the Menangkabau country, and the overseer told me that they are not natives of this particular region, but belong to the wild tribe of Lubus, which I should see farther up the valley, and that it is for this reason that this place is called Lubu Sikóping. They now build houses like those of other Malays. They are better-formed people than the Javanese, and closely resemble in their features the *Oranglaut*, or common Malays of the coast regions. Their favorite holiday-dress is chiefly a bright scarlet. Half an hour after I arrived here the inspector came. He had found the road so narrow in one or two places that the natives had to push out planks beyond the outer edge of the road to support the outside wheels of the carriage, and I was glad that I came on horseback, though, when I led the vicious brute, I had to keep a constant watch to prevent him from seizing my wrist in his teeth.

At 5 P. M. we walked out to enjoy the grand scenery in the vicinity. The level plateau here, which is one thousand five hundred feet above the sea, is bounded on the northeast side by an exceedingly steep, almost overhanging range of mountains, whose several crests appear to be five thousand feet above us. It was one of the most imposing sights I witnessed on that island of high mountains. Mount Ophir is just west of this place, and at sunset we saw it through a gap in the mountains near us, resting its lofty purple summit against the golden sky.

February 28th.—I find it much more agreeable to ride on horseback most of the time, because I can stop or turn round when I please, and the opziener has therefore given me a horse to go the next ten paals. For all that distance the scenery was much like that described last night, except that the valley kept widening as we progressed northward, and, therefore, the mountains, being farther from us, were not so imposing. When we had come to the limit of the overseer's territory, another living in the next district met us and travelled with us to his little house, where we dined on venison while he entertained us with tiger-stories. Only a few days before we arrived he had seen a tiger in the road but little more than a rifle-shot from his house; and, indeed, the deer that supplied the venison we were eating had been shot in his own garden, where it had evidently been chased by one of those ferocious beasts. At the opziener's houses there is a regular price for every thing furnished, and you order what you please, though one can seldom feast on venison, and must generally satisfy his hunger on chickens and eggs, and, to receive both of these different articles, he needs only to order the latter. In the houses of all officials of a higher rank than opzieners it would be considered no less than an insult to offer to pay for your lodging. From this place I rode with the inspector a distance of twenty-five miles to Rau, the chief village in this valley. We had not gone far before we came into herds of buffaloes, which are more than half-wild and said to be very dangerous, but the natives that accompanied us kept up a loud shouting, and the herd leaped to the right and left into the jungle and tall grass, and allowed us to pass on unmolested. The people here sometimes shoot them, but consider it a most dangerous kind of sport, for they say that when one is wounded, but not fatally, he will certainly turn and pursue the hunter, and, if he can overtake him, will quickly gore him to death.

On our way we crossed several long, covered bridges, one of which was so low and our horse so unmanageable, that we came near losing the top of our carriage before we could throw it back. Two or three of them were so bent down in the middle by only a buffalo and a native occasionally crossing them, that I was unwilling to risk myself in the carriage, and jumped out and crossed them on foot. One vibrated up and down in such a manner that I certainly expected at the next moment I should see the inspector, horse, bridge, and all, in the midst of the stream below. This stream begins at Lubu Sikëping, and, after flowing northwest to Rau, where it is called Sumpur, it curves to the northeast, and, receiving tributaries during its course, flows on till it empties into the Strait of Malacca. The coffee raised in this valley is transported in *padatis* from Lunda, a small village south of this place, over a high, difficult way to Ayar Bangis, on the west coast. Sometimes a hot simoom sweeps up the valley from the south, parching up the vegetation and causing a severe illness to those foreigners who are exposed to it. The mountains here are much lower on the east than on the west, and, as there are no deep clefts in the Barizan chain here, as in the Menangkabau country, the Sumpur is obliged to find its outlet to the east.

The soil here is not as fertile as farther to the north, where it is somewhat higher, the elevation of this point being only one thousand feet. Here we see the benefit of the transverse ranges that connect the Barizan to its parallel chain. At Bondyol, in the next valley to the south, where we were yesterday, we found the bottom of the valley abounding in rich vegetation, though that was three hundred feet lower than this place, because that valley is so short that the air has no room to become heated to a dry simoom, which can wither the vegetation as it sweeps along. It is, therefore, in this valley that the simoom is formed, not on the high mountains that border it or on the adjacent ocean.

March 1st.—Left Rau at 6 A. M., for we have another long day's journey before us. As yesterday, the road led along the bottom of the valley, but soon a range of mountains appeared before us, and we began to ascend along the side of a deep ravine. The rock here was exposed, and proved to be a soft sandstone covered with clay. Here we came to a third water-shed two thousand one hundred and fifty feet high, and could look back down the valley of Rau to the southeast. Its length in a right line, from this water-shed to that at the gorge near Lubu Siképing, is thirty geographical miles, but, instead of being straight, it curves to the northeast, and is of a crescent form, widest in the middle, and gradually narrowing toward the extremities. In its broadest part it is not more than six or eight miles wide. We now turned to the northwest, and began to descend into another valley, that of Mandéling. Here the mountains are quite devoid of forests, and only covered with a tall, rank, useless grass, the *Andropogon caricosum.*

At Marisipongi, the first village we came to in this valley, we found we were among an entirely new people, the Battas or Bataks. They also belong to the Malay race, but have an alphabet and a language of their own. Each of their villages usually consists of only a single street, which is straight, and not necessarily parallel to the road. Here it was market-day, and, while we stopped to rest, I had a good opportunity of observing them. The women generally wore only a sarong fastened at the waist and descending to the knee, the upper part of the body being wholly uncovered. As we passed, the younger women made up for this deficiency to the best of their ability with the scarf in which they were carrying their children. These young women have the odd custom of wearing from fifteen to twenty *iron* rings in each ear, and as many more on their arms above the wrist.

A great many persons of both sexes, and even some children, were afflicted with that unsightly malady, goitre, and had large swellings, generally on the neck, though I noticed one at the lower end of the breastbone. The cause assigned here by the Dutch officials for this disease is that these people have been accustomed to use very little salt, the iodine contained in that condiment being supposed to act as a preventive to the development of the disease. It is said to seldom or never appear among those Malays who have lived on the sea-coast for several generations, and I do not remember to have seen a single case in such a locality.

The market-place was nothing but a shed, and here a few Chinese and Arabs were displaying cotton cloth, knives, and ornaments, and the natives had brought dried and smoked fish, which they catch in these mountain-streams, also bananas, jambus or rose-apples, and a kind of fruit like that from which the guava jelly is made.

Rice is the chief article of food of the natives here, with dried fish and bananas, and a few eggs and chickens. From this village we rode to Kotanopan, our way again descending along a large foaming brook, in which the opziener of that district assured me the natives were accustomed to wash for gold, which they still obtain, though only in small quantities.

Here we passed the grave of a Batta. It consisted of a rectangular mound, with a wooden image of a horse's head on one end, and a part of a horse's tail fastened to the other—the mound forming his body. At each of the four corners was an image of a nude man or woman. Over the whole was a rude roof supported on four posts, and around the whole was placed a row of sticks four feet high, and a foot or two apart, bearing on their tops small flags of white cloth. This tendency to ornament graves we have already noticed among the aborigines of the Minahassa. It is also seen, but in a more revolting form, in the Papuan temple at Dorey.

March 2d.—From Kotanopan we have come to Fort Elout, after a journey of more than ordinary danger. For the first five miles our road was very good, but then we found it completely overgrown with tall grass. So long as it was over the level lands there was little danger, but soon it changed to the flanks of a spur, thrown out by the chain that formed the northeastern boundary of the valley. There it became very narrow, and the tall grass com-

pletely hid its outer edge. Besides, our horse was
wholly unaccustomed to a carriage, and only half-
trained, and every few moments took it into his head
to stop so short that we had to hold on to the carriage all the time, or at an unexpected moment find
ourselves going over the fender. The road was now
taking us out toward the end of the spur, the ravine
was growing deeper and deeper with an alarming
rapidity, and I began to wish myself out of the carriage, but the inspector was unwilling to stop the
horse for fear we could not get him started again. A
Malay was guiding our wild steed by the bit, and
away we were dashing at full gallop, when suddenly,
as we rounded the spur, the road, which was cut in
the rock, was so narrow that the outside wheels of
the carriage were just on its outer edge, and from
that verge the rock descended in such a perpendicular precipice that I could look from my seat in the
carriage down fully two hundred feet, with a boiling
torrent beneath me. It was evidently too late to
jump then, so I seized hold of the carriage, determined not to go off before my companion, the inspector, who, realizing at once our great danger, and
perceiving that the only thing that we could do was
to keep the horse going at the top of his speed,
shouted to the horse, and, in the same breath, threatened to take off the Malay's head if he should let go
of the bridle. Some fragments of rock had fallen
down into the road, and our fore-wheel, on the
inner side, struck these with such violence that I
thought certainly we should be thrown off the narrow shelf down the precipice. For two minutes we

RIDING ALONG A PRECIPICE.

seemed to hang in the air, and then the road widened. I drew a long breath of relief, and then bounded out over the wheel on to the solid ground, before I could fully satisfy myself that, thanks to a kind Providence and the force of gravitation, I was really safe.

The inspector said that he had travelled many thousand miles in Java, in all manners of ways, and through all manners of dangers, but was never so frightened before, and that he would not go back that way in a carriage for ten thousand guilders. If we had only known what we were coming to, we could have got out and walked, but it was already too late when we saw the danger. I determined to ride no farther in the carriage that day, and made our guide exchange places with me, and give me his horse. This dangerous place the natives call Kabawjatu, "where-the-buffaloes-fall." Only a short time before, a Malay was driving a single buffalo to market along this way, when he shied a little, went off headlong, and was dashed in pieces on the rocks beneath.

A short distance beyond this place we changed horses, at a little settlement of the Lubus. Their houses are scattered over the mountain-side, and not gathered into one place. They are ten or fifteen feet long, and eight or ten wide, and perched on high poles. The walls are made of bamboo, and the roofs are thatched with straw, like all that we have seen since leaving Lubu Siképing, instead of atap, which is used by all the natives farther south. The officials here informed me that these people eat bananas, and probably most fruits, maize, dogs, monkeys, and even *snakes*, but never rice; and this is the more strange because it is the staple article of food among their neighbors. They are yet slaves to their rajah, just as the people of all the tribes in this vicinity were before they were conquered by the Dutch, for the Lubus, so far as we know, remain as they were in the most ancient times. Here I enjoyed a magnificent view of the active volcano Seret Mérapi, the summit of which is five thousand nine hundred feet above the sea. It is not a separate mountain like the Mérapi of the Menangkabau country, but merely a peak in the Barizan chain. From its top a jet of opaque gas rose into the clear, blue sky, while small cumuli came up behind the coast-chain from the ocean, and seemed to settle on its highest summits, as if weary, and wishing to rest, before they continued their endless flight through the sky.

When we again came to the bottom of the valley, we found what seemed to us a wonder—a smooth, well-graded road, bordered on either side with a row of beautiful shade-trees. All the low land in this vicinity is used for sawas, and the rice, which was mostly two-thirds grown, waved most charmingly in the light wind, that reminded me of our summer-breezes. The inspector, who was an old gentleman, felt somewhat worn out with such incessant jolting, and, as I had been travelling without stopping for eight days, I was only too glad to have one day of rest also.

At sunset, as is always the custom in these tropical lands, we took an evening walk. The many fires now raging in the tall grass that covers the lower flanks of the mountains have so filled the air with smoke, that when the sun had sunk behind the serrated crest of the Barizan, the whole horizon for twenty degrees and to a considerable height was lighted up with one unvarying golden glow. Here the Barizan is composed of four or five parallel ranges, which rise successively one above the other until the last forms the highest elevation in that chain. These different ranges were of various shades of color; that the nearest to us, or the lowest, being the darkest, and those above it of a lighter and lighter hue up to the highest range, which had a bright border of gold along its crest; and from that line to where we stood the air seemed filled with a purple dust. As the daylight faded, the fires in the tall grass on the hill-sides became more distinct; sometimes advancing in a broad, continuous band, and sometimes breaking up into an irregular, beaded line. Soon afterward the moon rose as charmingly in the east as the sun just gloriously set in the west. First a diffuse light appeared along the mountaintops and whitened the fleecy cumuli hovering over their summits. Then that part of the sky grew brighter and brighter until the light of the full moon fell like a silver cascade over the serrated edge of the high mountains and rested on the tops of the hills below. An assistant resident is stationed here at Fort Elout, who has charge of this fruitful valley of Mandeling, which is wholly inhabited by the Battas. The territory between this valley and the west coast is also inhabited by this rude people. The Resident explained to us the trouble taken by the government and the expense it was incurring, in order to teach them to read and write, and cultivate the land. One time the older children burned all the books given them by the government, supposing that, of course if they had no books, they would not be required to go to school. Earthquakes are frequent here, and, but a short time since, seven shocks occurred in one day. All came from the south, exactly from the direction where the Seret Mérapi is seen burning. Most of them were accompanied by a noise, which preceded the shock long enough for the Resident to remark to a friend, " there comes another," before the shock itself was perceived. Here we saw many hanging birds'-nests, most ingeniously constructed. They were made of fine grass, woven into a mass having the form of a pear or gourd, from eight inches to a foot long. The smaller part is attached to the end of a drooping twig, and on the bottom at one side is the opening of a tube about an inch and a half in diameter. This rises vertically for four or five inches and then curves over and descends like a syphon. At the end of the short part of this syphon the tube is enlarged to a spherical cavity, and here the ingenious bird lays her eggs. In order to appreciate the remarkable skill required to make the nest, it would be necessary for one to see a series of them, from those which have been just begun to those that are nearly finished, for the tube which is to lead to the nest is not formed by blades of grass wound into rings or a helix, but is built up from a single direction until the two curving sides meet. Among the *sawas* are small artificial pools, where fish are raised as in China; a custom probably introduced by the

Chinese themselves. After these shallow pools have been used for this purpose a year or two, the fish are taken out, the larger ones sent to market, and the smaller ones transferred to another pond. The water in the first pool is then drained off, and its bottom becomes a fruitful rice-field. In this manner the natives allow their land to lie fallow, and at the same time make it yield a good crop.

March 4th.—At 6 A. M., started from Rau for Padang Sidempuan, at the northern end of this valley, which begins on the south at Marisipongi, where we first saw the Battas. All day our route has been in the bottom of the valley, at a general elevation of one thousand feet. Sometimes we passed over gentle undulations, but usually over one monotonous level area covered with tall grass, in which were interspersed large clumps of shrubbery. In one village there were two most enormous waringin-trees, under which the villagers had prepared a rude table. On this they had spread young cocoa-nuts, and bananas, apparently the only kinds of fruit they had to offer.

As we advanced, the mountains on our right dwindled until they formed hills, whose tops were only five or six hundred feet above the plateau in which we were travelling. Before us rose another great transverse ridge, in which towered up the peak of Lubu Rajah to a height of over six thousand two hundred feet above the sea. It is the highest mountain in the Batta Lands, as the Dutch call the high plateaus of Silindong and Toba which lie north of this transverse ridge, and are beyond the limits of the territory subject to the government of the Netherlands India. Soon after we arrived, the *controleur* received a letter from a Batta chief. It was nothing but a piece of young bamboo a couple of inches in diameter and about six inches long. On this had been scratched, with a blunt needle, characters of various shapes, quite intricate, but not having by any means the barbarous appearance of those used by the Chinese. The object of this letter was to inform the *controleur* that during a recent rain a bridge near the rajah's village had been washed away. Unlike the Chinese language, where every character is a word, the Batta is an alphabetic language, and one of their own invention. As spoken by the various branches of this tribe it differs only to the degree of dialects, and the language is, therefore, a unit. The religion of this people is a belief in evil spirits and omens. The place where their aboriginal civilization sprang up was probably in the neighboring plateau of Silindong and on the borders of Lake Toba. Thence they seem to have spread over all the area they now occupy in the interior and to the sea-coast on either side. In later times the people of Menangkabau, or Malays proper, extended their power along the coast and made the Battas an inland people.

The strangest fact concerning this people, who have come to such a state of civilization as to invent an alphabet of their own, is, that all of them, beyond the territory under the Dutch Government, are *cannibals*. Those living on this plain also feasted on human flesh until the Dutch conquered them, and obliged them to give up such a fiendish custom. The rajah of Sipirok assured the governor at Padang that he had eaten human flesh between thirty and forty times, and that he had never in all his life tasted any thing that he relished half as well. This custom has prevailed among the Battas from time immemorial.

From Marco Polo's writings we learn that, as early at least as in 1290, they were addicted to their present revolting habits.

Sir Stamford Raffles, who visited Tapanuli Bay in 1820, was informed that any one who should be convicted of the following five crimes must be cut up alive: For adultery; midnight robbery; in wars, where prisoners were taken; intermarrying in the same tribe; and for a treacherous attack on any house, village, or person. The facts which came to my knowledge while in this region, and the statements of the Dutch officials and of the natives themselves, entirely confirm this account of their customs and laws, except in regard to that against intermarrying. Such are yet the practices of the people in this immediate vicinity, and such, not many years ago, were those of all the people among whom we had been travelling for the last four days.

Here, and at several other places in the interior, I have seen young trees of a species of cinnamon, *kayu manis*, or "sweet wood" of the Malays. Its leaves and bark have a considerable aroma, but it is not the true cinnamon of Ceylon, nor that of Cochin China nor China. Cinnamons of one or more species occur also in Java, Borneo, Luzon, and Magindanao. As our carriage needed repairing, and both the inspector and I were becoming fatigued, we therefore rested at this place for a day.

March 6th.—Started early in the carriage for Lumut, in a westerly direction. Our road continued to ascend until we reached the water-shed formed by the Barizan, and were two thousand five hundred feet above the sea. We now passed out of the great valley of Mandéling, which is fifty-five miles long in a right line, but only from six to ten miles broad.

The descent from the water-shed toward the sea is gradual, but the road is execrable and exceedingly narrow at best, and wholly covered, except a narrow foot-path, with tall grass. Besides, our horses had never been harnessed to a carriage before, and, after many fruitless attempts to guide them, I said to the inspector that the only way we should be able to proceed would be to make the wild natives, who gathered to look on, haul us themselves. He replied that that would be perfectly impossible, for they respect no one but the governor. However, I noticed that they recognized our "American" as the one the governor had used in travelling that way once before—the only time a carriage had ever been seen on the road—and jumping out, directed our Malay attendants, who could speak their language, to say to them the governor wished us to take the "American" through to Siboga, and every man must help us obey his command. This chanced to strike them favorably, and their rajahs detailed some twenty to haul us as far as the next village. I selected three of the tallest and fleetest and placed them between the thills, and ranged others outside to haul, by means of long rattans fastened to the forward axle, and a suitable proportion behind to hold back by a rattan secured to the hind part of the carriage as we went down-hill. All being in their places, I jumped into the carriage. A wild yell was raised, and away we dashed down a gradual descent, as if we were drawn by a race-horse; the road became steeper and steeper, and we flew faster and faster; those behind had evidently forgotten what was expected of them. Those in front, who were outside of the thills, dropped the rattan and leaped aside for fear of the rattling wheels behind them, and those in the thills shouted out all sorts of implorings and execrations against those behind, who seemed to enjoy the discomfiture of their fellows too much to hold back at all. When we reached the bottom of the long hill, the men in the thills were the only ones near the carriage. The others were scattered at intervals all the way down the hill, but were coming on as fast as they could. All seemed in the best of temper, except those in the thills, who gave a spirited lecture to the others; but at once all formed as before, and took us up the succeeding hill. The inspector was in constant apprehension of some mishap, but I thought we might as well be drawn by wild men as wild horses.

Just before we arrived at each village, the rajah of that place met us with men enough to take us on to the next kampong, and sometimes we had forty or fifty of them drawing us at a time. On the level lands they usually took us along at a fast canter, shouting, and screaming, and leaping, as if they were half mad.

At noon we came to the famous suspension bridge of rattan, of which I had been hearing the most frightful accounts for the last hundred miles. At once I took off my shoes to avoid slipping, and hastened down the airy, oscillating way, without allowing myself to look down and become giddy at the fearful depth beneath me. At the middle it rests on the tops of tall trees, which grow up from a small island in the torrent far below. It has been constructed by first stretching across three large rattans. On them narrow strips of boards are placed transversely, and fastened at each end by strips of common rattan. Other rattans, starting from the ground at a little distance back of the bank, pass above the branches of high camphor-trees that grow on the edge of the chasm in which the torrent flows. Descending from these branches in a sharp curve, they rise again steeply at the farther end of the bridge. From these rattans vertical lines are fastened to the rattans below them, exactly as in our suspension bridges, and thus all parts are made to aid in supporting the weight. At each bank the bridge is some eight feet wide, but it narrows toward the middle until it is only two feet, where it vibrates the most. I had been directed to go over, if possible, at a hurried walk, and thus break up the oscillating motion, and particularly cautioned against seizing the side of the bridge, lest it might swing to the opposite side and throw me off into the abyss beneath. When I had gone half-way across the first span I found that one of the cross-boards, on which I was just in the act of placing my foot, had become

HANGING BRIDGE OF BAMBOO; SUMATRA.

loose and slipped over to one side, so that, if I had stepped as I had intended, I should have put my foot through, if indeed I had not fallen headlong and been dashed on the rocks in the torrent more than a hundred feet beneath me. I therefore stopped instantly, and allowed myself to swing with the bridge until it came to a state of rest, and then again went on slowly, and safely reached the opposite bank. My companions, who stood on the bank behind me, became greatly alarmed when they saw me stop in the midst of the long span, and were sure that I had either become giddy, or was frightened, and that, in either case, I would grasp hold of the side of the bridge contrary to their express orders.

The difficulty in crossing this bridge, which is as flexible as Manilla rope, is so great, not only because it oscillates to the right and left, but because there is a vertical motion, and its whole floor, instead of moving in one piece, is continually rolling in a series of waves. An official, who had taken very careful measurements of it in order to make an estimate of the cost of erecting a true bridge, for this airy way does not deserve such a substantial name, gave me the following figures: total length, 374 feet; height of the middle and lowest part of the first span above the torrent, 108 feet; height of the middle and lowest part of the second span, 137.5 feet. The inspector then came over safely, and we walked a short distance to a neighboring village while the natives were taking our carriage to pieces and bringing them over one at a time.

Although I am not one of those who allow themselves to be constantly tortured by presentiments and omens, I could not rid myself of an impression that some accident was going to happen to those who were bringing over the carriage, and went back to see for myself what they were doing. The wheels and top were over, and six natives were bringing the body, which, though quite large, was very light. They had already crossed the long span, and were coming on to the short one. "Is it possible," I said to myself, "that such a slight structure can hold such a weight at such a great leverage? We shall soon see, for they are rapidly coming to the middle of the second span." At the next instant there was a loud, sharp crack, like the report of a pistol. One of the large rattans that went over the high branches of the camphor-trees and supported the sides, had parted at one of its joints. The officer who had charge of the bridge, and was standing by my side, seized me by the shoulder in his fright. As soon as the rattan on one side broke, the bridge gave a fearful lurch in the opposite direction, but the natives all knew they must keep perfectly quiet and allow themselves to swing, and, finally, when it had become still, they came on carefully and safely reached the bank. The officer and I both believed that the moment one of the rattans broke, the others, having of course to support a much greater weight, would also break, and that we should hear a few more similar crackings, and see all the natives fall headlong down nearly one hundred and forty feet into the boiling torrent beneath, which is so rapid that only a few days ago a buffalo, that was standing in the side of the stream above the bridge, lost his footing and was carried down without being able to reach either bank.

The carriage was soon put together again, and a good number of natives detailed to haul us to the next village, and away we dashed along, and that fearful place was soon hidden from our view. From this point to Lumut our road extended over a hilly, undulating country, in which we crossed a number of small streams on rafts of bamboo.

Lumut we found to be only an opziener's station. A Malay teacher is also employed here by the government, but the general appearance of the people has changed little since they were accustomed to enjoy their cannibal feasts, and this is true of all the natives we have seen this side of Padang Sidempuan.

Most of the rajahs we have seen to-day have worn garments profusely ornamented with gold. The head-dress of each usually consisted of a short turban so wound around the head that the two ends hung down in front, and to these were fastened small, thin pieces of gold of a diamond or circular form. They also wear short jackets which are usually trimmed with a broad band of gold, though a few had silver instead. At the waist is worn a belt on which is worn in front a large diamond-shaped ornament four or five inches long, made of thin gold and ornamented with flowers and scrolls. When at Rau, we visited a native who was famous for his skill in manufacturing such golden ornaments. The leaves which he made on them were remarkably well-proportioned, and the details very correctly wrought in; and we admired his skill the more when he came to show us his tools, which consisted of a flat stone for an anvil, a hammer, and two or three large, blunt awls. Having beaten the gold out into thin sheets of the desired form, he made the leaves rise in relief by forming a corresponding groove on the opposite or inner side. In other cases he had formed the gold into small wire, which was bent into helices for ornaments to be placed on the front of such articles as buttons. At Fort de Kock this business is carried on so extensively as to form an important branch of the internal trade. The metal generally used there is silver, the coin imported by the Dutch, for we have no reason to suppose that that metal is found on this island. They make models of their houses, of leaves, flowers, and all the principal fruits, which are sent to Padang, where they find a ready demand among the foreigners, who send them as presents to their friends in Europe.

We have just been honored by a call from the two rajahs of this little village of Lumut. The bands of gold on their jackets were two inches broad—an indication that the precious metal must be obtained in all this region in very considerable quantities. Ever since entering the southern end of the valley of Mandéling, I have been repeatedly informed that the natives obtained gold by washing in their vicinity. At Fort Elout the Resident showed me a nugget, as large as a pigeon's egg, which a native had just found in a neighboring stream where they had certainly been at work for centuries. Washing seems to be almost the only mode adopted by the natives for obtaining gold, and I heard of only one place where they have ever attempted to take it from the rock. That place is in the mountains west of Rau.

March 7th.—Early this morning continued on for Siboga, with the satisfactory feeling that this day would be the last of our long and difficult journey. The road for ten miles led through a deep forest of gigantic camphor-trees, *Dryobalanops camphora*, the tall, straight trunks of which rose up like lofty columns. From their high branches hung down hundreds of the cord-like roots of a parasite. The "camphor-oil" is obtained from these trees by making a small cavity in the trunk near the ground, and the fluid dripping into this cavity is the "oil." After a tree has been dead for a long time, it is cut down and split up, and layers of pure camphor are found crystallized in thin plates in the fissures, where the wood in dying has slightly split open. This is known as "camphor barus," from Barus, a village on the coast a short distance to the north, because such crystallized camphor was formerly exported from that place. The Chinese and Japanese, who suppose it possesses the most extravagant healing properties, pay enormous prices for it, while, except that it is somewhat purer, it is probably not any better than that they make themselves by distillation from the wood of the *Cinnamon camphora*. The camphor-tree is not only valuable for the camphor it yields, but also for its timber, which is very straight and free from knots and other imperfections. This is a favorite region for tigers, and I have seen one or more skins at the house of each official. A short time since, an elephant came down here from the interior, but the natives failed to secure so valuable a prize. Herds of them are said to frequently appear in the Silindong plateau. The tusks of one taken here lately were sold for one thousand guilders (four hundred Mexican dollars). On our way we passed eight or ten houses of Battas, who had come down from the mountains. They were placed on posts like those we have been seeing; but the gable-ends, instead of being perpendicular, slant outward, so that the ridge-pole, which comes up high at each end, is much longer than the floor. Over a number of these streams we found long suspension bridges, but none were high as that over the Batang Taroh. Ascending to the crest of a mountain-range, some six or eight hundred feet in height, we found before us a grand view of the high mountains, stretching in a semicircle around the bay of Tapanuli; of the low land at their feet, and of a part of the bay itself. A steep, zigzag way took us down nearly to the level of the sea, and led us over the low land to the village of Siboga, a small Dutch settlement and military station at the head of the bay.

CHAPTER XIV.

RETURN TO PADANG.

Back of Siboga rises a high peak, and from its summit I was confident that I could enjoy a magnificent view over the whole bay. A native engaged to show me the way to its top, but after we had travelled a long distance I found he had even less idea of how we were to reach the desired spot than I had myself. Other natives gave me directions, but that day was too far spent for such a journey, and I therefore made my pretended guide travel with me the next day for nothing, as a punishment for his lying. Following up a stream back of the settlement, we took a minor valley to the south, and discovered a narrow path by which the Battas sometimes come down from the interior. This led up through a thick forest to a large place where that people had partially cleared the land by burning down the trees. In the irregular spaces between the stumps they had planted pineapples and yams, which were both thriving remarkably well. When we had gained that place I found the desired peak still above us. My attendant now begged me not to attempt to reach it, less, as I afterward learned, from his fear of the Battas than from his fear of the evil spirit who is said to inhabit that high point, and whom he believed we should certainly meet. But we gained the summit without meeting any unearthly intruders. There I found the whole bay and its shores spread out before me like a map. The broad coral banks bordering several of the points and islands were of a light-clay color in the dark-blue water, which was only here and there ruffled by the light morning breezes then moving over its limpid surface. This bay is said to closely resemble the bay of Rio Janeiro by those who have seen both. To the north it has a long arm, but on the south its boundary is sharply defined when viewed from the lofty point where I stood, while off the mouth of the bay was the high island of Mensalla, its hills making a sharply-serrated line against the sky.

On another occasion I made an excursion in a boat some six miles toward the northern end of the bay to look at some layers of coal. Leaving the boat we went a short distance up the side of a range of hills on the northwest side of the bay, and, crossing two small ridges that ran down to the shore, found the bed of a brook, which at that season was dry. In one of its sides were seen the layers of coal, approximately parallel to the surface of the hills, and resting on clay schists, to which they appeared perfectly conformable. Crossing another low ridge, we came down into the bed of another brook, where the same strata were again seen. The coal here is very impure, except near the middle layers, and appears to be of little commercial value; neither is the prospect flattering for finding other strata of a better quality beneath those seen at the surface. Although I looked carefully, I could detect no leaves or stems of plants, or any organic remains, by which the geological age of this coal could be determined; but the position of the layers parallel to the surface, or last folding the strata have undergone, agrees with its mineral characters in placing it, like the other coals of Sumatra, in the tertiary period.

As I came to Siboga from the south, over the low land around the bay, I noticed on my right a high, perpendicular cliff composed of recent strata that were horizontal, and which must have been deposited beneath the ocean, because the opposite side of the valley is open to the sea, with only hills at intervals along its shore, and even their forms indicate that they are of the same sedimentary origin. This cliff the natives call in Malay the *Ruma Satan*, or "the Devil's Dwelling." It was on the western declivity of the mountains which sweep round parallel to the shore. The Resident gave orders to the rajah of Sibuluan, a native village about four miles south of Siboga, to go with me and show me the way. When I came to that village I found the rajah was a young man, and evidently afraid of such an undertaking. In the first place, we must be exposed to the *cannibal* Battas, and even travel among them; but I assured him that that, so far from making me desire to turn back, only made me the more anxious to go on, for I liked to see all kinds of people, and I had no fear that the Battas would eat me. Finding he could not induce me to give up what he evidently considered a most venturesome journey, he summoned the largest man in his *kampong* and armed him with a long, rusty sword. Several others were also ordered to accompany us, though the rajah seemed to rely chiefly on the brave who carried his arms. As for me, the only weapon with which I was provided was a pocket-knife, but I think now that I underrated the danger then, and that if I were going on the same excursion again I should take a revolver at least. From Subuluan our course was along a large stream. Soon we came to a Batta village, where a capala and two men joined us, to act as our guides and also to increase my body-guard, which, even then, would have been far from formidable if any real danger had presented itself, and they had had a good opportunity to run away. The rough path that we were following came to a stream which I was compelled to wade, and found so deep that it rose to my arms. Besides, the current was so strong that I was glad to have the assistance of a native on either side. The sand and sharp gravel were thus washed into my shoes; and as I learned we should have to cross that stream some ten times, for such a road do these wild cannibals use, I quickly prepared myself to go barefoot.

We had now come into a deep gorge; the sun poured down his most scorching rays; the rocks and sand were so hot that it seemed they would blister my feet, and even the Malays complained. The next ford was just above a series of rapids. I was clad in a suit of blue flannel, which absorbed so much water that I found I was in great danger of being swept away by the torrent. I concluded that I had better adopt the costumes of the Malays. The rajah wore a new pair of *chilanas*, of the prevailing pattern, made in Achin. They are short-legged trousers, fastened at the waist and reaching nearly to the knee. I proposed that we exchange, but he declined to do that, and insisted on my keeping possession of my own habit, and using the article I desired, and in that costume I travelled till I came back to his village. In one place the torrent rolled up against a high precipice, but there chanced to be a horizontal crevice some distance above the water, and there, where scarcely a monkey would think of venturing, we were obliged to crawl along as best we could. This danger passed, we had to cross back and forth over rapids by leaping from rock to rock, some of which were above and some just beneath the surface of the boiling torrent. Then we came to an area of high grass. The tall native, in accordance with the rajah's orders, marching ahead with the sword grasped in his right hand, and its naked, rusty blade resting on his bare arm, was, indeed, the personification of bravery; but, as I had little faith in the necessity of such a doughty warrior, I began to ridicule his appearance to the rajah, when suddenly our brave gave an ugly nasal grunt, and, brandishing his sword high over his head, brought it down with a heavy cutting stroke on some object in front of him. "What is the matter?" every one asked. "A great snake was crossing the road!" an agreeable thing to hear, considering that I had no clothing on below the knee; but, while he was flourishing his weapon and getting ready to strike, the reptile had glided away in the tall grass.

The rajah now showed me a spot by the wayside where a Batta, who had been guilty of adultery, had been killed and eaten by his fellows not long before. All the others in the party confirmed the story in every particular. A little farther on was a Batta village consisting of four houses on high posts. One was small and stood apart from the others, and in that they stored their rice. To prevent the mice from reaching it, large projecting pieces of planks were placed on the tops of the posts. The walls, floor, and gable-ends of the dwelling-houses were made of plank, and the roof was a thatching of grass or straw. Having some curiosity to see the internal arrangements of a Batta house, I climbed up a ladder of five or six rounds at one end of the building, and took a place assigned me on the floor. There was no bench nor stool, nor any thing of the kind, so, according to Batta etiquette, I rested my back against the side of the house. The whole building was in one room, without a shadow of any partition. From the number of the inmates, I saw that probably four families dwelt in this single apartment, and this suspicion was strengthened when I noticed a rude fireplace, without any chimney, in each corner. On inquiry, I was informed that my conjectures were true. "But how do you know," I asked, "what part belongs to one family and what to another? Where is your partition?" One of them, who could understand a little Malay, gravely rose, and, coming to my side in answer to my query, pointed to a *crack* in the floor.

From this place the rajah had said I could obtain

an unobstructed view of the cliff, but when we arrived there a neighboring hill completely hid it from view. He then excused himself by saying that he had never been there before; and, when I informed him that I must go on until I could see it perfectly, the tears actually stood in his eyes from fear, he was so certain we should meet with the Evil Spirit. One of the Battas, who knew the way, offered to be my guide, and I released the rajah from the Resident's order to accompany me as far as I wished to go, and continued on, for I had no fear of meeting Apollyon in the next valley.

Two sections at right angles showed that the strata of this cliff were nearly horizontal, and composed of a light-colored clay, containing many coarse crystals of quartz. These materials had recently been formed by the decomposition of the adjoining syenitic rocks, and had been arranged into layers by the action of water. The height to the top of the cliff from the bed of the brook I judge to be eight hundred feet, and that is at least fifty feet above the level of the sea, making the whole elevation which this part of the island has recently undergone to be eight hundred and fifty feet.

When we returned to the Batta village, the rajah seemed greatly relieved, for he declared that he believed he should never see us again. Such are the superstitious terrors that constantly torture the imaginations of these ignorant people. On our return, a heavy rain set in, which completely drenched us and swelled the brook. Again and again the strong current came near sweeping us off the slippery rocks, while the lightning flashed in broad sheets and the thunders echoed and reëchoed in the deep ravine. The Malays who formed my guard then began to discuss in an undertone, without thinking that I overheard them, whether the Evil Spirit would not, after all, bring some dreadful misfortune on the white gentleman for daring to visit his abode. One suggested that the Battas might yet capture him on one of his dangerous excursions. Another said he would probably have an attack of fever (which I confess I myself considered probable), for after such exposure to the hot sun, and such a drenching, any man, even a native, is likely to find a keen burning in his veins the next morning. The rajah, however, replied to these unfavorable suggestions, that Tuan Allah would take pity on him, and not allow even the rain to harm him, for he was a good man, and it could not be very wicked in any one simply to go and see where the Evil Spirit lived. My feet and ankles had become so bruised from treading on the rough rocks in the bed of the torrent, and so cut from walking through the tall grass, that as soon as I reached my room I went to bed, and did not rise for thirty hours; but the rajah's predictions proved true, and I escaped without even an attack of fever.

A few days afterward, a rajah came from his village on the coast near Barus, or Barros, a small port about thirty miles toward Achin. He said that some neighboring Battas had taken two of his men, and had already *eaten* one of them, and were keeping the other to eat him also, and that he came to Siboga to ask the Resident that soldiers be sent to compel

those cannibals to deliver up their intended victim.
Such a request, of course, it was not possible for the
Resident to grant, however much he might wish to
do so, for the whole country is extremely mountainous, and covered with a dense, impenetrable forest;
and the moment these Battas have finished their attack, they instantly retreat into the interior without
allowing the Dutch the possibility of punishing
them, except by subjugating the entire country, and
that would be a work of the greatest difficulty, and
one that would require much time, and money, and
bring no adequate recompense. It is such a common
thing for the foreigners here at Siboga to hear that
one or more natives have been eaten in the neighboring mountains, that no one thinks of speaking of
it as any thing strange or even incredible. In the
Silindong valley two missionaries have been living
for some time, trying to educate and convert the
Battas. I met one of them with his bride at the
governor's residence when I arrived at Padang. The
lady had arrived but a short time before from Holland, and they were just then starting on their wedding tour to their future residence among the cannibals. The other missionary is now at this village,
and I have just been present at his wedding. His
wife is a young lady of not more than seventeen
summers, and what is stranger than all in both of
these matches is, that neither of these gentlemen
had seen his betrothed before she arrived, except in
a miniature, which of course might or might not be
a good likeness. It may relieve the curious for me
to state that all parties are entirely satisfied.

This missionary tells me that he knew of a Batta who had been guilty of stealing an article of only very little value according to their ideas of wealth, yet he was seized, his arms extended at full length and fastened to a bamboo, a sharpened prop placed under his chin, so that he could not move his head, and in this condition he was bound fast to a tree. The knife was then handed to the native who had lost the article, and he was ordered to step forward and cut out of the living man what piece he preferred. This he did promptly; the rajah took the second choice, and then the people finished the cold-blooded butchery, and thus their victim died. This revolting feast, he assures me, took place but a short distance from the village where he resides. How any lady can think of going to live among such dangers I cannot conceive; but Madame Pfeiffer, according to her account, went considerably farther than the place where these missionaries reside, and even reached the northern end of the Silindong valley; but I am assured here, and she states nearly the same thing in her book, that the Battas only permitted her to return because they regarded her as a witch. Three years after she performed that journey, three French priests were butchered and devoured, before they had come near to the farthest place she had reached alone. No Malay would have ever escaped who had gone so far into their country.

The parts that are esteemed the greatest delicacies are the palms of the hands, and, after them, the eyes. As soon as a piece is cut out it is dipped, still warm and steaming, in *sambal*, a common con-

A NATIVE OF THE ISLAND OF NIAS.

diment, composed of red or Chili peppers and a few grains of coarse salt, ground up between two flat stones. Formerly it appears to have been the custom to broil the human flesh, for Mr. Marsden states that, in December, 1780, a native of Nias, who stabbed a Batta at Batang Taroh, the river I crossed on the suspension bridge, was seized at six one morning, and, without any judicial process, was tied to a stake, cut in pieces with the utmost eagerness while yet alive, and eaten upon the spot, partly *broiled*, but mostly raw.

It is probably on account of the difficulty of penetrating their inland and elevated country, and from the natural ferocity of these people, that the Mohammedan priests of the neighboring country of Menangkabau have failed to induce the Battas to adopt their religion. The first white men who went up far into the interior appear to have been Mr. Ward and Mr. Burton, two English missionaries, about the year 1820.

They started from this place, and reached the Silindong valley. Their object was to reach Lake Toba, but they were only obliged to return on account of their becoming seriously ill. The kindly manner in which they were treated is very different from the reception all other white men have received at the hands of these cannibals.

It appears that the next white men who went up into the interior of this country were two American missionaries, Henry Lyman and Samuel Munson, graduates of Amherst College, and natives of Massachusetts. In 1835 they sailed from Batavia to Padang, and thence came directly up the coast to the Batu Islands, Pulo Nias, and this bay. From this village they went up into the interior toward Lake Toba, and when about fifty miles distant they were attacked and killed by the Battas.

Considering the friendly reception given the former missionaries, I do not think this journey promised such an unhappy issue.

The Battas certainly do not eat human flesh for lack of food, nor wholly to satisfy revenge, but chiefly to gratify their appetites. The governor at Padang informed me that these people gave him this odd origin of their cannibal customs: Many years ago one of their rajahs committed a great crime, and it was evident to all that, exalted as he was, he ought to be punished, but no one would take upon himself the responsibility to punish a prince. After much consultation they at last hit upon the happy idea that he should be put to death, but they would all eat a piece of his body, and in this way all would share in punishing him. During this feast each one, to his astonishment, found the portion assigned him a most palatable morsel, and they all agreed that whenever another convict was to be put to death they would allow themselves to gratify their appetites again in the same manner, and thus arose the custom which has been handed down from one generation to another till the present day.

For many years after the discovery of a passage to the East by sea, pepper formed the principal article of trade, and even Vasco de Gama, who made this great discovery, appears not to have been satisfied with the results and prospects of his voyage until he had fully loaded his ships with it. At that time it was worth about seventy-five cents per pound in Europe. For a century afterward, so completely was this trade monopolized by the Portuguese and Dutch Governments, that it constantly commanded even a higher price. Except salt, perhaps no other condiment is so universally used; and yet the natives, who cultivate it for the rest of the world, never use it themselves, just as we have already seen is the case with those Malays who raise cloves and nutmeg and mace.

It was used by the Romans more than two thousand years ago; and Pliny is surprised that people should go all the way to India to obtain a condiment that had nothing to recommend it but its pungency (*amaritudo*).

In the early part of this century a very considerable trade in pepper was carried on by American vessels, chiefly from Boston and Salem, with this island, especially between this place and Achin, a region generally known to our sailors as "The Pepper Coast." Serious troubles often arose between their crews and the natives, and in 1830 nearly all the officers and crew of the ship Friendship, of Salem, were overpowered and murdered but a little farther north.

The region where the pepper-vine is now mostly cultivated is south of Palembang, on the banks of the river Ogan. In the archipelago it does not grow wild, and is only cultivated on Sumatra and a few of the Philippines. Its Javanese name, *maricha*, is pure Sanscrit, and this as well as its distribution indicates that it was introduced from India.

Here, at Tapanuli, are many natives of Achin, and their darker color and greater stature at once mark them as another people, and indicate that they are the descendants of natives of India and Malays, and this is completely in accordance with what we know of their history. The village of Achin is situated at the northwestern extremity of the island, on a small river two miles from where it empties into a bay, which is well sheltered by islands from the wind and sea in all seasons. On account of its good roadstead, and its being the nearest point to India in the whole archipelago, Achin appears to have been, for ages before the arrival of Europeans, the great mart for the Telinga traders from the eastern shores of the southern part of India.

There they brought cotton fabrics, salt, and opium, and obtained in exchange tin, gold, pepper, cloves, nutmegs, mace, betel-nuts, sulphur, camphor, and benzoin. When the Portuguese first arrived, in 1509, under Sequiera, at the neighboring city of Pedir, Achin was tributary to that city, but in 1521 an energetic prince came to the throne; in eighteen years he had conquered all the neighboring kingdoms, and his city became the great commercial emporium for all the western part of the archipelago. This prosperity it continued to enjoy for a hundred and fifty years. Its fame even reached Europe, and the proudest sovereigns were anxious to obtain the

THE ENGLISH APPEAR IN THE EAST. 449

favor of the King of Achin, and make commercial treaties with him.

Here the English first appeared, in 1602, under Sir James Lancaster, who commanded a squadron of four ships, and was furnished with a letter from Queen Elizabeth* to the king, who had been a fisherman, and had only obtained the throne by murdering the prince who would have lawfully in-

---

* Queen Elizabeth's letter is as follows: "We for them" (the East India Company) "do promise, that in no time hereafter you shall have cause to repent thereof, but rather to rejoice much, for their dealing shall be true and their conversation sure, and we hope that they will give such good proof thereof that this beginning shall be a perpetual confirmation of love betwixt our subjects in both parts, by carrying from us such things and merchandise as you have need of there. So that your highness shall be very well served, and better contented, than you have heretofore been with the Portugals and Spaniards, our enemies, who only and none else of these regions have frequented those your and the other kingdoms of the East, not suffering that the other natives should do it, pretending themselves to be monarchs and absolute lords of all those kingdoms and provinces, as their own conquest and inheritance, as appears by their lofty titles in their writings. The contrary whereof hath very lately appeared unto us. That your highness, and your royal family, fathers and grandfathers, have, by the grace of God, and their valor, known, not only to defend your own kingdoms, but also to give war unto the Portugals in the land which they possess, as namely: in Malacca, in the year of human redemption, 1575, under the conduct of your valliant Captain Ragamacota (*Rajah makuta*) with their great loss and the perpetual honor of your highness' crown and kingdom. And now, if your highness shall be pleased to accept unto your favor and grace and under your royal protection and defence, these our subjects, that they may freely do their business now and continue yearly hereafter, this bearer, who goeth chief of the fleet of four ships, hath order, with your highness' license, to leave certain factors with a settled house or factory in your kingdom, until the going thither of another fleet, which shall go thither on the return of this—which left factors shall learn the language and customs of your subjects, whereby the better and more lovingly to converse with them."

herited it. Such was the humble appearance of the English in the East two centuries and a half ago.

Little probably could even the far-seeing queen herself have imagined that one of her successors should reign over the hundred and fifty millions of Hindustan; that her Eastern merchants would soon give up the trade in pepper with Sumatra, and in spices with the Moluccas, for the far more lucrative commerce in silks and teas with China, and especially that to the then unexplored continent of Australia citizens of her own kingdom would migrate, and there lay the foundation of the most enterprising, flourishing, and, what promises to be within the next century, the greatest power in all the East.

When we started from Padang it was planned that a man-of-war should come to Siboga and take us back; but we have been obliged to wait here ten days, and now she has come only to take the Resident, and go to Singkel, the farthest point up the coast held by the Dutch.

The captain of the steamer on which I came from Surabaya to Batavia, however, has chanced to arrive in a little prau, in which he has been visiting several places along the coast for the purpose of ascertaining the facilities for obtaining timber to be used in constructing some government buildings at Padang. He is now on the point of sailing to the Batu Islands and thence to Padang, and proposes that I share the dangers of such a voyage in his little boat, an offer which I gladly accept, but Mr. Terville, the inspector, prefers to wait for the return of the steamship. Our boat is about thirty feet long by eight broad, and instead of being covered by a flat deck, has a steep roof, which descends on either side to the railing like the Javanese junks. Aft, where the tiller sweeps round, the deck is horizontal, but, as the stern is nearly as sharply-pointed as the bow, there is little room to sit. We have one mast, with a large, tattered mainsail and two jibs.

At midnight there was a little breeze from the land and we weighed anchor and stood to sea. In the morning we found ourselves becalmed about five miles from Tunkus Nasi, a sharp, conical island, which forms the southern extremity of Tapanuli Bay. Somewhat more to the west was the high plateau-like island of Mensalla. On its northwestern shore there is a waterfall, where the water leaps down some two hundred feet directly into the sea. It is so high that when I was at Siboga, people who have been at Barus assured me they have been able to see it when the sun shone on it, though the distance is some sixteen miles. At sunset we were so far down the coast that it was time for us to change our course to the south if we would visit the Batu Islands.

Our Malay captain was anxious that we should keep on our course to Padang; my friend said he cared very little to go to those islands, and when I looked at the ragged mainsail and realized that it would probably disappear in a moment if a heavy squall chanced to strike us, I gave my vote to continue on near the shore. Besides, the sky looked threatening, and we were evidently in a miserable vessel to live out a fresh gale and a heavy sea. Near midnight I was aroused by our boat pitching and rolling heavily, and the captain shouting out to his Malay crew all sorts of orders in rapid succession. Soon he came down to inform us, in the most trembling tones, it was so dark that it was not possible to see any thing, and in a few moments we should all be drowned. I hurried on deck, more from a habit of always wishing to see what is going to happen, than from fear. A thick, black mass of clouds was rolling up from seaward and spreading over the sky with alarming rapidity. The mainsail was taken in and only the main-jib was set, when the first gust struck us. Immediately, as if rolled over by a gigantic hand, our boat careened until her lee-rail was completely under water, and I thought, for a moment, she would certainly capsize. The main-jib burst into ribbons, and at last we righted. The flying-jib was then set, when she came near upsetting again. We were then only about a mile from the land, and the wind was directly on shore, so that it was impossible to save ourselves by running before it. Nothing could be done to keep off the rocks excepting to heave-to and trust to our anchor. All the cable possible was paid out, and yet the tempest continued to drive us toward the land. Another gust came, and as the lightning flashed I could see that we were not half a mile from a high island with precipitous shores, encircled by a coral reef, where the heavy swell rolling directly in from the ocean was breaking apparently twelve or fifteen feet high. I knew that at the rate we were drifting we must strike on it in fifteen minutes, and that to a certainty our frail boat would be broken into fragments in an instant. There was no possibility of escape, for the most expert swimmer could not possibly have saved himself in such a frightful surf. I coolly concluded that that would be the last of my dangers and resigned myself to my fate. Soon, however, the horizon became somewhat clearer, and, better than all, our anchor had evidently struck into good holding-ground and was keeping us from drifting. In an hour more the tempest was over, though the heavy swell continued to roll in as before. In the morning we found ourselves not far from Ayar Bangis, and put in there while our crew mended the sails. This is the port to which the coffee raised in the valley of Rau, in the interior, is brought down, to be hence shipped in praus to Padang, where it is placed in the government storehouse and sold at auction four times a year, viz., in March, June, September, and December. Natal, about twenty-five miles north of here, is the chief port to which is brought the valuable coffee raised in the fertile valley of Mandéling, of which Fort Elout is the capital. All this part of Sumatra abounds in very valuable timber, and the Resident here showed us some magnificent logs which his natives are sawing into planks. If we had such timber in our country we would use it for the nicest kinds of veneering.

As the storm continued, we remained for a day among the islands off Ayar Bangis. They are mostly low, and nearly all composed of coral rock. The natives live on fish and the cocoa-nuts which they raise in great numbers on these low coral islands.

The chief value of the cocoa-nuts here, as in the eastern part of the archipelago, is for the oil they yield; considerable quantities of that article are brought to Padang from these, the Batu and other islands off this part of Sumatra.

At sunset, next day, we were near Pasaman, a small place on the coast, west of the lofty peak of Ophir. Thousands of small, fleecy cumuli at that time covered the sky, and, as the sun neared the horizon, all these clouds were changed into the brightest gold. Indeed, the whole sky seemed literally paved with small blocks of gold, most of which were bordered with a narrow margin of purple. One end of this great arch seemed to rest on the distant horizon, the other on the crests of the lofty mountains east of us, but especially on the top of Mount Ophir, whose western side was lighted up with tints of gold and purple of surpassing richness.

All this glorious display in the heavens was so perfectly repeated, even to the minutest details, on the calm sea, that it was difficult to tell which to admire more, the sky or the ocean. Of all the rich sunsets I enjoyed while in the tropical East, this was by far the most magnificent, and never did I imagine it was possible for any one, while here on earth, to behold a scene that would so nearly approach the splendor of the Celestial City, described in the apocalyptic vision as being "of pure gold, like unto clear glass."

The next morning we were near Tiku, a village at the mouth of the small stream that flows out from the lake in the bottom of the great crater of Manindyu. The circular mountain-range which forms the walls of this great crater was clearly seen, and the deep rent through it, by which the waters collected in the bottom of the crater find a passage out to the sea. Twenty miles south of Tiku is Priaman, the place to which most of the coffee from the Menangkabau, or, as the Dutch prefer to call it, the Padang plateau, is brought to be sent in praus to Padang. On the evening of the fifth day the Apenburg, on Ape Hill, which marks the approach to Padang, and the shipping in the road, near by, were in full view. One large and very fine ship was flying the American ensign. In a few hours more I found myself again in the palace of the governor, and thus the expedition through the land of cannibals was safely over.

The American ship was owned by one of the largest and most enterprising firms in Boston. Her captain and his lady were on shore, and I soon hurried to their boarding-place; and, at once, we almost felt ourselves back in New England, and forgot that we were far from America, in a land of palms, and of one long, endless summer.

The chief article exported from this place to the United States is coffee. It is a very variable crop. During the last nine years it has varied in quantity from six thousand piculs (eight hundred thousand pounds) in 1857, to seventy-two thousand piculs (nine million six hundred thousand pounds) in 1858.*

The king's birthday—the great national holiday with the Dutch—now occurred. In the morn-

* For a detailed list of the quantities exported each year, and the average price, see Appendix D.

ing there was a grand parade on the lawn, in front of the governor's palace, of all the European and native troops, numbering in all some four or five thousand, but many others are stationed in small bodies at various places in the interior. They were organized in battalions on the French plan, and their appearance and manœuvring were very creditable. There was a small mounted force, much like our flying artillery. This, I was informed, proved to be one of the most efficient parts of the army in their contests with the natives—the paths in the interior always being so narrow and so extremely uneven that only very light cannon can be brought into use. After the parade the governor, as the representative of the king, received the congratulations of all the officials in that region. The day ended with a grand ball, to which, I may add, the mestizo belles were not only invited, but came, and took as prominent a part as the ladies who had the envied fortune to be born in Europe. At every little post the highest official receives the congratulations of his brother-officers in similar manner, and all are required to appear in full dress with cocked hats.

After having served in our own gigantic war, where a sash, a pair of small shoulder-straps, a few bright buttons, and a gold cord round a slouched hat, were sufficient to indicate the rank of even a major-general, I was quite dazzled by the brilliant uniforms of even the most petty officials in the Dutch service. The army officers wear epaulets, and broad bands of gold lace on the pantaloons, collars, and cuffs. The backs of their coats are figured over in the most extravagant fashion. The civil officers present a similar gaudy display in silver. The object of all this is to impress the natives with a high idea of the wealth and power of the Dutch Government, and of the great dignity of those who are honored by being selected to administer it; and exactly these ideas are conveyed to the minds of the natives by such displays. Their own rajahs and princes never appear in public without making the most dazzling show possible; and the mass of the people, therefore, have come to think that their rulers mu·t be weak and poor, and even more worthy of their contempt than their respect, if they do not make a most imposing appearance on all great occasions.

CHAPTER XV.

THE PADANG PLATEAU.

As I had seen only a small portion of the *Padangsche Bovenlanden*, or Padang plateau, I again set off for the interior, following the same route that I had taken before, namely, north, over low lands to the left of the Barizan chain. As the governor's "American" had not arrived from Saboga, he kindly borrowed for me a "bendy," that is, a small, heavy, two-wheeled chaise. He gave me an order allowing me to use two horses if I pleased; and, by the time I had travelled twenty miles, I was glad to avail myself of the privilege. A bamboo was fastened across the thills and allowed to project four or five feet on one side, and the additional horse was then placed beside the other, the usual mode of driving tandem in this country. To complete the odd style of harnessing these half-tamed steeds, the natives arranged the reins so that I was obliged to hold two in the left hand and but one in the right. The result was, that the outer horse was as loose as those harnessed in a similar manner in Russia, and altogether beyond my control. Whenever we came to a slight descent, he would always spring into a full gallop, and the one in the thills would follow his example.

Then came a few severe shocks against the large stones in the road, and we found ourselves at the bottom of the hill. One time the shocks were so severe that my footman, who had a seat behind, and a good place to hold on with both hands, was missing when I reached the bottom of the hill, and, on looking round, I found the bendy had flung him off some distance upon the rough stones. When we reached Kayu Tanam, thick clouds, that had been gathering on the adjacent lofty peaks, rolled down and poured out a perfect flood of rain. The drops were so large, and fell with such momentum, that it seemed like standing under a heavy shower-bath. The lightning gleamed as it only does in tropical lands, and the thunder roared as if the great Barizan chain on my right was splitting open again, and forming another immense "cleft." I was wondering that my horses were not frightened amid such terrific peals, when suddenly a piercing flash dazzled my eyes, and the same instant came a sharp crash like the sudden breaking of a thousand heavy timbers, and for a moment I was quite bewildered. Both horses reared until they nearly stood on their hind feet, and then plunged forward in a perfect state of fright. The road there chanced to be straight, and I let them go at the top of their speed for a mile or two, when they again became somewhat manageable, and in this way we flew along high up the side of a great ravine and came into the deep cleft. Ascending the cañon, we came to Padang Panjang, and the next day to Fort de Kock. The waterfall opposite where we entered the cleft was considerably swollen by the heavy rains, and a small stream, separate from the main fall, was shooting over the high edge of the precipice. On a steep declivity near by, a small stream had coursed part way down, completely hidden from view by the thick sheet of vegetation that covered the rocks, until, striking some obstacle, it flew off into the air in a great jet, which appeared to come out of the solid rock.

From Fort de Kock my course was nearly west a day's ride to Paya Kombo. At first the road led over a level or slightly undulating land which abounds in villages, and is highly cultivated. A number of small streams that rise on the northern flanks of the great Mérapi, flow northward across the plain, and then turn to the east and join to form the Batang Agam. Nine miles out we came to a range of jagged hills, the scanty soil on their sides only serving to make their sharp, projecting rocks more conspicuous and unsightly, like a tattered garment thrown over a skeleton. This rock I found to be a highly crystalline marble of a blue color, completely split up by joints and fissures into cubical blocks, whose outer surfaces have everywhere become greatly roughened by the action of rain and heat. Subsequently I had an opportunity of learning that it makes a very valuable kind of white lime.

We presently found ourselves descending into a beautiful valley, through which the Agam, already a considerable stream, courses rapidly along. The road immediately approached its banks, crossed it over a high stone bridge, and then ran along a narrow terrace cut in a high precipice of the limestone cliff, whose feet were bathed in the small river. On the level land and hills in this region, the only rock which outcropped was a red sandstone, composed of strata that have been considerably plicated in many places; but they are evidently of a recent formation and unconformable to the older crystalline limestone on which they rest. Passing the Mérapi, we rode down a gradually descending plain that lies on the north of Mount Sago.

Early in the afternoon we came to Paya Kombo, where an assistant resident is stationed. His residence is the finest building I have seen in Sumatra. He greeted me kindly, and introduced me to the assistant resident stationed at Fort Van der Capellan, the next chief place I was designing to visit. Thus I found a pleasant companion, and one who could explain the peculiarities of the country I should see during the next two days.

April 2d.—Rode from Paya Kombo to Bua with the Resident of this district. A short distance from Paya Kombo we crossed a large and very beautiful stone bridge that had been planned and superintended by a government official who had never received the slightest training in architecture. Our course was nearly southwest, and the road slowly ascended, for we were really coming upon the flanks of Mount Sago. It then changes to the east, and again to the south, as we made a circuit round the eastern side of the mountain. This part of the road was built on a steep acclivity, that descended to the deep valley of the Sinamu on our left. The higher hills on the opposite side of the valley are probably of limestone. When we came round to the south side of Mount Sago, before us lay the charming valley of Bua, perhaps the most beautiful valley in Sumatra. On our left was a range of hundreds of sharp peaks, a continuation of the limestone chain noticed yesterday between Fort de Kock and Paya Kombo. Near their feet is the Sinamu, now a small river, flowing away to the southeast. At Paya Kombo this stream flows to the southeast, which is its general course for about twenty-five miles after it passes Mount Sago; it then changes to the east, and is known as the Indragiri. It is a fair sample of the tortuous course of all the streams in the mountainous parts of Sumatra. They wind to and fro so abruptly, that sometimes the traveller comes to the banks of a river without suspecting for a moment that it is the very one which he was following in a wholly different direction the day before. The only way it is possible to realize the irregularities of these streams, is to examine a map of this region on a very large scale. On our left was another high range walling in the narrow valley, the bottom of which curves gradually upward as it approaches either side. The level parts of the valley are all changed into beautiful sawas, which are now filled with young rice-blades of a bright green. Riding down the valley for four or five miles, we came to the *controleur's* house at Bua. It is situated near the west side of the valley, facing the north. Thick clouds, that had been hiding the top of Mount Sago, now vanished into pure air, and the old crater-walls came grandly into view. They are so deeply notched on the southern side, that I could look directly up into the crater from the *controleur's* residence in the valley. The sharp limestone needles, on the east side of the valley, also were more distinct. They were only three miles away, and yet I counted no less than twenty separate peaks in a straight line, at right angles with my vision, in fifteen degrees along the horizon. Looking up from the village of Bua toward Mount Sago, the view has a charming ideal effect—such as one might expect to see in a composite painting, where wonderful details of scenery from different localities are harmoniously combined.

April 3d.—At 6 A. M. went with the *controleur* and rajah, and about forty natives, to a large cave west of Bua, in the limestone range that forms the western boundary of the valley. Coming to a small stream that flows out of this chain, we followed its course upward, until we found it issuing from beneath a high arch that opened into a large cavern. Here the strata of the limestone were more distinct than I have seen elsewhere. They have a dip of about 20° west, their strike being northwest and southeast, the general direction of the chain. Immediately within the arch the roof of the cave rose into a dome, apparently more than one hundred feet high at the centre. Flocks of swallows had made this their building-place, and, disturbed by the smoke of our torches, they made the cavern resound with their sharp chirping. On the walls were many stalactites that closely resembled the luxuriant orchids and parasites of tropical forests, as if Nature were here reproducing in stone the wonders of the vegetable kingdom. After crossing the stream two or three times we came to the end of this grand hall, and climbed up what appeared to be a waterfall, but was, in reality, solid stone. The water, flowing over the steep ledge of limestone, had in time deposited over its rough edges an incrustation, which, of course, took exactly the form of the running water that made it.

Having reached the top of this petrified fall, we passed on our hands and knees through a small hole, and found ourselves in another large hall of an elliptical form. At the farther end was a small rivulet gurgling its way among the large rocks that covered the floor of the cave. I had been told that this water was so hot that a man could not hold his hand in it; but, on trying it with the thermometer, I found the mercury only rose to 92° Fahrenheit, not quite up to blood-heat (98°). It abounded, however, in small fish about four inches long, several of which the natives caught with their hands. They all had eyes that were apparently well formed, though this place seemed to us absolutely cut off from daylight.

Returning to the outer cave, we proceeded a short way by wading in the bed of the stream, but the cavern now diminished into an irregular tunnel, and the water that flowed through it was too deep for us to go on in safety, and we were therefore obliged to return. The *controleur* informed me that one of his predecessors had gone on and come out again in the plain near Fort Van der Capellen, so that the cave is really a tunnel, which passes completely through the whole chain; and the distance from its mouth at this place to the opening at its opposite end must be at least five miles in an air line. While the natives were in the water, and each held a blazing torch, I ordered them to range themselves a few feet apart in a long line. The light reflected from the changing surface of the flowing stream beneath, and the wide irregular rocks and stalactites above, and the dark half-naked bodies of the natives themselves, made it appear as if I had come into the abode of evil demons; and this delusion became complete when one shouted, and the rest joining in prolonged their cry into a wild yell that echoed and reëchoed again and again, coming back to us like the answering, remorseful shriek of hundreds of evil spirits that were imprisoned forever deep within the bowels of the mountain.

In the inner part of the larger cave I was directed to look up in a certain direction, when soon a long, narrow band of yellow light gleamed from an opening, and, darting into the cave, partially lighted up some of the long stalactites that hung from the roof. Then came two bright flames waving to and fro, which showed me the forms of two natives who had climbed up some other chamber, and had come out through an aperture far above us into the apartment where we were standing.

The Resident was travelling to inspect the coffee-gardens, and would go back up the valley to Suka Rajah, the "Rajah's Delight," a large coffee-garden in the ravine that leads up into the old crater of the Sago. I therefore hired coolies to haul my bendy over the mountain to Fort Van der Capellen, and thence to Padang Panjang, while I accompanied the Resident and *controleur* on horseback. After we had rested awhile at a small summer-house, I continued on foot up the ravine as far as coffee-trees are planted, a coolie from the valley following me, and continually begging me to return, for fear we might be attacked by a tiger. I told him to go back and let me proceed alone; but we were already so far away that he did not dare to leave me. The whole interior of this crater is covered with a dense forest, in which there are many trees, showing that it has constantly remained inactive for many years, and this is corroborated by what we know of the history of this part of Menangkabau; for, when "the volcano" is spoken of, it is probable that the Mérapi is meant, and not the Sago, on the one side, nor the Singalang on the other.

As I could not reach to the bottom of the crater by following up the ravine, I determined to try to ascend one of the ridges on its sides, and possibly look down into it from an elevated point. That part of the steep mountain-side was covered with tall grass, and the "tufa," or red clay, formed by the decomposition of the volcanic rock, ejected from this vent, was very slippery after the recent shower. Yet, by grasping the grass and small shrubbery, I made my way up nearly to the rim of the crater, but did not get the unobstructed view I wished. To obtain this, it is necessary to ascend the mountain on the north side. I was, however, far more than repaid for my labor, by the magnificent landscape spread out before me to the south and southeast. At my feet began the Bua Valley, which, at a distance of ten or twelve miles, expanded into a plain bordered on the west by the high mountains of the Barizan chain, and on the east by that of the Padang Lawas, which yet farther on curved round to the southwest and united with the Barizan in the gigantic peak of Mount Talang. Winding to and fro down the Bua Valley, was occasionally seen the silver surface of the Sinamu, and beside that and the other streams were many broad overflowed sawas, which gave the valleys the appearance of abounding with hundreds of little lakes. This is the grandest and most comprehensive view I have enjoyed in Sumatra, and this spot is well named "The Rajah's Delight." At an elevation of about four thousand five hundred feet we found it very chilly by night, not so much from the difference of temperature, as indicated by the thermometer, as on account of a strong wind and a thick mist that enveloped us. This coffee-garden is considered the best in this region; but the Resident informs me that there are one or two at the same, or a somewhat greater elevation, on the Mérapi, which are finer. The large crops raised here are probably due to the elevation and to the soil, which has been formed from decomposing volcanic rock, and enriched by the vegetable mould that has accumulated for centuries.

April 4*th*.—Continued on horseback along the southern flanks of Mount Sago to its western side, when we came to the head of a valley bounded by steep acclivities. A thick mist unfortunately concealed the view from this point, the finest, it is said, in the whole region. A steep, zigzag path brought us down to a small stream, and, ten miles in a southwesterly direction, we came to the Resident's house at Fort Van der Capellen. The more direct and frequented road between Paya Kombo and this place lies between Mount Sago and Mount Mérapi; and those two great elevations are so separate that Tangjong Allam, the highest point on the road, is only three thousand four hundred feet, about two hundred feet above Fort de Kock. Four miles beyond, we passed through a village where there is a waringin-tree of enormous dimensions. Its trunk is so large that I found it required eight natives to embrace it by joining hands! It is not, however, a single, compact trunk, like that of a pine, but is composed of an irregular bundle of them bound together. Besides this, there are three other great trunks which support the larger limbs, this species of *Ficus* being very closely allied to the banyan-tree of India.

Two miles west of this place, on the acclivity of one of the limestone ranges already described, lies Pagaruyong, now a small kampong, but in ancient times one of the capitals of the great Malay kingdom of Menangkabau. Its early history only comes down to us in obscure legends. One is that Noah and his "forty companions" in the ark discovered dry land at Lankapura, near the present city of Palembang, by seeing a bird which had escaped from their vessel alight at that place. From that spot two brothers, Papati-si-batang (a name of Sanscrit origin), and Kayi Tumangung (a name of Javanese origin), who were included in the forty that had escaped the deluge, came to a mountain named Siguntang-guntang, which was described as dividing Palembang from Jambi, and thence to Priangan, a word in Javanese signifying "the land of wood-spirits," or fairies, and at present the name of a kampong on the road from this place to Padang Panjang, and situated on the flanks of the Mérapi, near the wooded region. There is little doubt that this kampong is the same as the ancient one of the same name, for that was described as being "near the great volcano."

Another legend represents the founder of the Menangkabau empire to have been Sang Sapurba (a name compounded of both Sanscrit and Javanese words), who is also said to have come from Palembang, which we know was a Javanese colony. The Javanese and Sanscrit origins of these names at once suggest the probability that a larger part of the civilization which rendered this empire so superior to all others in Sumatra, was not indigenous, but introduced from Java, and at a period subsequent to the introduction into that island of Hinduism and its accompanying Sanscrit names from India. The names of many of the most remarkable mountains and localities in this region are also found to be of similar origin, and greatly strengthen this probability. The word Menangkabau itself signifies in Javanese "the victory of the buffalo;" and, as it has been one of the favorite sports of the Javanese from time immemorial to make buffaloes fight with tigers, we may presume this locality acquired its name from its being the frequent scene of such a bloody pastime.

When Europeans first arrived on the northern

coast of the island, in 1509, this empire was evidently in its decline; and though the rajahs of Achin, Pedir, and Pasé, acknowledged the sultan of this country as their superior, they only paid him a small tribute, and were really independent princes. The empire at that time included on the east coast the area between the rivers of Palembang and Siak, and on the west coast from Manjuta, near Indrapura, as far north as Singkel, at the mouth of the river of that name, which is the outlet of the great Lake Aik Däu, in the Batta Lands.* Afterward the Rajah of Achin, whose daughter the sultan had married and slighted, took possession of the west coast, as far south as Bencoolen. In 1613 his successor claimed no farther south than Padang, and he actually governed no place south of Barus.

In 1680 the Sultan Alif died, leaving no heir. Dissensions at once arose, and the empire was ultimately divided between three princes, who each claimed to be the regular successor to the throne, and assumed all the extravagant titles of the previous sultans. These princes severally resided at Suruasa (on the Dutch maps Soeroeasso), which is situated two miles south of Pagaruyong, on the banks of a small stream that flows southward and empties into the Ombiling, at Pagaruyong (on the Dutch maps Pager Oedjoeng), and at Sungtarap (in Dutch Soeng Tarap), a kampong three miles north of Fort Van der Capellen. The Dutch treated the Prince of Suruasa with the greatest distinction, but

---

* Vide Marsden's "History of Sumatra," p. 322 *et seq.*

whether that place or Pagaruyong was the more ancient site is undecided.

The first European who reached this region was Sir Stamford Raffles in 1818. He had the good fortune to discover at Suruasa two inscriptions on stone in the Kawi, or ancient Javanese character, thereby proving that the early civilization of Java was transplanted to this land. At Pagaruyong he also discovered a Hindu image, "chastely and beautifully carved, corresponding with those discovered in Java, and evidently the work of similar artists and the object of a similar worship." Thus the ancient religion, as well as the ancient language of Java, was adopted to some extent by the early inhabitants of this country.

There appears to be no reason why we should suppose that Mohammedanism was first introduced into Java and thence brought to this land, as there is in the case of the Hinduism that prevailed here centuries ago. We may rather infer that soon after that religion had found followers on the north coast, its teachers were not long in making their way into the Menangkabau country, the influence and reputed wealth of which must have been pictured to them in the most glowing colors as soon as they first landed at Achin.

About the year 1807 three native pilgrims returned from Mecca to their homes on the shores of Lake Korinchi, which is situated about thirty miles southeast of the great mountain of Talang. As they had just left the grave of their prophet, they burned with zeal to discipline their lax countrymen, and to make them conform more nearly to the rigid requirements of the faith they had pretended to adopt. Believing, like true Mohammedans, that no argument is so convincing as the sword, these zealots began a warfare as well as a reform. This religion is the more remarkable, because, so far as we know, it is the only one that has ever been originated in the whole archipelago.

In 1837 these religious conquerors came into collision with the Dutch, and, after a severe contest of three years, were completely conquered, and not a vestige of their rigorous laws can now be discerned. Such harsh measures were evidently distasteful to the lax Malays, and now on all market-days and festive occasions they array themselves in as gaudy colors as they did before the zealous pilgrims of Korinchi came back from Mecca.

The skilful work of these people in silver and gold has already been described. This they did not learn from foreigners, but have practised for ages. They were also very skilful in the manufacture of kris-blades, cannon, and matchlocks—mining, smelting, and forging the iron entirely themselves. Marsden says their principal mine was at Padang Luar, probably Padang Luwa or Lawa, a kampong on the level land near Fort de Kock, and about a mile north of that place. It was taken to Selimpuwong (on the Dutch maps Salimpawang), a small kampong between Mount Mérapi and Mount Sago, on the road leading northward from this place to Paya Kombo, where it was smelted and manufactured. Their cannon were often mentioned by the earliest Portuguese navigators. They were manufactured here and sold to the more warlike nations at the northern end of the island. The barrels of their matchlocks were made by winding a flat bar of iron spirally around a circular rod and welding it into one piece; and Marsden, who probably saw some of these guns, describes them as being of the "justest bore." They also manufactured an inferior kind of powder. These arts they may have learned from the Chinese, who practised them long before they were known in Europe, and who probably came down the coast to the Malay peninsula and this island centuries before the Portuguese sailed around the Cape of Good Hope.

At present, all the natives, except the militia, within the limits of the Dutch territory, are absolutely forbidden by the Dutch Government to have powder or fire-arms of any description in their possession, and the penalty against importing them and selling them to the natives is very severe. Without such a law, no foreigner would be safe in any part of the archipelago. The iron that these people now use appears to be wholly imported from Europe. They need little except for knives, and the steel for those comes mostly from Padang.

This evening the guard reported a fire in a neighboring kampong, and a bright light was seen some miles off on the flanks of the Mérapi. Although I have now been in the archipelago nearly a year, it is the first fire I have seen; and this appears the more remarkable, when we consider the highly inflammable materials of which the native huts are built, the walls being of bamboo and the roof of atap. However, when they do take fire, they blaze up and disappear like a bundle of straw.

April 6th.—The Resident gave me a span of horses and a covered carriage to drive to the banks of a stream flowing to the southeast, and a servant followed with another horse for me to use in fording the stream and continuing my journey southward to the southern end of Lake Sinkara. There has been much rain during the past week, and coming to the river we found it so swollen and rapid that the moment a horse or man stepped into it he would certainly be swept away. I was, therefore, obliged to follow up its course a mile or two, till I came to a village where the natives had made a rude bridge between two high trees that leaned toward each other from the opposite banks of the torrent. The bottom of the bridge consisted of only two large bamboos, but there was another on either side to enable one to maintain his balance while crossing. No place could be found where it was possible to bring over the horse, and I was obliged, therefore, to send him back and finish that day's journey of twenty miles on foot.

After crossing the stream I turned to the eastward, and, passing over a number of sharp ridges, came down to the road we had left. This conducted us along a small, rapid river, which we found to be the Ombiling, the only outlet of Lake Sinkara. At several places I noticed large wheels for raising water to inundate the rice-fields. On the rim were fastened pieces of bamboo at a slight angle, which filled as they touched the surface of the stream and poured out their contents when they came to the highest point. In all particulars these wheels are exactly like those used in China for the same purpose, and perhaps were introduced by immigrants or merchants from that land. We crossed the foaming Ombiling on a bridge near where the lake pours out its surplus water down a ravine and forms that stream. Before the Dutch came up into this region the natives had made a suspension bridge here, near Samawang, similar to the one I crossed over the Batang Taroh. Governor Raffles has described it in his memoirs, and has also noticed the water-wheels just described, so that they must have been in use for a long time, and could not have been introduced by Europeans nor by the Chinamen who have established themselves at the principal places in this region since it became subject to the Dutch.

Mid-day was passed when I reached the kampong of Samawang, near the bridge, and I was so worn out with my long walk over the mountains and fording the swollen streams, that I was glad to crawl into a little dirty hut and beg an old Malay woman to cook me a little rice, for I had yet ten miles farther to go, and pouring showers frequently came over the lake. My repast consisted of rice, a smoked fish, a few grains of coarse salt and some red pepper ground up together between two flat stones. As I satisfied my hunger, I could but contrast my simple meal with the royal feasts I had been taking with the governor at his residence at Padang less than a week before, but, as Shakespeare says, "Hunger is the best sauce," and I enjoyed my hard fare more than many pampered princes do the choicest viands. From this place there is a well-built road along the eastern side of the lake to the kampong of Sinkara on the southern shore. The lake is ten miles long and about three miles wide. It is parallel to the Barizan chain in this place, and extends in a northwest and southeast direction. Its surface is about seventeen hundred feet above the sea. Its most remarkable character is its great depth at one place, near the cleft of Paningahan, where the plummet runs down eleven hundred and eighty-two feet, nearly a quarter of a mile, so that its bottom, at that spot, is only about five hundred feet above the level of the sea. West of the Sinkara is the great Barizan chain, with its acclivities rising immediately from the margin of the lake, and its peaks generally attaining an elevation of fifteen hundred feet above the lake, or three thousand two hundred feet above the sea. On the eastern side, and on the northern end of the lake, are hills of less than half that height, mostly composed of syenite. The Barizan chain, as shown in the cleft of Paningahan, is composed of chloritic schists interstratified with marble, and overlaid in most places with lava, pumice-stone, and volcanic sand or ashes. These strata of schists and limestone undoubtedly rest on gigantic rocks, for such are found outcropping on the opposite or coast side of the range. The basin of Lake Sinkara, therefore, occurs where a great fault has taken place. Five miles east of the lake, and a short distance south of the kampong Pasilian, is Mount Sibumbun, which, as well as the cleft of Paningahan, has been carefully examined by Mr. Van Dijk, of the Government Mining Corps, on account of the copper-mines they contain. Sibumbun is a peak of greenstone rising out of syenite. Westward, one passes from the granite into marble, and then on to a sandstone of a late formation, which contains layers of coal that is probably of the same age as that I saw at Siboga.

The whole geological history of this part of Sumatra may be summed up as follows: On the syenite and granite, layers of mud and coral were deposited; then the whole was raised and plicated; and after this period was deposited the sandstone, the strata of which we have already noted as being unconformable to the rocks on which they rest, and more nearly horizontal. If, as Mr. Van Dijk thinks, and is very probable, the marble in the cleft of Padang Pangjang is formed from corals, at least not older than the eocene age, it follows that the mountain-ranges of Sumatra have been formed within a comparatively recent period. The process of covering these strata by lava, pumice-stone, and volcanic sand and ashes, has been going on since historic time.

The most remarkable thing in this kampong of Sinkara, is the *bali*, or town-hall. Either end, on the inside, is built up into a series of successive platforms, one rising over the other. On the outside these elevated ends resemble the stern of the old three and four decked frigates which the Dutch generally used when they first became masters of these seas, and such as can yet be seen used as hulks in the ports of the British colonies. The exterior of the *bali*, as well as the better private houses, are painted red, and ornamented with flowers and scroll-work in white and black.

While at this village I noticed a native leading a large dog-like monkey from place to place. On inquiring, the servants told me that he was trained to pick off cocoa-nuts from the bunches in the trees, but I doubted whether he could know what ones to select, and therefore watched him myself. His master brought him to the foot of the tree, gave a peculiar jerk to the rope, and at once he began to climb up. Reaching the top, he seated himself on the base of a leaf and immediately began wrenching off those nuts that were fully grown, by partially twisting them. After he had taken off all the ripe nuts on one side of the tree, he went round to the opposite side and broke off the ripe ones there also, without once attempting to pull off those that were partly grown. This selecting the ripe nuts from the large clusters seemed to be the result of his own instinct, and not of any signal from his master, so far as I could detect.

The shore at the southern end of the lake is very low and marshy, and wholly devoted to rice-fields. Here were enormous flocks of herons, that made the sawas perfectly white wherever they alighted. Over these low lands is built the road that leads to Solok, six miles distant in a southeasterly direction.

April 8th.—Rode to Solok. On the way passed twenty-seven women going to the burial of a native prince. Their costume was peculiar, even in this land. It consisted simply of the common sarong open at the right hip, and fastened at the waist to a narrow scarf about the neck, and a turban around the head. About three miles from Sinkara, the way passed over a slight elevation, and again I came down into a low land which was one great fertile sawa. Rice here is abundant and very cheap, and the Resident states that many of the natives prefer to use that which is at least a year old, and that a few have small quantities which they have kept for several years. The kernels of this rice are smaller than those of the kind grown in our Carolinas; but that has been tried here, and found to yield less by a considerable number of pounds per acre than the native variety.

This region was known, before it was conquered by the Dutch, as the Tiga Blas country, or the country of the "Thirteen Confederate Towns," because the thirteen villages in this vicinity had entered into a compact to afford mutual aid and protection. In a similar manner all the territory that previously belonged to the single kingdom of Menangkabau was divided up into petty confederacies when the Dutch conquered the country, and the several areas thus ruled are now marked on the Dutch maps as the district of the "Five, Ten, or Twenty Kottas." At present, though most of the natives live in villages, many houses are scattered over the cultivated lands. Before the conquest they all lived in villages that were generally surrounded by a stockade and a thick hedge of bamboos. The Dutch generals who subdued them destroyed these rude fortifications, that the villagers might have no defences and less facilities to revolt.

Many of the kampongs in this region were then situated on the hills, but have since been removed to the plains for the same reason. Near Solok, the inner range that forms the western buttress of the plateau rises up above the surrounding plain like a great wall, that curves round to the west and unites with the Barizan chain in the great Talang, which attains an elevation of about eight thousand five hundred feet. A short distance north of it is a cleft, through which the Resident is now building a road to Padang. About twelve miles to the north are two other clefts, near Paningahan, formed by the throes of a volcano near that kampong; and farther north is the cleft at Padang Panjang, all four occurring within less than thirty miles in a straight line.

On the southeastern declivity of Talang, at the height of six thousand feet, is a small tarn, whence issues the Solok River, that empties into Lake Sinkara, the source of the Ombiling, which curves to the east and southeast, and unites with the Sinamu, that we have already traced from Paya Kombo down the Bua Valley. From their juncture begins the Indragiri, which, pursuing an easterly course over the low lands that form the eastern side of Sumatra, empties into the Java Sea nearly opposite the Linga Islands. This tarn, therefore, may be regarded as the source of the Indragiri; and within a circle of half a mile radius rise three streams that flow in wholly different directions—two, the Indragiri and Jambi, emptying into the Java Sea, and the third mingling its waters with those of the Indian Ocean.

April 10*th*.—Rode on horseback from Sinkara north to Samawang, at the outlet of the lake, and thence continued on foot in a westerly direction to

Batu Bragon, at its northern end, and in a north-westerly direction to Padang Panjang.

On the west side of the lake, from the mouths of the deep ravines, extend bands of naked stones, which form, as it were, paved highways—the highways, indeed, that Nature has made for man to go up among her sublime mountains.

Between Samawang and Batu Bragon I crossed several beds of these dry torrents. The boulders in them were mostly of lava, and rapidly falling apart into a coarse, sharp-edged shingle. Fragments of syenite also appeared. These stones had been washed down from the neighboring hills, and were piled up in long winrows, as if they had been as light as chaff —so great is the transporting power of these mountain torrents, that only exist during the heavy rains.

From Batu Bragon the road ascended the flanks of the Mérapi, which are under the highest state of cultivation—most of them terraced for rice, but some sugar-cane is also raised here. To press out its juices, two cylinders of wood are placed perpendicularly in a wooden frame, and several spirals are made on each, so that they will exactly fit into each other like the cogs of two wheels. One of these is turned round by a long lever drawn by a buffalo, the other cylinder revolving at the same time, but, of course, in the opposite direction. The stalks of the cane are put in on one side, and the juices are gathered in a large vessel beneath. This they boil into a syrup, and, some say, crystallize it into sugar.

Again and again, as I was ascending to Padang Panjang, I turned to enjoy once more the magnificent view to the south. Near me were green rice-fields waving in the sunshine, and far beneath these was the large blue lake surrounded by high dark mountains; on their lofty peaks were gathering black clouds, from which occasionally a heavy, suppressed muttering rolled along, betokening the severity of the coming storm. The next day I returned to the governor's residence at Padang.

Some time before I came from Java, a Malay prau, in the employ of Chinamen, had visited the Pagi Islands, to purchase cocoa-nut oil and tortoise-shell, and had induced a man and woman, represented in the accompanying illustration, to go with them to Padang. The sarong of the woman was made of the leaves of the cocoa-nut palm and banana, torn up into strips, and fastened at one end to a long rattan, which was wound several times round the waist. When these leaves are green, they form a respectable covering, but, in the hot, tropical sun, they soon wither into mere strings. For a baju a similar garment of banana-leaves was used. The head-dress was yet more peculiar. It was made of banana-leaves, folded, as shown in the engraving, into the form of a cocked hat. This is usually ornamented at the top with a tuft of grass, and it is always worn crosswise. The only clothing of the man was a strip of bark, about four inches wide, and ten or twelve feet long, passing round the waist, and covering the loins, as shown in the cut. Boys go entirely naked until they are about eight years old. Neither the man nor woman cared for rice, but they were fond of bread, though they had never seen any before. Their

NATIVES OF THE PAGI ISLANDS.

usual food at home was sago, boiled in salt water, and covered with grated cocoa-nut. When the governor gave the man a fowl, and asked him to cook it after his own fashion, he built a small fire in the back yard, and, as soon as it was well blazing, tied the bird's wings and legs, and thrust it alive into the flames, in order to burn off the feathers. The governor provided them with many presents for their rajahs and friends, and, at the first opportunity, sent them back to their islands. Soon after their return, another native came to Padang in the same way. He was there when I came back from the interior, and, at the governor's invitation, he made us a visit. He was of the pure Malay type, not differing to a marked degree in stature or general proportions from the Sumatran Malays who came with him. His breast and abdomen and the backs of his hands were tattooed. Both sexes are ornamented in this way. The process is begun when they are six or seven years old, and continued at intervals for a long time. This man said that each village had a style of its own. It is done with a sharpened copper wire, and the substance pricked in is said to be the smoke of a gum, mingled with the sap of some plant, as the juice of the sugar-cane. He had no idea of the origin of this custom; nor of its use, except to distinguish the people of the various villages.

Some time before I set out on my last journey, the governor had offered to give me a small gun-boat, somewhat larger than a pilot-boat, but manned with nearly twenty Malays, to go off to these islands, taking this man, who had learned some Malay during his stay at Padang with me as an interpreter. An unexpected event, however, made it necessary to send that boat up the coast, and it would be some days before another would come; so I concluded to take the mail-boat for Bencoolen, and commence a long journey directly across the island to Palembang, and, reaching Banca, go up to Singapore on the steamer which touches at that island while on her way to Singapore from Batavia.

While travelling in the interior of Sumatra, we have seen that the mountains, which extend from one end of the island to the other, range themselves, generally, in two parallel chains, that wall in a long, narrow plateau. The island of Engano is the summit of the southeastern peak in another similar mountain-chain, extending in a northwesterly direction, parallel to those already described. After sinking beneath the level of the sea, this chain reappears in the Pagi, Mantawi, and Batu groups, Pulo Nias, Pulo Babi, and the Cocos Islands.

The plateau in the interior, we have also found, is divided into a number of separate valleys, by transverse ranges, which yoke together the principal chains. In a similar manner transverse ranges appear in Pulo Kapini, one of the Batu Islands, and in the Banyak Islands. These transverse ranges are seen also in the high and well-marked promontories which jut out from the Barizan, or coast-chain of Sumatra, at those places. A third projecting part of the coast is seen at Indrapura. As the valleys in the interior become plateaus, when we compare them to the present sea-level, so is the long, narrow area between these islands and Sumatra a plateau, when compared with the bed of the unfathomable ocean outside of them. In the same manner, then, as the Kurile and Japan Islands, the Lew-Chews, and Formosa, are but the more elevated parts of a great mountain-chain that rises on the eastern edge of the continent of Asia, so these islands are only the tops of another great chain which rises on a part of the southern border of the same continent, and indicates where the wide and deep basin of the Indian Ocean commences.

CHAPTER XVI.

CROSSING SUMATRA.

April 17*th*.—Took the steamer at Padang for Bencoolen. Nearly all the way we had a heavy wind from the southeast, though the southeastern monsoon has not yet begun in the Java Sea. The western limit of this monsoon region, I judge, after many inquiries, may be considered to be the Cape of Indrapura, but both monsoon winds prevail occasionally as far north as Padang. Farther north the winds are constantly variable. At Tapanuli Bay I was informed that heavy "northers" occasionally prevail for several days; and I was earnestly advised not to go off to the adjacent island of Mensalla in a ship's boat, though the sea was calm for two or three days at a time.

April 18*th*.—At 2 P. M. we entered Bencoolen Bay. It is an open roadstead, and the swell raised by the steady southeast trades of the Indian Ocean rolls in and breaks for the first time on the shore, there being no chain of islands to the seaward to protect this part of the coast, as there is farther north. We were able, however, to anchor in the bay off the city. Landing here is difficult, on account of the surf, and especially as the shores are mostly fringed with coral reefs. The city is located on a low bluff, on the south side of the bay.

By a treaty with the Dutch in 1824 this territory was ceded them by the English, in exchange for Malacca and the adjoining country. It is at present under a Resident, who is appointed by the government at Batavia, and is not under the Governor of Padang. The residency commences at the southeastern extremity of the island, and includes the area between the Barizan chain and the sea-coast, from that point as far north as Mokomoko. Its population numbers one hundred and twenty thousand five hundred and fourteen, and is divided as follows:—Europeans, one hundred and seventy-four; natives, one hundred and nineteen thousand six hundred and ninety-one; Chinese, five hundred and ninety-six; Arabs, six; other Eastern nations, forty-seven.

April 19th.—The Resident gave me a large prau to go to Pulo Tikus or Rat Island, a small coral island, about six miles off Bencoolen. On its shore-side the reef curves in at one place, and forms a little bay. All round it, on the edges of the reef, were a number of old anchors, heavy enough for the largest frigates. They had been placed there by the English, who moored their ships at that place, and carried off the pepper from Bencoolen in praus. If Bencoolen had a good harbor or roadstead, it would be an important place, but it has none, and there is no good opportunity to make one.

On Pulo Tikus we found a few fishermen, from

whom I obtained a number of the same species of shells that I had gathered before at the Spice Islands and other places in the eastern part of the archipelago. The common nautilus-shell is occasionally found there, and a very perfect one was given me that had been brought from Engano. It is, however, probable that the animal does not live in these seas, and that these shells have floated from the vicinity of the island of Rotti, off the southern end of Timur, where, as already noticed, these rare mollusks are said to live in abundance.

Bencoolen is also well known throughout the archipelago as having been the residence of Sir Stamford Raffles, who was governor of the English possessions, on this coast, from 1818 to 1824. From 1811 to 1816, while the whole archipelago was under the English, Sir Stamford was governor-general, and resided near Batavia, and it was contrary to his most earnest representations that Java and its dependencies were ceded back to the Dutch; and the great, direct revenue which those islands have yielded to Holland, since that time, has proved, in an emphatic manner, the correctness of his foresight. Ever since I arrived at Batavia, I have frequently heard his name mentioned by the Dutch officials, and always with the greatest respect.

Governor Raffles's taste for natural history was very marked. During his visit to London, before coming here, he founded the Zoological Society, and began the Zoological Gardens, which now form one of the chief inducements to strangers to visit that great and wealthy metropolis. When he sailed from this port, his ship was nearly loaded with the animals of the region, living and mounted, but, the same evening, when not more than fifty miles from the coast, she took fire, and her crew and passengers barely escaped with their lives. Not only all Sir Stamford's specimens, but all his official documents, and the many private papers he had been gathering during twelve years, were irreparably lost. Such a strange fatality seems to attend the shipment of specimens in natural history from the East, but I trust that mine may be an exception to this rule.*

April 20*th*.—Rode to Ujang Padang, a low bluff about twenty feet high, on the north side of Bencoolen Bay. It is composed of a stiff, red clay, resting on other layers of lead-colored clay, which are stratified, and contain many fossils of recent shells, a few of which appeared in the lower strata of the red clay. These fossiliferous strata probably extend for some distance north and south, but are concealed by the overlying strata of red clay, for they reappear again at the foot of a bluff between this point and Bencoolen.

From Cape Indrapura southward, a strip of low, comparatively level land borders the shore, but north of that point the ocean comes up to the bases of the hills and mountains. South of that point there are a few small islands near the shore, but north of it

---

* While this work is going to the press, the specimens referred to have all arrived in perfect order, though the ship that brought them was obliged to put in twice in distress, having one time been nearly dismasted by a cyclone, that kept her on her beam ends for eight hours.

the sea is studded with them; and especially north of Padang there are very many shallow, dangerous coral reefs, not indicated on most maps. South of Indrapura the coast has either been elevated more than the area north of it, which has remained beneath the sea, or the northern part of the coast has been depressed, while the southern part has nearly maintained its former level. The sand and clays of which this strip of low alluvial land is composed came from the disintegration and decomposition of the rocks that form the Barizan chain. They have been transported to their present position by the many small streams that flow down the southwestern flanks of those mountains to the sea. The transporting power of a stream depends, of course, chiefly on its volume, and the rapidity with which it flows. A glance at the maps of Sumatra will show that the larger streams are north of Cape Indrapura. Again, as the streams south of that point flow, for a part of their course, through level lands, they are not as rapid as those north of it, which empty at once into the sea, without making a circuitous or zigzag course through the alluvial lands, or deltas, which they themselves have formed.

April 21st.—Commenced my overland journey on horseback, the only mode of travelling in this region. Our company to-day consists of the Resident, a rajah, and many attendants; and we have come here to Suban, to look at the deposits of coal in this vicinity. From Bencoolen to Taba Pananjong, at the foot of the Barizan, the road is nearly level, being over the strip of low land that we followed along the Bencoolen River, having the sharply-pointed Sugar-Loaf Mountain on our right, until we came to a second pointed hill belonging to the same eruptive formation. In one place we saw the recent tracks of an elephant, and the natives, who are good judges, think they were probably made yesterday. Soon after, a spot was pointed out to me where, not long before, were found fragments of the clothing, and a part of the body of a native, who, while travelling along this, the most frequented road in this region, had been torn to pieces by the tigers. Near by is a rude trap for these destructive beasts. It consists of a small place, enclosed by a paling, with two large trees placed horizontally, the one above the other, so that when the tiger puts his head between them to seize the kid within the paling, the upper beam falls on him and holds him fast by its great weight. The natives then, hearing his roaring, come up and quickly dispatch him with their lances. When eighteen paals (about seventeen miles) from Bencoolen, we left the main road, which is well built, and followed a narrow footpath for six paals over a succession of small ridges that jut out from the main coast-chains. They were so near together that we were continually either scrambling down a steep declivity to the bottom of a little valley, or climbing up the opposite side. The soil is a red clay, like that noticed in the cliffs at Ujang Padang, and has been formed by the decomposition of the volcanic rocks which it covers. Heavy showers have occurred in this vicinity to-day, and descending or ascending these declivities is very difficult. It would be dangerous to travel here with any but these active and sure-footed ponies. With men on their backs they will climb up places that our horses at home, which are accustomed to level roads, would not like to ascend alone. In certain spots along this path were many piles of the excrements of elephants, where they came to feed on the branches of young trees. Half an hour before sunset we arrived here, at Suban, a village of four houses, and were glad to rest and take some food after a very fatiguing day's journey. Near by is a large stony brook, where I have enjoyed a refreshing bath in the cool, clear mountain-stream.

April 22*d*. — Early this morning we walked about half a mile up the stream, making our way over the huge boulders in its bed. Soon we came to strata of coal, associated with layers of clay and sandstone. I was searching particularly for a limestone mentioned by Van Dijk, who has examined the geology of this region, as being of the same age as the coal, and containing fossils of a recent period. Not finding it in this direction, I returned and continued down the stream for half a mile, crossing from side to side over the slippery rocks and through the torrent until the banks became high, perpendicular walls, and the water was deeper than the waist.

Finding I could proceed no farther without a raft of bamboo, I returned a quarter of a mile, ascended the steep bank, and followed down the stream for about a mile, but could not find any outcropping of the rock I was seeking. When I reached Suban again, I felt a peculiar smarting and itching sensation at the ankles, and found my stockings red with blood. Turning them down, I found both ankles perfectly fringed with blood-suckers, some of which had filled themselves until they seemed ready to burst. One had even crawled down to my foot, and made an incision which allowed the blood to pour out through my canvas shoe. All this day we have suffered from these disgusting pests. Our horses became quite striped with their own blood, and a dog that followed us looked as if he had run through a pool of clotted gore before we reached the highway again. Of all the pests I have experienced in the tropics, or in any land, whether mosquitoes, black flies, ants, snakes, or viler vermin, these are the most annoying and disgusting. There is something almost unendurable in the thought that these slimy worms are lancing you and sucking out your life-blood, yet the Resident informs me that he has travelled many times through the forests in this region when these animals were far more numerous and tormenting than they have been to-day. Sometimes he has known them to drop from the leaves upon the heads and into the necks of all who chanced to pass that way.

Returning two paals toward the highway, we took a path through a magnificent forest in a more easterly direction, for about the same distance, to Ayar Sumpur, a brook where the coal again appears on its sides and in its bed. The layers seen at Suban were not more than two or three feet thick, but here they are from six to ten. Between this place and Suban coal again outcrops on the banks of the Kamuning.

In all these places it is near the surface, being only covered with a few feet of red clay. That at Ayar Sumpur appears decidedly better than that found near Siboga.* From this place to where the coal could be taken down the Bencoolen River is a distance of only four Java paals. From there it could be transported to Bencoolen on bamboo rafts, the distance by the river being twenty-six and a half paals. The enormous quantity found here is estimated at over 200,000,000 cubic yards. The quantity and the quality of this deposit will make it of value, in case the government owning this part of the island should have its supply from Europe cut off by a war, but the disadvantage of not having a good roadstead at Bencoolen, where this coal could be taken on board vessels, renders it doubtful whether it would be found profitable to work this mine, except in case of great emergency, and then it might be found preferable to bring it from Borneo. Coal is also found at Dusun Baru, in the district of Palajou, on the banks of the Ketaun River, in the district of Mokomoko, and again in the district of Indrapura. At all these places it agrees in its mineral characteristics and outcrops very regularly at a distance of about ten miles from the sea-coast. About five miles farther inland, at Bukit Sunnur and at Suban, another and superior kind of coal appears, which may be somewhat older than the former. This latter coal agrees in its mineral characteristics with that found a few

---

* This accords with Van Dijk's statement, that while the purity of English coals is represented by 81.08, that of the Orange-Nassau mines in Borneo would be represented by 98.46, and this by 69.47.

miles east of the lake of Sinkara. All the coal in the vicinity of Suban is near the surface, sometimes only covered with four or five feet of red clay. Any private company who would like to work this mine would receive every assistance from the general and local governments.

On our return from Agar Sumpur we noticed the tracks of a rhinoceros, tiger, and deer, which had all passed along that way last night. In the path, from place to place, the natives had made pits eight or ten feet long, and about three wide and five or six deep. Each was covered over with sticks, on which dirt was laid, and dry leaves were scattered over the whole so as to perfectly conceal all appearance of danger. It is so nearly of the proportions of the rhinoceros, for whom it is made, and so deep, and the clay in which it is made is so slippery, that he generally fails to extricate himself, and the natives then dispatch him with their spears. The Resident tells me that the natives have also killed elephants by watching near a place where they come often to feed, and when one is walking and partly sliding down a steep declivity they spring up behind him and give a heavy blow with a cleaver on the after-part of the hind-legs, six or eight inches above the foot, but that this dangerous feat is very rarely attempted.

Reaching the main road, we soon arrived at Taba Pananjong. All the kampongs in this region are small, frequently consisting of only eight or ten houses, but they are all very neat and regularly arranged in one row on each side of the road, which is usually bordered with a line of cocoa-nut-trees. The natives are called Rejangs, and form a distinct nation from the Malays of Menangkabau. They have an alphabet and language peculiar to themselves, but belong to the same Malay race as all the others in the island of Sumatra. In order that I might see them dance, the Resident invited the rajah to come to the house of the *controleur* in the evening and bring with him the "*anak gadis*," literally "the virgins," of the village, but really the unmarried females. They were all clad in a sarong, fastened high round the waist, and over the shoulders was thrown a sort of scarf, which was so folded that one end would hang down behind, between the shoulders. Their dance consisted in little more than stretching both arms back until the backs of the hands nearly touched each other, and holding the edges of the scarf between the fingers. This peculiar figure they take in order to give their busts the fullest appearance possible, and captivate some one of the young men looking on. From this position they changed their hands to near the shoulders, the arms being extended and the forearms being turned back toward the head. The hands were then twisted round, with the wrist for a pivot.

Several young men appeared quite charmed and eagerly joined in the dance. The postures they assumed were quite similar. It is on such festive occasions that marriage contracts are generally made. The price of a bride, *jujur*, is fixed by the Dutch Government at twenty guilders, eight Mexican dollars, that is, the parents cannot now recover more than that sum for their daughter in case their son-in-law is unwilling to pay a larger sum. When the English were here in the beginning of this century, the *jujur* was as high as a hundred or a hundred and twenty dollars. Some of the "virgin children" I noticed had reached middle age, but the rajah explained to me that no man is willing to part with his daughters at a less price than the twenty guilders his neighbor receives for each of his, for fear of appearing to acknowledge that he thought his neighbor's daughters were more fascinating than his own; and a young man, being obliged to pay the same sum for any bride, of course chooses one who, according to his fancy, possesses the greatest charms, and no one who is not young is supposed to be charming.

Another common mode of marrying among these people is termed *umbil anak*, "taking a child." A father chooses a husband for his daughter and takes the young man to live in his family. When this young man can pay a certain sum to the father, he removes his wife and family to his own house, but until that time he and his family are regarded as servants or debtors. As tokens of their virginity, the anak gadis wear silver on their forearms, and broad bands of silver on their wrists. In the Lampong country to the south, instead of small, solid rings, they wear large rings made of hollow tubes, sometimes in such a number as to cover both arms from the wrist to the elbow. Here they occasionally have silver chains on their necks, and in their ears ornaments somewhat similar in form to those worn in the Menangkabau country, but much smaller, and the part that passes through the ear is no larger than a quill.

These natives also make many fine imitations of fruit and flowers in silver, like those of the Padang plateau. Their sarongs and scarfs they manufacture themselves, and ornament very skilfully with figures and leaves wrought in with silver-thread.

April 20*th*.—Rode this morning from Taba Pauanjong over the Barizan or Coast Range, which here, as elsewhere, is generally higher than the ranges parallel to it on the east, and therefore forms the water-shed between the east and west coasts. The road had been well built, but was extremely muddy and badly washed away in some places by the heavy rains which have lately occurred in this vicinity. It is, however, sufficiently good for the natives to use their *padatis*, or carts drawn by buffaloes, but most of the men I met were carrying their produce to market on their backs.

All the mountains are covered with a most dense forest, but the low lands which spread from their bases to the sea appear quite unfertile, especially when compared with the low lands of Java. The morning air was still and clear, and troops of large black monkeys made the valleys and ravines continually resound with their loud trumpeting. From the top of the pass, which is from two thousand five hundred to three thousand feet in height, a magnificent view is obtained, to the southwest, of the low lands extending to Bencoolen, and also of Pulo Tikus in the distance, and the heavy surf breaking on its coral reefs and sparkling brightly in the sunshine. On the opposite or interior side of the chain was spread out before me the lovely and highly fertile valley of the River Musi, which takes its rise a little farther to the north. In the midst of this valley was the kampong and Dutch post Kopaiyong. Beyond the valley rose an active volcano, Mount Ulu Musi, with three peaks. The largest and the oldest was quiet, and beyond it was a second and somewhat smaller cone, evidently of a more recent origin than the former, but also inactive. Beyond this cone was a third, yet smaller, from the top of which great quantities of steam and other gases were ascending in dense volumes.

From this pass our descent was as rapid as our ascent had been on the coast side, until we came down to the banks of the Musi, and the valley in which the village of Kopaiyong is situated. The height of this plateau above the sea is from fifteen to eighteen hundred feet. It is a complete analogue of the plateau about the lake of Sinkara, and all the others between the Barizan and its parallel chains to the northward. Its soil is a fine, black loam. Its chief products are tobacco and coffee, which both thrive here very well. This is considered, and no doubt rightly, a very healthy place. There are no "wet or dry seasons," as in Java, but showers occur here every few days, generally in the afternoon. Although the soil and climate of this valley are so favorable for the development of civilization, yet the natives in all this region, until a few years ago, only clothed themselves with the bark of trees. This plateau has lacked, however, one inducement toward promoting industry and civilization which that of Menangkabau possesses, and that is gold. In the coast region, the houses of the natives have high, sharp roofs, and are covered with atap, but here they are larger and lower; and the roofs are nearly flat, and covered with bamboos split into halves and placed side by side, with the concave side upward. Over the edges of these are placed other pieces of bamboo, with the concave side downward. This is the only place in the archipelago where I have seen this simple and easy mode of making a roof.

April 24*th*.—Finding myself very ill from over-exertion during the past two days, and that the next two days' journeys must be long and fatiguing, I rest here and enjoy the cool, refreshing air of Kopaiyong for a day. The *controleur* informs me that the volcanic cone northeast of us was formed during an eruption which took place only a year ago, and that, for some time previous to the eruption, heavy earthquakes occurred here very frequently; but since the gases that were pent up beneath the mountain have found a vent, only one earthquake has been experienced, and that was very slight. This is the most active volcano I have seen. A great quantity of white gas is now rising most grandly. At one moment it appears like a great sheaf, and at the next instant slowly changes into a perpendicular column, and this again becomes an immense inverted cone, which seems supported in the sky by resting its apex on the summit of the volcano beneath it. The whole amount of trade at this place in a year amounts to one hundred thousand guilders (forty thousand dollars). The traders are Chinamen, Arabs, and a few Dutchmen. They obtain from the natives coffee and tobacco, and give them in return cotton goods, knives, and various kinds of trinkets. The population of this region appears to be only a small fraction of what it is on the Padang plateau; if it were as large and industrious, the upper valley of the Musi would soon be transformed into one great garden, and Bencoolen, to which its products must be taken to be shipped abroad, would immediately become a port of the first importance. I had seriously contemplated undertaking the journey from Solok to this place, and if it had not been necessary for me to return to Padang, I should have attempted it, notwithstanding it would have been necessary to have travelled the whole distance on foot, and to have met constant hinderances and annoyances from the natives, who are extremely jealous of all foreigners. The distance from Solok, in a straight line, is nearly two hundred geographical miles, but by the zigzag and circuitous route which I would have been obliged to take, it would have been nearly three hundred.

The house of the *controleur* at this place is covered with an atap of bamboo splints, made in the same way as the common atap of palm-leaves, but it is much neater, and said to be far more durable.

April 25th.—As there are no white people at the place where I am to lodge to-night, the *controleur* was so kind as to send a servant yesterday with an ample supply of eatables, and orders to the rajahs on the way to receive me kindly when I reached their respective villages.

At 6 A. M. started with a guide and a coolie for Kaban Agong, a distance of nine paals in a southeasterly direction, along the Musi, which, in this part of its course, is only a small stream with slight falls at short distances. The valley south of Kopaiyong may be quite wide, but we soon passed into such a dense jungle that I was unable to obtain any view of the mountains on either hand. Kaban Agong is a small kampong of twenty or twenty-five houses, and, except the two or three occasionally seen near each other in the cleared places, or ladangs, the whole country is an unbroken wilderness.

The houses of the village were quite regularly arranged in two rows, and in the middle of the street between them is a small circular house, with open sides, and seats around it for the coolies, who are travelling to and fro, to stop and rest under a shelter from the sunshine. Here the rajah received me, and brought such fruits as his people raised. The coolie, who marched beside my horse, carried my Spencer's breech-loader, which I had been careful to have ready loaded and capped. It caused the natives to manifest the greatest respect for us, especially when my servants declared that I needed only to put it to my shoulder, pull the trigger, and there would be a constant stream of bullets. From Kaban Agong to Tanjong Agong (eight paals) we passed over a more open and hilly country. The road here diverged from the left bank of the Musi, and took a more easterly course. Here more sawas appeared, but the people are in great poverty. Many of the hills are covered with the common rank prairie-grass, which we saw covering large areas in the northwest part of the Mandéling Valley, and in many other places.

In such open prairies the sun poured down a most

scorching heat, and even my Malay attendants complained bitterly; indeed, I find I can bear such excessive heat better than they. From the tops of the low hills I enjoyed fine views of the Barizan or coast chain. The outline of many of its peaks shows that they were formerly eruptive cones, but now they are more or less washed down or changed in form by rains and streams. As we came near this village, Tanjong Agong, the road was filled with the tracks and excrements of a herd of elephants that passed this way yesterday or the day before. Two days ago two of these beasts came into the sawas, near this place, and the natives succeeded in shooting one. Tanjong Agong is a small village, of only eighteen or twenty small houses, each of which is placed on posts six or eight feet high. A ladder leads up to a landing, which is enclosed by a fence and a gate, to prevent the tigers from entering their houses. The natives keep hens, and would have dogs, but they are all destroyed by the tigers. These ravenous beasts infest the whole region in such numbers, and are so daring, that the rajah, who can speak Malay very well, assures me that, during last year, *five* of the people of this little village were torn to pieces by them while working in the sawas, or while travelling to the neighboring kampongs. No native here ever thinks of going even the shortest distance by night, except when sent on the most urgent business; and it is chiefly for this reason that I always commence my day's journey so early.

The house in which I lodge is built of bamboo, and surrounded with a paling of sharpened stakes, which also include the stable. It has lately been built by order of the Dutch Government for the accommodation of any official or other foreigner travelling in this country. Before the paling was completed, the *controleur* of the district visited this place, and put his horse into the stable. At midnight he heard a loud howling and neighing, and the natives shouting out to each other to come with their arms. A tiger had come out of the adjoining forest, and had sprung upon his horse from behind, and the natives were attacking him with their lances. He lost his horse, but had the privilege of carrying away the tiger's skin. Those who complain of the scarcity of game ought to come here. It is not by any means inaccessible, and both tigers and elephants are exceedingly abundant.

April 26th.—At $6\frac{1}{2}$ A. M. continued on through a more open and somewhat cultivated country. The Musi here makes a great bend to the southwest, and the path leads eastward over a gently-rising elevation, on the top of which is a large and most thriving coffee-garden, and near by are rice-fields which yield abundantly. This garden has been very lately planted, and yet all the trees that are old enough to bear are nearly loaded down with fruit. The rice-fields show that an abundance of food could be raised here, and the only thing that is wanting is people to do the work. The elevated situation of this country makes it very healthy for foreigners. If any one could obtain a grant of land here, and also the privilege of bringing a large number of Chinamen, he would certainly realize a fortune, for coffee can be here cultivated with little care, and rice, the staple article of food among that people, can be raised in any quantity. Such a privilege could not be obtained at present, but the liberal tendency of the government of the Netherlands India promises that it may be, at no distant time in the future. Such an enterprise would not have the character of an experiment, for the facility with which coffee and rice can be grown has already been shown on this plantation, and the cost of transporting it to Padang or Palembang would be very light. Sumatra undoubtedly contains large quantities of gold, but the true source of her wealth is not the precious metal she possesses, but the crops of coffee she produces.

From the top of this mountain I took my last view of the Barizan chain, which had been constantly in sight since I passed through the Strait of Sunda on my way to Padang. In the ladangs in this region the walls of the huts of the natives are mostly made of bark. While coming down from this low mountain-range, we had a splendid view up a valley to the southward, and of the low but sharply-crested chain which limits on the south the area drained by the Musi. At the foot of this elevation a stream courses southward to the Musi, and on its banks are a native village, and a Dutch post and fort. Here, as elsewhere, I rode up to the house of the *controleur*, whom I had previously notified of my coming. He had gone a number of miles southward, to the limit of his district and the Pasuma country, where I now learned a war was going on. His good lady was at home, and, to my great surprise, welcomed me in pure English. To be able to converse in the interior of Sumatra, in my native tongue, was indeed a pleasure I had not anticipated. The distance from Tanjong Agong to this place is eleven paals, about ten miles.

April 27th.—Continued down the north bank of the Musi, which here flows to the northwest. For three or four paals the path (for it cannot properly be styled a road) was very narrow, and built on the steep side of a mountain, at the foot of which the Musi boils in a series of rapids. When within six or seven miles of Tebing Tingi, we found the valley much broken, and soon it became flat, and changed in many places into morasses. Here we came to a small stream, over which was a bamboo bridge, supported by rattans fastened to the limbs of two high, overhanging trees. This was so weak that my guide directed me to dismount and pass on foot. At 2 A. M. we arrived at Tebing Tingi, where an assistant resident is stationed, who received me politely, and urged me to remain with him several days. Distance made to-day, seventeen paals. The whole distance from Kopaiyong to this place, forty-five paals, I have travelled with the single horse given me by the *controleur* of that village. Such is the generous manner in which the Dutch officials treat those who come to them properly recommended by the higher authorities.

After crossing the Barizan chain, and coming down into this valley of the Musi, I have noticed that the natives are of a lighter color, taller, and more gracefully formed than those seen in the vicinity of Bencoolen. The men always carry a kris or a lance when they go from one kampong to another. The same laws and customs prevail here as in the vicinity of Bencoolen, except that the jugur, or price of a bride, is considerably higher. The anak gadis here also wear many rings of large silver wire on the forearm, and gold beads on the wrist, in token of their virginity. The Resident states to me that the native population does not appear to increase in this region, and that the high price of the brides is the chief reason. As the price is paid to the girl's parents, and not to herself, she has less inducement to conduct herself in accordance with their wishes; and, to avoid the natural consequences of their habits, the anak gadis are accustomed to take very large doses of pepper, which is mixed with salt, in order to be swallowed more easily. Many are never married, and most of those who are, bear but two or three children, after they have subjected themselves to such severe treatment in their youth.

April 27th.—Rode five or six paals up the Musi, and then crossed it at the foot of a rapid on a "racket," or raft of bamboo, the usual mode of ferrying in this island. In the centre of the raft is a kind of platform, where the passenger sits. One native stands at the bow, and one at the stern, each having a long bamboo. The racket is then drawn up close to the foot of the rapids, and a man keeps her head to the stream, while the other pushes her over. As soon as she leaves the bank, away she shoots down the current, despite the shouts and exertions of both. We were carried down so swiftly, that I began to fear we should come into another rapid, where our frail raft would have been washed to pieces among the foaming rocks in a moment; but at last they succeeded in stopping her, and we gained the opposite bank. Thence my guide took me through a morass, which was covered with a dense jungle, an admirable place for crocodiles, and they do not fail to frequent it in large numbers; but the thousands of leeches formed a worse pest. In one place, about a foot square, in the path, I think I saw as many as twenty, all stretching and twisting themselves in every direction in search of prey. They are small, being about an inch long, and a tenth of an inch in diameter, before they gorge themselves with the blood of some unfortunate animal that chances to pass. They tormented me in a most shocking manner. Every ten or fifteen minutes I had to stop and rid myself of perfect anklets of them.

I was in search of a coral-stone, which the natives of this region burn for lime. My attendants, as well as myself, were so tormented with the leeches, that we could not remain long in that region, but I saw it was nothing but a raised reef, chiefly composed of comminuted coral, in which were many large hemispherical meandrinas. The strata, where they could be distinguished, were seen to be nearly horizontal. Large blocks of coral are scattered about, just as on the present reefs, but the jungle was too thick to travel in far, and, as soon as we had gathered a few shells, we hurried to the Musi, and rode back seven miles in a heavy, drenching rain.

All the region we have been travelling in to-day

abounds in rhinoceroses, elephants, and deer. If the leeches attack them as they did a dog that followed us, they must prove one of the most efficient means of destroying those large animals. It is at least fortunate for the elephant and rhinoceros that they are pachyderms. While passing through the places where the jungle is mostly composed of bamboos, we saw several large troops of small, slate-colored monkeys, and, among the taller trees, troops of another species of a light-yellow color, with long arms and long tails. On the morning that I left Tanjong Agong, as we passed a tall tree by the roadside, the natives cautioned me to keep quiet, for it was "full of monkeys," and, when we were just under it, they all set up a loud shout, and at once a whole troop sprang out of its high branches like a flock of birds. Some came down twenty-five or thirty feet before they struck on the tops of the small trees beneath them, and yet each would recover, and go off through the jungle, with the speed of an arrow, in a moment.

While nearly all animals have a particular area which they frequent—as the low coast region, the plateaus of these tropical lands, or the higher parts of the mountains—the rhinoceros lives indifferently anywhere between the sea-shores and the tops of the highest peaks. This species has two "horns," the first being the longer and more sharply pointed, but the Java species has only one. The natives here know nothing of the frequent combats between these animals and elephants, that are so frequently pictured in popular works on natural history. The Resident has, however, told me of a combat between two other rivals of these forests that is more remarkable. When he was *controleur* at a small post, a short distance north of this place, a native came to him one morning, and asked, if he should find a dead tiger and bring its head, whether he would receive the usual bounty given by the government. The Resident assured him that he would, and the native then explained that there had evidently been a battle between two tigers in the woods, near his kampong, for all had heard their howls and cries, and they were fighting so long that, he had no doubt, one was left dead on the spot. A party at once began a hunt for the expected prize, and soon they found the battle had not been between two tigers, as they had supposed, but between a tiger and a bear, and that both were dead. The bear was still hugging the tiger, and the tiger had reached round, and fastened his teeth in the side of the bear's neck. The natives then gathered some rattan, wound it round them, just as they were, strung them to a long bamboo, and brought them to the office of the Resident, who gave a full account of this strange combat in his next official report.

These bears are popularly called "sun" bears, *Helarctos Malayanus*, from their habit of basking in the hot sunshine, while other bears slink away from the full light of day into some shady place. The Resident at Bencoolen had a young cub that was very tame. Its fur was short, fine, and glossy. It was entirely black, except a crescent-shaped spot of white on its breast, which characterizes the species.

Governor Raffles, while at Bencoolen, also had a

tame one, which was very fond of mangostins, and only lost its good-nature when it came to the table, and was not treated with champagne. When fully grown, it is only four and a half feet long. It is herbivorous, and particularly fond of the young leaves of the cocoa-nut palm, and is said to destroy many of those valuable trees to gratify its appetite.

April 30th.—At 6 A. M. commenced the last stage of my journey on horseback. My course now was from Tebing Tingi, on the Musi, in a southeasterly direction, to Lahat, the head of navigation on the Limatang. The distance between these two places is about forty paals, considerably farther than it would be from Tebing Tingi down the Musi to the head of navigation on that river; but I prefer to take this route, in order to learn something of the localities of coal on the Limatang and its branches, and of the unexplored Pasuma country. We crossed the Musi on a raft, and at once the road took us into a forest, which continued with little interruption all the way to Bunga Mas, a distance of twenty-four paals. Most of this forest rises out of a dense undergrowth, in which the creeping stems and prickly leaves of rattans were seen. These are various species of *Calamus*, a genus of palms that has small, reed-like, trailing stems, which are in strange contrast to the erect and rigid trunks of the cocoa-nut, the areca, the palmetto, and other palms. It seems paradoxical to call this a palm, and the high, rigid bamboo a species of grass. When they are growing, the stem is sheathed in the bases of so many leaves that it is half an inch in diameter. When these are stripped off, a smooth, reed-like stem of a straw-color is found within, which becomes yellow as it dries. The first half-mile of the road we travelled to-day was completely ploughed up by elephants which passed along two days ago during a heavy rain. The piles of their excrements were so numerous that it seems they use it as a stall. Every few moments we came upon their tracks. In one place they had completely brushed away the bridge over a small stream, where they went down to ford it; for, though they always try to avail themselves of the cleared road when they travel to and fro among these forests, they are too sagacious to trust themselves on the frail bridges.

In the afternoon, the small boughs which they had lately broken off became more numerous as we advanced, and their leaves were of a livelier green. We were evidently near a herd, for leaves wilt in a short time under this tropical sun. Soon after, we came into a thicker part of the forest, where many tall trees threw out high, overarching branches, which effectually shielded us from the scorching sun, while the dry leaves they had shed quite covered the road.

Several natives had joined us, for they always travel in company through fear of the tigers. While we were passing through the dark wood, suddenly a heavy crashing began in the thick jungle about twenty paces from where I was riding. A native, who was walking beside my horse with my rifle capped and cocked, handed it to me in an instant, but the jungle was so thick that it was impossible to see any thing, and I did not propose to fire until

I could see the forehead of my game. All set up a loud, prolonged yell, and the beast slowly retreated, and allowed us to proceed unmolested. The natives are not afraid of whole herds of elephants, but they dislike to come near a single one. The larger and stronger males sometimes drive off all their weaker rivals, which are apt to wreak their vengeance on any one they chance to meet. Beyond this was a more open country, and in the road were scattered many small trees that had been torn up by a herd, apparently this very morning.

Although they are so abundant here in Sumatra, there are none found in Java. They occur in large numbers on the Malay Peninsula, and there is good reason to suppose they exist in the wild state in the northern parts of Borneo. This is regarded as distinct from the Asiatic and African species, and has been named *Elephas Sumatrensis*.

Three paals before we came to Bunga Mas, a heavy rain set in and continued until we reached that place. Our road crossed a number of streams that had their sources on the flanks of the mountains on our right, and in a short time their torrents were so swollen that my horse could scarcely ford them. Bunga Mas is a *dusun*, or village, on a cliff by a small river which flows toward the north. Near the village is a stockade fort, where we arrived at half-past six. The captain gave me comfortable quarters, and I was truly thankful to escape the storm and the tigers without, and to rest after more than twelve hours in the saddle.

This evening the captain has shown me the skin

of a large tiger, which, a short time since, killed three natives in four nights at this place. The village is surrounded by a stockade to keep out these ravenous beasts, and the gate is guarded at night by a native armed with a musket. One evening this tiger stole up behind the guard, sprang upon him, and, as a native said who chanced to see it, killed him instantly with a blow of her paw on the back of his neck. She then caught him up and ran away with him. The next day the body was found partly eaten, and was buried very deeply to keep it out of her reach. The second evening she seized and carried off a native who was bathing in the stream at the foot of the cliff. The captain now found he must try to destroy her, and therefore loaded a musket with a very heavy charge of powder and two bullets. The gun was then lashed firmly to a tree, and a large piece of fresh meat was fastened to the muzzle, so that when she attempted to take it away she would discharge the piece, and receive both bullets. The next morning they found a piece of her tongue on the ground near the muzzle of the gun, and the same trap was set again; but the next night she came back and took away a second man on guard at the gate of the *dusun*. The captain now started with a corporal and eight men, determined to hunt her down. They tracked her to a place filled with tall grass, and closing round that, slowly advanced, until two or three of them heard a growl, when they all fired and killed her instantly. It proved to be a female, and she had evidently been so daring for the purpose of procuring food for her young.

May 1*st*.—The rain continued through the night, and only cleared away at daylight. In two hours I started, though I found myself ill from such continued exertion and exposure to a burning sun and drenching rains, and, more than all, from drinking so many different kinds of water in a single day. I was accompanied by a soldier who was one of the eight who went out to hunt the tiger that killed so many natives in such a short time. He repeated to me all the details of the whole matter, and assured me that a piece of the brute's tongue was found on the ground just as the captain said, and that, when they had secured her, they found that a part of her tongue was gone.

We had not travelled more than half a mile before we came upon the tracks of two tigers, a large one and a small one, probably a female and her young, which had passed along the road in the same way we were going. The perfect impressions left by their feet showed they had walked along that road since the rain had ceased, and therefore not more than two hours before us, and possibly not more than ten minutes. We expected to see them at almost every turn in the road, and we all kept together and proceeded with the greatest caution till the sun was high and it was again scorching hot. At such times these dangerous beasts always retreat into the cool jungle.

For eight paals from Bunga Mas the road was more hilly than it was yesterday. In many places the sides of the little valley between the ridges were so steep that steps were made in the slippery clay for the natives, who always travel on foot. Seven paals out, we had a fine view of the Pasuma country. It is a plateau which spreads out to the southeast and east from the feet of the great Dempo, the highest and most magnificent mountain in all this region. The lower part of this volcano appeared in all its details, but thick clouds unfortunately concealed its summit. Considerable quantities of opaque gases are said to have poured out of its crater, but it does not appear to have undergone any great eruption since the Dutch established themselves in this region. It is the most southern and eastern of the many active volcanoes on this island. Like the Mérapi in the Padang plateau, the Dempo does not rise in the Barizan chain nor in one parallel to it, but in a transverse range. Here there is no high chain parallel to the Barizan, as there is at Kopaiyong, where the Musi takes its rise, and also north of Mount Ulu Musi continuously through the Korinchi country all the way to the Batta Lands. Another and a longer transverse elevation appears in the chain which forms the boundary between this residency of Palembang and that of Lampong, and which is the water-shed, extending in a northeasterly direction from Lake Ranau to the Java Sea. The height of Mount Dempo has been variously estimated at from ten thousand to twelve thousand feet, but I judge that it is not higher than the Mérapi, and that its summit therefore is not more than nine thousand five hundred feet above the level of the sea.

The Pasuma plateau is undoubtedly the most densely-peopled area in this part of the island. Its soil is described to me, by those who have seen it, as exceedingly fertile, and quite like that of the Musi valley at Kopaiyong, but the natives of that country were extremely poor, while the Pasumas raise an abundance of rice and keep many fowls. During the past few years they have raised potatoes and many sorts of European vegetables, which they sold to the Dutch before the war began. The cause of the present difficulty was a demand made by the Dutch Government that the Pasuma chiefs should acknowledge its supremacy, which they have all refused to do. The villages or fortified places of the Pasumas are located on the tops of hills, and they fight with so much determination that they have already repulsed the Dutch once from one of their forts with a very considerable loss. No one, however, entertains a doubt of the final result of this campaign, for their fortifications are poor defences against the mortars and other ordnance of the Dutch.

Soon after the tracks of the two tigers disappeared, we came to a kind of rude stockade fort, where a guard of native militia are stationed. The paling, however, is more for a protection against the tigers than the neighboring Pasumas. A number of the guard told me that they hear the tigers howl here every night, and that frequently they come up on the hill and walk round the paling, looking for a chance to enter; and I have no doubt their assertions were entirely true, for when we had come to the foot of the hill the whole road was covered with tracks. The natives, who, from long experience, have remarkable skill in tracing these beasts, said that three different ones had been there since the rain ceased; but one who has not been accustomed to examine such tracks would have judged that half a dozen tigers had passed that way. There are but a few native houses here at a distance from the villages in the ladangs, and those are all perched on posts twelve or fifteen feet high, and reached by a ladder or notched stick, in order that those dwelling in them may be safer from the tigers.

At noon we came down into a fertile valley surrounded with mountains in the distance, and at 2 P. M. arrived at Lahat, a pretty native village on the banks of the Limatang. The *controleur* stationed here received me politely, and engaged a boat to take me down the Limatang to Palembang. The Limatang takes its rise up in the Pasuma country, and Lahat, being at the head of navigation on this river, is an important point. A strong fort has been built here, and is constantly garrisoned with one or two companies of soldiers. One night while I was there, there was a general alarm that a strong body of Pasumas had been discovered reconnoitring the village, and immediately every possible preparation was made to receive them. The cause of the alarm proved to be, that one of the Javanese soldiers stationed outside the fort stated that he saw two natives skulking in the shrubbery near him, and that he heard them consulting whether it was best to attack him, because, as was true, his gun was not loaded. The mode of attack that the Pasumas adopt is to send forward a few of their braves to set fire to a village, while the main body remains near by to make attack as soon as the confusion caused by the fire begins. This is undoubtedly the safest and most effectual mode of attacking a kampong, as the houses of the natives are mostly of bamboo, and if there is a fresh breeze and one or two huts can be fired to windward, the whole village will soon be in a blaze. Though this seems to us a dastardly mode of warfare, the Pasumas are justly famed for their high sense of honor, their bitterest enemy being safe when he comes and intrusts himself entirely to their protection. When the Dutch troops arrived here, an official, who had frequently been up into their country, volunteered to visit the various kampongs and try to induce them to submit, and in every place he was well received and all his wants cared for, though none of the chiefs would, for a moment, entertain his proposals.

My journey on horseback was finished. The distance by the route taken from Bencoolen is about one hundred and twenty paals, or one hundred and twelve miles, but I had travelled considerably farther to particular localities that were off the direct route. I had chanced to make the journey at just the right time of year. The road is good enough for padatis and to transport light artillery. For most of the time a tall, rank grass fills the whole road except a narrow footpath, but the government obliges the natives living near this highway to cut off the grass and repair the bridges once a year, and I chanced to begin my journey just as most of this work was finished. The bridges are generally made of bamboo, and can therefore be used for only a short time after they are repaired. Indeed, in many places, they are frequently swept away altogether, and are not rebuilt until the next year. From what I have already recorded, those who glory in hunting dangerous game may conclude that they cannot do better than to visit this part of Sumatra. To reach it they should come from Singapore to Muntok on the island of Banca, and thence over to Palembang, where the Resident of all this region resides, and obtain from him letters to his sub-officers in this vicinity. From Palembang they should come up the Musi and Limatang to Lahat, when they will find themselves in a most magnificent and healthy country, and one literally abounding in game.

CHAPTER XVII.

PALEMBANG, BANCA, AND SINGAPORE.

May 4th.—At 7 A. M. I bade my host, the *controleur*, good-by, and began to glide down the Limatang for Palembang.

It was a cool, clear morning, and I enjoyed a fine view of Mount Dempo and the other high peaks near it. The current at first was so rapid that the only care of my men was, to keep the boat from striking on the many bars of sand and shingle. To do this, one stood forward and one aft, each provided with a long bamboo. We soon shot into a series of foaming rapids, and here the river bent so abruptly to the right and left that I thought we should certainly be dashed against a ragged, precipitous wall of rock that formed the right bank at that place, but we passed safely by, though the stern of the boat only passed clear by a few inches. My boat was about twenty feet long and five broad, flat-bottomed, and made of thin plank. Its central part was covered over with roof of atap, like the sampans in China, and on this was another sliding roof, which could be hauled forward to protect the rowers from rain or sunshine. From Lahat to the mouth of the Inem River relays of natives stood ready on the bank to guide our boat. This service they render the Dutch Government instead of paying a direct tax in money.

A short distance below Lahat, on the right bank, is a remarkably needle-like peak called Bukit Sirilo. Near this hill the Limatang makes a long bend to the north, and after we had left it two or three miles behind us I was quite surprised to find we had turned sharply round, and that it was now two or three miles before us. A short distance above the Sirilo we passed a fine outcropping of coal in the left bank. The government engineers have examined it, and found it to be soft and bituminous, but containing too large a proportion of incombustible matter to be of any great value. The strata dip toward the coast. The Resident of Tebing Tingi informed me that a similar coal is found on the Musi below that place. I believe that strata of recent limestone, containing corals, which I observed above Tebing Tingi, underlie this coal, and that it is, therefore, of very recent geological age. At 4 P. M. we came to Muara Inem, a large kampong of two thousand souls, on the Inem, at its juncture with the Limatang. Here I had the pleasure of meeting the *controleur*, whom I had met in the Minahassa, and who had been my fellow-traveller from Celebes to Java. During the latter third of my way down the Limatang to this point, the country is well peopled, and forms a marked contrast with the sparsely-populated regions through which I have been travelling since leaving Bencoolen.

At one kampong we saw three women in a small, flat-bottomed canoe, each sitting erect and paddling with both hands. In this way they crossed the river with a surprising rapidity, considering the simple apparatus they used. The readiness with which they paddled indicated that this is no very uncommon mode of crossing rivers in this land.

As the villages became larger and more frequent, more and more cocoa-nut trees appeared, and soon we passed several large bamboo rafts, bearing sheds that were filled with this fruit, and in one place two natives were seen quietly floating down the river on a great pile of these nuts in the most complacent manner. At first I expected to see the nuts fly off in all directions and the men disappear beneath the surface of the river, but as we came nearer I saw the nuts were fastened together in small bunches by strips of their own husks, and these bunches were bound into a hemispherical mass large enough to float the two men. The nuts on the raft were to be taken down to Palembang, where the cocoa-palms do not flourish. During the day we saw two or three large troops of monkeys. This is a very pleasant time to pass down these rivers, because they are now high, and instead of seeing only walls and bluffs of naked mud on either hand, the banks are covered with grass down to the water's edge, and the bamboos and trees, that grow here in tropical luxuriance, lean over gracefully toward the rapid river, and lave the tips of their lowest branches in the passing current.

May 5th.—The *controleur* kindly took me in his large barge, with twenty men to paddle and two men to steer, some five miles up the Inem River to Lingga, where there is an outcropping of coal in the river bank. The coal found there is very light, almost as soft as charcoal, and evidently of a very recent geological age. A similar but somewhat better coal is found five or six miles farther up this river. At Karang Tingi, three miles up the river from Muara Inem, the rajah of that district gave me a bottle of petroleum, which is about as thick as tar, and, according to the examinations of the Dutch chemists, does not contain much paraffine, naphtha, nor material suitable for burning in lamps. It is found about six miles back from the river. At Karang Tingi we noticed a number of boys enjoying an odd kind of sport. They were sliding down the high slippery bank on their naked backs.

At Muara Inem the *controleur* showed me a large garden filled with trees, from which the "palm-oil" is manufactured. It is a low palm, and the fruit is not much larger than the betel-nut. I understood him to say that it was the *Elais Guineensis*, and had been introduced from the Dutch possessions on the west coast of Africa. The oil is contained in the husk, and is used in manufacturing soap and candles.

May 6th.—Very early this morning started with the *controleur* down the Limatang in his barge, with twenty men. During last night the river rose here four or five feet, and the current is now unusually strong. From Muara Inem, to where it empties into the Musi, it is very crooked, constantly bending to the right in nearly equal curves, the current, of course, being strongest in the middle of each bend. This constant curving gives an endless variety to its scenery.

A VIEW ON THE RIVER LIMATANG, SUMATRA.

The water, being high, enabled us to see the cleared places that occurred from time to time on the bank; though generally only a thick wood or dense jungle appeared on either hand, yet I never for a moment was weary of watching the graceful bending of the reeds and tall bamboos, and of the varied grouping of these with large trees. In two places the river makes such long bends, that artificial canals have been made across the tongues of land thus formed. One of these cuts, which was less than a hundred yards long, saved us going round half a mile by the river. Every four or five miles we came to a large kampong, and exchanged our boatmen for new ones, so that all day long we swiftly glided down the smooth stream, one relay of men not getting weary before they were relieved by another, and the strong current also helping us onward. The kampongs here are free from the filth seen in those farther up in the interior. The houses are all placed on posts five or six feet high, for sometimes the whole country is completely flooded. Many of them are built of well-planed boards, and have a roofing of tiles. When the sun had become low, we came to the large kampong of Baruaiyu. At all these villages there is a raft with a house upon it, where the boatmen waited for us. Fastening our boat to one of these, we took up our quarters in the rajah's house. Like those built by our Puritan forefathers, it had one long roof and one short one, but it was so low that a tall man could scarcely stand up in it anywhere. The floor, instead of being level, rose in four broad steps, and the whole building formed but one large apartment with two small rooms at the rear end.

May 7th.—A severe toothache and the bites and buzzing of thousands of mosquitoes made me glad to see the dawn once more, and again be floating down the river. Before we came to the chief village of each district, where we were to exchange boatmen, we always met the boat of the rajah of that place, and were greeted with shouts and a great din from tifas and gongs.

The rajahs in this region are divided into three grades, and their ranks are shown by the small hemispherical caps they wear. Those of the highest rank have theirs completely covered with figures wrought with gold thread; those of the second rank have theirs mostly covered with such ornaments; and those of the third rank wear only a gold band. They all carry krises of the common serpentine form. Those that have the wavy lines alike on each side of the blade are regarded as the most valuable. The handles are usually made of whale's-teeth, and very nicely carved; and the scabbards are frequently overlaid with gold. Those that have been used by famous chiefs are valued at all sorts of enormous prices, but are never sold. They also frequently wear a belt covered with large diamond-shaped plates of silver, on which are inscribed verses of the Koran, for the natives of this region are probably the most zealous and most rigid Mohammedans in the archipelago.

The staple article of food here is rice. They also raise much cotton from seed imported from our

Southern States. Having gathered it from the ripe bolls, they take out the seeds by running it between two wooden or iron cylinders, which are made to revolve by a treadle, and are so near together, that the seeds, which are saved for the next season, cannot pass through. The fibres are very short, compared to the average product raised in our country, but it serves a good purpose here, where they make it into a coarse thread, which they weave by hand into a cloth for kabayas and chilanas.

The marriage rites and laws here are nearly the same as those I have already described at Taba Pananjong, except that the price of a bride here is just that of a buffalo, or about eighty guilders (thirty-two dollars). Unless a young man has a buffalo or other possessions of equal value, therefore, he cannot purchase a wife. Near Baruaiyu there is a peculiar people known as the Rembang people, who live in four or five villages at some distance from the river. They are very willing to learn to read and write their own language, but will not allow themselves to be taught Dutch or Malay. Last night the river rose still higher, and now it has overflowed its banks, which appear much lower than they are between Lamat and Muara Inem. During the day we have had several showers. At 5 P. M. we arrived at Sungi Rotan, the last village on the Lamatang before its confluence with the Musi. It is a small and poor village, the land here being generally too low for rice, and the cocoa-nut palms yielding but little compared to what they do higher up. Farther down toward Palembang they yield still less. This is the limit of the *controleur's* district in this direction. It extends but a short distance up the Inem and up the Limatang above Muara Inem, and yet it contains no less that ninety-one thousand souls.

The *controleur* came here to settle a difficulty between the people of this and a neighboring village. The other party had occupied a portion of the ricelands belonging to this people, and the trouble had risen to such a pitch, that the government had to interfere, to prevent them from beginning a war. I said to the rajah that, beyond Lamat, I had passed for miles through a beautiful country, and that it seemed to me he would do well to migrate there; but he evidently disliked such a suggestion, and the *controleur* asked me not to urge him to adopt my view, for fear that he might think the government designed sending him there, and because he and all his people would rather die than go to live in any distant region.

May 8th.—At 6½ A. M. started for Palembang. My own boat, which I sent on directly from Muara Inem, arrived here yesterday a few hours before us, having been three days in coming down the same distance that we have made in two. We soon stopped at the request of one of the boatmen to examine a small bamboo box which he had set in a neighboring bayou for crawfish. Several were found in it. Their eyes seemed to emit flashes of light, and appeared to be spherical jewels of a light-scarlet hue. I found them palatable when roasted. The boatmen also found some *Ampullariæ*, which they said they were accustomed to eat, and I found them palatable also

We soon floated out of the narrow Limatang into the wide and sluggish Musi, and changed our course from north to east. There are great quantities of rattan along the lower part of the Limatang and the Musi, and the natives gather only a small fraction of what they might if they were not so indolent. Last night, at Sungi Rotan, the mosquitoes proved a worse pest than the night before, and they have continued to annoy us all day.

In the afternoon I had a slight attack of fever, almost the only one I have had since I was ill immediately after my arrival in Batavia, a few days more than a year ago. After three large doses of quinine I fell asleep, my boatmen saying that we should not reach Palembang till morning, which entirely agreed with my own wishes, as I did not care to call during the evening on the assistant Resident, whom I had already notified of my coming. When the last dose had disappeared I soon became oblivious to all real things, and was only troubled with the torturing images seen in a fever-dream. While these hideous forms were still before my mind's eye, I was suddenly aroused by a loud noise, and, while yet half awake, was dazzled by a bright light on the water, and, on looking out, saw that we were near a large house. On the brilliantly-lighted portico above us were festoons of flowers, and, while I was yet gazing in wonder, inspiriting music sprang up and couple after couple whirled by in the mazy waltz. I put my hand up to my head to assure myself that I was not the victim of some hallucination, and my boatmen, apparently perceiving my state of mind, informed me that we had arrived at Palembang, and that a sister of one of the officials had lately been married, and her brother was celebrating the happy occasion by giving a grand "feast," or, as we should say, a ball.

The bright light, the enlivening music, and the constant hum of happy voices, instantly banished all possibility of my entertaining the thought of remaining for the night in my dark, narrow cabin; and at once, with no other light whatever than that reflected on the water from the bright ballroom, I prepared myself to meet the Resident in full dress. He was greatly surprised to see me at such a late hour, but received me in a most cordial manner, and at once commenced introducing me to the host and hostess, the bride and bridegroom, and all the assembled guests. The chills and burning fever, from which I had been suffering, vanished, and in a moment I found myself transferred from a real purgatory into a perfect paradise.

Palembang occupies both banks of the Musi for four or five miles, but there are only three or four rows of houses on each bank. Many of these houses were built on bamboo rafts, and, when the tide is high, the city seems to be built on a plain, but at low water it appears to be built in a valley. The tide here usually rises and falls nine or ten feet, but in spring fourteen feet. This is the greatest rise and fall that I have seen in the archipelago. It is said that in the river Rakan, which empties into the Strait of Malacca, at spring tides the water comes in with a bore and rises thirty feet. The principal part of Pa-

WOMEN OF PALEMBANG.

PALEMBANG — HIGH WATER.

lembang is built on the left bank. There are a large and well-constructed fort, and the houses of the Resident, assistant Resident, and other officials. The Resident and the colonel commanding the fort are now in the Pasuma country. On the left bank is the Chinese quarter, and very fine imitations of the more common tropical fruits are made there in lacquer-ware by those people. Below the fort, on the right bank, is the large market, where we saw a magnificent display of krises, and enormous quantities of fruit. The name Palembang, or, more correctly, Palimbangan, is of Javanese origin, and signifies "the place where the draining off was done." The "draining off" is the same phrase as that used to describe water running out of the open-work baskets, in which gold is washed, and the word Palembang is regarded generally as equivalent to "gold-washing" in our language. The Javanese origin of the first settlers in this region is further shown by the title of the native officials and the names of various localities in the vicinity. The natives have a tradition that Palembang was founded by the Javanese government of Majapahit, but the Portuguese state that it was founded two hundred and fifty years before their arrival, or about A. D. 1250.

Back of the Resident's house is a mosque with pilasters and a dome, and near by a minaret, about fifty feet high, with a winding external staircase. It is by far the finest piece of native architecture that I have seen in these islands, and is said to be decidedly superior to any of the old temples in Java. Its history appears to be lost, but I judge it was built not long after the arrival of the Portuguese. The architects were probably not natives, but the Arabs, who have not only traded with this people, but succeeded in converting them to Mohammedanism. Palembang Lama, or Old Palembang, is situated on the left bank, a mile or two below the fort. Landing with the natives under a waringin-tree, I followed a narrow path over the low land for a mile, and came to the grave of a native queen. All possible virtues are ascribed to her by the natives, and many were on their way to this shrine to make vows and repeat their Mohammedan formulas, or were already returning homeward. Those who were going stopped at a little village by the way to purchase bunches of a kind of balm which they placed in the tomb. After meeting with many worshippers, I was quite surprised to find the grave was only protected by an old wooden building. The coffin was a rectangular piece of wood, about a foot and a half wide, and five feet long, in which was inserted at the head and foot a small square post, about two feet high. Near the grave of the queen were those of her nearest relatives. This is regarded as the oldest grave that can be identified in this vicinity. It is supposed to have the power to shield its worshippers from sickness and all kinds of misfortune. The Mohammedanism of this people, therefore, even when it is purest, is largely mingled with their previous superstitions.

Nearer Palembang we visited the tombs of later princes. A high wall encloses several separate buildings from twenty to thirty feet square, and surmounted by domes, and within are the coffins, much like that already described. Other massive rectangular tombs are seen outside. None of these appear to be very old.

From Palembang to the mouth of the Musi is about fifty miles, and yet there is plenty of water for the largest steamers to come to the city. The Musi is therefore the largest river in Sumatra; and Palembang gains its importance from its position as the head of navigation on this river, which receives into itself streams navigable for small boats for many miles. On the south is the Ogan, which, in its upper part, flows through a very fertile and well-peopled region, and which, from the descriptions given me, I judge is a plateau analogous to that at Kopaiyong, near the source of the Musi. This region of the Ogan produces much pepper. North of the Musi is the country of the Kubus, who have been described to me here and at Tebing-Tingi as belonging to the Malay race. They are said to clothe themselves with bark-cloth, and to eat monkeys and reptiles of all kinds. They shun all foreigners and other natives, and are very rarely seen. They appear to be very similar in their personal appearance and habits to the Lubus that I saw north of Padang, and perhaps form but a branch of that people.* It was to this place that the author of the "Prisoner of Weltevreden" came on his filibustering expedition, and was seized and carried to Batavia, whence he escaped. The open-hearted and generous manner in

* The total population of this residency is estimated at 527,050, of which 132 are Europeans; about 522,345 natives; 2,790 Chinese; 1,716 Arabs; and 67 from other Eastern nations.

which I have been everywhere received and aided, both by the government and by private persons, as has constantly appeared on these pages, convinces me that any American, whose character and mission are above suspicion, will be treated with no greater kindness and consideration by any nation than by the Dutch in the East Indian Archipelago.

May 13*th.*—Took a small steamer for Muntok, on the island of Banca, where the mail-boat from Batavia touches while on her way to Singapore. Muntok is a very pretty village. The houses, which mostly belong to Chinamen, are neatly built and well painted. The streets are kept in good repair, and the whole place has an air of enterprise and thrift. Here I had the pleasure of making the acquaintance of the chief mining engineer on the island. One morning we rode out a few miles to a granite hill, from the top of which I had a fine view over the Strait of Banca to the low, monotonous coast of Sumatra. There are but few elevations on Banca, and none of any considerable height. All are covered with a thick forest. The rocks of which Banca is composed are chiefly granite, and a red, compact sandstone or grit. The tin is disseminated in small particles through the whole mass of granite, which has slowly disintegrated and decomposed, and the clay and sand thus formed have been washed into the nearest depressions. The tin, being the heaviest of these materials, has settled near the bottom of each basin, when they have been somewhat assorted by the action of water. The upper strata being removed, the particles of tin are found in the lower strata, and obtained by washing, just as in the process of washing similar alluvial deposits for gold. When the beds of all the basins on the island have been thoroughly washed, the yield of tin will be at an end, because it does not occur, as at Cornwall, in veins in the granite, but only in small scattered grains. The washing is almost wholly done by Chinese, who chiefly come from Amoy.

The income of Banca* has been for some time over three million guilders per year, after deducting the salaries of all the officials on the island, and the annual expense of the garrison. The chief engineer thinks that about two-thirds of all the tin on the island has now been taken out, but that the present yield will continue for some years, and a less one for many years after. This tin-bearing range of granite begins as far north on the west coast of the peninsula of Malacca as Tavoy. It has been obtained at Tenasserim, and on the island of Junk Ceylon, and large quantities are annually taken out at Malacca. It is also found on the Sumatra side of the strait, in the district of Kampar. The range reappears in the islands of Banca and Billiton, and again in Bali, at the eastern end of Java.

May 14*th*.—In the evening the steamer arrived from Batavia. For fellow-passengers I found the captain and doctor of an English ship that had lately been burned in the Strait of Sunda while bound from Amoy to Demarara with a cargo of coolies. A passenger from her was also on board, who had written

* The population of the island is 54,339. Of these, 116 are Europeans; 37,070 natives; 17,097 Chinese, and 56 Arabs.

a book on Cochin China, giving his experience while a captive in that land.

May 18*th*.—We continue, this morning, to pass small islands, and now, by degrees, we are able to make out many ships and steamers at anchor in a bay, and soon the houses by the bund or street bordering the shore begin to appear. We are nearing Singapore. A year and fourteen days have passed since I landed in Java. During that time I have travelled six thousand miles over the archipelago, and yet I have not once set foot on any other soil than that possessed by the Dutch, so great is the extent of their Eastern possessions.

The activity and enterprise which characterize this city are very striking to one who has been living so long among the phlegmatic Dutchmen. Singapore, or, more correctly, Singapura, "the lion city," is situated on an island of the same name, which is about twenty-five miles long from east to west, and fourteen miles wide from north to south.

When the English, in 1817, restored the archipelago to the Dutch, they felt the need of some port to protect their commerce; and in 1819, by the foresight of Sir Stamford Raffles, the present site of Singapore was chosen for a free city. In seven years from that time its population numbered 13,000; but has since risen to 90,000. Its imports have risen from $5,808,000 in 1823 to $31,460,000 in 1863, and its exports from $4,598,000 in 1823 to $26,620,000 in 1863.

As soon as I landed, I found myself among American friends, and one of them kindly introduced me to the Governor of the Straits Settlements, who received me in the most polite manner and kindly offered to assist me in any way in his power. At my request, he gave me notes of introduction to the Governor of Hong Kong and the admiral commanding her Majesty's fleet in the seas of China and Japan. A few days of rest after my long journeys over Sumatra soon glided by, and I was ready to continue my travels.

From Singapore my plan was to proceed directly to China, but finding in port a French ship which was bound for Hong Kong, via Saigon, the capital of Cochin China, I engaged a passage on her in order to see something also of the French possessions in the East. Just as we were ready to sail I met a gentleman who had lately returned from a long journey to Cambodia, whither he had gone to photograph the ruins of the wonderful temples in that land. He had a specimen for me, he said, which I must accept before I knew what it was, a condition I readily complied with, but when the "specimen" appeared I must confess I was not a little surprised to find it was an enormous *python*. It had been caught by the natives of Bankok after it had gorged itself on some unfortunate beast, but that was some time before, and the brute was evidently ready for another feast. My cans containing alcohol were already on board the ship, but I took the monster with me when I went off to her late in the evening, designing to drown it in its box and then transfer his snakeship to a can. The captain, with the greatest politeness, met me at the rail, and showed me my state-room in the after-cabin, and the sailors began to bring my baggage, when first of all appeared the box containing the python! I shouted out to the cabin-boy that that box must be left out on deck, and then, in a low tone, explained to the captain that it contained an enormous snake. "*Un serpent? un serpent?*" he exclaimed, raising up both hands in horror, in such an expressive way as only a Frenchman can, and proceeding to declare that he ought to have known that a passenger who was a naturalist would be sure to fill the whole ship with all sorts of venomous beasts. All the others were little less startled, and shunned me in the half-lighted cabin, as if I were in league with evil spirits, but I quieted their fears by ordering a sailor to put the box into a large boat that was placed right side up on the main deck and promising to kill the great reptile to-morrow.

May 24th.—Early this morning we made sail, and I concluded to let my troublesome specimen remain until we were out of the harbor, but now, in the changing of the monsoons, the winds are light and baffling and we finally came to anchor once more; and a sailor who got up into the boat said something about "*le serpent.*" I was on the quarter-deck at the time, and determining at once not to be troubled more with it, jumped down on the main-deck, ran to the side of the boat, and seizing the box gave it a toss into the sea, but just as it was leaving my hands I thought to myself, "How light it is!" and the sailor said, "*Le serpent n'est pas encore!—pas encore!*" We all looked over the ship's side and there was the box floating quietly away, and it was evident that the monster had escaped. Every one then asked, "Where is he?" but no one could tell. I assured the captain that he was in the box when I put it on the sampan to come off to the ship. "Is he on board?" was the next question from the mouths of all. We looked carefully in the boat and round the deck, but could detect no trace of him whatever, and all, except myself, came to the conclusion that he was not brought on board, and then went back to their work. The box in which he had been confined was about a foot and a half long by a foot high and a foot wide, and over the top were four or five strips of board, each fastened at either end with a single nail. On inquiring more closely, the sailor told me that before I seized the box, the side with the slats was one of the perpendicular sides, and had not been placed uppermost, as it ought to have been. "Then," I reasoned, "he is here on board somewhere beyond a doubt, and I brought him here, and it's my duty to find him and kill him."

We had four horses on deck, and the middle of the boat was filled with hay for them, and under that it was probable the great reptile had crawled away. In the bottom of the boat, aft, was a triangular deck, and, as I climbed up a second time, I noticed that the board which formed the apex of the triangle was loose, and moved a little to one side. Carefully raising this, I espied, to my horror, the great python closely coiled away beneath, the place being so small that the loose board rested on one of his coils. I wore a thin suit, a Chinese baju, or loose blouse, a pair of canvas shoes, and a large sun-hat.

Throwing off my hat, that I might go into the dreadful struggle unimpeded, I shouted out for a long knife, knowing well that what I must try to do was to cut him in two, and that he would attempt to catch my hand in his jaws, and, if he should succeed in doing that, he would wind himself around me as quick as a man could wind the lash of a long whip around a fixed stick, and certainly he was large enough and strong enough to crush the largest horse. The cook handed me a sharp knife, more than a foot long, and, holding the board down with my feet, I thrust the blade through the crack, and, wrenching with all my might, tried to break the great reptile's back-bone, and thus render all that part of the body behind the fracture helpless. Despite my utmost efforts, he pulled away the knife, and escaped two or three feet forward, where there was more room under the deck. By this time there was the greatest confusion. The captain, evidently believing that discretion is the better part of valor, ran below the moment he was satisfied that I had indeed discovered the monster, seized a brace of revolvers, and, perching himself upon the monkey-rail, leaned his back against the mizzen-rigging, and held one in each hand, ready to fire into the boat at the slightest alarm. The sailors all gathered round the boat, and stood perfectly still, apparently half-stupified, and not knowing whether it would be safest for them to stand still, climb up in the rigging, or jump overboard. The first mate armed himself with a revolver, and climbed on to the stern of the boat. Indeed, every moment I expected to hear a report, and find

myself shot by some of the brave ones behind
me. The second mate, who was the only real man
among them all, seized a large sheath-knife, and
climbed into the boat to help me. I knew it would
not do to attempt to strike the monster with a
knife where he had room enough to defend himself; I therefore threw it down, and seized a short
handspike of iron-wood, the only weapon within my
reach, and told the second mate to raise the deck,
and I would attempt to finish my antagonist with
the club, for the thought of escaping while I could,
and leave for others to do what belonged to me,
never entered my mind. As the deck rose I beheld
him coiled up about two feet and a half from my
right foot. Suffering the acutest agony from the
deep wound I had already given him, he raised his
head high out of the midst of his huge coil, his red
jaws wide open, and his eyes flashing fire like live
coals. I felt the blood chill in my veins as, for an
instant, we glanced into each other's eyes, and both
instinctively realized that one of us two must die on
that spot. He darted at my foot, hoping to fasten
his fangs in my canvas shoe, but I was too quick for
him, and gave him such a blow over the head and
neck that he was glad to coil up again. This gave
me time to prepare to deal him another blow, and
thus for about fifteen minutes I continued to strike
with all my might, and three or four times his jaws
came within two or three inches of my canvas shoe.
I began now to feel my strength failing, and that I
could not hold out more than a moment longer, yet, in
that moment, fortunately, the carpenter got his wits

together, and thought of his broad-axe, and, bringing it to the side of the boat, held up the handle, so that I could seize it while the reptile was coiling up from the last stunning blow. The next time he darted at me I gave him a heavy cut about fifteen inches behind his head, severing the body completely off, except about an inch on the under side, and, as he coiled up, this part fell over, and he fastened his teeth into his own coils. One cut more, and I seized a rope, and, in an instant, I tugged him over the boat's side, across the deck, and over the ship's rail into the sea. The long trail of his blood on the deck assured me that I was indeed safe, and, drawing a long breath of relief, I thanked the Giver of all our blessings.

This was my last experience in the tropical East. A breeze sprang up, and the ship took me rapidly away toward the great empire of China, where I travelled for a year, and passed through more continued dangers and yet greater hardships than in the East Indian Archipelago.

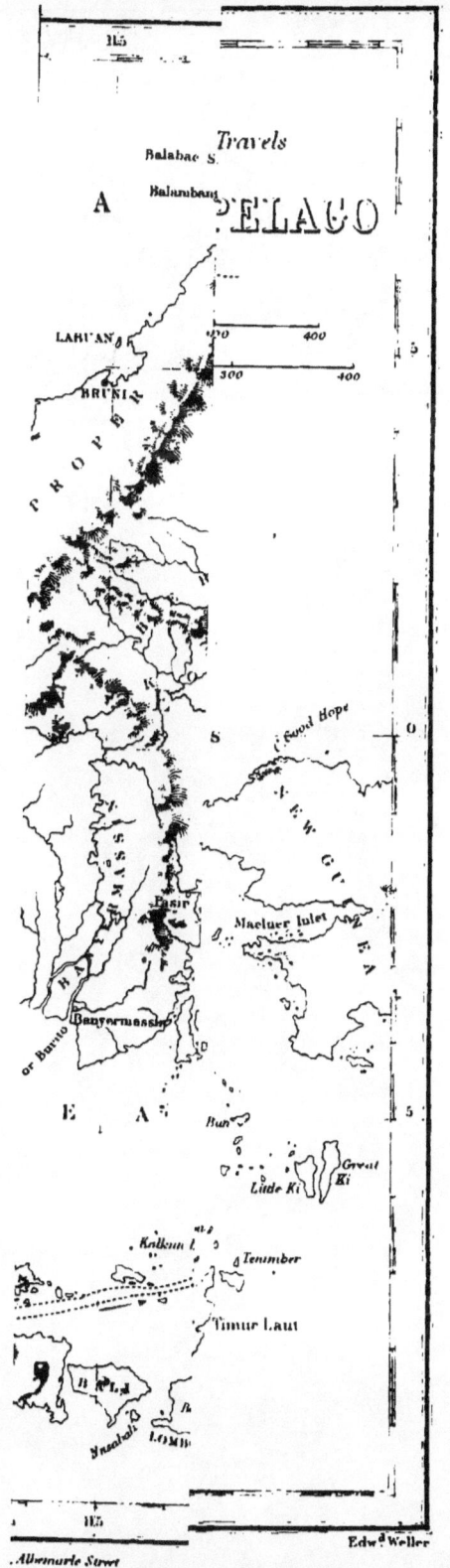

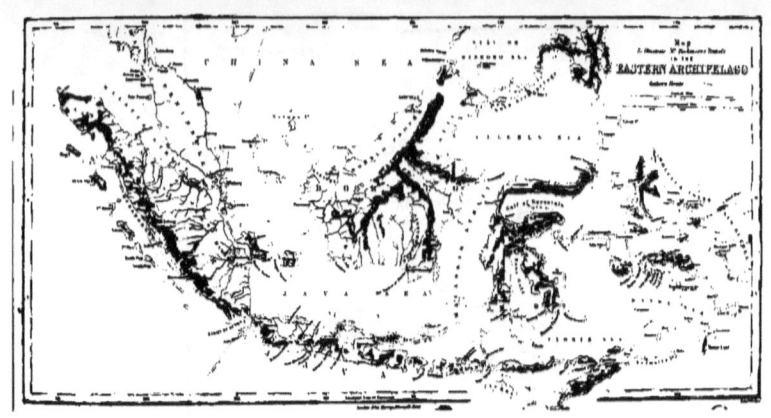

APPENDIX A.

Area of the Principal Islands, according to Baron Melville van Carnbée.

	Square English geographical miles.		Square English geographical miles.
Java and Madura	38,251.2	Timur	9,808.0
Sumatra	128,560.0	Sandal-wood Island	3,784.0
Pulo Nias	1,200.0	Tenimber Islands	2,400.0
Babi	480.0	Aru Islands	1,040.0
Pagi	560.0	Islands of Banda	17.6
Banca	3,568.0	Ceram	4,944.0
Billiton	1,904.0	Buru	2,624.0
Borneo	203,888.0	Gilolo	5,016.0
Celebes	57,248.0	Bachian	800.0
Buton	1,379.2	Ternate	11.2
Bali	16,848.0	Amboina	2,128.0
Lombok	10,560.0		
Sumbawa	4,448.0	Total area of the Netherlands India	445,411.2
Floris	4,032.0		

APPENDIX B.

Population of the Netherlands India, 1865.

ISLANDS.	Europeans.	Natives.	Chinese.	Arabs.	Other Eastern nations.	Total.
Java and Madura	27,105	13,704,535	156,192	6,764	22,772	13,917,368
"West Coast" of Sumatra, including the islands from Nias to the Pagis	1,188	872,173	3,172	54	1,116	877,703
Residency of Bencoolen	174	119,691	596	6	47	120,514
" " Lampong	52	88,113	180	8	4,666	93,019
" " Palembang	132	522,345	2,790	1,716	67	527,050
Banca	116	37,070	17,097	56	....	54,339
Billiton	34	12,786	1,781	....	1,223	15,824
Rhio	136	10,454	19,972	2	119	30,683
Borneo (the parts under the Dutch Government)	328	802,889	26,393	1,736	597	931,843
Celebes	1,176	292,619	4,385	42	....	298,222
Residency of Amboina	1,219	104,841	311	85	817	107,273
" " Banda	545	5,876	153	12	....	6,586
" " Ternate	732	2,062	427	70	....	3,291
The Minahassa	550	102,423	1,437	11	....	104,418
Timur	190	Unknown.	752	3	....	945
Bali and Lombok	....	863,725	....	....	....	863,725
Total	33,677	17,641,602	235,535	10,565	31,424	17,952,803

APPENDIX C.

A Table of Heights of the Principal Mountains in the Archipelago.

Place.	Height in Eng. feet.	Place.	Height in Eng. feet.
AMBOINA.		MINAHASSA.	
Salhutu (highest peak on the island)	4,010	Mount Massarang	4,150
TERNATE (peak of)	5,510	Mount Tompasso	3,850
TIDORE (peak of)	5,440	Mount Saputan	5,960
MINAHASSA.		Mount Mahawut	4,171
Mount Klabat	6,560	Mount Sempo	4,904
Mount Sudara	4,390	Mount Katawak	3,970
Mount Batu Angus	2,290	Mount Kawin	3,430
Mount Lokon	5,140	Lake of Tondano	2,272

HEIGHTS IN JAVA.

Mount Krawang	5,771	Sindoro	10,316
Salak	7,244	Merbabu	10,219
Mandalawangi	9,940	Sumbing	10,947
Gedeh	9,750	Lawu	10,727
Sedaratu	9,591	Dorowati	8,480
Alun-alun	9,100	Kawi	9,408
Papandayang	7,477	Arjuno	10,947
Pasir Alang	8,387	Sémiru	12,235
Taman Saät	7,908	Budolembu, highest peak in the Tenger Mountains	8,705
Chikorai	9,233		
Telaga Bodas	5,874	Boromo	7,545
Highest edge of Galunggong	5,320	Ajang	9,890
Galunggong	3,825	Raon	10,177
Slamat	11,329		

HEIGHTS IN SUMATRA.

Padang Hill (Apenberg)	341
Kayu Tanam	403
Padang Panjang	2,432
Fort Gugur Sigandang, the highest point on the *col* between Singalang and Mérapi	3,677
From this place to Matua is the plateau of Agam—Matua is	3,389
Bambang	2,028
Pisang	1,685
Kumpodang (where we crossed the brook and found a *controleur* making a bridge, etc.)	670
Bondyol	735
Water-shed just before coming to Libu Siköping	2,132
Libu Siköping	1,511
Rau	972
Water-shed between Rau and Kota Nopan	2,132
That above Kota Nopan	1,351

APPENDIX.

	Feet.
Water-shed between Tobing and Uraba	2,451
Last hills crossed before coming down to Eik Bediri	600 to 800
Dundgus Nasi (island passed in coming from Siboga)	800
Mount Talang (Crawfurd's Dictionary)	10,500
Mount Singalang	9,634
Mount Mérapi	9,570
Mount Sago, about	5,862
Mount Ophir	9,770
Mount Kalabu (west of Rau)	5,115
Mount Seret Mérapi	5,860
Mount Pitya Kéling	680
Lubu Rajah	6,234
Height of the plateau of Toba, about	4,000
Sinkara, greatest depth	1,193
Bottom of Silindong Valley	3,144
Bukit Gedang, the edge of the old crater crossed in going down to Manindyu	3,624
Lake of Manindyu	1,541
Tanjong Alam, on the road from Fort van der Capellen to Paya Kombo	3,428
Paya Kombo	1,704
Height of Silindong Valley (e. g., at Uta Galong)	3,144
Height of Toba Valley about	4,000
Mount Indrapura, estimated at	12,255
Mount Lusé, in the territory of Achin, in 3° 40′ N. (Crawfurd)	11,250
Mount Lombok, according to Melville van Carnbée, by triangulation, about	12,363

APPENDIX D.

Coffee sold by the Government at Padang.

YEAR.	Total quantity.	Exported to U. S.	Average price.
	Piculs.	*Piculs.*	*Guilders.*
1856	125,000	65,521	30.84
1857	150,000	6,037	33.78
1858	185,000	72,010	25.25
1859	145,000	46,285	32.09
1860	151,000	19,536	34.59
1861	150,000	18,715	34.67
1862	135,000	15,971	41.15
1863		23,745	
1864	164,400	48,543	39.56

APPENDIX E.

Trade of Java and Madura during 1864.

COUNTRIES.	No. of ships.	Tonnage.
ARRIVALS.		
From Holland	197	143,250
From other parts of Europe	69	34,193
From the United States	24	12,610
From the Cape of Good Hope	7	4,132
From India	18	9,060
From China, Manilla, and Siam	128	45,067
From Mauritius	4	1,034
From Japan	4	843
From Australia	68	29,548
From the eastern parts of the archipelago	2,138	141,462½
Total	2,657	423,083½
DEPARTURES.		
For Holland	396	267,260
For other parts of Europe	9	3,338
For the United States	3	2,258
For India	8	4,755
For China, Manilla, and Siam	73	22,508
For Japan	5	1,878
For Australia	20	4,338
For the eastern parts of the archipelago	2,245	151,066½
Total	2,759	577,401½

TOMB OF THE SULTAN—PALEMBANG.

See page 131.

APPENDIX F.

A List of the Birds collected by the Author on the island of Buru.

Pandion leucocephalus, Gould,
  B. of Aust., vol. i., pl. 6.
Baza Rheinwardtii, Schleg. and Müll.,
  P.Z.S.,* 1860, p. 342.
Tinnunculus moluccensis, Hornb. and
  Jacq., P.Z.S., 1860, p. 343.
Ephialtes leucospila, Gray,
  P.Z.S., 1860, p. 344.
Caprimulgus macrourus, Horsf.,
  P.Z.S., 1863, p. 22.
Hirundo javanica, Sath.,
  P.Z.S., 1860, p. 345.
Cypselus mystaceus, Sess.,
  P.Z.S., 1863, p. 22.
Eurystomus pacificus, Gray,
  P.Z.S., 1863, p. 25.
Todiramphus collaris, Bon.,
  P.Z.S., 1863, p. 23.
Todiramphus sanctus, Bon.,
  P.Z.S., 1863, p. 23.
Alcyone pusilla, Gould,
  B. of Aust., vol. ii., pl. 26.
Nectarinia zenobia, Gray,
  P.Z.S., 1863, p. 32.
Nectarinia proserpina, Wall.,
  P.Z.S., 1863, p. 32.
Dicæum erythothorax, Sess.,
  P.Z.S., 1863, p. 32.
Tropidorynchus bouruensis, Wall.,
  P.Z.S., 1863, p. 31.
Acrocephalus australis, Gould,
  B. of Aust., vol. iii., pl. 37.
Sylvia flavescens, Gray,
  P.Z.S., 1860, p. 349.
Cysticola rustica, Wall.,
  P.Z.S., 1863, p. 25.
Cysticola ruficeps, Gould,
  B. of Aust., vol. iii., pl. 45.

Motacilla flavescens, Shaw,
  P.Z.S., 1860, p. 350.
Criniger mysticalis, Wall.,
  P.Z.S., 1863, p. 28.
Minueta bouruensis, Wall.,
  P.Z.S., 1863, p. 26.
Rhipidura tricolor, Gray,
  P.Z.S., 1860, p. 351.
Rhipidura bouruensis, Wall.,
  P.Z.S., 1863, p. 29.
Rhipidura, sp.
Monarcha loricata, Wall.,
  P.Z.S., 1863, p. 29.
Muscicapa, sp.
Campheya marginata, Wall.,
  P.Z.S., 1863, p. 31.
Artaurus leucogaster, Gray,
  P.Z.S., 1860, p. 354.
Dicrurus amboinensis, Gray,
  P.Z.S., 1860, p. 354.
Calornis obscura, Gray,
  P.Z.S., 1860, p. 355.
Calornis metallica, Bon.,
  P.Z.S., 1860, p. 355.
Munia molucca, Blyth,
  P.Z.S., 1860, p. 355.
Platycercus dorsalis, Quoy and Gaim,
  (P. hypophonius, Gray)
  P.Z.S., 1860, p. 356.
Eos rubra, Wagl.,
  P.Z.S., 1860, p. 356.
Trichoglossus cyanogrammus, Wagl.,
  P.Z.S., 1860, p. 357.
Eclectus puniceus, Gm.,
  P.Z.S., 1860, p. 357.
Eclectus polychlorus, Scop.,
  P.Z.S., 1860, p. 358.
Tanygnathus affinis, Wall.,
  P.Z.S., 1863, p. 20.

* 'Proceedings of the Zoological Society of London.'

Geoffroius personatus, Gray,
P.Z.S., 1860. p. 358.
Eudynornis ransomi, Bon.,
P.Z.S., 1860, p. 359.
Centropus medius, Müll.,
P.Z.S., 1863, p. 23.
Cuculus caroides, Müll.,
P.Z.S., 1860, p. 359.
Cuculus assimilis, Gray,
P.Z.S., 1858, p. 184.
Cacomantis sepulchris, Bon.,
P.Z.S., 1860, p. 359.
Ptilonopus superbus, Steph.,
P.Z.S., 1858, p. 184.
Ptilonopus prasinorrhous, Gray,
P.Z.S., 1858, p. 185.
Ptilonopus viridis, Gm.,
P.Z.S., 1863, p. 31.
Treron aromatica, Gray,
P.Z.S., 1863, p. 33.
Carpophaga perspicillata, Gray,
P.Z.S., 1860, p. 360.
Carpophaga melanura, Gray,
P.Z.S., 1860, p. 361.
Macropygia amboinensis, Gray,
P.Z.S., 1860, p. 361.
Macropygia, sp.
Chalcophaps moluccensis, Gray,
P.Z.S., 1860, p. 361.
Megapodius Forsteri, Temm.,
P.Z.S., 1860, p. 362.
Megapodius Wallacii, Gray,
P.Z.S., 1860, p. 362.
Glareola grallaria, Temm.,
P.Z.S., 1863, p. 35.

Ardetta flacicollis, Sath.,
Gould, B. of Aust., vol. vi., pl. 65.
Ardea novæ-hollandiæ, Sath.,
Gould, B. of Aust., vol. vi., pl. 53.
Herodias immaculata, Gould,
B. of Aust., vol. vi., pl. 58.
Butorides javanica, Blyth,
P.Z.S., 1863, p. 35.
Limosa uropygialis, Gould,
B. of Aust., vol. vi., pl. 29.
Sphoeniculus magnus, Gould,
B. of Aust., vol. vi., pl. 33.
Sphoeniculus subarquatus, Gould,
B. of Aust., vol. vi., pl. 32.
Sphoeniculus albescens, Gould,
B. of Aust., vol. vi., pl. 31.
Actitis empusa, Gould,
B. of Aust., vol. vi., pl. 31.
Totanus griseopygius, Gould,
B. of Aust., vol. vi., pl. 38.
Numenius uropygialis, Gould,
B. of Aust., vol. vi., pl. 43.
Gallinula mystacina, Temm.
Rallus pectoralis, Cuv.,
Gould, B. of Aust., vol. vi., pl. 76.
Rallus, sp.
Dendrocygna guttulata, Gray,
P.Z.S., 1863, p. 36.
Sterna velox, Rüpp.,
P.Z.S., 1860, p. 366.
Sula fusca, Gould,
B. of Aust., vol. vii., pl. 78.

NOTE.—For lists of birds collected on the Banda Isles, Ternate, and Celebes, see 'Proceedings of the Boston Society of Natural History.' For a list of the shells collected in the Moluccas and other scientific papers, see 'Memoirs and Proceedings of the Boston Society of Natural History,' and the 'American Journal of Science for 1868,' et seq.

INDEX.

A.

Abreu, Antonio d', sent to search for the Spice Islands, 23; is the first to reach the Bandas, 215; pillars of discovery erected by, 256.

Achin, country, people, and trade, 448; English appear at, 449.

Alfura, name whence derived and its signification, 203, and *note*; bloody laws of, in Ceram, 205; of Kaibobo, 207; drunken revels of, 209, 210; of Buru, their customs and belief, 271–273, of the Minahassa, 365.

Amahai, bay of, described, 202; village of, *ib.*

Amboina, residence of Rumphius, 13; island and city described, 130–132; famous for its shells, 133; life of foreigners at, 211; trade of, 249.

Amuk, defined, 383.

Anak gadis, or virgin children, 497, 507.

Anoa depressicornis, an antelope, 325.

Ants, abundance of and trouble caused by, 288, 289.

Army, headquarters of Javanese, 43; Dutch, in Sumatra, 456.

Arrack, how made, 68.

Arriens, governor of the Moluccas, 213; kind invitation given the author, *ib.*; visits Banda, 213 *et seq.*

Aru Islands, account of, 244.

Assilulu, visit to the village of, 149–161.

Ayar Bangis, port of, 453.

B.

Baba, island of, described, 127.

Babirusa, skulls of, 150; distribution of, *ib.*; young one seen at Kayeli, 292; author hunts for, on Limbi, 325; one commits suicide, 331.

Bachian, island of, described, 299; great python killed on, 334; fauna of, 380.

Baju, a, described, 34.

Bali, described, 93; fauna of, *ib.*; separation from Java, 93, 94; fauna of, 94; religion of, 95, 96.

Bali, a town hall, 477.

Bamboo, used by the Malays, 86.

Banana, tree and fruit described, 84, 85; native name for, 159; different kinds, *ib.*

Banca, description and geology of, 534; income of, 535.

Banda, author arrives at, 128, and revisits, 214; description of the group, 214, 215; early inhabitants of, 216; religion of, *ib.*; natives of, exterminated by the Dutch, 217; convicts banished to, 217, 218; the group only walls of a crater, 224; compared with that of the Tenger Mountains, *ib.*; nutmeg parks on, 227; residency of, 242.

Banteng, the *Bos sondaicus*, 72.

Bantiks, a people near Menado, 343.

Barros, João de, history of, 97, *note*; his description of Celebes, 97; describes the many languages spoken in the Moluccas, 163; his description of the Bandas, 215, 216.

Barus, a port in Sumatra, 442.

Batavia, purpose of going to, 13; foundation of, 24; police of, 383.

Batta, grave of a, 417; Lands, a description of, 423; are cannibals, 424; referred to by Marco Polo, 425; by Sir Stamford Raffles, *ib.*; draw the author's carriage, 426, 427; author visits a village of, 440; houses of, *ib.*; eat a man, 442; missionaries among, 443; Madame Pfeiffer among, 444; kill two American missionaries.

445; origin of their cannibal customs, 446.
Barbosa, Odardo, cited, 63; history of, 100, *note;* describes the natives of Celebes, 100.
Bears, of Sumatra, 510, 511.
Bencoolen, bay of, 486; history of, 487, 489.
Benzoin, a resin, 63.
Betel-nut; tree described, 180; mode of chewing the, 181.
Birds.—Bird that guarded the double cocoa-nut tree, 15; of Java, 80, 81; trade in, on the coast of New Guinea, 242; luris, *ib.;* crown pigeons (*Megapodiideæ*), 242; doves (*Columba ænea* and *Columba perspicillata*), fruit planted by, 243; of paradise found at Aru Islands, 244; Pigafetta's account of, *ib.;* king-fishers at the Bandas, 246; *Pitta vigorsi*, a rare species, *ib.; Carpophaga luctuosa*, a white dove, 255, 268; the prince parrot (*Platycercus hypophonius*), description of, *ib.;* luris, red (*Eos rubra*), 256, 259; king-fishers at Buru, 258; hunting luris, 259; parrakeets, *ib.; Trichoglossus cyanogrammus*, *ib.;* luris, Moore's description of, 260; *Tanygnathus macrorynchus*, a large, green parrot, 268; *Carpophaga perspicillata*, a long-tailed dove, *ib.; Muscicapidæ*, *ib.; Monarcha loricata*, *ib.; Tropidorynchus bouruensis*, 269; *Anas rajah*, or "prince duck," 283; author incurs great danger in procuring, *ib.; castori rajah*, 289; *Megapodius Forsteni*, *ib.; M. Wallacei*, *ib.;* mode of shooting, skinning, and preserving, 288, 289; *Corvus enka*, 335; *Dicrurus*, *ib.*
Birgos latro, the great hermit crab, 148.
Bleeker, Dr., on the geology of Laitimur, 247; on the ichthyology of Lake Linu, 344.
Bloodsuckers, author tortured by, 492, 493, 508.
Boats, with outriggers, 57; see also *lepper-lepper.*
Bonang, the, described, 190.
Bonoa, situation of, 253.
Bosche, Governor Van den; entertains the author at Padang, 387.
Bos sondaicus; the ox of Madura, 72.
Bread-fruit, tree and fruit described, 92.
Breech-loader, Sharpe's, 43.

Bridge, suspension, made of rattan, 428, 430; of bamboo, 474; of rattan, 475.
Bua, valley of, 462; cave of, 463, 464.
Buffalo, the, described, 35; habits of, 35, 36; color of, 36; fights with tigers, 36; wild ones in Sumatra, 413.
Buru, described, 256; history of, 270, 271; Alfura of, and their customs and belief, 271–273; alternation of seasons in, 298.
Buton, description and geology of, 380, 381.

C.

Camphor-trees, described, 433; kinds of, *ib.*
Campong, a, described, 132.
Cannibals; mode of eating men, 444; see also Battas.
Cassowary, eggs of, 150; habitat of the, *ib.*
Cauto, Diogo de, history of, 98, *note;* his description of Celebes, 98, 99.
Celebes; description and history of, 97–100; northern peninsula of, 322; gold-mines in, 379; fauna of, 380.
Cemetery, Chinese, at Batavia, 35.
Ceram, described, 201, 202; head-hunters of, 203; Alfura, *ib.;* landing on the south coast of, 207, alternation of seasons in, 298.
Ceram-laut, natives of, 242; elevation of, 243.
Cervus rufa, 80; *mantjac*, *ib.*
Chair, to travel in, described, 141, 142.
Chilachap, port of, 57.
Christmas Island, passed, 13.
Cinnamon, kinds of, and their distribution, 425.
Cleft, of Padang Panjang, 390–392; 459, 460.
Clove, tree and fruit described, 153; distribution of, 153, 154; quantities obtained in previous years, 153; mode of gathering the, 155; names for, 156; history of, 157; yield of, in Saparua, Haruku, and Nusalaut, 197.
Clypeastridæ, abundant at Saparua, 186.
Coal, near Siboga, 436; near Bencoolen, 492–495; abundance of, 494; on the Limatang, 521; on the Inem, 524.
Cock-fighting, Malay passion for, 61.
Cocoa-nut, the double, 14; palm, de-

scribed, 81-83; oil, mode of making, 83; kind eaten by Malays, 82, 83; importance of, 84; beaches lined with trees of, 149; a portable fountain, *ib.*; abundance of, on the upper Limatang, 523; rafts of, *ib.*

Cocoa-trees at Amboina, 138; history of, 138, 139.

Coffee, store-houses for, at Menado, 346; history of, 347-349; how brought to Padang and when sold, 453; exports to the United States, 455, and Appendix D.; where large quantities could be profitably raised, 504, 505.

Coir, a rope made of gomuti fibres, 370.

Controleur, duties of, 67; in Ceram summons the head-hunters, 203.

Cooking, Eastern mode of, 31.

Coral, *Meandrinas*, or "brain corals," 285; different kinds of, and appearance beneath the sea, 285-287; *Fungidæ, Gorgonias*, raised reefs, 508.

Cotton, raised by the natives on the Limatang, 527.

Crawfurd, Mr. John, cited, 96; in regard to Mount Tomboro, 108.

D.

Damma, described, 126; hot springs in, 126, 127.

Deer, author hunts, on Buru, 290-292; their venison smoked and made into *dinding*, 292; *Axis maculata*, 387; hunted by tigers, 413.

Diaz, Bartholomew, his discovery of southern extremity of Africa, 22.

Dilli, city of, 122; name whence derived, 124.

Diving, skilful, 103.

Draco volans, described, 144.

Dugong found at Aru Islands, 244.

Duku, the, described, 90.

Durian tree and fruit described, 91, 92.

E.

Earl, Mr., cited in regard to a plateau, 95; people near Dilli, 116.

Earthquake, experienced by the author at Amboina,167-169; diseases caused by several, 169, 170.

Elephants, native mode of killing, 495; author comes near a stray one, 513; distribution of, *ib.*

Elizabeth, Queen; her letter to the rajah of Achin, 449, *note.*

Eugene Sue, describes Rahden Saleh, 38.

Exquisite, an Eastern, described, 42.

F.

Feest Kakian, a revel of the head-hunters, 210.

Fever, Batavia, described, 39.

Fishes; large one caught at Limbi, 332; *Ophiocephalus striatus*, 354; *Anabas scandens, ib.*; *Anguilla Elphinstonei, ib.*

Fishing, boats used by Malays, 52; Malay mode of, 89.

Floris described ''; cannibals of, *ib.*

Flying-fish, 106; can fly during a calm, 122.

Forest, home in a tropical, 261; nature's highway through, 263.

Fountain, "youth's radiant," quoted from Moore, 297.

Fringilla oryzivora, the rice-bird, 80.

G.

Gallus bankiva, 60, 61; other species of, 60.

Galunggong, Mount; eruption of, 75, 76; compared with the Tenger Mountains, 77.

Gambang, of Java, 190.

Gambling, Malay vice of, 61.

Geology, of Timur, near Kupang, 119, 120; of the Banda group, 241; of Amboina, 247; of Buru, 263, 293; of Bachian, 299; of the Minahassa, 376; of Gorontalo, 379; of Buton, 381; of a cliff at Tapanuli Bay, 441; of the Padang plateau, 477; of the cliffs of Bencoolen Bay, 489, 490; of the region near Tebing Tingi, 508; of the region of the upper Limatang, 522; of Banca, 534.

Gillibanta, passed, 187.

Gilolo, west coast of, 310; Alfura of, 311; "the bloodhounds" of, *ib.*

Goitre, prevalent in the interior of Sumatra, 416; probable cause of, *ib.*

Gold-mines in Celebes, 379; geological age of, *ib.*; mines in Sumatra, 404-406; distribution of, 406; ornaments of, 431, 432; mode of obtaining, 432.

Gomuti palm, fibres of, 350; made into a rope, 370; *tuak* or wine of, 371.

Goram, situation of, 243.

Gorontalo, bay of, 377; country and tribes near, 378.
Gresik, village of, 56.
Gunong Api, of Sapi Strait, 106, 107; of Banda, 214–219; author ascends, 228; description of, 228–234; account of eruptions of, 237; the one near Wetta, 245; of Banda compared to Ternate, 317.

H.

Haruku, one of the Uliassers, 178; north coast of, 182; population and description of, *ib.*
Head-hunters, of Ceram, 203; clothing, 203, 204; dance of, *ib.*; of Sawai Bay, 205, 206.
Hinduism, history of, 62.
Hitu, a part of Amboina, 130; remarkable appearance of hills on, 131; excursion along the coast of, 141.
Horse, author thrown from a, 341; of Sumatra, 409.
Hospital, at Batavia, 39.
Houtman, commander of first Dutch fleet to the East, 24; arrives at Ternate, 307.
Hukom, Biza, Kadua, Tua, and *Kachil,* meaning of, 338.
Hunting in the tropics, 139.

I.

Ice, used in the East, 31; whence brought, and where manufactured, 31.
Inkfish, an *Octopus,* author dines on, 172.

J.

Java, Sea, 19; meaning of the word, 21; described by Ludovico Barthema, 23; compared with Cuba, 77–79; description of, 77, 78; population of, 78; imports and exports, 79; forests, *ib.*; fauna, 79–81; flora, 81–89; separated from Sumatra and Bali, 93, 94.
Jewels, from the heads of wild boars, 151; Rumphius's account of, 152.
Jukes, Mr., cited on the geology of Sandal-wood Island, 112; Timur, 119.
Junghuhn, Dr., cited, 52, 53, 109.

K.

Kayéli, bay of, 256; village of 257; description of, 269; history of, 270; a threatening fleet arrive off, 283.
Kayu-puti, trees and oil described, 282, 283; distribution of, 283.
Kema, village of, 323; great python killed near, 334.
Ki, some account of the group, 243.
Kissa, described, 125.
Klings, whence their name, 63; early voyages of, to the archipelago, 405.
Kloff, Captain; describes the natives of Kissa, 125.
Korinchi, reformers of, 471.
Kubus, the tribe of, described, 533.
Kupang, village of, 113; bay of, *ib.*; population of, 114; oranges of, *ib.*

L.

Ladangs, native gardens, 264.
Lepers, author visits a village of, 343; description of the, 343–346; description of the disease, 345.
Lepper-lepper, a native boat, 165; dangerous voyage in, 165, 166.
Letti, described, 125.
Limatang, river of, 518, 520, 521; author descends, 521–533.
Limbi, an island near Kema, 324; author visits for Babirusa, 324–332.
Living, Eastern mode of, 32.
Lombok, the, described, 264.
Lombok, island of, separated from Bali, 93; fauna of, 94; flora, *ib.*
Lontar, one of the Banda Islands, 214; shores of, 219; author visits it, 223–227; beautiful nutmeg-groves of, 225.
Lotus, fragrant, 358; land of, by Tennyson, 366.
Lubus, tribe of, 411; habits, 419.

M.

Macassar, harbor of, 100; praus of, 100, 101; city of, 103–105; tombs of princes near, 105.
Madura, a low island, 55; Strait of, 56; cattle of, 60; south coast of, 71; whence its name, *ib.*; coffee-trees on, 72; manufacture of salt on, 72.
Magellan, Ferdinand, his discovery of the Spice Islands, 305–307.
Maize, history of, 265–267.
Makian, island of, described, 299; eruptions of, 299, 300.
Malabrathrum, a gum, 62.
Malay, first sight of, 18; language of, 20; physical characteristics of, 33,

34; passion for gambling, *ib.*; are mostly Mohammedans, *ib.*; language affected by the Portuguese, 122; speak many dialects, 162, 163; migrations of, from Gilolo, 313.

Mango, tree and fruit described, 89, 90, 148.

Mangostin, described, 88, 89.

Manindyu, lake of, 397; crater of, 399, 401; village of, *ib.*

Marco Polo, his account of Java, 21.

Marriage, feast at Kayéli, 274; Mohammedan laws in regard to, 275; at Amboina, 275–278; Malay ideas of, 279.

Matabella, situation of group, 243; Wallace's description of, *ib.*

Menado, village of, 342; bay of, 346, 351; Tua, an island, 346.

Menangkabau, kingdom of, 394; former capitals of, 468; history of, 469–474; arts in, 472, 473.

Minahassa; the most beautiful spot on the globe, 316; mode of travelling in, 335; population of, and area, 339; cataract in, 356; mud-wells and hot springs in, 358–364; Alfura of, 365; most charming view in, 369; products of, 370, 375; graves of the aborigines of, 373; Christianity and education in, 375; geology of, 376.

Mittara; small island near Ternate, 317.

Mohammedan religion, first converts to, 51; at Gresik, 56; jealousy, 159; requires the shaving of the head, 273; filing the teeth, 274.

Moluccas, history of the, 146; population and how divided, 195; Catholicism in, 307, 308; Christianity introduced, 308; of what islands composed, 309.

Monkeys, of Sumatra and Java, 408, 409; large troops of, 410; sagacity of, 478; a flock of, 509.

Monsoons, calms during the changing of, 16; name whence derived, 44; east and west, *ib.*; rainy, 45; sky thick in the eastern, 120; eastern at Amboina, Ceram, Buru, and New Guinea, 128, 129; western boundary of, 486.

Mosque, Mohammedan, in Samarang, 50.

Mount, Ungarung, 45; Slamat, *ib.*; Sumbing, 46; Prau, residence of the gods, 46–48; Japara, 48; Tenger, 73; Bromo, 74; Tomboro, eruption of, 108–110; Tompasso, 357; Singalang, 393; Mérapi, *ib.*; Ophir, 404; Seret Mérapi, 420, 422; Lubu Rajah, 423; Sago, 461–468; Talang, 480; Ulu Musi, 499; Dempo, 516.

Mud-wells, in the Minahassa, 359–364.

Müller, Dr. S., ascended Gunong Api of Banda in 1828, 236.

Musa paradisiaca, the banana-tree, 85; *textilis*, 340.

N.

Natal, port of, 453.

Nautilus, shells of, purchased at Kupang, 119; said to be common on Rotti, *ib.*; those secured at Amboina, 134, 135.

Navigating mud-flats, 57.

Nusalaut, name whence derived, 178; author visits, 187; surrounded by a platform of coral, 187; natives of, in ancient costume, *ib.*; description and population of, 188.

Nutmeg-tree, when found, 215; gathered by the natives, 216; description of tree and fruit, 222; mode of curing the fruit, 222, 223.

O.

Orangbai, an, described, 136.

Orang-utan, habits of, 408, 409.

Ophir, whence the gold of, 405.

Opium, mode of selling and smoking, 279–282; history of, 280.

P.

Padang, city of, 385; Panjang, 392; Sidempuan, 423.

Padangsche Bovenlanden, or Padang plateau, 390; native houses in, 393; dress of the natives of, 394; author travels in, Chap. XV.; geology of, 477.

Puhli, described, 66.

Pagi Islands; natives of, and their habits, 482, 483.

Palembang, author arrives at, 529; description and history of, 530, 531; mosque of, 531; Lama, 532.

Pandanus, a screw-pine, 84.

Papandayang, Mount, eruption of, 74, 75.

Papaw, tree and fruit described, 85.

Papua, natives of, 311, 312; taxes levied on, 314; author thinks of going to, 315.

Pasuma, plateau and people of, 516–519.
Pedatis, described, 68.
Pepper, an article of trade, 446–448; distribution of and native names for, 447, 448.
Periplus of the Erythræan Sea, 62.
Pigafetta, his account of birds of paradise, 244; account of the Philippines, 308.
Piña-cloth, how made, 143.
Pine-apples, introduction and history of, 142.
Piper betel, leaves of, chewed by the Malays, 181.
Pirates, in the Moluccas, 318; from China, ib.; from Mindanao, 319; Malays escape from, 320; a surprise of, ib.; praus of, 321; a challenge from, ib.; Dutch cruise for, 322.
Plough, kind used by Malays, 36; mode of using, 36, 37.
Pompelmus, a gigantic orange, 19.
Ponies, Javanese, 65.
Post-coaches of Java, 64.
Pumice-stone, great quantities of, 110.
Python, one seen near Kema, 333; stories concerning, 333–335; author presented with one, 537; it escapes, 539; author has a deadly struggle with, 541.

R.

Raffles, Sir Stamford, history of, 488.
Railroads in Java, 49.
Rambutan, described, 89.
Ranjaus, 86.
Rattan, kinds of, 511; how gathered, 511, 512.
Reef, first coral, visited, 123; author's boat strikes on one, 183; waves breaking on a, 199.
Reinwardt, Professor, cited, 53; ascended Gunong Api of Banda, in 1821, 236; predicts an eruption, 312.
Rejangs, customs and laws, 496–498.
Reynst, Gerard, arrival at Banda, 236.
Rhinoceros, native pits for, 495; distribution of, 509.
Rice, manner of gathering in Java, 66.
Rivers; Musi and its valley, 499; Inem, 521, 522.
Roads, post, in Java, 64.
Roma, described, 126.
Roses, abundance of, in the Minahassa, 352, 366.
Rotti, island of, 116; people of, ib.

Ruma negri, a public house, 355; beautiful one, 366.
Ruma Satan, or Devil's Dwelling, author visits, 437–442.
Rumphius; his "Rariteit Kamer" referred to by Linnæus, 13; grave of, 250; sketch of life of, 251.

S.

Saccharum, sinensis, 69; officinarum, ib.; violaceum, ib.
Sacrifice, human, 117.
Saleh, Rahden, palace of, 37, 38; manners and acquirements of, 38; described by Eugene Sue, ib.
Salt, manufacture in Madura, 72; Java, 72, 73; Borneo and Philippines, 73; quantity of, ib.; prices of, 73, note.
Samarang, arrive at, 45; described, 48.
Sambal, described, 32.
Sandal-wood Island, description of, 113; horses of, ib.
Sandy Sea, the, 74.
Saparua, name whence derived, 178; island described, 184; history, ib.; town of, 184, 185; bay of, 186.
Sapi, described, 60.
Sarong, description of the, 18, 34.
Sawai bay, people of, 205.
Sawas, described, 66; fertility of, 67.
Schneider, Dr., cited, 120, 247.
Schools, in the Spice Islands, 193; how supported, ib.; welcome to the Resident, 194; classes of, 195.
Sclater, Mr., cited, 94.
Semao, island of, 113.
Sequiera, first brings Portuguese into Eastern Archipelago, 23.
Shells, collecting, at Kupang, 117–119; Trochus mamoratus, 175; Strombus latissimus, 176; Scalaria pretiosa, 185; Cypræa moneta, 186; best place in the Spice Islands to gather, 198; harp, ib.; Mitra episcopalis and papalis, 199; Tridacna gigas, found on hills, 248; Auricula in Ceram, 255; Rostellaria rectirostris, ib.
Siboga, author comes to the village of, 434; country about, 435, et seq.; coal near, 436.
Singapore, history and description of, 536.
Sinkara, lake of, 476; kampong, ib.
Siri, Malay name for the Piper betel, 181.
Snakes, swimming, 14.
Springs, Damma, 126; in Java, 127; hot, in the Minahassa, 360–364.

INDEX.

Strait, Sunda, 13–19; Sapi, passed through, 106–108.
Styrax benzoin, described, 63.
Sugar-cane, kinds of, 69; history of, 69, 70.
Sugar-Loaf Island, passed, 121.
Sulphur, from volcanoes, 53.
Sumatra, grand mountains of, 43; author travels in, 384–532; Dutch army in, 456; Hinduism in, 471; Mohammedanism in, 471; unimproved areas in, 502; true source of the wealth of, 505.
Sumbawa, seen, 107; Mount Tomboro in, 108.
Sundanese, a language of Java, 25.
Surabaya; business of, 56; shipping at, *ib.*; harbor of, 57; situation of, *ib.*; population of, *ib.*; dock-yard, 58; machine-shops, *ib.*; artillery works, 59; streets of, 60.
Surakarta, residence of Javanese princes, 26.
Surf, on south coast of Ceram, 208; revolt in, 257.

T.

Tandu, a, described, 49.
Tanjong O, feared by the natives, 200; Flasco, beautiful sunset seen at, 377.
Tapanuli, bay of, 434, 436; geology of a cliff near, 441; natives that come to the bay of, 448.
Teak, durability of, and different purposes used for, 59; abundant in Java, 79; distribution of, 267.
Telegraph-lines in Java and Sumatra, 65.
Tenger Mountains, seen, 73; Sandy Sea in, 74; Bromo in, *ib.*; compared with the Bandas, 241.
Ternate, island and village of, described, 300, 303, 304; history and account of the eruptions of, 300–309; the prince of, and his territory, 309, 310; trade of, 315; author experiences four earthquakes at, in four days, 316; houses of foreigners at, 317.
Tidore, peak and village of, 312, 313; prince of, 313.
Tifa; a kind of drum, 137; discordant sounds of, 179; mode of beating, 180.
Tigers, ravages of, 413; native traps for, 491; natives destroyed, 503, 504;

fight with a bear, 510; abundance of, 513–517.
Timur, different races on, 115; southeast monsoon in, *ib.*; northwestern coast of, 121.
Timur-laut, described, 127; natives of, at Banda, 218.
Tin, distribution of, 535.
Tobacco, history of, 265, 266.
Tondano, lake of, 367, 368; village of, 368; Klabat, mantled with clouds, 369; tragedy occurred near, 372.
Trees.—Upas, 54; *Antiaris toxicaria*, 54, 55; unchar, 55; *Artocarpus incisa*, and *integrifolia*, 92, 93; *Carophyllus aromaticus*, the clove, 153; Palmyra palm, 222; *Borassus flabelliformis*, *ib.*; *Myristica moschata*, the nutmeg, *ib.*; *Tectona grandis*, the teak, 267.
Tripang, described, 101–103.

U.

Uliassers, described, 178.

V.

Valentyn, his description of an earthquake wave, 240; history of Buru, 270; history of Ternate, 304; describes the eruption of Mount Kemaas, 336, 337.
Valley of Poison, 53.
Van Dijk, cited, 476, 492, 494.
Vidua, Carlo de, sinks in a solfatara, 354.
Viverra musanga, 79, 80.

W.

Wakasihu, visit to the village of, 161–164; rajah of, 161; shells gathered at, 162.
Wallace, A. R., cited, 94, 95; list of the birds of paradise, 341, *note.*
Wetta, described, 124.
Wilkinson, Sir Gardner, cited, 62.

X.

Xavier, St. Francis, visits the Moluccas, 307.

Z.

Zoological gardens, at Batavia, 38; at Samarang, 60.

THE END.

www.ingramcontent.com/pod-product-compliance
Lightning Source LLC
Chambersburg PA
CBHW021226300426
44111CB00007B/440